Crisis and legitimacy

This book is dedicated to the memory of my teacher,
Alexander M. Bickel, 1924-74,
who first opened my mind to these problems

Crisis and legitimacy

The administrative process and American government

James O. Freedman
Associate Provost and Professor of Law
University of Pennsylvania

Cambridge University Press

Cambridge
London   New York   Melbourne

Published by the Syndics of the Cambridge University Press
The Pitt Building, Trumpington Street, Cambridge CB2 1RP
Bentley House, 200 Euston Road, London NW1 2DB
32 East 57th Street, New York, NY 10022, USA
296 Beaconsfield Parade, Middle Park, Melbourne 3206, Australia

First published 1978

Printed in the United States of America
Typeset by Freedmen's Organization, Los Angeles, California
Printed and bound by Hamilton Printing Company, Rensselaer, New York

Library of Congress Cataloging in Publication Data

Freedman, James O.

Includes bibliographical references.

1. Independent regulatory commissions – United States.
2. Administrative procedure – United States.
3. Legitimacy of governments.   I. Title.
KF5407.F73   342'.73'066   78–51683
ISBN 0 521 22036 7

Contents

The nature of the informal administrative process

Conclusion

Permissions

The author gratefully acknowledges permission of the following publishers to reprint all or portions of the author's previously published work:

To the Administrative Law Review for Freedman, "Expertise and the Administrative Law Process," 28 Administrative Law Review 363 (1976).

To the Temple University Law Quarterly for Freedman, "The Administrative Process and the Elderly," 46 Temple Law Quarterly 511 (1973).

To the University of Chicago Law Review for Freedman, "Summary Action by Administrative Agencies," 40 University of Chicago Law Review 1 (1970) and Freedman, "Delegation of Power and Institutional Competence," 43 University of Chicago Law Review 307 (1976).

To the Stanford Law Review and Fred B. Rothman and Co. for Freedman, "Crisis and Legitimacy in the Administrative Process," 27 Stanford Law Review 1041 (Copyright 1975 by the Board of Trustees of the Leland Stanford Junior University).

To the University of Pennsylvania Law Review and Fred B. Rothman and Co. for Freedman, "The Uses and Limits of Remand in Administrative Law: Staleness of the Record," 115 University of Pennsylvania Law Review 145 (1966) and Freedman, "Administrative Procedure and the Control of Foreign Direct Investment," 119 University of Pennsylvania Law Review 1 (1970).

Preface

Everyone who writes a book knows that the author of the Book of Ecclesiastes was right. Of making many books there assuredly is no end. And yet every writer nurtures still the secret hope that his book will achieve what most books do not: a modest place in the literature of his field. I must confess my own hope that this book will persuade its readers of the importance of understanding the recurrent sense of crisis attending the federal administrative agencies and of the necessity of developing a theory of the legitimacy of the administrative process. I hope, too, that this book will illuminate the darkness that sometimes obscures a more complete understanding of the role that the administrative process plays in the governance of a modern democracy.

I have tried throughout these pages to give evidence of my conviction that a scholar's most fundamental obligation is to recognize that one of the most important words in the English language is "perhaps."

For the past thirteen years I have been privileged to teach administrative law at the University of Pennsylvania Law School. I am grateful to the three remarkable men who have served as dean during that period for making the school such a hospitable environment for the pursuit of scholarly work: Jefferson B. Fordham, Bernard Wolfman, and Louis H. Pollak, as well as to my colleague Clarence Morris for his support and the inspiration of his example.

I am also grateful to the Administrative Conference of the United States, which supported some of the research that went into this book, and to the National Endowment for the Humanities, which awarded me a Fellowship for Independent Study and Research that permitted me the freedom of a sabbatical year to complete the manuscript. Finally, I am deeply grateful to Clare Hall, Cambridge University, for inviting me to spend the 1976–77 academic year there as a Visiting Fellow. The atmosphere of stimulating collegiality that President Robert W. K. Honeycombe and his colleagues have created at Clare Hall made the year one of the most productive and pleasant of my life.

I owe a substantial intellectual debt to the work of a number of senior scholars in the field of administrative law, particularly Kenneth Culp Davis, Henry J. Friendly, Walter Gellhorn, and Louis L. Jaffe. No one seeking to understand the administrative process in the twentieth century can ever acknowledge fully the intellectual indebtedness that my generation of scholars owes to the contributions, rich in vision and wisdom, of Felix Frankfurter, professor and judge.

At an important point in my thinking about the nature and meaning of the recurrent sense of crisis in the administrative process, I happened to be introduced to *The Structure of Scientific Revolutions* (1962) by Thomas Kuhn. Although my analysis and mode of description must justify itself in its own terms, I suspect that the resemblance it bears to Kuhn's provocative approach reflects the powerful imprint that his book made on my mind. Only after I had completed the first draft of this book did I come upon Arthur Koestler's essay, "Literature and the Law of Diminishing Returns," in *The Heel of Achilles* (1974), which develops the similar argument that recurrent patterns can be found in the evolution of literary style.

Earlier versions of some of the chapters in this book have appeared in the Administrative Law Review, the Cambridge Law Journal, the Stanford Law Review, the Temple Law Quarterly, the University of Chicago Law Review, and the University of Pennsylvania Law Review. I am grateful to those journals for their editorial suggestions and for permission to reprint material that they originally published.

A number of students gave me significant assistance in the preparation of this book. I am happy to acknowledge the contributions of Henry S. Bryans, Louis Corsi, Richard A. Friedman, and James Morris of the University of Pennsylvania Law School, and of Douglas Ginsburg of the University of Chicago Law School. My copy editor, Claire Komnick, saved me from many infelicities of style, although I daresay that many remain through no fault of hers. My secretary, Margaret Massiah, faithfully typed numerous drafts of the manuscript of this book. Mrs. Colin Serby of Bishop's Stortford, Hertfordshire, flawlessly typed the final manuscript.

During the extended period in which I wrote this book, my family tolerated my compulsive demands and irritating eccentricities with love and understanding. To my wife, Sheba, my daughter, Deborah, and my son,

Jared, I owe the thanks of a husband and father. To Richard G. Lonsdorf I owe the gratitude of a friend for all the ways in which his companionship has sustained my spirit and enriched my life.

James O. Freedman

Clare Hall
Cambridge, England
August 1977

Introduction

1

Crisis and legitimacy in the administrative process: a historical perspective

The rise of administrative bodies probably has been the most significant legal trend of the last half-century and perhaps more values are affected by their decisions than those of all the courts, review of administrative decisions apart.

Justice Robert H. Jackson, in *FTC v. Ruberoid Co.* (1952)

When Alexis de Tocqueville published his remarkable study of democracy in America, he expressed a nineteenth-century European's admiration for the ease with which Americans did without government. It is not likely that a contemporary European observer, retracing Tocqueville's footsteps, would be led to express a similar admiration.

The steady growth in the role of the federal government since Tocqueville's time has been one of the most distinctive and important developments in American history. As the role of the federal government in national life has expanded, the center of gravity of the powers it exercises has gradually shifted, from the legislature in the first half of the nineteenth century, to the judiciary in the second half of the nineteenth century, to the executive and administration in the twentieth century. The characteristic pattern that underlies this shift can be seen in the nation's assertion of public control over the railroads, first by the enactment of restrictive legislation, then by emphasis upon judicial remedies, and finally by resort to administrative regulation.

This shift in the center of gravity of governmental powers has become so pronounced that contemporary political scientists, with increasing regularity, describe America as an administrative state. The distinguishing quality of the modern administrative state is its reliance upon the administrative process as a principal instrumentality for the achievement of national policies.

3

Roots of the modern administrative process

The growth of the administrative process in the United States occurred gradually, as the original thirteen states matured into a continental nation, increasingly industrialized and urbanized, facing economic and social problems that required responses more technologically expert, more institutionally flexible, and more procedurally expeditious than either the Congress or the federal courts could provide. The creation of administrative agencies was designed to supply these institutional deficiencies in the formulation and administration of public policy.

Although the rise of the administrative process is often identified with the presidency of Franklin D. Roosevelt, in fact reliance upon administrative agencies to meet emerging national problems long antedates the New Deal. It is as old as the Republic itself. The First Congress of the United States, meeting in 1789, enacted legislation authorizing administrative officers to "estimate the duties payable" on imports and to adjudicate claims to military pensions for "invalids who were wounded and disabled during the late war." The forerunner of the Patent Office was created in 1790, of the Office of Indian Affairs in 1796. The General Land Office was established in 1812. The administrative process thus has deep historical roots.

Approximately one-third of the federal administrative agencies were created before 1900, notably the Civil Service Commission in 1883 and the Interstate Commerce Commission in 1887. By 1891, the Pension Office of the Department of the Interior, with six thousand employees and more than a half-million cases pending for adjudication, was, according to its commissioner, the "largest executive bureau in the world."[1] Still another third of the federal agencies were created between 1900 and 1930, notably the Federal Reserve Board in 1913, the Federal Trade Commission in 1914, and the United States Tariff Commission in 1916. During these same decades, many state governments, responding to the influence of the Granger and Progressive movements, created administrative agencies to regulate banking, bridges, canals, ferries, grain elevators, insurance, railroad freight rates, and warehouses.

Reliance upon the administrative process was thus an established practice by the time that Roosevelt became President in 1933. But it nevertheless seems natural to associate the dominant position of the administrative process in modern government with President Roosevelt because the New Deal radiated a faith in the capacity of the administrative process perhaps exceeding that of any previous administration.

Faced with the devastating consequences of a major depression, the New Deal created a large number of administrative agencies to attack the nation's economic and social problems. These agencies, almost all of which eventually wrought major changes in American life, included the Federal Deposit Insurance Corporation (1933), the Tennessee Valley Authority (1933), the Federal Communications Commission (1934), the Securities and Exchange Commission (1934), the National Labor Relations Board (1935), and the Civil Aeronautics Board (1938).

In 1937, the President's Committee on Administrative Management reported critically to President Roosevelt that Congress had created more than a dozen major independent regulatory agencies since 1887, and went on to complain that "Congress is always tempted to turn each new responsibility over to a new independent commission. This is not only following the line of least resistance. It is also following a 50-year-old tradition."[2]

The tradition persists to this day. The demonstrated utility of the administrative process in meeting serious national problems during the New Deal years undoubtedly influenced the decision to create additional administrative agencies to meet the problems of controlling materials, manpower, prices, and production presented by World War II. In the decades since the war, the creation of new administrative agencies to deal with emerging national problems has continued apace. Under Democratic and Republican Presidents alike, Congress has regularly chosen to rely upon administrative regulation – rather than upon civil remedies, criminal penalties, subsidies to the private sector, or the free market, for example – to implement public policies in new and complex areas of federal concern. These areas have included atomic energy (the Atomic Energy Commission, 1946), military conscription (the Selective Service Commission, 1948), space exploration (the National Aeronautics and Space Administration, 1958), shipping (the Federal Maritime Commission, 1961), employment discrimination (the Equal Employment Opportunity Commission, 1965), environmental protection (the Environmental Protection Agency, 1970), occupational safety (the Occupational Safety and Health Review Commission, 1970), and consumer product safety (the Consumer Product Safety Commission, 1972).

The continuing growth in the administrative process has led to a corresponding increase in the prominence of administrative law in the decisions of the Supreme Court. The role of the Supreme Court in the shaping of American administrative law dates at least from the decision in *The Brig Aurora* in 1813.[3] At one time, in 1957, decisions involving review of administrative action constituted the largest single category of cases decided by the

5

Court on the merits, about one-third of the total.[4] In the decades of the 1960s and 1970s, however, the Court considered proportionally fewer administrative law cases as other classes of litigation, particularly those involving criminal procedure and civil rights, assumed a heightened national importance and claimed a greater share of the Court's attention.

By the time of the nation's bicentennial in 1976, the federal administrative process had achieved a considerable status. It embraced more than sixty independent regulatory agencies as well as perhaps several hundred administrative agencies located in the executive departments. Administrative agencies exercised regulatory responsibilities in scores of important and sensitive areas. The decisions rendered by the federal administrative agencies were many times the number rendered by the federal courts and probably affected the lives of more ordinary citizens more pervasively and more intimately than the decisions of the federal courts. In virtually every relevant respect, the administrative process has become a fourth branch of government, comparable in the scope of its authority and the impact of its decision making to the three more familiar constitutional branches.

The United States thus has increasingly become an administrative state. Americans have sought to understand the implications of this fact for the character of American democracy, the nature of American justice, and the quality of American life. These implications have often been troubling – even though the administrative process had deep historical roots, even though its growth has been gradual and evolutionary, and even though that growth has occurred only by deliberative acts of democratic choice. If the United States is to realize the promise and respect the limitations of the administrative process, the quest for understanding its implications must be regularly renewed.

The recurrent sense of crisis

Erik Erikson once wrote that "in every field there are a few very simple questions which are highly embarrassing because the debate which forever arises around them leads only to perpetual failure and seems consistently to make fools of the most expert."[5] This observation has particular applicability to the administrative process, where the kinds of questions to which Erikson refers concern the status, the soundness, and ultimately the legitimacy of the administrative process: What justifies the exercise of such extensive lawmaking powers by groups that lack the political accountability of the legislature? What justifies the exercise of such decisive adjudicatory powers by groups

6

whose members lack the tenure and independence of the judiciary? What explains the failure of the administrative agencies, as the recurrent generalization would have it, to achieve a significant measure of effectiveness in performing their regulatory tasks?

Questions such as these have usually been based upon the premise that there is a "crisis" in the administrative process. Each generation has tended to define the crisis in its own terms, usually by focusing upon a major question that has attracted its attention and reforming impulses.

For many years, the dominant concern was the anomaly of the existence of administrative agencies in a government founded upon a commitment to the separation of powers. That concern later became closely joined to a concern over the constitutionality of the delegation of power. Slowly, these questions gave rise to the creation of a satisfactory explanation in theory, which rationalized the position of the administrative agencies, accommodated their existence to the constitutional structure, and set limits to the powers that might properly be delegated.[6] Thus the initial concerns were stilled for the moment. But they soon were replaced by new ones, each in its own time phrased in the idiom of crisis.

During the early years of the twentieth century, one such concern focused on the role of the courts in reviewing administrative action. As the theoretical responses to this concern became increasingly elaborated, particularly in the magisterial work of John Dickinson,[7] they gained a general acceptance by lawyers, legislators, and citizens. A second question, which followed closely upon the debate over judicial review, involved the procedures by which administrative agencies reached their decisions. No single phrase can capture the variegated procedural styles that the scores of federal administrative agencies followed during the period from 1920 to 1945, when this concern was dominant. But it is surely fair to say that many agencies paid scant attention to the matter at all while others followed ad hoc schemes that departed widely from the judicial-type procedures that traditional theory regarded as the finest fruit of centuries of Anglo-American legal experience. This concern over procedure grew in intensity until it was substantially satisfied by passage of the Administrative Procedure Act[8] in 1946, and by the Supreme Court's increased readiness to enforce the requirements of procedural due process.

There have been other significant areas of concern as well, although none can properly be described as having been dominant during a particular historical period. These are concerns that have been so consistently troubling to those who study and participate in the administrative process that the terms

7

by which they are commonly described have almost become clichés. They include phenomena such as these: the failure of agencies to develop standards that, in Judge Friendly's phrase, are "sufficiently definite to permit decisions to be fairly predictable and the reasons for them to be understood";[9] the tendency of agencies to become "captives" of the industries they are charged with regulating; the agencies' lack of demonstrable and relevant expertise; the blight of *ex parte* influence and communication; and the failure of agencies to protect the interests of the consumer. Many of these concerns were captured in the catchphrase of Justice Jackson, who, in a notable dissent, referred to a pervasive "malaise in the administrative scheme."[10]

Virtually every President since the period of the New Deal has been sufficiently disturbed by the functioning and status of the federal administrative agencies to order at least one major study seeking recommendations for improvement. President Roosevelt commissioned two such studies: the Report of the President's Committee on Administrative Management, which concluded that the agencies constituted "a headless fourth branch of government" and should be abolished, with their responsibilities being absorbed by the executive branch; and the Report of the Attorney General's Committee on Administrative Procedure, which accepted the role of administrative agencies in the structure of American government but recommended reforms in administrative procedure that eventually became the basis of the Administrative Procedure Act.[11]

Presidents Truman and Eisenhower enlisted the experience of former President Hoover in creating the Commission on Organization of the Executive Branch of Government, which proposed that the adjudicatory functions of the Federal Trade Commission and the National Labor Relations Board be taken away and given to a newly created Administrative Court of the United States.[12] John F. Kennedy, while still the President-elect, asked James M. Landis, formerly dean of the Harvard Law School and a member of several agencies, to prepare a report on the state of the administrative process. The Landis Report was scathing in its criticisms of the agencies for their inefficiency and their failure to formulate policy effectively.[13] President Nixon appointed the President's Advisory Council on Executive Organization, also known as the Ash Council, which recommended that the major regulatory agencies be replaced in their collegiate form by single administrators whose decisions would be reviewable by a new administrative court.[14]

That so many Presidents have felt compelled to seek comprehensive assessments of the administrative process and that the resulting studies have so consistently proposed changes of such a fundamental, even radical, character is suggestive of a persisting sense of uneasiness and concern about the problematic place of administrative agencies in the machinery of modern government. To these presidentially inspired studies must be added a series of searching critiques of the administrative process, published within approximately a decade of each other, by three of the most thoughtful of recent administrative agency members, Philip Elman of the Federal Trade Commission, Louis J. Hector of the Civil Aeronautics Board, and Newton N. Minow of the Federal Communications Commission.[15]

The history of the modern administrative process can be seen, then, as having been marked by an extended sense of crisis. At each stage of this history, the sense of crisis has been phrased in terms of a dominant concern. Eventually, each dominant concern has subsided in intensity as a satisfactory theoretical explanation has been fashioned or responsive legislation enacted, only to be succeeded by a differently formulated concern that has become dominant in its place.

The emergence of each new concern has not, of course, caused the earlier ones to disappear completely. They have remained and continued to trouble new generations of lawyers and scholars. But they have come to be regarded as part of the inevitable, even intractable, imperfections that attend all human endeavors, requiring periodic attention and adjustment, rather than as glaring anomalies that call into question the central justifications for the administrative process itself.

The enduring sense of crisis historically associated with the administrative agencies seems to suggest that something more serious than merely routine criticism is at work. As one examines this history, one begins to believe that the dominant concern of any given period is in fact only the manifestation of a deeper uneasiness over the place and function of the administrative process in American government, and that each generation – however earnestly and plausibly it has formulated its uneasiness – has in fact been speaking to this same underlying problem. This may explain why, despite the fact that each generation has fashioned solutions responsive to the problems it has perceived, the nation's sense of uneasiness with the administrative process has persisted.

The criticism that historically has been directed toward the administrative agencies is significantly different in tone and quality from the criticism, robust though it often has been, that regularly has attended the manner in which Congress and the courts carry out their respective responsibilities. Those institutions have been challenged primarily with questions concerning the proper limits of their undoubted powers, the wisdom of particular decisions as a matter of policy or the national good, and the efficiency of the processes by which they reach their decisions. Most of these criticisms have been directed at actions and defects existing at the margins of institutional power, at temporary aberrations and malfunctions rather than at the legitimacy of the institutional power. On those few occasions when the criticism has been directed at the legitimacy of the institutional power itself, the power has survived wholly intact, its legitimacy undiminished.[16]

By contrast, the criticism of the administrative agencies has been animated by a strong and persisting challenge to the basic legitimacy of the administrative process itself. Criticisms of this character are stated in the reports commissioned by Presidents Roosevelt, Truman, Kennedy, and Nixon, as well as in an extensive body of literature analyzing the federal administrative process.[17] That such criticism has so often been phrased in terms of crisis suggests that it is too serious, too fundamental, perhaps too deeply implicated in principle, to be met by theoretical constructs or by incremental adjustments of the kind that governments routinely rely upon when anomalies or inefficiencies of recent appearance or temporary duration seem to require a response.

The subject of legitimacy is concerned with popular attitudes toward the exercise of governmental power. Such attitudes focus upon whether governmental power is being held and exercised in accordance with a nation's laws, values, traditions, and customs. That the legitimacy of the federal administrative process should still be in question at this late date may be surprising. But institutions of which so much is demanded, no matter how deep their historical roots, can hardly be expected to gain and sustain public acceptance when the very basis of their existence and their legitimacy is so consistently and forcefully challenged. Institutional legitimacy is an indispensable condition for institutional effectiveness. By endowing institutional decisions with an inherent capacity to attract obedience and respect, legitimacy permits an institution to achieve its goals without the regular necessity of threatening the use of force and creating renewed episodes of public resentment. Since the authority of any institution, as Max Weber so effectively argued, rests ultimately upon a popular belief in its legitimacy,[18] substantial, persisting challenges to the legitimacy of governmental institutions must be regarded with concern, for such challenges threaten to impair the capacity of government to meet its administrative responsibilities effectively.

But how do governmental institutions achieve a status of legitimacy in the American political setting? Why have the federal administrative agencies failed to achieve a status of legitimacy as complete as that of other governmental institutions? And what steps can Congress or the administrative agencies take to enhance the legitimacy of the administrative process?

The recurrent sense of crisis attending the federal administrative process results from the failure of many Americans to appreciate the relevance of four principal sources of legitimacy to the role that administrative agencies play in American government. The legitimacy of the administrative process may be supported by public recognition that administrative agencies occupy an indispensable position in the constitutional scheme of government. The policies and performance of administrative agencies may further be accepted as legitimate to the extent that the public perceives the administrative process as embodying significant elements of political accountability. In addition, the effectiveness of administrative agencies in meeting their statutory responsibilities may enhance their legitimacy by strengthening public support in a nation that always has been impressed by effective performance. Finally, the legitimacy of the administrative process may be enhanced by the public's perception that its decision-making procedures are fair.

Part I of this book examines sources of crisis in the administrative process. These sources include the failure of administrative agencies to conform to the constitutional scheme of separation of powers, the departures that the administrative process makes from judicial norms, public ambivalence toward economic regulation, public concern with bureaucratization, public skepticism of administrative expertise, the fact that administrative agencies lack a direct political accountability, and the problems created for administrative policy making by broad delegations of legislative power. Part I argues that these sources of crisis impair the legitimacy of the administrative process, often unfairly because many of the judgments underlying these sources of crisis are misconceived as conclusions of historical fact, misinformed as judgments of administrative practice, or indiscriminately general as assessments of agency performance.

Part II suggests that the quality of administrative justice – the fairness of an agency's procedures, its interest in the protection of individual rights, its commitment to the attainment of just results – is an essential source of administrative legitimacy. Part II evaluates formal and informal administrative processes in order to demonstrate the integrity of the procedures by which the federal administrative agencies discharge their important decision-making responsibilities and to expose areas where improvement is desirable.

Questions of legitimacy give rise to an intricate and perplexing inquiry,

11

filled with theoretical and practical subtleties. Government has little choice but to confront these subtleties if, as Charles L. Black, Jr., has written, it is to command "among its citizens an adequately strong feeling of the legitimacy of its measures, of their authentic governmental character as distinguished from their debatable policy and wisdom."[19] The failure of the federal administrative agencies to still the recurrent sense of crisis with respect to their legitimacy – to persuade the American people "of their authentic governmental character" – thus presents questions worthy of a serious quest for understanding, even if because of the difficulty of such questions, the quest should finally lead, in Erikson's phrase, "only to perpetual failure."

I

Sources of crisis in the administrative process

2

Separation of powers and the American imagination

There is no doubt that the development of the administrative agency in response to modern legislative and administrative need has placed severe strain on the separation of powers principle in its pristine formulation.

Justice Byron R. White, in Buckley v. Valeo (1976)

Reverence for the doctrine of the separation of powers is an American tradition. The roots of the doctrine reach backward to the thought of Plato, Aristotle, Cicero, Machiavelli, Locke, and Blackstone; but it is Montesquieu's statement of it, in *The Spirit of the Laws*, that is usually regarded as having influenced the Framers of the United States Constitution most decisively. Montesquieu expressed the view that when "the legislative and executive powers are united in the same person, or in the same body of magistrates, there can be no liberty."[1] Although the theory had been stated in several state constitutions adopted earlier than 1789,[2] its classic American expression is in the great phrases of the U.S. Constitution providing separate institutions for the exercise of the legislative, the executive, and the judicial powers. The decision of the Framers to rest the structure of the new nation upon the theory of the separation of powers represented, as Arthur M. Schlesinger, Jr., has written, "a distinctive American contribution to the art of government."[3]

The question, of course, was the meaning, the content, the intention of that contribution. It was Madison, in a series of remarkable essays of such timeless pertinence that they might have been written today, who gave the most important contemporaneous interpretation of that contribution. "The accumulation of all powers, legislative, executive, and judiciary, in the same hands, whether of one, of few, or many, and whether hereditary, self-appointed, or elective, may justly be pronounced the very definition of tyranny," he wrote in *The Federalist*.[4]

15

For Madison, the central concern was to devise an instrument of government that would respond to the ancient wisdom "that power is of an encroaching nature, and that it ought to be effectively restrained from passing the limits assigned to it."[5] That instrument was the system of checks and balances, upon which the Constitution was made to rest. The "great security against a gradual concentration of the several powers in the same department," Madison wrote, "consists in giving to those who administer each department the necessary constitutional means and personal motives to resist encroachments of the others."[6] The goal, he believed, was to design institutional arrangements so that "ambition [would] be made to counteract ambition."[7]

The fact that the theory of the separation of powers was written into the Constitution by men of the undoubted stature of the Framers gave it a weight and a dignity, a momentum for respect, that subsequent generations could not readily resist. Some consequences of this fact became evident when courts were asked to interpret the meaning of the Framers' creation. The Supreme Court, in *Kilbourn v. Thompson*, a leading nineteenth-century decision, wrote that it is "essential to the successful working of this system that the persons intrusted with power in any one of [the three] branches shall not be permitted to encroach upon the powers confided to the others, but that each shall by the law of its creation be limited to the exercise of the powers appropriate to its own department and no other."[8] The carefully literal reading that the Court in *Kilbourn* gave to the grand phrases of the Constitution is striking; it suggests something of the dutiful recitation of a received verity.

Perhaps the most significant twentieth-century judicial expression of the intention of the separation of powers doctrine appears in Justice Brandeis's dissent in *Myers v. United States*: "The doctrine of the separation of powers was adopted by the Convention of 1787, not to promote efficiency but to preclude the exercise of arbitrary power. The purpose was, not to avoid friction but, by means of the inevitable friction incident to the distribution of the governmental powers among three departments, to save the people from autocracy."[9] Here the tone is more profound and philosophical than in *Kilbourn*, more consonant with Madison's attempt to ground the separation of powers in a view of man's nature. But it is also suffused with a reverential belief that the separation of powers is a hallowed bulwark against the tyranny to which, as history was believed to have taught, the accumulation of power tends.

There can be little question that the theory of the separation of powers – born from a psychological understanding of the nature of man and adopted by the Framers as part of the nation's experiment in fashioning institutional defenses against tyranny – retains an enduring hold on the American imagination. It has come to function as something of an idealized archetype, bequeathed to present generations by farsighted realists of past generations. That temper is quite perfectly reflected in a celebratory passage in Justice Frankfurter's concurring opinion in the *Steel Seizure* case:

The Founders of this Nation were not imbued with the modern cynicism that the only thing that history teaches is that it teaches nothing. They acted on the conviction that the experience of man sheds a good deal of light on his nature. It sheds a good deal of light not merely on the need for effective power, if a society is to be at once cohesive and civilized, but also on the need for limitations on the power of governors over the governed.

To that end they rested the structure of our central government on the system of checks and balances. For them the doctrine of separation of powers was not mere theory; it was a felt necessity. Not so long ago it was fashionable to find our system of checks and balances obstructive to effective government. It was easy to ridicule that system as outmoded – too easy. The experience through which the world has passed in our own day has made vivid the realization that the Framers of our Constitution were not inexperienced doctrinaires.[10]

The administrative process does not, of course, strictly conform to the Framers' theory of the separation of powers. Administrative agencies were deliberately created as instruments of blended powers. In many instances they were expressly created to combine legislative, executive, and judicial powers. The protection of the people's liberties that was to come from the "inevitable friction" among those exercising the separated powers was compromised for the notable strengths – particularly versatility in the development and enforcement of policy – that a combination of powers would permit.

The anomalous position of administrative agencies in a system of government so deeply committed to the theory of the separation of powers has naturally been the subject of intense consideration. That consideration has often turned to criticism of a fundamental kind. The President's Committee on Administrative Management, reporting to Roosevelt in 1937, wrote that administrative agencies "constitute a headless 'fourth branch' of the Government, a haphazard deposit of irresponsible agencies and uncoordinated powers. They do violence to the basic theory of the American Constitution that there should be three major branches of the Government and only

17

three.''[11] The committee recommended that ''[a]ny program to restore our constitutional ideal of a fully coordinated Executive Branch responsible to the President must bring within the reach of that responsible control all work done by these independent commissions which is not judicial in nature.''[12]

Although criticism of this character has diminished in intensity in recent decades, particularly since enactment of the Administrative Procedure Act in 1946, the conceptual concern that it expressed has not been laid to rest. It is not an overstatement to assert, as Kenneth C. Davis has, that ''[p]robably the principal doctrinal barrier to the development of the administrative process has been the theory of separation of powers.''[13]

That the legitimacy of the administrative process has so regularly been called into question because of its inconsistency with the theory of the separation of powers is not without its ironies. Two of Madison's most important essays on the theory of the separation of powers are defenses of the proposed Constitution against criticism that the powers it assigns to the legislative, the executive, and the judiciary departments are not kept sufficiently separate and distinct to satisfy the theory.[14] Madison replied that the criticism would be serious if it were valid – ''no further arguments would be necessary to inspire a universal reprobation of the system,'' he wrote – but argued that a rigid and formalistic conception of the separation of powers was ''warranted by neither the real meaning annexed to that maxim by its author nor by the sense in which it has hitherto been understood in America.''[15] Neither the British Constitution, upon which Montesquieu built his theory,[16] nor the constitutions of the several states, kept the departments of power separate and distinct, ''notwithstanding the emphatical and, in some instances, the unqualified terms in which this axiom has been laid down.''[17] For Madison the theory was most responsibly stated in the requirement of the New Hampshire constitution that ''the legislative, executive, and judiciary powers ought to be kept as separate from, and independent of, each other *as the nature of a free government will admit; or as is consistent with that chain of connection that binds the whole fabric of the constitution in one indissoluble bond of unity and amity.''[18]

Madison thus regarded the theory of the separation of powers as a ''political maxim''[19] that cautioned against excessive and unwise concentrations of power but did not preclude one branch of government from participating in functions assigned primarily to another. His view was shared by his contemporaries, with the significant exception, possibly, of James Wilson.[20] Two distinguished scholars of the formative stages of American administrative law have observed, "The latitude with which the doctrine [of the separation of powers] must be observed in a work-a-day world was steadily insisted upon by those shrewd men of the world who framed the Constitution and by the statesman who became the great Chief Justice."[21]

The Supreme Court, in turn, has recognized that the Constitution does not prescribe a rigid separation of powers among the essential branches of government. In *Buckley v. Valeo* the Court, taking note of the specific manner in which the Constitution contemplates that powers will sometimes be shared, stated: "The President is a participant in the law-making process by virtue of his authority to veto bills enacted by Congress. The Senate is a participant in the appointive process by virtue of its authority to refuse to confirm persons nominated to office by the President."[22]

The Court, in fact, has never regarded the theory of the separation of powers as merely an abstract and inflexible legal doctrine. Instead, it consistently has considered as paramount the policies that the theory is designed to serve. The Court has given content to the theory by estimating the relationship of these policies to the particular questions before it, and by fashioning safeguards to secure the essential constitutional balance that the principle of the separation of powers was designed to preserve. Nothing better illustrates this process of accommodating the goals of the theory with the needs of effective government than the long series of decisions by which the rules governing the delegation of legislative power have been created.[23] The Court has always shaped its reading of the theory by reference both to its fundamental purposes and to the perception, lucidly stated by Woodrow Wilson, that government is "not a machine, but a living thing" and "[n]o living thing can have its organs offset against each other as checks, and live."[24]

The conventional understanding of the separation of powers can be seen, then, as an apotheosized version of the theory that the Framers understood and chose to incorporate into the new nation's Constitution. The lines of the popular version have a conceptual purity and immutability that Madison and his contemporaries would have seen only as naïve and unwise. It is surely ironic that the administrative process should be criticized as violating the theory of the separation of powers by those whose conception of that theory is more Madisonian than Madison's. Ironic or not, the simplistic version of the theory of the separation of powers still informs the American imagination, and has done much to nourish the continuing skepticism about the legitimacy of the administrative process.

Any attempt at understanding the nature of the recurring sense of crisis attending the administrative agencies must begin with an appreciation of the fact that the simplistic conception of the separation of powers embedded in the public imagination – a conception quite at odds with the Framers' sophisticated understanding of the doctrine – has unfairly called into question the legitimacy of the administrative process.

3

The departure from judicial norms

[T]he assumption that the methods of natural justice are ex necessitate those of Courts of justice is wholly unfounded.

> Lord Shaw, in *Local Government Board v. Arlidge* (1915)

If the doctrine of the separation of powers is one of the fixed stars in the constellation of American values, the trial-type procedures by which the judicial process decides disputes are another. The American people traditionally have regarded the adversary procedures of the judicial process as one of the finest achievements of Anglo-American legal development. Their faith in the fitness of courts for the resolution of almost any kind of dispute, private or public, indeed, had formed the basis of one of Tocqueville's most celebrated observations. The substance of that faith remains powerful more than a century later. Because the administrative process makes significant and unfamiliar departures from judicial norms, it has aroused a sense of uneasiness as to its fundamental fairness. What considerations could possibly justify the intentional departure from procedures that have served the cause of justice so well and protected the rights of the individual for so long? The edge of misgiving that informs that question has been an important factor in sustaining the recurrent sense of crisis attending the federal administrative process.

The departures that the administrative process has made from judicial norms are the products of practical experience, not of theories that, in Madison's derisory phrase, are "the offspring of the closet."[1] The repeated decisions of Congress, particularly in the twentieth century, to invoke the distinctive methods of the administrative process in addressing a widening range of social and economic problems constitute a cumulative judgment that the procedural methods of the judicial process are not adequate to meet many of the regulatory needs of an industrialized nation. That judgment reflects several considerations.

Although it long has been recognized that trial-type proceedings serve the interests of society well when factual disputes are sharp and issues of credibility prominent, as they typically are in criminal prosecutions and negligence cases, the methods of a trial are not well suited to tasks more legislative, supervisory, or "polycentric" in nature, such as the regulation of commercial competition and trade practices, the anticipation and management of industrial growth, the administration of welfare programs, or the allocation of a limited resource to one or a few among many applicants.[2] Determining whether a proposed rate structure is "just and reasonable" or whether a new service to a community is required by the "public interest, convenience, or necessity" are tasks calling for administrative or managerial judgments quite different in their imaginative demands and creative scope from the typical judicial tasks of "finding" a nonrecurring historical fact and "applying" the relevant legal rule to it.[3]

Those who conceptualized the modern administrative process understood that the effective discharge of responsibilities such as these could not be achieved within the case-by-case constraints of judicial procedures. These responsibilities demanded a more extensive and versatile set of procedural possibilities – rule making, adjudication, industry-wide conferences, advisory opinions – and greater flexibility in their employment, by formal and informal means, than the historic limitations of the judicial process permitted.

The early advocates of the administrative process also sought a format in which the public interest could be represented and vindicated formally, rather than only coincidentally. They placed upon administrative agencies the explicit responsibility of employing their expertise and independence to define and assert a larger view of the public interest than private parties, motivated by self-interest, could be expected to express. In adversary proceedings of the classic judicial kind, the parties have an incentive to present only partial versions of the facts. Moreover, the rules of evidence often prevent consideration of relevant information and exploration of suggestive areas of inquiry. In his famous speech on "The Causes of Popular Dissatisfaction with the Administration of Justice," delivered in 1906, Roscoe Pound attacked the adversary system for many of these reasons. It promoted a "sporting theory of justice," he said, with the result that "we take it as a matter of course that a judge should be a mere umpire, to pass upon objections and hold counsel to the rules of the game, and that the parties should fight out their own game in their own way without judicial interference."[4]

Thus trial-type proceedings were hardly a desirable method for developing a comprehensive national policy in an area of administrative regulation or for formulating and enforcing an informed conception of the public interest. In order to remedy the deficiencies of trial-type proceedings, the administrative process intentionally departed from judicial norms in developing new models of institutional decision making. The departures from judicial norms that characterize administrative rule making have been considerably less disturbing to popular conceptions of justice than the departures made in the procedures for resolving adjudicatory questions of the kind traditionally settled by the courts. Therefore, this discussion focuses primarily upon adjudicatory proceedings in order to suggest the justifications for the departures that the administrative process makes from judicial norms.

Certain departures from judicial norms can be seen in the early developments of the administrative adjudicatory process. In this new administrative model, the hearing examiner was authorized to call and to cross-examine witnesses and to participate actively in the development of a record that reflected fully the public interest issues involved. He was expected to order the parties to supplement the record in areas where he considered it deficient, regardless of whether the parties themselves might prefer to restrict the record within narrower bounds.[5] The Social Security Administration even gave the hearing examiner responsibility for representing both the claimant and the government in developing the testimonial record, as well as the duty of making the eventual adjudicatory decision. In sustaining the constitutionality of this inquisitorial procedure, the Supreme Court said that it was not "persuaded by the advocate-judge-multiple-hat suggestion" because "it assumes too much and would bring down too many procedures designed, and working well, for a governmental structure of great and growing complexity."[6]

Those who created the modern administrative process also sought to free it from many of the formal restrictions of the judicial process. As Justice Frankfurter, an early advocate of the more spacious potentialities of the administrative process, once wrote in another context: "Only fragments of a social problem are seen through the narrow windows of a litigation."[7] The administrative process therefore has relaxed the enforcement of the common law rules of evidence, including the limitations on the use of hearsay, by permitting the introduction of any evidence as long as it was not irrelevant, immaterial, or unduly repetitious. And in order to gain the strengths of the legislative process in informing the mind of the decision maker, the administrative process has devised rule-making proceedings for the resolution of many issues that courts would have decided within the more constricted confines of trial-type proceedings.

But the most dramatic departure that the administrative process has made from judicial norms has been in authorizing agencies to combine investigative, prosecuting, and adjudicatory functions in order to strengthen the coordinated development of regulatory policy. This means that an administrative agency has the opportunity to participate in each of the decisive stages of administrative lawmaking. It also means that an agency can act as investigator and prosecutor in issuing a complaint, and eventually as judge in deciding whether the allegations in the complaint have been proved at a hearing.

The departures that the administrative process thus has made from judicial norms have been recommended by the renewed capacity they have given government to respond to social and economic problems too complex to yield to trial-type proceedings of the kind traditional in courts. They have been justified, finally, by the greater authority they have put at the service of the nation's regulatory aspirations.

But those who created the modern administrative process understood, almost from the start, that the departures it made from judicial norms would arouse anxiety and that pressures to judicialize its procedures would inevitably arise. Felix Frankfurter was typical of many Progressive and New Deal intellectuals in urging that efforts to impose judicial procedures upon the administrative process be resisted. As professor and judge, he insisted that reliance upon administrative agencies reflected a legislative realization that "the regulatory needs of modern society demand law-enforcing tribunals other than the conventional courts"[8] and that agencies must be recognized on their own terms as "collaborative instrumentalities of justice" with the courts.[9] He called for a "candid recognition that the administrative process has had a different development and has a different operation from that of our courts because the two derive from different needs."[10] Frankfurter spoke for several generations of social reformers in arguing that the American legal tradition must accept the procedural and institutional departures that administrative agencies have made from judicial norms as growing out of the special nature of their origin and responsibilities, much as the

24

common law had come to accept the more flexible and innovative remedies of equity as collaborative methods for protecting the rights of the individual.

As Frankfurter and his contemporaries expected, pressures to judicialize the emergent administrative process soon appeared, finding vigorous, sometimes exaggerated, expression in the early decades of the twentieth century.[11] Elihu Root, in his presidential address to the American Bar Association in 1916, noted that the United States was "entering upon the creation of a body of administrative law quite different in its machinery, its remedies, and its necessary safeguards from the old methods of regulation by specific statutes enforced by courts."[12] He could see "no withdrawal from these experiments" because delegation of legislative power to administrative agencies was the only way that modern government could deal effectively with the increasingly complex conditions of an industrialized society.

But others thought the experiments had gone too far. John Lord O'Brian, in 1920, called attention to the "system of non-judicial process" that administrative agencies relied upon, having deliberately abandoned "American settled habits of judicial procedure," and found it "alien to our jurisprudence."[13] The American Bar Association, which has regularly proposed that the methods of judicial trials be introduced to a greater degree in the conduct of administrative proceedings, asserted in 1934 that the rise of the administrative process constituted a "fifth column" imported from the Continent, and created the danger that judicial methods of procedure would meet "the fate of the Merovingian kings."[14] And Roscoe Pound, the dean of the Harvard Law School, who earlier had decried the defects of the adversary system, warned in 1938 that administrative justice was deteriorating into "administrative absolutism," which he identified as "a Marxian idea much in vogue now" in which the traditional concept of law as a body of authoritative grounds for decision was regarded as illusory.[15]

Challenges of this character continued to be heard throughout the 1930s, as the pattern of New Deal legislation made clear that reliance upon the administrative process was systematically increasing. Many of these challenges could be dismissed as little more than disguised assaults upon the economic and social philosophy of the New Deal itself. But when challenges of a similar character, albeit phrased more temperately, came from the courts, they could not be dismissed as readily.

The Supreme Court of the period was plainly dubious that the characteristic procedures of the administrative process were as reliable as the more traditional methods of the judicial process. An important example of such judicial skepticism can be seen in the doctrines of jurisdictional and constititutional fact, announced in *Crowell v. Benson*[16] and *Ohio Valley Water Co. v. Ben Avon Borough.*[17] These related doctrines required that a court make an independent determination of the facts essential to an administrative agency's constitutional authority to act, precisely because of what the Court in a later decision called the greater "security inherent in our judicial safeguards."[18] Even as prominent a supporter of the administrative process as Justice Brandeis, who had dissented from the Court's announcement of the jurisdictional and constitutional fact doctrines, remarked upon the "difference in security of judicial over administrative action" in the course of an opinion for the Court in *Ng Fung Ho v. White* holding that an individual facing an administrative order of deportation was constitutionally entitled to a judicial trial *de novo* on the factual question of citizenship.[19]

By requiring an independent judicial determination of certain kinds of facts, decisions such as these limited the authority and questioned the legitimacy of the administrative process. But they did not – and this was a notable aspect of their holdings – compel administrative agencies to modify their distinctive procedures. Gradually, the sense of uneasiness created by the departures that the administrative process made from judicial norms subsided in intensity. As judicial suspicions that the growth of administrative government would undermine the judicial process proved unfounded, the administrative process gained increasing acceptance as a necessary part of the nation's legal institutions. Enactment of the Administrative Procedure Act in 1946, with its grant of independence to impartial hearing examiners and its creation of a virtually complete internal separation of inconsistent functions, broadened this acceptance by demonstrating that the administrative process could protect the rights of the individual at least as punctiliously as the judicial process did, a conclusion that the experience of many European legal systems seemed to support.

Nevertheless, the nation's acceptance of the administrative process was not yet as complete as its acceptance of the judicial process. The departures that the administrative process made from judicial norms nurtured a residue of reservation that, in the 1960s and 1970s, found renewed expression in a consistent progress of Supreme Court decisions. Ignoring Justice Frankfurter's informed warning that the differences in origin and function of administrative agencies "preclude wholesale transplantation of the rules of procedure, trial and review which have evolved from the history and experience of courts,"[20] the Court required administrative agencies to follow a gradually enlarged range of formal procedures drawn from the trial-type

26

model of the courts, often without sufficient sensitivity to the possibility that arrangements less judicial in nature might be better suited to wisely remedying the constitutional defects at issue.[21] In a related development, the lower federal courts showed an inclination to require administrative agencies to follow trial-type procedures in rule-making proceedings, despite the fact that neither the Administrative Procedure Act nor any substantive legislation imposed such requirements,[22] as well as to chastise an occasional hearing examiner for conducting a hearing more actively than would be appropriate for a federal judge.[23]

The tendency of these decisions has been to judicialize the administrative process rather than to strengthen and refine those of its qualities that are most distinctively administrative. The dangers of distortion inherent in this tendency – that administrative agencies, as they are compelled to follow judicial norms more closely, will lose a measure of their capacity for effective decision making – is not often addressed.[24] As this tendency toward judicialization has become more pronounced, in defiance of Justice Frankfurter's admonition, the legitimacy of the administrative process inevitably has suffered. Those concerned with the legitimacy of the administrative process cannot avoid wondering how persuasively the independent existence of an administrative process that is substantially judicialized can be justified in light of the stature of the judicial process as the more authentic instrument of judicialized decision making.

What accounts for the tendency in the 1960s and 1970s to impose trial-type procedures upon administrative agencies? The most probable explanation requires reference to a number of related cultural developments. These were years disfigured by the assassinations of John F. Kennedy and Martin Luther King, Jr., by the divisiveness of the Vietnam War, and by the tawdry dishonor of Watergate. The level of social hostility – between minority groups and whites, between women and men, between young and old – increased steadily. As ennobling efforts were mounted to reverse deeply rooted patterns of discrimination and injustice, the rhetoric of the period encouraged individuals to identify themselves as members of separate groups (often racial, sexual, or ethnic in nature) before they defined themselves as members of the larger American community. Faced with this situation, Americans did what societies often do when social conflict threatens to disturb an existing sense of stability and commonality: They turned to procedural formality to establish a degree of confidence that the government's authority, particularly to the extent that it had the capacity to favor one group at the expense of another, was exercised fairly.

27

In addition, the deceptions and misjudgments that characterized the nation's conduct of the Vietnam War bred a widely shared loss of confidence in the integrity of government officials and in the capacity of government to reach wise decisions in secret. The demand that the decision-making processes of the government be more open, that they provide an effective opportunity for ordinary citizens to contest the government's proposals before they became fixed as matters of policy, was rooted in this distrust of official ideology, motivation, and action. For persons skeptical of the government's honesty and the benevolence of its intentions, trial-type hearings of an adversary character were the most familiar and traditional method for openly challenging the wisdom of proposed governmental action.[25]

Finally, Americans had become deeply distressed by the increasing influence that bureaucracy had over their daily lives. Of particular concern was the "insolence of office" that bureaucracy too often generates, with its formalistic adherence to rigid rules and its ritual indifference to the individual personalities of those whose interests it governs. An insistence upon trial-type hearings was an understandable response to the characteristic style of many governmental bureaucracies: Whatever their limitations, trial-type procedures are an effective device for compelling bureaucracy to pay attention to the specific circumstances of particular individuals.

Whether or not these developments supply a complete explanation, the fact that administrative agencies increasingly have been required to follow trial-type procedures in recent years is instructive in its ironies. These requirements have been announced at a time when students of judicial administration have been advocating that whole classes of litigation – for example, automobile accident claims, wage-earner bankruptcies, divorces, the adoption of children, and traffic offenses – should be removed from the courts and placed in administrative agencies precisely because trial-type hearings threaten by their procedural complexity to overwhelm the capacity of courts to act at all. In addition, many thoughtful observers of the judicial process have again been expressing doubts, in a manner reminiscent of Roscoe Pound and legal realists such as Jerome Frank,[26] about the capacity of trial-type hearings for determining the truth. Thus Judge Marvin Frankel, in his 1974 Cardozo Lecture, argued that the "search for truth fails too much of the time" in trial-type proceedings because many of the rules of the adversary system "are not geared for, but are often aptly suited to defeat, the development of the truth."[27]

Despite the pause that these ironies should give, the virtues of trial-type proceedings ought not be dismissed too quickly. In many administrative

28

contexts, trial-type proceedings have served the cause of justice well. When the civil liberties of an individual are involved – for example, when the government seeks to dismiss an employee on a ground carrying a moral stigma, or proposes to return a paroled prisoner to custody for his lapses, or challenges a person's right to continue to practice his profession – reliance upon trial-type hearings, with the precise focus that confrontation and cross-examination exact, can serve as an invaluable means of exposing error and prejudice.[28] Even in hearings of a primarily legislative character, there may be particular issues that are explored most appropriately by trial-type procedures. The administrative process regularly has demonstrated that it is capable of adjusting its approach to take account of such differentiated necessities as they occur.

But when an administrative hearing involves issues essentially legislative in nature – for example, rate making, resource allocation, or social and economic planning – the special virtues of trial-type proceedings are not only less suitable than other forms of procedure, they also distort the administrative process by which the agency is striving to reach a sound result, substituting the passive impartiality of judicial procedures for a vigorous administrative exploration of the public interest.

The danger, of course, is that public uneasiness about the departures that the administrative process makes from judicial norms might sweep such discriminating distinctions as these to the side and lead to wholesale requirements that trial-type procedures be followed for the decision of every issue in administrative hearings. If administrative agencies are to redeem Justice Frankfurter's vision that they be "collaborative instrumentalities of justice," the choice between permitting them to depart from judicial norms and requiring them to conform to trial-type procedures must be governed by considerations of substantive appropriateness, not by the reassuring attraction of familiar traditions that may be inapposite to the task at hand.

In the 1970s the Supreme Court seemed to modify its course of requiring that the administrative process be conducted according to judicial norms. At the same time, as the financial and social costs of adversary procedures have become more evident, the American people have begun to consider the desirability of relying upon many nonjudicial and informal methods of dispute settlement, such as the Scandinavian institution of the ombudsman, for protecting the individual against erroneous or arbitrary governmental action. It is possible that these developments will encourage a greater understanding of the distinctive style of the administrative process and create a greater appreciation of the reasons for supporting the departures it makes from judicial norms. Perhaps, too, these developments will cause Americans to reflect upon the fact that most of the European nations and most of the world's great intellectual disciplines do not follow trial-type procedures for the achievement of their goals, even though their commitment to the attainment of justice and the search for truth is as strong as that of the American legal system.

The intentional departures that the administrative process has made from the judicial norm of adversary proceedings thus have been an enduring source of public uneasiness. These departures have played a significant part in sustaining doubts about the legitimacy of the administrative process. Although the trial-type procedures by which the judicial process traditionally has settled disputes will undoubtedly continue to hold an important place in the American imagination, they must be seen in a balanced perspective. The recurrent sense of crisis attending the federal administrative agencies will be better understood only when public misgivings about the departures that the administrative process has made from judicial norms are acknowledged openly, and the departures discussed in terms of their appropriateness for particular administrative functions, rather than resisted merely because they are not traditional.

4

Public perceptions and administrative performance

The felt necessities of the time, the prevalent moral and political theories, intuitions of public policy, avowed or unconscious, even the prejudices which judges share with their fellow-men, have had a good deal more to do than the syllogism in determining the rules by which men should be governed.

Oliver Wendell Holmes, Jr., *The Common Law* (1881)

The problematic status of the administrative agencies in the U.S. government implicates more than just the theory of separation of powers and the departure from judicial norms. It also reflects at least three additional concerns: our failure as a society to resolve a basic ambivalence toward the idea of regulation, public concern with bureaucratization, and public skepticism of administrative expertise.

Public ambivalence toward economic regulation

Although administrative agencies have existed since the founding of the nation, the homage that the nineteenth century paid to the doctrine of laissez faire and to the social implications of Darwinism gave particular assurance that governmental intervention into private economic activity would be limited. Charles F. Dole, expounding his generation's conception of citizenship in 1891, could write that the "rule is to leave trade as free as possible of restrictions" because "legislators and congressmen are not generally wise enough to meddle with other people's business, and always do this at great risk."[1]

The nineteenth century's prevailing skepticism toward governmental intervention in the economy gradually gave way to new attitudes in the early decades of the twentieth century. Influenced by the thought of William James, John Dewey, Lester Ward, and Thorstein Veblen, Americans were

31

now prepared to consider the possibility that the government could make effective use of the new social sciences in economic planning. First under Theodore Roosevelt, then under Woodrow Wilson, the United States began the process of enlarging its reliance upon administrative agencies to regulate private economic activity in the larger interests of the nation.[2]

But the decision to rely upon administrative agencies as dominant instrumentalities of modern government probably stems most directly from the impact of the Depression on American life. In 1933, when Franklin D. Roosevelt became President, the economy of the nation lay stricken; factories and stores were closed; one out of every four American workers was unemployed; hunger marchers paraded in the streets of many cities.[3]

President Roosevelt addressed the national emergency vigorously. He launched a frontal attack on the nation's economic problems, central to which was the creation of an armada of administrative agencies to carry out national policies. Was there a need to even the balance between management and labor at the bargaining table? Roosevelt established the National Labor Relations Board. Were investors being defrauded in the sale of securities? Roosevelt established the Securities and Exchange Commission. Was there a need to stop the "cut throat" competition that was causing anarchy in hundreds of trades and industries? Roosevelt established the National Recovery Administration.

The New Deal's decision to rely so heavily upon administrative agencies as the vehicle of economic recovery and social reform reflected practical considerations that had long been recognized. Administrative agencies could respond more promptly and flexibly than Congress or the courts to changes in the conditions being regulated.[4] Because of their expertise and specialization, they were far more likely than Congress to recognize subtle changes in industrial activity and to appreciate their regulatory implications. Because of their relative freedom from judicial norms of procedure and from the heritage of the common law, they were far more likely than courts to respond with innovative vigor, as well as a sympathetic commitment, to the purposes of the legislation they were administering.[5] In addition, administrative agencies were far more capable institutionally than Congress or the courts of discharging ongoing tasks such as supervision and inspection, whose constant performance is often essential to the effective achievement of many governmental programs.

Although the remedies of the New Deal demonstrated the utility of the administrative process in meeting serious national problems, it seems clear in retrospect that the prominence that President Roosevelt gave to the administrative process was not the result of any well-thought-out philosophy of governmental action.[6] Roosevelt was a pragmatist rather than a dogmatist. He was eager to reverse the nation's economic decline by whatever measures would work. He was devoted to improvisation and trial-and-error experimentation, willing to replace one approach with another if it bore greater promise of success.[7] His test for the acceptability of the administrative process as an instrument of governmental action was its effectiveness in promoting the directing economic growth; he had little interest in its possibilities as theory suggested them. The desperation of the nation's circumstances, the imperative need for action, would probably have denied him the luxury of pursuing such an interest even if his temperament had so inclined him.[8]

The provenance of the modern administrative process in the aggressive pragmatism of the New Deal has had significant implications for its status and legitimacy. The New Deal represented a national commitment – born of the social consensus of the time and broadly supported by a majority of Americans ever since – that there should be increased governmental intervention in the economy. The apparent success of the variegated responses that Roosevelt fashioned to meet the nation's exigencies served to obscure the fact that he lacked a coherent philosophy of when, and to what degree, such governmental intervention was appropriate – except, of course, that it should stop somewhere short of complete governmental planning of economic activity and decisions.[9]

To the present day, Americans have failed to develop or agree upon a coherent philosophy of governmental activism in economic matters. A majority of the American people seek a more powerful role for the government in the planning of economic growth at the same time, paradoxically, that they fear the consequences of a more powerful government for a free market economy. The nearest approach our society has made to achieving a philosophy in such matters has been to secure general agreement for the proposition that the appropriate extent of governmental activism in planning and controlling the economy lies somewhere between the polarities defined by Adam Smith and Karl Marx, between the polemical positions, as it were, of Milton Friedman and John Kenneth Galbraith.[10] An ideology of such imprecision may befit a pragmatic people, but it is hardly adequate to delimit the perennial debate that our society conducts on the proper role of government in regulating the economy.

Administrative agencies, as the symbols of our belief that some degree of governmental regulation of the economy is necessary and appropriate, inevitably become a focal point in that debate. The imprecision of the ideology that justifies the existence of administrative agencies reflects the basic ambivalence of our society toward the process of regulation. When a nation cannot find the intellectual wherewithal to formulate a coherent ideology on an issue as fundamental to its values as the balance to be struck between a free market and state regulation, such regulation as it does authorize will always be subject to philosophic as well as pragmatic question. And as long as the legitimacy of governmental regulation is subject to question, the legitimacy of administrative agencies assigned to carry out specific tasks of regulation will of course also be challenged.

The ambivalence that has frustrated our attempts as a society to arrive at a coherent ideology of governmental activism has also caused Congress to legislate most economic regulation in-evasive generalities, leaving to the respective administrative agencies the essential tasks of evolving regulatory policies. The question, for example, of what standard should govern the awarding of radio and television broadcast licenses by the Federal Communications Commission is properly a matter of high concern in a nation committed to limiting the growth of monopoly and preserving the values embodied in the First Amendment. Yet the only standard supplied by Congress in the Federal Communications Act of 1934 is that of "public convenience, interest, or necessity."[11] Delegations of a similar generality – sharing, as they do, an injunction to regulate in the "public interest" – are commonplace in federal and state administrative law.[12]

One result of the simplification implicit in such broad delegations of legislative power has been to make administrative agencies, rather than Congress, the arena for debate and decision on complex policy questions of fundamental importance to our democracy. This consequence has had distressing implications for the legitimacy of the administrative process. Many agencies have been criticized sharply for their failure to develop coherent policies in the course of their regulatory activities,[13] a criticism that had adversely affected their status as effective instruments of governmental regulation. Yet when Congress has failed to adopt a set of social preferences for resolving those fundamental and complex issues that typically lie behind broad delegations of power, an administrative agency, itself now exposed to the conflicting political forces that led Congress to shrink from a decisive response in the first instance, can hardly be expected to do better. Indeed, on several well-publicized occasions when an administrative agency has

34

taken a bold step toward clearly resolving a complex policy issue, Congress has immediately issued a stern rebuke that restored the status quo ante upon which the contending political forces had come to rest.[14]

In addition, by failing to provide many administrative agencies with either a coherent ideology of regulation or with clear statutory standards by which to act, Congress has left the agencies vulnerable to the private interests they were created to regulate. Statutory vagueness in the delegation of power may be appropriate when an agency is first created to deal with a problem not yet fully understood. But when such vagueness is permitted to persist over decades, it becomes first a signal of Congress's refusal to provide the agency with a sense of mandate, and then a temptation to private groups to exert pressure and influence.

Given these circumstances, it should not be surprising that the best-organized and most politically powerful private interests – interests that would play an active and cooperative role in the regulation of their industry even if Congress had provided more definitive indications of a policy[15] – should gain a considerable measure of influence over the making of administrative policy. The tendency of administrative agencies to become the captives of those they ostensibly regulate has long been noticed and has had a deleterious effect on the legitimacy of the administrative process by calling into question its independence and integrity. What has not always been noticed is the degree to which the causes of this tendency lie with the American people and Congress rather than with the administrative agencies alone.

Any inquiry into the sources of the recurrent perceptions of crisis in the administrative process must take account of the dominant political ideologies that have surrounded the growth of the administrative process as a principle instrument of modern government. Just as such an inquiry must come to terms with simplistic conceptions of the theory of separation of powers and the desirability of judicial procedures, so must it come to terms with the continuing ambivalence of the American people toward the process of governmental regulation of the economy and with the discrepancies that that ambivalence has caused between our professed ideals and the instruments of administration that we have created to achieve them.

Public concern with bureaucratization

More than a generation has passed since the creative early years of the New Deal, when a great many new administrative agencies acted with a reforming dynamism rarely seen on so grand a scale. The agencies that came to birth during the New Deal years, no less than those that already were well established parts of American life by then, have now come to maturity.

As a general rule, administrative agencies can be described as passing through several stages of existence, although the description is inevitably crude and something of a caricature. They are usually born amid high hopes that government, at last, has taken effective action in creating a new mechanism to carry out the nation's goals in an area requiring dedicated attention. Fired by the public support that brought them into being, they act with enthusiasm, vigor, and adaptive flexibility. But these same agencies come to adolescence surrounded by charges that they have begun to lose their former sense of mission and vitality, that they have become complacent and tired. The problems within the agencies' jurisdiction often prove more intractable than their creators anticipated, the task of continually confronting resistant social phenomena becomes increasingly frustrating, particularly when an agency has achieved early successes, and the intensity of the public support that they enjoyed initially begins to wane as new problems engage the nation's attention. Agencies then enter upon maturity, a period in which their processes become institutionally routinized and greater emphasis seems to be placed upon conformity to bureaucratic norms than upon innovative achievements. And finally – in one of the few reliable laws of governmental behavior – administrative agencies hardly ever die.[16]

An obvious example of this progression would be the National Labor Relations Board, established in 1935, which in its early years brought to the administration of the Wagner Act precisely the dynamic and sympathetic impulses that President Roosevelt and the New Deal Congress that enacted it must have intended. But now that it has "matured," it demonstrates a more routinized approach to its responsibilities. A second example would be the Interstate Commerce Commission, created in 1887 to regulate the railroad industry in its relationships with farmers and shippers. Whatever the strength of the commission's early performance under the pioneering chairmanship of Judge Cooley, for the past half-century it has been regarded as the complacent protector of industry interests rather than a creative regulator of the industry's marketplace.

The reasons that cause administrative agencies to make this Weberian passage from charisma to bureaucracy are complex. The social conditions that give the agencies their initial momentum tend to change their shape – often precisely because of the agency's effectiveness in confronting them – and the necessity for acting with urgency and imagination becomes relaxed. Moreover, the problems that remain after years of agency efforts are often the most difficult, politically sensitive, and intractable ones.

In addition, as the layers of an agency's internal bureaucracy multiply, as the number of its field offices grows, as the multitude of private groups with which it must cooperate increases, as the persons at the top find each successive enforcement effort less challenging and less exciting than the one that came before, as public support becomes more attenuated, as prudence becomes increasingly necessary if the agency is to survive the resentment and political repercussions that energetic enforcement typically engenders – as all of these invariable consequences occur, the ability of an administrative agency to maintain its initial level of creativity and enthusiasm gradually diminishes.[17]

Manuel Cohen, a former chairman of the Securities and Exchange Commission, has described this phenomenon, with the unfairness and exaggeration that inhere in phrases of shorthand summary, as a tendency toward "bureaucratic ossification."[18] For many Americans, the administrative agencies give all too much evidence of what Harold Laski described as the signifying characteristics of bureaucracy – "a passion for routine in administration, the sacrifice of flexibility to rule, delay in the making of decisions and a refusal to embark upon experiment."[19]

More than that, the pervasive bureaucratization of the administrative agencies comes at a time when Americans are experiencing a profound uneasiness over the influence of bureaucracy in their lives. Because of the prominent position they occupy in so many areas of public concern, the administrative agencies of the federal government are a natural focal point for that uneasiness.

The trend toward bureaucratization in Western society – described by Weber more than a half-century ago – seems now to have reached a culmination in the United States. Americans are confronted by bureaucracies, public and private, at virtually every turn. An individual cannot avoid repeated encounters with bureaucracies, whether he be a businessman, a governmental civil servant, a corporate employee, a union member, a university teacher, a college student, a hospital patient, an applicant for government benefits, a welfare recipient, or a political party worker.

Bureaucracies, in the Weberian model, are rational organizations, non-political and highly expert, acting through a hierarchy, governed by an authoritative statement of permissible means and normative ends, settling conflicts by reference to objective criteria, applying rules *sine ira et studio* –

37

without hatred or passion.[20] It was the very impersonality and specialization of bureaucracies that Weberian theory regarded as the guarantors of their impartiality, consistency of action, and freedom from caprice. Weber wrote in a characteristic passage:

Experience tends universally to show that the purely bureaucratic type of administrative organization – that is, the monocratic variety of bureaucracy – is, from a purely technical point of view, capable of attaining the highest degree of efficiency and is in this sense formally the most rational known means of carrying out imperative control over human beings. It is superior to any other form in precision, in stability, in the stringency of its discipline, and in its reliability. It thus makes possible a particularly high degree of calculability of results for the heads of the organization and for those acting in relation to it.[21]

But for the individual who must relate to them, usually in a role of subordination or dependence, bureaucracies too often appear concerned primarily with formalistic adherence to their own rules, rather than with seeking a personalized response to the peculiarities of his specific circumstances. As bureaucracies attempt to attain the Weberian ideals of precision, reliability, and efficiency, they exert upon their functionaries a constant pressure to conform to disciplined patterns of categorization. Robert K. Merton, a leading student of bureaucracy, has taken graphic note of the consequences of this pressure:

Adherence to the rules, originally conceived as a means, becomes transformed into an end-in-itself. . . . Discipline, readily interpreted as conformance with regulations, whatever the situation, is seen not as a measure designed for specific purposes but becomes an immediate value in the life-organization of the bureaucrat. This emphasis, resulting from the displacement of the original goals, develops into rigidities and an inability to adjust readily. Formalism, even ritualism, ensues with an unchallenged insistence upon punctilious adherence to formalized procedures. This may be exaggerated to the point where primary concern with conformity to the rules interferes with the achievement of the purposes of the organization, in which case we have the familiar phenomenon of the technicism or red tape of the official.[22]

As the process of bureaucratization has gone forward, the traditional conception of the client whose individual needs supply the raison d'être of an organization's efforts has become greatly attenuated. Many employees of bureaucracies no longer regard themselves as serving clients at all, even though the stated mission of their organizational endeavors has not changed; welfare agencies are perhaps the best example. The coercive structure of bureaucracy – by suppressing or ignoring individual distinctions in order to ensure the efficient performance of its functions – has increasingly transformed an idealistic devotion to those in need of the organization's services and skills into patterns of behavior variously described as "trained incapacity" (by Veblen), "occupational psychosis" (by Dewey), and "professional deformation" (by Warnotte). These patterns affirm the widening social distance between bureaucracies and the individual. Thus those millions of persons who must deal regularly with bureaucracies, even when they do not find themselves confronted with "the insolence of office," often regard the experience as frustrating, unpleasant, and demeaning.

The fact that administrative agencies are bureaucracies has not only made them a focus of public concern; it has also adversely affected their capacity to make effective use of many of their most creative employees. Although many administrative agencies have been successful in attracting and retaining the services of highly able staff experts, they have not always been able to provide them with a satisfying intellectual environment in which to work.

The pervasive demands that large bureaucracies make upon their members can be dispiriting, as sociologists have frequently documented.[23] The organizational imperatives that govern the shape and direction of a bureaucracy's functioning often require its employees to forfeit a significant measure of their autonomy as individuals, as well as the sense of fullness in personal achievement that greater independence would permit. Because employees of bureaucracies must conform their conduct and constrict their initiatives to the needs of the organization, the problem of motivation becomes an acute concern for managers. The oppressive impact that bureaucracies often have upon their employees' personalities, particularly upon their sense of themselves and their pride in their competence and accomplishments, can thus be great.[24]

In a famous passage in his study of the Federal Trade Commission, Gerard C. Henderson observed that the

... science of administration owes its being to the fact that most government affairs are run by men of average capabilities, and that it is necessary to supply such men with a routine and a ready-made technique, and to confine them to a formal procedure which may indeed at times clip the wings of genius, but which will serve to create conditions under which average men are more likely to arrive at just results.[25]

Henderson's judgment may well be right as a general matter, but the conditions he describes have tended to create an atmosphere of discord between the impulses and creative intellectuals and the bureaucratic demands of the administrative agencies that have employed them.[26] Moreover, the identifying characteristic of bureaucratic policy making is its intentional reliance

39

upon collective work-products – passed through several levels of consideration and modified at each, bearing the marks of many hands and many compromises – rather than upon the clear vision of a single individual.[27] As a consequence, many of the administrative agencies' most talented employees have become frustrated by their inability to translate fluently their expertise into decisive agency action. The turnover of expert personnel in public bureaucracies has accordingly been greater than has been the case in many other institutional settings.

In addition, bureaucracies are affected by the temper of the times in which they function. The collective morale and self-esteem among members of a bureaucracy can be damaged severely by critical and disparaging public attitudes toward bureaucratic organizations. When the larger public resents the influence and authority of bureaucracy, the motivation and sense of significant opportunity for accomplishment of those employed by bureaucracies are greatly diminished.[28] Although assertions of this kind are not readily proved, it seems likely that public attitudes of uneasiness toward bureaucracy have adversely affected the commitment to excellence and the enthusiasm of many employees of the federal administrative agencies.

The manner in which public attitudes toward a social phenomenon have gradually changed is sometimes best understood by examining the intellectual careers of representative individuals. Among those active in public service, William O. Douglas has been something of a paradigmatic figure in his progressive disillusionment with the powerful role that the federal bureaucracy has played in American life. Once a New Deal child of light in his enthusiasm for administrative government, Justice Douglas slowly became increasingly alarmed at the ways in which bureaucracies constricted the capacity of individuals to control their own lives.[29] In his dissenting opinion in *Wyman v. James*, a decision permitting a social caseworker to visit a welfare recipient's home upon penalty of loss of benefits if entry were refused, Justice Douglas expressed his matured views in a manner that many Americans would undoubtedly endorse:

The bureaucracy of modern government is not only slow, lumbering, and oppressive; it is omnipresent. It touches everyone's life at numerous points. It pries more and more into private affairs, breaking down the barriers that individuals erect to give some insulation from the intrigues and harassments of modern life.[30]

It is not surprising that many Americans, in responding to the increasing bureaucratization of their society, should make the administrative agencies of the federal government a particular focus of their uneasiness and concern.

As the federal government has steadily enlarged its role as provider of welfare benefits, supplier of market subsidies, and grantor of contracts, greater numbers of Americans have become dependent upon "the new property" dispensed by its bureaucratic processes.[31]

That the federal bureaucracy cannot be evaded once it occupies a regulatory area, as any number of private bureaucracies often can be by the transfer of one's trade to a competitor, may further contribute to making the administrative agencies a focal point of public concern. In addition, many Americans are strongly persuaded, as Justice Douglas seems to have been, that administrative bureaucracies present a more serious threat to the civil liberties and privacy of the individual than private bureaucracies do.

Given the extent and intensity of public concern with the impact of bureaucracy on private lives, it is understandable that some of the most influential novels of the past three decades have turned on the relationship of an individual to a large bureaucratic organization. In books such as *The Naked and the Dead* by Norman Mailer, *The Caine Mutiny* by Herman Wouk, *Catch-22* and *Something Happened* by Joseph Heller, and *One Flew over the Cuckoo's Nest* by Ken Kesey, American writers have portrayed various kinds of bureaucracies – the U.S. Army and Navy, business corporations, mental hospitals – as impersonal institutions thwarting the freedom, the idealism, and the creative energies of the individual. William H. Whyte's book *The Organization Man*, one of the most widely discussed nonfiction works of the 1950s and 1960s, elaborated a similar theme. The popularity of these books, perhaps like that of Kafka's classic novels *The Trial* and *The Castle*, derived in substantial part from the antibureaucratic sensibility that informed them.

It would be foolish to deny that the uneasiness that Americans feel about the coercive and dehumanizing influence of bureaucratic organizations upon many important conditions of their lives rests upon a clear view of the realities. And it is understandable that the federal administrative agencies, as prominent and powerful bureaucracies, are an object of that uneasiness. But it is important to recognize that complaints about bureaucracy and its excesses are not unique to the twentieth century. One of the "facts" that the Declaration of Independence submitted to a candid world to prove that "the history of the present King of Great Britain is a history of repeated injuries and usurpations, all having in direct object the establishment of an absolute Tyranny over these States," was that he had "erected a multitude of New Offices, and sent hither swarms of Officers to harass our People, and eat out their substance." In *The Old Regime and the French Revolution*,

Tocqueville noted that long before the climactic events of 1789, the central government's habit of maintaining an administrative surveillance from Paris over almost everything that happened in France had become "almost an obsession." He quoted a government official's remark, made in 1733, that

> . . . the amount of office work imposed on our heads of government is quite appalling. Everything passes through their hands, they alone decide what is to be done, and when their knowledge is not as wide as their authority, they have to leave things to subordinate members of their staffs, with the result that the latter have become the true rulers of the country.[32]

But it is important to recognize that the causes of the concern engendered by the fact that administrative agencies function as bureaucracies transcend the agencies themselves. They are a fundamental attribute of the process of advanced industrialization through which the United States, in common with most of the nations of the Western world and many of the nations of the communist world, is passing.[33] To suggest that these causes are peculiar to administrative government, as commentators sometimes do when they refer to a crisis in the administrative process, is to ignore their scope and complexity. Such a course impedes constructive analysis and unfairly impairs the status and legitimacy of administrative agencies.

Finally, it is important to remember that the principal reason that administrative government is so largely bureaucratic government is that bureaucracy as an organizational form makes an essential contribution to American society. The American people have required the federal government to administer a large number of complicated regulatory and welfare programs, and they add to the number each year as their perceptions of social need deepen and enlarge. Administrative government has grown because the American people have chosen, after deliberative national debate, to create increased governmental protections against the hazards of unrestrained economic activity and to provide a wider range of social services to the young, the unemployed, the poor, the ill, and the elderly. These programs and their accompanying administrative and bureaucratic machinery have resulted from political decisions taken by the elected representatives of the people.

In a nation of more than two hundred million persons, spread across a great continent, the administration of these programs could not be achieved without reliance upon bureaucracy and its methods. Many of the failures and defects in these programs are undeniably attributable to the fact that the federal agencies that administer them are organized and function as bureaucracies. But no other form of organization could perform these tasks as well as administrative bureaucracy, for all its inherent faults and rigidities, has done.[34] It is easy – too easy – to point to bureaucracy as one of the causes of the "crisis" in the administrative process, but those who complain of the bureaucratic nature of the administrative process rarely suggest realistic alternatives to its use. Here, as elsewhere, perfectionist visions of the best have been the needless enemy of the good. The American experience with administrative government has not always been satisfying or congenial, but it is consistent with Weber's confident assertion that "the decisive reason for the advance of bureaucratic organization has always been its purely technical superiority over any other form of organization."[35]

To conclude that bureaucracy is an essential part of administrative government is not to accept passively or uncritically its most egregious aspects and regressive faults. The task of controlling and limiting the undesirable influences of administrative bureaucracy upon the quality of American life remains. Efforts to extend opportunities for public participation in the administrative process, to establish methods for citizen protection such as the Freedom of Information Act and the Ombudsman, to increase the accountability of administrative agencies to the larger public, and to decentralize the administration of particular federal functions, are all appropriate responses to this task. Many others are necessary.

It is interesting to reflect that Weber himself understood the fear of many European social philosophers that bureaucracy could fracture the integrity of the individual and destroy a society's sense of community. Yet he retained the hope that the rationality of bureaucratic administration would protect the individual against the chaos and anxieties of social disorder. The tensions that Weber felt between his conviction that bureaucratic organization was indispensable to industrialized societies and his fear that bureaucracy might ultimately destroy the human spirit are with us still.

Another native European social philosopher, Erik Erikson, has wisely suggested in his Jefferson Lectures that "American democracy, if it is to survive within the superorganizations of government and commerce, of industry and labor, is predicated on personal contacts within groups of optimal size – optimal meaning the power to persuade each other in matters that influence the lives of each."[36] Until we create a society in which greater opportunities for such personal and communal interaction are made possible institutionally, the influence of all bureaucratic organizations – not just those of the federal government – is likely to remain a source of profound public concern.

43

Public skepticism of administrative expertise

Several intellectual assumptions of the New Deal period have played a significant part in sustaining the recurrent sense of crisis attending the federal administrative agencies. Those "present at the creation" of the New Deal held a distinctive set of views on administration as a mode – indeed, a style – of modern government. Most notable among these views were a commitment to expertise as a principal justification for the administrative process, and a belief that independence from the executive and legislative branches would be a guarantor of the integrity of the process. These views constituted an idealized conception of the administrative process that, in natural course, created high public expectations for the performance of the federal administrative agencies.

As the New Deal has receded further into the past, the public attitudes that encouraged and supported that idealized conception of the administrative process have gradually changed. Many of the recent criticisms of the administrative process reflect a gathering skepticism of the uses of expertise in government and of the desirability of independence in policy-making units of government. The manner in which public skepticism of administrative expertise has contributed to the recurrent sense of crisis in the administrative process is the subject of this discussion. The manner in which public skepticism of agency independence has contributed to that sense of crisis is the subject of Chapter 5.

The New Deal and administrative expertise

Reliance upon expertise as a principal attribute of administrative regulation antedates the New Deal by many decades. But it is convenient to begin with the New Deal because so much of the nature of the modern administrative process takes its shape from the philosophy of Franklin D. Roosevelt and his contemporaries.

The New Deal believed in experts. Those who rationalized its regulatory initiatives regarded expertise and specialization as the particular strengths of the administrative process. Thus James M. Landis, in a classic discussion of the administrative process written in 1938, argued that with

. . . the rise of regulation, the need for expertness became dominant; for the art of regulating an industry requires knowledge of the details of its operation, ability to shift requirements as the condition of the industry may dictate, the pursuit of energetic measures upon the appearance of an emergency, and the power through enforcement to realize conclusions as to policy.[37]

This, clearly, is the expression of a sentiment with an unusually optimistic, even naïve, tone.

For Landis, as for many who celebrated the capacity of the administrative process to apply expertise to social problems, Andrew Jackson could not have been more wrong in believing that a democratic government would be strengthened by preventing civil servants from enjoying a long continuance in office. "But expertness cannot derive otherwise," Landis wrote. "It springs only from that continuity of interest, that ability and desire to devote fifty-two weeks a year, year after year, to a particular problem." And, as Landis made clear, such expertness could hardly be acquired by ordinary citizens. "To hope for an adequate handling of the problem of allowable trade practices by the sudden emergence of a host of Pyms and Hampdens," said Landis, "was too delightfully visionary to be of much practical value."

A similar view was held by Felix Frankfurter, perhaps the paradigmatic intellectual figure of the New Deal. Frankfurter shared Landis's faith in disinterested expertise as a mechanism of social regulation. As early as 1912, he wrote to Learned Hand that "we are singularly in need in this country of the deliberateness and truthfulness of really scientific expertness."[38] Frankfurter believed that if public regulation was to be effective as an instrument of social and economic reform, it would have to rely, as the British had, upon "a highly trained and disinterested permanent service, charged with the task of administering the broad policies formulated by Parliament and of putting at the disposal of government that ascertainable body of knowledge on which the choice of policies must be based."[39] He thus expressed a view that many others in the Progressive movement of the period, most notably Herbert Croly, Robert LaFollette, and Walter Lippmann, shared.

The premise that administrative agencies have a substantive expertise in their areas of regulatory responsibility was readily accepted by the courts and has become the basis of a considerable body of administrative law, particularly in the areas of primary jurisdiction and the scope of judicial review. On more than one occasion the Supreme Court has sustained administrative decisions by a generous reference to the administrative expertise – the accumulated and specialized experience – that it believed, or was prepared to assume, informed the agency's action. Thus the Court, in a typical reference to administrative expertise, once wrote: "'Cumulative experience'

45

begets understanding and insight by which judgments not objectively demonstrable are validated or qualified or invalidated.''[40]

The premise of administrative expertise has had an obvious usefulness to the courts in allocating institutional responsibility for decision making between courts and agencies. It has permitted courts to sustain administrative decisions against challenge by finding a significant measure of reasonableness in the results that agencies have reached and by crediting the rest – which the court may not fully understand in its technical or specialized complexity – to administrative expertise.

The New Deal recognized that there was a danger in excessive reliance upon experts. They possessed the possibility, as Frankfurter himself well understood, of becoming ''a new type of oligarchy, namely government by experts.''[41] It was this danger to which Lord Hewart addressed himself in a leading book of the period, somberly entitled *The New Despotism*.

Indeed, the possibility of such a dismaying prospect when experts were given roles of policy-making prominence tended to emphasize the democratic dilemma of accommodating a ''neutral'' expertise with political responsiveness. But those who framed the modern administrative process believed that any latent dangers could be controlled, primarily by the development of high professional standards of performance; the use of effective and fair procedures in the application of the experts' knowledge; public scrutiny; informed criticism by the bar; and an insistence, as Frankfurter put it, that ''the final determinations of large policy . . . be made by the direct representatives of the public and not by the experts.''[42]

These views on the utility of expertise comprised a part of an idealized conception of the promise of the administrative process. ''Administrative government,'' Justice Douglas wrote in 1940, ''is here to stay. It is democracy's way of dealing with the overcomplicated social and economic problems of today.''[43] And expertise, he hardly needed to add, was one of the identifying virtues of administrative government.

Current skepticism of administrative expertise

It would be difficult today to assemble men of the stature of Landis, Frankfurter, and Douglas to celebrate the possibilities of administrative expertise with a similar lack of serious reservation. For the past several decades, the administrative process has been subjected to considerable criticism – much of it calling into question the fundamental premise of expertise upon which the New Deal rested so much of the agencies' justification.

The slogan of the War on Poverty – that government policies should be framed and administered with the "maximum feasible participation" of those they are intended to serve – anticipated a number of related developments that were to form a discernible pattern during the 1960s and 1970s. Those developments shared a common premise: that expertise alone is not a sufficient guarantor of the formulation of sound public policy or even of the consideration of a sufficiently wide variety of views.

This premise underlies developments such as the significant steps that courts have taken to enlarge the bounds of citizen standing and intervention at the agency level and to relax the requirements for standing to challenge administrative action in the courts. These developments have been accompanied by an increased judicial readiness to apply the Constitution's requirements of procedural due process to certain areas of American life in which it was formerly assumed that the fundamental "fairness" of administrative decision making rested upon what Juctice Frankfurter once called "the protections implicit in the office of the functionary whose conduct is challenged."[44] The protections to which he referred included the expertise – broadly conceived to embrace a professional competence and conscientiousness, as well as a personal honorableness – of the functionary. The Supreme Court's decisions applying the due process clause to welfare agencies, prisons, and public schools reflect a widely held sense that society can no longer rely upon finding these protective qualities in administrative officials.

At the same time, there has been increased public interest in devising new statutory and institutional means of ensuring that the exercise of administrative expertise is more readily subject to citizen influence as well as public scrutiny. This public concern lies behind the Freedom of Information Act, the Government in the Sunshine Act, and the Privacy Act of 1974. It is also reflected in the heightened public interest in the Scandinavian concept of the ombudsman.

Though disparate in origin, these developments of the past decade can be seen as sharing the common premise that administrative regulation cannot be accepted as effective or benign merely because those who have the power of decision are denominated as, or even are, expert. In addition, these developments can be seen as reflecting a belief that protections beyond the asserted expertise of the administrator are necessary if the administrative process is to serve the public interest adequately. In short, a persuasive case can be made that public attitudes toward expertise as an engine of administrative regulation have become more skeptical in the generation since the New Deal so optimistically proclaimed that reliance upon administrative expertise would increase the effectiveness of modern government.

What accounts for these changes in public attitude? What accounts for the increased public skepticism toward administrative expertise? At least three factors deserve consideration.

The first of these factors may be no more than a heightened expression of a traditional American distrust of experts. Something in the temper of the American character – perhaps its pragmatism, perhaps its heritage of Yankee common sense, perhaps its belief in equality among men – has never been quite at ease with persons whose identity is defined by their superior command of a difficult, often recondite, subject matter. Nicholas Murray Butler, whose professional life acquainted him with many experts, gave expression to this native wariness of experts when he told a Columbia University commencement that "an expert is one who knows more and more about less and less."

A deep strain of resentment toward "experts" has marked our history. This strain may indeed be part of a larger pattern of anti-intellectualism in American life, as Richard Hofstadter has persuasively argued in his important book, *Anti-intellectualism in American Life*. But it has been given expression by many intellectuals themselves. Woodrow Wilson, surely one of the most intellectual of American politicians, asserted during his 1912 campaign for the presidency:

What I fear is a government of experts. God forbid that in a democratic country we should resign the task and give the government over to experts. What are we for if we are to be scientifically taken care of by a small number of gentlemen who are the only men who understand the job. Because if we don't understand the job we are not a free people. We ought to resign our free institutions and go to school to somebody and find out what it is we are about.[45]

And then, in a remarkably unlikely addendum, Wilson, the former university president, said:

I want to say I have never heard more penetrating debate of public questions than I have sometimes been privileged to hear in clubs of workingmen; because the man who is down against the daily problem of life doesn't talk about it in rhetoric; he talks about it in facts. And the only thing I am interested in is facts.

Wilson's remarks sound many of the historically stereotyped themes: the expert as a person who is out of touch with the common man's reality; the expert as a person who participates in American life only from a distant remove that deprives him of a practical understanding of the job that must be done; the expert as the embodiment of paternalism; the expert as a person who is strong on rhetoric but weak on performance.

The possibility that we are currently experiencing a renewed expression of this traditional American distrust of experts should scarcely be surprising, given both the intensity of the nation's concern with defining and achieving conditions of social equality and the depth of conviction among a part of the population that the Vietnam War represented a special instance of the arrogance and failure of "the best and the brightest." Moreover, resentment is commonly a companion of dependence, and dependence upon experts has become increasingly necessary as the complexities of governing a continental nation have multiplied.

Joined to this traditional American distrust of experts, as a second factor that has contributed significantly to the growing skepticism of administrative expertise, is a public perception that administrative agencies are in fact something less than expert. Criticism of the purported expertise of administrative agencies – of their failure to live up to the New Deal's idealized conceptions of their capacities – has steadily increased in recent decades, as the Hoover Commission Report, the Landis Report, and the Ash Council Report, among other reports, attest.

The explanation for this discrepancy between New Deal aspirations and the agencies' actual performance is undoubtedly complicated, compounded as it is of a number of factors not easily verified or understood. The failure of many administrative agencies to persuade the public and the groups they regulate that they possess a relevant expertise may be attributable in part to the quality of the most visible agency representatives, that is, those whom successive Presidents have appointed as members. Although Presidents by tradition have made conscientious efforts to appoint persons with expert qualifications to a few specific administrative agencies – for example, the Federal Reserve Board, the Atomic Energy Commission, and the Securities and Exchange Commission – too often agency members have been persons appointed for political considerations who did not possess the qualifications to be regarded as experts before they began their service.

In addition, agency members have tended to serve for periods of time too brief to support a claim that they had acquired expertise on the firing line. Even those agency members who have served for substantial periods of time may have acquired no more than a routinized experience, rather than expertness. These facts may suggest why so few members of administrative agencies have attained recognition and respect for the quality of their performance. Finally, the fact that rapid turnover in agency membership has caused frequent changes in the direction of major agency policies, often in the wake of the election returns, has created considerable public doubt that agency members are impartial and disinterested experts, rather than value-oriented individuals addressing value-laden questions.

The range of the federal administrative agencies is too broad and diverse to permit students of the administrative process to draw a fair generalization as to the relative degree of expertise that does exist among agency members. But this cautionary perception has not prevented many Americans from concluding that most administrative agencies have lacked in fact the expertise that in theory they were supposed to possess.

A third factor that may help to explain the growing public skepticism of administrative expertise concerns the nature of the questions that administrative agencies are required to confront. It is possible that many Americans have come to believe that a technical expertise is neither adequate nor appropriate for the resolution of controversial questions of public policy of the kind that Congress has delegated regularly to administrative agencies. This belief is underscored whenever Congress, in requiring an agency to decide such questions, gives it no more guidance than a statutory standard of vaguely defined breadth. A direction to act in the "public interest" is, of course, the classic example.

The agencies themselves, it must be said, have sometimes contributed to this source of skepticism by their immodest style in approaching the momentous task of giving substantive content to legislative generalities. Thus the Federal Communications Commission, in a grand flourish of enthusiasm, once wrote:

As guardian of the public interest, we are entrusted with a wide range of discretionary authority and under that authority we may not only appraise the facts and draw inferences from them, but also bring to bear upon the problems an expert judgment from our analysis of the total situation as to just where the public interest lies.[46]

Many Americans are undoubtedly skeptical of a scheme that grants an administrative agency such considerable authority. They believe instead that the responsibility of ascertaining "just where the public interest lies" often calls more properly upon the generalist qualities of the citizen – and of those electorally responsible to him – than it does upon the expert judgment of the administrator, whether he be a lawyer, an economist, or an engineer.[47]

This skepticism has particular applicability to momentous issues such as the proper role of the government in regulating a sensitive or strategic industry, the desirability of encouraging competition or providing protection from it in a particular sector of the economy, and the proper role of communications media in a democratic society. As to issues such as these, many Americans may feel about administrative expertise the same way that Learned Hand felt about an absolutist power of judicial review: that "it would be most irksome to be ruled by a bevy of Platonic Guardians."[48]

The legislative decision to "take things out of politics" by delegating significant issues of public policy to an administrative agency does not change the nature of the issues to be decided. It merely changes the forum in which they will be decided from one that draws its strength from its political responsiveness to one that takes its definition from its expertise and independence. This is, of course, a significant change. Even James M. Landis recognized that an agency's "relative isolation from the popular democratic processes occasionally arouses the antagonism of legislators."[49] Government by what John Stuart Mill called "the wisest" and others would call "the elite" represents, in the minds of many, an anomaly in democratic practice.

These considerations may ultimately reflect the American people's conviction that fundamental questions of public policy and social values must be decided by an electorally responsive political process, rather than be treated as merely technical or instrumental issues appropriate for professionalized resolution. They may further symbolize the New Deal's failure to persuade the American people that the expertise administrators apply to large issues of public policy is truly objective or impartial – a premise routinely questioned in judicial proceedings. If policy making is properly regarded as an essential function of politics, then public skepticism of administrative expertise may finally imply the belief that a legislative decision to "purify" the political process by committing large issues of public policy to the expertise of the administrative process is inconsistent with democratic precepts.

The future of administrative expertise

Despite the fact that the American people thus may feel uneasy about the problematic role of administrative expertise, they are not likely to reduce in any significant degree the nation's reliance upon the administrative process in the foreseeable future. Given the technical complexity and scope of so many of the nation's problems, the historical tendency to resort to the administrative process and its accompanying promise of expertise and specialization for practical solutions or governance will undoubtedly remain strong. Indeed, despite Woodrow Wilson's asserted fear of a government of experts, and despite his yearning for facts of a kind that experts could not satisfy, the role of experts in government grew considerably during his administration, as it had for more than a decade before that. The Federal Trade Commission and the Federal Reserve Board, among other administrative institutions, were both created during Wilson's presidency.[50]

The American people, quite like Wilson, have regularly overcome their native distrust of experts whenever reliance upon administrative expertise seemed to suggest the promise of gaining greater command over a troubling problem of modern industrial or social life. But the likelihood that the American people will continue to rely upon administrative agencies for the resolution of national problems does not mean that the factors contributing to the current skepticism of administrative expertise may safely be ignored. Experts *have* their limitations. The task is not to eliminate administrative reliance upon experts, which is neither possible nor desirable in an advanced industrial nation, but to assess properly the limitations of experts so that we may construct institutional mechanisms that permit wise use of the experts' specialized knowledge and skills. Unless we place the limitations of administrative expertise in a realistic perspective, we may discover too late that our administrative law and institutions rest upon unrealistic assumptions no longer credible to the American people.

In a wise and subtle essay published in 1930, Harold Laski outlined the limitations of the expert.[51] The expert, he said, tends "to make his subject the measure of life, instead of making life the measure of his subject." He therefore sacrifices "the insight of common sense to intensity of experience." Indeed, "the more highly expert he is, the more profoundly he is immersed in his routine, the less he is likely to know of the life about him." The consequence is "an inability to discriminate, a confusion of learning with wisdom." And because the expert lacks a "flexibility of mind" as he approaches the margin of his special competence, he "dislikes the appearance of novel views" that may call into question the validity of his own knowledge and conclusions. Laski concluded: "My point may perhaps be made by saying that *expertise* consists in such an analytic comprehension of a special realm of facts that the power to see that realm in the perspective of totality is lost."

Laski's description of the expert as an idealized social type, however just, is too abstract to bear a direct relationship to the reality of the federal administrative process. Even if Laski's description can be understood as suggestive only, it will seem at least ironic to those who are skeptical of administrative expertise precisely because they perceive the members of administrative agencies as lacking in expertise. Such persons are not likely to find satisfaction in the assurance that experts have their limitations.

To the extent that skepticism of administrative expertise is based on the premise that agency members have often lacked expertise in the substantive areas that they have been appointed to regulate, it misses the mark in a crucial respect. The pertinent and enduring expertness of an administrative agency as to matters of technical substance can more properly be understood as deriving primarily from its staff, and not from the shifting membership of those who temporarily serve as commissioners. It is, indeed, the experience and specialization of a large and dedicated staff that has permitted agencies to channel the diverse expertise of many individuals into the process of institutional decision making – one of the unique contributions of the modern administrative process. If Laski's observations on the limitations of the expert are relevant to the federal administrative process at all, they are more appropriately applied to the agency staff than to agency members.

The question, then, is how administrative agencies can best create decision-making processes that permit agency members, who are themselves not likely to be experts in any professional sense, to perform the necessary function of moderating the staff's assertions of expertise in the course of retaining their ultimate authority over the formulation of policy.

The performance of this function requires agency members to use the staff's expertise wisely but not uncritically: to measure the staff's expertise against the counsels of common sense, to place the staff's expertise within the context of a wider experience with the world of affairs, to coordinate the staff's various kinds of expertise into a coherent program, and to estimate the extent to which the staff's technical expertise must share the direction of agency policy with values drawn from the world of political and social experience. "The amateur," as Laski noted in speaking of such tasks, "brings to [decisions] the relevance of the outer world and the knowledge of men. He disposes of private idiosyncrasy and technical prejudice."

To perform this function effectively, agency members must possess the intellectual capacity to integrate diverse streams of information and opinion into a single current of policy, the moral capacity to question whether the experts' emperors may sometimes wear no clothes, and the executive

capacity to establish dominion over the wayward tendency of career subordinates to evade control by converting the bureaucratically familiar into the
self-evidently necessary. In addition, agency members must have the
competence to serve as sympathetic mediators between the values expressed
by Congress in the agency's enabling legislation and the staff's expert
recommendations for realizing those values.

Such personal capacities are not commonly found. Yet it is precisely these
generalist qualities of mind and temperament that we seek most insistently
– and find with gratifying frequency – in our judges. What Karl Llewellyn
once wrote of our judicial system has an appropriate applicability to our
administrative system:

For we have a legal system which entrusts its case-law-making to a body who are specialists only in being unspecialized, in being the official depositaries of as much
general and balanced but rather uninformed horse sense as can be mustered. Such a
body has as its function to be instructed, case by case, by the experts in any speciality,
and then, by combination of its very nonexpertness in the particular with its general
and widely buttressed expert roundness in many smatterings, to reach a judgment
which adds balance not only, as has been argued so often and so hard, against the
passing flurries of public passion, but no less against the often deep but too often
jug-handled contributions of any technicians.[52]

Thus those who point to the absence of a technical expertise in agency
members may actually be directing attention to the desirability of an expertise of a different kind – an expertise in the art of skepticism about expertise,
a competence in the worldly art of the politically acceptable and socially
wise. It is expertise of this special character that Presidents should seek in
making appointments to the administrative agencies.

For a number of reasons, this conception of the agency member as generalist may become more significant in the years ahead. Public skepticism of
administrative expertise is undoubtedly part of a larger crisis of accountability now attending many of our governmental institutions, including the
presidency, the Congress, and the Supreme Court. It may also be a part of a
larger revolt against traditional authority now attending many of our cultural
and social institutions.[53] The concern that Congress has vested in administrative agencies the duty of applying expertise to policy questions more
appropriately settled in a politically responsive forum both states an issue of
enduring significance for democratic theory and comprises an important
element in the present crisis of institutional accountability.[54]

The contemporary impulse to temper the exercise of administrative expertise with a greater degree of citizen participation in the administrative

process is perhaps best understood as a response to that crisis of accountability, just as many believed that the New Deal's aggressive reliance upon experts was best understood as a statement that citizen participation in the decision-making processes of the federal bureaucracy was unneeded and unwanted. This impulse represents a pragmatic attempt to retain the benefits of administrative expertise and yet, at the same time, to create greater institutional opportunities, of a kind not unlike those offered by more politically responsive institutions, for participation in administrative decision-making processes.

Whether this attempt will succeed in achieving a better accommodation between the uses of administrative expertise and the precepts of democratic theory, it is too early to say. But it seems likely that the administrative universe that we have conventionally known, in which important private interest groups have played the dominant collaborative role in the process by which agencies have defined the "public interest,"[55] will gradually be modified in favor of a structure permitting more extensive participation by a wider range of individuals and groups. These newly admitted participants in the administrative process can be expected to urge upon the agencies the opinions and designs of their own experts.

In an administrative universe restructured in this manner, the agency member who is not a technical expert becomes an essential guarantor of the common sense and political acceptability of proposals that originate from experts, whether they be agency staff members or private retainers. As Laski so well understood:

In convincing the non-specialist Minister that a policy propounded is either right or wrong, the expert is already half-way to convincing the public of his plans; and if he fails in that effort to convince, the chances are that his plans are, for the environment he seeks to control, inadequate or mistaken.

The agency member who is not an expert thus performs one of the defining acts of the statesman: He serves, in Laski's words, as "the broker of ideas without whom no bridges can be built between the expert and the multitude."

Public skepticism of administrative expertise undoubtedly has been one of the factors that has contributed to the recurrent sense of crisis attending the administrative process. Although the New Deal sensibly recognized that increased reliance upon experts was an essential step in the development of modern administrative government, too often it stressed its faith in the uses of administrative expertise with a naïve, if idealistic, optimism. Because administrative expertise has been burdened with unrealistic expectations, the administrative process has been institutionally incapable of living up to the New Deal's idealized conception of its role.

The public rhetoric of the New Deal period tended to suggest that reliance upon a technical administrative expertise could somehow be regarded as a substitute for the exercise of a widely informed policy judgment by broadly trained generalists. The question of whether it is wise for a democratic government to rely so heavily upon the knowledge of experts has been answered in the only way that the needs of a complex industrial nation would permit. What remains unanswered is the question of whether those generalists who serve as members of administrative agencies can devise effective institutional means for placing the staff's expert contributions in the perspective of a broader set of social experiences and political values.

That task, as bureaucratic theory teaches, is not easily accomplished. Well before Franklin D. Roosevelt and his contemporaries celebrated the capacities of administrative expertise, Weber expressed doubt that generalists ever could effectively control experts. "Generally speaking," he wrote, "the trained permanent official is more likely to get his way in the long run than his nominal superior, the Cabinet minister, who is not a specialist."[56] And yet the task must be addressed if modern government is to meet public skepticism of administrative expertise.

By mastering that task, administrative agencies will affirm the fundamental principle that control of administrative policy making remains the responsibility of informed generalists who recognize the limitations of the claims of expertise. In so doing, they will also reduce the force of one of the most persistently troubling sources of the recurrent sense of crisis attending the federal administrative process.

The performance of the federal administrative agencies almost certainly will continue to be affected by public ambivalence toward the process of regulation, public concern with bureaucratization, and public skepticism of administrative expertise. Unless these concerns are perceived in their proper perspective, they will limit the effectiveness and impair the legitimacy of the administrative process.

Debate about the appropriate role of the federal government in regulating economic activity is a healthy element in democratic discourse. But the basic ambivalence of the American people toward governmental intervention in the economy has prevented the development of a coherent philosophy of governmental regulation and has had disturbing consequences for the legitimacy of the administrative agencies created to carry out those tasks of regulation that have been authorized. The impact of those consequences will be diminished only when Congress assumes the essential task of formulating the nation's regulatory policies, instead of delegating this task to administrative agencies without providing them with adequate standards.

The pervasive bureaucratization of the federal administrative process – as profoundly disturbing as it properly is – must be understood as part of a larger trend toward bureaucratization common to most of the advanced industrialized societies of the world. One can hardly expect administrative agencies, which are among the most prominent of governmental bureaucracies, to be immune from the force of such a historical trend. It is important to recognize, however, that in a nation as large as the United States, administrative bureaucracy, for all its faults, performs an essential organizational function. The challenge of controlling and limiting the undesirable influences of administrative bureaucracy upon American life therefore remains an important one, calling for efforts to extend opportunities for public participation in the administrative process, to establish methods for protecting citizens against administrative abuse, to increase the accountability of administrative agencies to the public at large, and to decentralize the administration of federal programs whenever feasible.

Public skepticism of administrative expertise also reflects wider social and historical trends. The perception that experts have their limitations, particularly in the lawmaking processes of a democracy, is of course a just one. But the proper response is not to condemn administrative institutions that must continue to draw upon the judgment of experts in performing complex regulatory tasks. Rather, it is to meet public skepticism of administrative expertise by developing effective institutional methods of placing the expert contributions of an agency's staff in the broader social and political perspectives of the agency's members.

The public perceptions discussed in this chapter – ambivalence toward the process of regulation, concern with bureaucratization, and skepticism of administrative expertise – are examples of those "felt necessities of the time" that Justice Holmes believed decisively influenced the character of legal institutions. Often these perceptions have been simplistic, inaccurate, or unfair, and thereby have impaired the legitimacy and the effectiveness of the administrative process. Public perceptions that are informed and realistic, however, can strengthen the role of administrative agencies in modern government and thereby enhance the legitimacy of the administrative process.

5

Agency independence and political accountability

One disquieting symptom is the frequency with which, when a new reform is suggested, ways are sought to "keep it out of politics." Politics is the democratic way of governing; is it becoming necessary, then, to keep government itself out of politics?

John Maurice Clark, *Social Control of Business* (1926)

Closely related to the New Deal's views on the importance of agency expertise was the New Deal's belief that the integrity of the administrative process would be protected by granting it independence from the executive and legislative branches of government. This belief, like the belief in expertise, formed an essential part of the idealized conception of the administrative process that shaped so much of the New Deal's attitude toward the problems of modern government. Public uneasiness over the idea of agency independence and its problematic implications for political accountability has been a significant factor in causing the recurrent sense of crisis attending the federal administrative process.

Before discussing this aspect of agency independence, it is necessary to distinguish it from a second aspect of administrative independence that periodically has caused public concern. This is agency independence from control by the regulated industries. Often critics of particular administrative agencies will argue that the regulated industry has "captured" the agency, that "administrative action reflects predominantly the solution desired by the industrial group."[1] That there should sometimes be a basis for such charges is hardly surprising, given the facts that administrative agencies and those whom they regulate have certain kinds of advantages each over the other, that employment opportunities generally move from both agency to industry and industry to agency, that long-term dealing with the problems of an industry inevitably leads to a greater sympathy and understanding for the industry's attitudes, and that living on terms of harmony with one's

58

formal adversary is, for many regulators, a more comfortable and rewarding way of professional life than engaging in perpetual combat, however sublimated it may be beneath the forms of legal actions.

Although scholars may contend over the ways in which this tendency works itself out, those who are part of a regulated industry are well aware of the wisdom of exploiting its possibilities. Richard Olney, attorney general of the United States under President Cleveland, made the point in replying to a friend in the railroad business who had urged him to seek abolition of the Interstate Commerce Commission, then only five years old:

The Commission, as its functions have now been limited by the courts, is, or can be made, of great use to the railroads. It satisfies the popular clamor for a government supervision of railroads, at the same time that the supervision is almost entirely nominal. Further, the older such a commission gets to be, the more inclined it will be found to take the business and railroad view of things. It thus becomes a sort of barrier between the railroad corporations and the people and a sort of protection against hasty and crude legislation hostile to railroad interests. . . . The part of wisdom is not to destroy the Commission, but to utilize it.[2]

A more astute description of the way in which an administrative agency can be expected to become oriented toward the industry it regulates probably has not been written.[3]

Scholars disagree about the effect of "industry captivity" upon administrative performance and about the prospect of ameliorating the problem by statutory innovations such as limitations upon prior and subsequent employment of agency members within the regulated industry. But agency independence from "industry captivity" was not the primary concern of the New Deal theorists. The focus of their concern was the manner in which the effectiveness of the administrative agencies in achieving their regulatory missions might be enhanced by insulating them from political control by the executive and legislative branches of government.

The theory of political independence

The theme that independence from the political process enhances the quality of administrative performance had been sounded by political scientists well before the time of the New Deal.[4] Indeed, it had occupied a prominent place in the reforming impulses of the Progressive Era, when men such as Herbert Croly, Louis D. Brandeis, and Walter Lippmann argued that the regulatory tasks of government could be better performed if they were taken out of politics and committed to the professionalized administration of non-partisan experts. But those who rationalized the New Deal's reliance upon the administrative process gave a particular stress to what James M. Landis called the "desire to have the fashioning of industrial policy removed to a degree from political influence."[5]

By granting administrative agencies an effective independence from the normal political processes, Congress would ensure that administrators were free to be impartial in their judgments, guided by their most conscientious visions of what constituted wise regulation, and committed only to protecting the public interest. Independence, in Joseph B. Eastman's expressive phrase, would permit administrators to be "masters of their own souls, and known to be such."[6] In addition, administrative agencies that were independent were far more likely to achieve continuity, coherence, and stability in the development of regulatory policy than agencies that were subject to the political direction of the President and the mercurial tempers of political fortunes, as the executive departments were.

Beyond these reasons for establishing economic regulation in a nonpolitical setting, the fact that administrative agencies were to exercise functions previously exercised by all three branches of government counseled granting them an independence at least from the political branches. The need for independence from the political branches was especially pronounced when agencies exercised judicial powers: Individuals were entitled to expect that adjudicatory proceedings involving their rights and liberties would be decided in a forum of judicial detachment, insulated from the intrusion of partisan influences.

Although the New Deal's emphasis upon the independence of the administrative process was thus recommended by theory, it undoubtedly had a political attractiveness as well. By placing administrative agencies beyond the formal control of the President, the New Deal may have hoped to allay congressional and public apprehensions about the extensiveness and daring of the program of economic regulation upon which it proposed to embark. Agency independence may have been politically attractive for the further reason that it implied the judicialization of administrative procedures, a consequence that gave a measure of reassurance to the legal profession. Finally, it is possible that those who shaped the New Deal's idealized conception of the administrative process believed that reliance upon administrative agencies independent of the President would be seen politically – even if the view was not wholly accurate historically – as symbolizing a fresh approach to the overwhelming economic problems that the nation faced.

For all of these reasons, Congress throughout the first decades of the twentieth century believed it desirable to free the administrative process from political constraints. The principal means by which it sought to implement this desire with respect to the President was to grant members of the independent regulatory agencies an assured tenure, backed by a substantial statutory protection against removal without cause. In addition, Congress provided that the terms of office for agency members would extend beyond the terms of the appointing President, that the expiration dates of the members' terms of office would be staggered, and that the proportion of agency members that the President could select from one political party would be limited to a simple majority.

In *Myers v. United States*,[7] decided in 1926, Congress's attempts to limit the President's power of removal received a setback. The Supreme Court held that Congress could not constitutionally limit the power of the President to remove a postmaster appointed, with the Senate's consent, to a four-year term. A unilateral power of removal, the Court said in broad terms, was part of the President's executive power "to take Care that the Laws be faithfully executed." But within a decade, in *Humphrey's Executor v. United States*,[8] the Court limited the sweeping implications of *Myers* and endorsed the authority of Congress to impose statutory limitations upon the President's freedom to remove members of the independent regulatory agencies from office.

Humphrey's Executor involved an attempt by President Franklin D. Roosevelt to remove the holdover Republican chairman of the Federal Trade Commission because, as the President wrote to him, "I do not feel that your mind and my mind go along together on either the policies or the administering of the Federal Trade Commission, and, frankly, I think it is best for the people of this country that I should have a full confidence." The Court sustained the constitutionality of the statutory provision limiting the President's removal power to certain specified causes because "it is quite evident that one who holds his office only during the pleasure of another, cannot be depended upon to maintain an attitude of independence against the latter's will." The Court stressed that the "character of the office" required a member of the Federal Trade Commission to perform quasi-judicial and quasi-legislative functions rather than any executive functions for which the President might properly have a special concern. The decision in *Myers* was not controlling, the Court explained, because it applied only to "purely executive officers."

As a result of the decision in *Humphrey's Executor*, Congress may constitutionally protect the independence of members of administrative agencies against executive control by limiting the President's power of removal to the unlikely instances in which he is prepared to assert that a statutory ground of cause (typically inefficiency, neglect of duty, or malfeasance in office) exists. The principle of the independence of the federal administrative agencies that served as one of the justifications for the New Deal's faith in the administrative process thus became more firmly established in the law because, ironically, of President Roosevelt's attempt to violate the independence of an incumbent commissioner on grounds of policy.[9]

The independence of the major regulatory agencies is also protected from improper interference by Congress, although the fabric of the supporting theory is not as fully textured as it is in the case of the President. The Administrative Procedure Act, specific enabling statutes, and many agency rules prohibit members of Congress, no less than other citizens, from making off-the-record attempts to influence the decision of particular administrative proceedings, upon penalty of reversal of the agency's decision or disqualification of the agency's members and of the other individuals involved. Judicial decisions further limit the extent to which Congress may seek to influence administrative decisions, either by questioning agency members in committee hearings as to their intentions in pending cases or by exerting pressures upon agency members to reach specific conclusions.[10] In addition, the tendency of the courts to impose an increasing number of judicial procedures upon the administrative process can be seen as reflecting a desire to protect the integrity of the independent administrative agencies by emphasizing their underlying similarity to the nonpolitical character of the courts.

Political independence in practice

It is important not to overstate in theory the degree of independence that exists in fact. There are many qualifying conditions upon agency independence: in the view of some commentators so many that the theory of independence must be regarded as "fanciful" and a "myth."[11] At the least, the independence of administrative agencies from the President and Congress has not been secured in the complete sense contemplated by the idealized conception of the administrative process that constituted such an important part of New Deal thinking.

Despite the Supreme Court's endorsement in *Humphrey's Executor* of Congress's authority to insulate the administrative process from executive control, the President has retained significant opportunities to influence the conduct of the federal administrative agencies – through the power of appointment, through control of agency budget proposals, through authority over the process of legislation – and few Presidents have been hesitant in seizing these opportunities as frequently and vigorously as they could.

The influence of the President begins with his power to appoint members of administrative agencies, a power that has invariably been exercised with political and policy considerations in mind. Because of the high turnover that routinely occurs in the membership of the federal administrative agencies, most Presidents have been able to name a majority of the members of the major regulatory agencies before the completion of their first term in office, thereby achieving significant changes in the direction of agency policy within a short period of time. The President's power to appoint agency members is subject, of course, to confirmation by the Senate, but very few nominations have been rejected in the past half-century, although doubtless some were never made because of the difficulties they were expected to face in the Senate. The President's power to appoint agency members also embraces the power to refuse to reappoint incumbent members upon the expiration of their terms, a power that a President need exercise only occasionally in order to remind agency members of his authoritative influence over their administrative careers.

The opportunities of the President to influence the independent regulatory agencies are increased by his power to designate (or demote) the chairmen of the major regulatory agencies. Because of this power, the reality is that the chairman of an independent agency holds his position as chairman at the pleasure of the President. The significance of this presidential prerogative has been enhanced by the implementation of a series of reorganization plans, recommended originally by the First Hoover Commission and later by the Landis Report, that increased the administrative authority of most agency chairmen over internal agency management, including the appointment and supervision of personnel, the determination of the use and expenditure of funds, and the distribution of work load among agency employees.[12]

In addition, the President has retained a power of removal in fact despite the restriction that *Humphrey's Executor* sustained in theory. When Presidents have simply requested the resignations of agency members whom they wished to remove, without supplying an elaborated statement of cause, they have usually received them, perhaps because the agency members involved were not prepared to risk the publication of a more explicit statement by the President. President Ford, for example, was able to procure the resignation of John H. Powell as chairman and a member of the Equal Employment Opportunity Commission in 1975 after expressing in only general terms his belief that the divisions and lack of harmony within the agency required the resignation.

Conversely, although there are no statutory restrictions on the power of the President to remove members of the Federal Power Commission, the Federal Communications Commission, or the Securities and Exchange Commission – perhaps because those agencies were created in the period between *Myers*, which held that Congress could not limit the President's removal power, and *Humphrey's Executor*, which held that Congress could – Presidents have not found it advisable to exploit their apparent freedom with respect to those three agencies. When Congress has imposed limitations upon the President as well as when it has not, political realities have conditioned and determined presidential use of the removal power to a greater degree than the restrictions or silences of the formal legislation.

The President's opportunities to influence the policies of the independent regulatory agencies are enlarged by the common (but not invariable) statutory requirements that agencies must obtain the approval of the attorney general before they may institute judicial proceedings to enjoin illegal practices, to enforce subpoenas, or to compel obedience to administrative orders. In addition, the statutory provision by which the attorney general is charged generally with the supervision of all litigation to which an administrative agency is a party (again with certain exceptions) gives an executive official, rather than the agency, the authority to decide whether to petition the U.S. Supreme Court for a writ of certiorari to review a lower court decision that the agency regards as detrimental to its objectives; it also gives the attorney general, rather than the agency, the authority to decide what position the United States will take on the merits in the event that the Court grants a writ.[13] These requirements ensure that the government has an opportunity to take consistent positions on similar issues as they may arise in many agencies, but they also increase the dependence of the independent administrative agencies upon the authority of the President.

In addition, many Presidents – perhaps realizing that they will be blamed for failures in agency performance even though an agency is independent – have taken a special interest in the manner in which the administrative agencies perform their functions. President Kennedy, in an early message to Congress, asserted that ''the President's responsibilities require him to know and evaluate how efficiently these agencies dispatch their business, including any lack of prompt decision of the thousands of cases which they are called upon to decide, any failure to evolve policy in areas where they have been charged by the Congress to do so, or any other difficulties that militate against the performance of their statutory duties.''[14] President Kennedy's message, based on the President's constitutional duty to take care that the laws are faithfully executed, stresses the importance of the President's responsibility to inform Congress when he believes that agency policies are inconsistent with the legislative will and to make recommendations for improving agency performance.

In a few instances, Congress has authorized the President to participate directly in the decision-making processes of administrative agencies, particularly when decisions bear upon areas especially confided to him by the Constitution, such as the conduct of foreign affairs. Thus decisions of the Tariff Commission recommending that the statutory tariff levels be increased or decreased must be approved by the President before they can become effective, as must decisions of the Civil Aeronautics Board involving the allocation of foreign or overseas airline routes.[15]

Apart from unusual situations such as these, Presidents have understood that they may not appropriately attempt to influence the decision of particular administrative proceedings required by law to be determined on the record, except of course by authorizing an executive department to appear formally as an intervenor. But many Presidents have believed that they could properly go beyond President Kennedy's description of their responsibilities and plainly indicate their views on the general direction that the policies of the federal government should take. Because of the absence of clear guidelines as to the appropriate degree of interest that a President may take in the direction of agency policy, Presidents have usually erred on the side of activism.

On one occasion, President Ford invited the chairmen and members of the major regulatory agencies to the White House to outline his views on the need for deregulation of many areas of economic activity and to invite their cooperation in achieving that goal. On another, President Eisenhower sent a letter to the Senate Foreign Relations Committee expressing his hope that the United States would take prompt action to permit commencement of the Saint Lawrence Seaway project. He forwarded a copy of the letter to the chairman of the Federal Power Commission, which had pending before it a power application necessary for undertaking the project. The commission approved the application.[16] The force of presidential will and prestige is so great and the limits to the appropriate exercise of presidential persuasion sufficiently unclear that few agencies can long persist in pursuing a course contrary to the President's firm desires.

But the chief instrument of executive influence over the administrative process probably is the Office of Management and Budget (OMB), which must approve agency budget requests and legislative recommendations before they are submitted to Congress. Before granting its approval, OMB scrutinizes agency requests closely in order to assure itself that they are consistent with the President's policies. Without its approval, an agency's proposals stand small likelihood of achievement. In addition, OMB has the authority to control agency spending of appropriations already made, a power that it administers with a careful eye to the substantive purposes for which the agency seeks to spend the appropriations. The classically literate conclusion of William L. Cary, former chairman of the Securities and Exchange Commission, is not overstated: OMB stands as "the Cerberus at the gate" of any program that an agency proposes to undertake or to strengthen.[17]

At the time that *Humphrey's Executor* was decided, many persons believed that additional restrictions upon the President's authority were probably unnecessary because the realities of modern government, particularly the size of the federal bureaucracy and the breadth of the President's responsibilities, would serve to prevent him from effectively influencing the work of the administrative process, except perhaps in an occasional and sporadic manner. That belief rested upon the judgment that any person responsible for the conduct of foreign affairs, the formulation of domestic policy in scores of substantive areas, the maintenance of good relationships with Congress, the performance of ceremonial duties as head of state, and the discharge of political tasks as head of party, could not possibly attend as well to the day-by-day performance of the administrative agencies.[18] That judgment remains sound with respect to the President as an individual, but it does not take account of the dramatic growth in the institutional competence and political authority of the Office of Management and Budget in exercising power in the name of the President. The power that OMB exercises over purse and program in coordinating budgetary requests to Congress now gives the President a substantial capacity to influence the policy initiatives and performance of regulatory agencies that in theory are independent of executive control.[19]

With respect to Congress, too, the idealized conception of the independence of the administrative process has been less than fully realized in practice. Because administrative agencies exercise delegated legislative powers and make decisions of great political and economic consequence, Congress has understandably been tempted to encroach upon the independence of the administrative process. It has done so by several means.

The Legislative Reorganization Act of 1946 authorizes each standing committee of Congress to exercise continuing review of the performance of administrative agencies enforcing laws that fall within the jurisdiction of each committee. These committees also control agency requests for new legislation to carry out their mandates more completely. Most administrative agencies answer to at least six congressional committees, three in the Senate and three in the House. Congress plainly has a proper interest in supervising how effectively administrative agencies exercise the legislative powers delegated to them, but the existence of this legislative power of oversight does ensure that agencies independent in theory will inevitably feel a substantial measure of accountability to the political concerns of Congress.[20]

Related to this power of oversight in the opportunity it gives Congress to influence agency policies is the control that Congress has over agency appropriations. The power of the purse has traditionally been a decisive source of legislative authority over administrative policy making. By taking particularized account of an agency's various activities in responding to appropriations requests, by specifically directing how new funds must be spent, by permitting an expansion of the agency's staff or requiring that it be cut back, Congress can strengthen the achievement of those administrative objectives that it supports and weaken the pursuit of those with which it disagrees.[21]

Congress also has the authority to enact legislation nullifying or overriding particular administrative decisions, as it did, for example, in passing the Federal Cigarette Labelling and Advertising Act of 1965, superseding the more stringent trade regulation rule that the Federal Trade Commission had promulgated. The importance of that legislative authority lies as much in the potential for public rebuke that it threatens as in its actual invocation. Usually, however, Congress stops short of enacting such legislative reversals, and instead holds public hearings or investigations in an effort to compel the agency itself to moderate a course disturbing to powerful interests, legislative or private, or to concede the error of its ways.[22] Congress doubtless understands that in administrative agencies no less than in courts, the law-interpreting process is an ineluctable part of the law-implementing process. But in summoning agency members to explain to skeptical legislators how they reached a particular decision, especially in adjudicatory proceedings, Congress has not always exercised a wise restraint of the kind that the Constitution requires it to observe with respect to federal judges.

In addition to these institutional mechanisms that make agencies dependent upon Congress for legislation and appropriations, individual congressmen, under pressure from constituents to produce favorable results, rarely hesitate to make inquiries of administrative agencies about the status of particular cases, thereby indicating their interest in the outcome without violating any of the formal prohibitions on *ex parte* communications; many agencies receive several thousand letters and telephone calls of this character every year.

Finally, the Senate has the power to confirm or to refuse to confirm nominations (and renominations to new terms) of members of administrative agencies. This power has not commonly been used to deny confirmation to a President's nominee. But Congress often has seized upon confirmation hearings as an occasion for reviewing an agency's policies and performance and emphasizing its status as an agent of Congress, as well as for seeking to commit the nominee publicly to a set of substantive views about the direction that the agency's policies should take.

Thus serious discrepancies have developed between the idealized conception of the administrative process that has come forward from the New Deal and the more terrestrial reality that has characterized the actual practice of the President, the Congress, and the agencies. The discrepancies are particularly marked with respect to the claims that the idealized conception makes for the independence of the administrative process, just as they were with respect to the related claims that it made for administrative expertise.

Although the major regulatory agencies are independent in theory, they remain subject in fact to effective sources of influence and control by all three branches of government. Their independent status is qualified by the President's unique powers of persuasion as well as by his dominance of the Office of Management and Budget, by Congress's supervisory authority and its control of agency legislation and appropriations, and by the federal courts' traditional power of judicial review. The independence of the administrative process is at best contingent, rather than absolute, in character.

The discrepancies between the theory of independence and the fact of its practice have made it difficult to sustain public confidence in the independence of the administrative process. These discrepancies have been significant factors in generating misgivings as to the value of independence in administrative agencies and in creating public doubts about the legitimacy of the administrative process.

Misgivings about political independence

Misgivings about the independence of the administrative process have taken several forms, none of them finally persuasive.

First, that administrative agencies are independent rather than subject to formal executive control is sometimes said to encourage Presidents in the belief that they need not be conscientious in making appointments to the agencies. Thus Philip Elman, who served with distinction as a member of the Federal Trade Commission, has argued that although a President will be "reluctant to appoint incompetent Commissioners to executive agencies, for their failure will be his failure," he may be quite prepared to use appointments to the independent agencies to pay off political debts, since the independence of the agencies will shield him from responsibility for their failures of performance.[23]

As an argument against administrative independence, Elman's point has an intuitive plausibility to it, but the political practice of the past several decades does not confirm its thesis. The general quality of presidential appointments to the independent regulatory agencies undeniably has been less impressive than desirable, but the general quality of appointments to executive department positions of equivalent responsibility (particularly at the subcabinet level) has not obviously been stronger. The comparative conscientiousness with which Presidents have made appointments to the independent administrative agencies as well as to high-level executive positions is probably better explained by such factors as the degree of the President's interest in specific substantive areas, the fortuitous conjunction of a vacant position and the obligation to reward a political ally or discharge a political debt, and the pressures of clientele interests than it is by any simple reliance upon the fact of independence from, or subjection to, the control of the executive.

Second, independence from executive control is often said to have failed as a device for encouraging the federal administrative agencies to formulate policy and to undertake long-term program planning. If the statement is meant to apply to every independent agency, it cannot be sustained. A sufficient number of independent agencies have been successful in formulating policy and enforcing it effectively to render such an indiscriminately broad indictment unjustified. But the statement nevertheless is valid to a considerable extent. Indeed, the failure of many independent agencies to achieve the formulation of coherent policies has been one of the most criticized deficiencies of the modern administrative process.

The question, however, is whether agency independence is one of the primary causes of these failures. The fact that some independent agencies have not so failed suggests that it is not. Moreover, the argument that those independent agencies that have failed to formulate policy effectively would have succeeded in doing so had they been less independent and subject to greater executive control is not supported by the experience of many executive agencies that are within the President's power of direction. Although many executive departments have successfully developed and enforced policy in a systematic and creative manner, others have failed in the same way that some of the independent administrative agencies have failed. The capacity of a governmental agency to formulate and implement policy effectively undoubtedly turns upon many more factors – including legislative support for the agency's efforts, public attitudes toward the agency's mission, and the nature of the problems the agency must address – than simply whether the agency is independent of, or subject to, the control of the executive.

Third, that administrative agencies are independent of executive control is frequently regarded as responsible for denying them the political support of the President, thereby limiting their capacity to resist the pressures of congressional committees and special-interest groups with the same stamina and assurance that executive agencies can. The consequence, it is said, is that the independent agencies are forced to rely upon the industries they regulate for the political support that any governmental institution finds it essential to have, a posture that increases their vulnerability to "industry captivity."

It is generally true that agencies that enjoy the political support of the President will formulate policy more courageously and self-confidently and enforce their mandates more effectively than those that do not. But the experience of the federal administrative agencies does not support the conclusion that executive agencies are more likely than independent agencies to receive the political support of the President merely because they are subject to executive control. Independent agencies often have had vigorous support from the President. The National Labor Relations Board, for example, received strong political support from President Roosevelt because he was committed to its mission of encouraging unionization and collective bargaining. Conversely, agencies subject to executive control sometimes have found it difficult to attract any measure of significant support from the

President. Although the Food and Drug Administration, for example, is an executive agency, Presidents invariably have tended to deny it the political support it has needed to do its work well. However, the fact that an agency is subject to executive control has not guaranteed that the political support of the President will protect it from the domination of the private interests it regulates, as the special histories of the Department of Agriculture, the Federal Highway Administration, and the Corps of Engineers suggest.[24]

The fact that an agency is independent of executive control does not necessarily mean that it will be denied the political support of the President, any more than the fact that it is subject to executive direction necessarily means that the President will give it his active support. A President's decision to lend his political support to the work of any particular governmental agency is usually the result of a complicated process of choice, mingling idealistic and expediential factors. The ultimate decision probably depends upon the President's political priorities of the moment and his own relationships to the regulated industry and its critics to a much greater degree than it does upon whether the agency is independent of, or subject to, his formal control.

Public misgivings about the independence of the administrative process thus take forms that finally prove unpersuasive, as these three examples suggest. But misgivings so persistent cannot be readily dismissed if public doubts about the legitimacy of the administrative process are to be understood and addressed. The fact that public misgivings about the independence of the administrative process persist despite the unpersuasiveness of the forms in which they so often are phrased suggests that these misgivings are rooted in a source not adequately articulated or rationalized. The most plausible source of that character is the perceived anomaly of granting significant governmental authority to unelected officials not directly accountable through the political process.

Political accountability and American government

Political accountability is an important value in American society. The process by which the governed pass political judgment upon the governors is at the heart of the democratic idea. Justice Holmes once dismissed a claim that the government must provide an administrative hearing before increasing taxes by emphasizing the power of electoral redress that citizens have ''over those who make the rule.''[25] But in the case of the independent administrative agencies, as many critics have stressed, citizens cannot invoke the electoral process to enforce political responsibility directly upon "those who make the rule."

Typical of such critics was the President's Committee on Administrative Management, which reported to Franklin D. Roosevelt in 1937 that the independent regulatory commissions were more accurately called the "irresponsible" regulatory commissions because they did not conform to basic requirements of democratic accountability. "Power without responsibility," the Committee said, "has no place in a government based on the theory of democratic control, for responsibility is the people's only weapon, their only insurance against abuse of power."[26] A generation later, in 1971, President Nixon's Advisory Council on Executive Organization (the Ash Council) reached similar conclusions. The independent administrative agencies lacked "the political accountability required to insure public responsibility," it said, and argued that the "overseeing of economic regulation by responsible public officials, necessary to assure effective discharge of agency responsibilities, cannot exist if the decision-makers are immune from public concerns as expressed through their elected representatives."[27]

The reports of these two committees have properly been criticized as unmeasured condemnations of administrative independence, primarily because they lack any obvious reliance upon supporting studies or upon the informed judgment of serious scholars. But the similar conclusions of more careful students, particularly Marver H. Bernstein, cannot be dismissed on these grounds. Bernstein concluded his comprehensive analysis of the independent regulatory commissions by asserting that

. . . the theory upon which the independence of the commission is based represents a serious danger to the growth of political democracy in the United States. The dogma of independence encourages support of the naïve notion of escape from politics. . . . Because it is based upon a mistaken concept of the political process which undermines the political theory of democracy, the commission has significantly antidemocratic implications.[28]

In many respects, the assertion is overstated. Although the independent administrative agencies are nonmajoritarian in the precise sense that they are not directly accountable to the people through electoral and political processes, they are hardly free from substantial constraints imposing a form of accountability. Their accountability to the public will is constrained by the delegation doctrine, by the requirements that they promulgate rules to guide their discretion and provide reasons to justify their decisions, by the extensive regime of legislative supervision and executive influence that prevails in fact despite the agencies' independence in theory, by the opportunities for public participation that many administrative hearings afford, and by the pervasive discipline of judicial review designed to ensure that agency actions are consistent with the instructions of a democratically elected Congress. Independence from political accountability, like independence from executive control, is a matter of degree.

Nevertheless, direct elections remain the paradigmatic means of enforcing political accountability in a democracy. In practical terms, the fact that direct elections can render only an undifferentiated judgment upon a political performance comprising thousands of discrete choices means that elections often are not likely to be any more effective in enforcing responsibility, particularly for specific decisions, than the range of constraints to which administrative agencies are subject. But none of the influences that constrain administrative agencies can rival a popular election in its symbolic affirmation of a direct accountability to the people.[29] The fact that the independent administrative agencies are not majoritarian institutions directly accountable through the political process has impaired the sense of legitimacy that they, in common with all governmental institutions, must have in order to function effectively.

These concerns about the legitimacy of the administrative process probably could be stilled by a system providing for the direct election of agency members. At one time a number of states, reacting to Populist sentiment, did provide for the direct election of members of important administrative agencies, such as railroad commissions and public utility commissions. (Huey Long's political career began with his election to the Louisiana Railroad Commission.) But most states eventually abandoned the experiment as unwise,[30] and direct elections of agency members at the federal level would surely be impractical today.

If doubts about the legitimacy of the administrative process are to be met by attempting to increase the political responsiveness of the independent agencies, the simplest course would be to abolish their independence from executive control, so that agency members are accountable to the President in the same manner as cabinet officers and other members of the executive branch. Perhaps particular agencies could be made more politically responsive by means short of abolishing their independence, for example, by requiring that they engage in regular discussions with executive departments having similar responsibilities or by permitting the President, subject to congressional veto and judicial review, to modify agency actions that he deems inconsistent with the achievement of his own national policy goals.[31]

It is doubtful, however, that the adoption of any of these courses would significantly enhance the administrative process's responsiveness to the people in the sense demanded by the critics of administrative independence. None of these courses would create a political accountability that was more than indirect in character, and none could guarantee that increasing an agency's accountability to the President would necessarily increase his interest in, or support for, the policies that the agency sought to pursue.

But there is a more important point. The recurrent public concern with the fact that the independent administrative agencies lack a direct political accountability is surely a curious, and perhaps an ironic, phenomenon in light of the central role that nonmajoritarian institutions play in American democratic practice.

One of the enduring themes of American political thought, beginning with the fundamental contributions of James Madison in *The Federalist*, has been the conviction that simple majoritarian means cannot alone create governmental institutions sufficiently stable to impose coherence upon the fluid, often volatile, politics of a dynamic and heterogeneous nation. From the beginning, Americans have understood that majorities, although essential to the democratic idea, are not always everything, and that for many purposes reliance upon qualities such as expertise, professionalism, independence, seniority, continuity, and tenure is more sensible, more *functional*, than reliance upon pure political accountability. For these reasons, reminiscent of the writings of Burke, Tocqueville, and Bryce, the American political system tests the temper of political opinion by the periodic selection of representative officials, rather than by town meetings or by continual recourse to plebiscites on subjects of topical controversy. It governs by a combination of electorally responsive officials and nonmajoritarian structures, sometimes overlapping in a disorderly fashion, in order to accomodate political accountability to institutional stability.[32]

Moreover, Americans have always understood that because majorities often are coalitions of a number of minorities, an effective political system must devise means for assembling and maintaining these majorities – for permitting them to coalesce and to govern as effective majorities between the necessary tests of public opinion that democratic theory properly requires and that periodic elections provide. This task can only be achieved by the intervention of mediating institutions themselves not sensitive to episodic shifts in public opinion. A part of the genius of the American political system has been the constant interplay it has encouraged between elected officials who are politically accountable and mediating institutions that are nonmajoritarian in character.

Among the most prominent of these nonmajoritarian institutions are the President's cabinet and the federal bureaucracy. A President could hardly take care that the laws be faithfully executed without relying upon the peculiar strengths of both of these institutions. Nor could Congress organize its deliberative efforts effectively without relying upon the mediating institution of the committee system, which is also a nonmajoritarian device. Woodrow Wilson's youthful judgment that "Congressional government is Committee government" is only somewhat less true today than it was when he expressed it in 1885.[33]

Nonmajoritarian institutions such as the President's cabinet, the federal bureaucracy, the congressional committee system, and political parties complement the nation's politically responsive institutions, at once strengthening and limiting them, by supplying elements of institutional stability, continuity, and dependability in the formulation and enforcement of policies that might otherwise be washed away by turbulent eddies in short-term majoritarian sentiments.

Of course, the most significant of the nation's nonmajoritarian governmental institutions is the Supreme Court. The Court's freedom from the political accountability that direct elections represent or that supervision by elected officials can impose has given rise to an extensive and searching literature. The special urgency that infuses that body of literature derives from the felt necessity of clarifying and establishing the Court's democratic legitimacy in light of the fact that it is a nonmajoritarian institution.[34]

Thus the status of the independent administrative agencies as nonmajoritarian institutions is scarcely an anomaly in the American political system. Those who question the legitimacy of the administrative process on the ground of the nonmajoritarian character of the independent agencies, without also questioning the legitimacy of all of the other governmental institutions that are nonmajoritarian, are guilty of drawing what the Supreme Court's equal protection decisions call an underinclusive classification. In an important and perceptive book, Robert A. Dahl has written that "Americans have been indoctrinated to believe in both Madisonian and populistic democracy" and that "they have never fully reconciled the two." The pragmatic willingness of the American people to tolerate the philosophic antinomy represented by a government based on two doctrines not fully reconciled has been one of the renewing strengths of the American political process. Given the important part that nonmajoritarian institutions traditionally have played in the American system of government, it would be difficult, indeed, to demonstrate, as Dahl concludes, that "a full shift to populistic democracy would therefore increase the legitimacy of governmental decisions."[35]

That the nonmajoritarian character of the independent administrative agencies is not an anomaly does not, of course, mean that their independence from direct political accountability is necessarily a virtue. Even Joseph B. Eastman, a fierce defender of administrative independence, acknowledged that the exact degree of an agency's independence from the political branches should be adjusted in light of how well the agency was meeting the needs that brought it into existence in the first place.[36] In deciding whether and how to make such adjustments, abstract appeals to the importance of political accountability, especially when they are phrased in simplistic majoritarian terms, are not likely to be very helpful. The question of whether the specific degree of independence that any particular agency enjoys is a virtue must be decided by pragmatic calculations of the kind that have been one of the characteristic strengths of American political thought – and have given us a political system, uniquely representative and stable, composed of both majoritarian and nonmajoritarian institutions.

In the idealized conception of the administrative process that characterized the New Deal's philosophy of governmental regulation, expertise and independence were seen as compensatory substitutes for political accountability. So much seems clear at least in retrospect. As the American people's faith in expertise and independence has declined, public concern that the independent administrative agencies are not politically accountable in a direct sense has increased. Perhaps any institutional arrangement that sought to take important public issues out of politics and lodge them in governmental agencies formally independent of executive control would finally provoke skepticism in a nation committed to principles of democratic accountability. In any event, that skepticism has done much to sustain the recurrent sense of crisis attending the federal administrative process.

Yet the ways in which the independent administrative agencies function in fact – and particularly the ways in which they relate to the political branches – are quite different from what theory, uninformed by experience, might predict. The independent agencies are subject to a considerable measure of control and influence by the President and by Congress. Moreover, there is little empirical evidence to support the view that the failures of the independent administrative agencies are properly attributable to their formal independence from executive control.

To be sure, the independent administrative agencies are not majoritarian in character, but that does not distinguish them from some of the most significant and necessary institutions in our governmental system, which has always been a complicated but pragmatic blend of majoritarian and nonmajoritarian elements. The independent administrative agencies quite obviously were not anticipated by James Madison in *The Federalist*, but they are nonmajoritarian institutions of the kind that he regarded as essential to the construction of an effective and stable government.

If the recurrent sense of crisis attending the federal administrative agencies is to be understood properly, then the legitimacy of the administrative process must be judged not by its consistency with simplistic majoritarian conceptions of political accountability but by the contribution it makes to Madison's vision of a "non-tyrannical republic."

6

Delegation of power and institutional competence

The legislature cannot transfer the power of making laws to any other hands; for it being but a delegated power from the people, they who have it cannot pass it over to others.

John Locke, Second Treatise on Civil Government (1690)

The first sentence of the Constitution, after the Preamble, provides: "All legislative Powers herein granted shall be vested in a Congress of the United States. . . ."[1] From the beginning of the Republic, Congress has regularly chosen to delegate portions of that power to others, primarily the administrative agencies it has created and the President. The Supreme Court has almost always sustained the constitutionality of such delegations, while at the same time asserting the continuing vitality of earlier pronouncements of an apparently contradictory character, such as the familiar statement from *Field v. Clark*: "That Congress cannot delegate legislative power to the President is a principle universally recognized as vital to the integrity and maintenance of the system of government ordained by the Constitution."[2] In this respect the Court has behaved much like Byron's Julia who, as Justice Jackson once recalled, "whispering 'I will ne'er consent,' – consented."[3]

Because the results the Court has reached have often seemed inconsistent with the principles it has stated in reaching them, the nondelegation doctrine has long been regarded as theoretically unsatisfactory.[4] And since, as a practical matter, the Court has generally sustained even the broadest transfers of legislative power, some commentators have criticized the Court for permitting greater delegations of legislative authority than is wise for effective governance,[5] thereby contributing to "the atrophy of institutions of popular control."[6] Others have characterized the doctrine as "almost a complete failure" in effectively preventing the delegation of legislative power.[7] Still others believe that the Supreme Court's permissive interpretation of the

78

doctrine, by permitting Congress to withhold from administrative agencies a clear mandate to achieve national policies, has invited encroachments upon agency independence,[8] thereby contributing significantly to recurring public perceptions of a crisis in the administrative process. In any event, the tendency of Congress to delegate legislative authority in terms often best described as evasive generalities is an expectable consequence of an ambivalence toward the act of economic regulation itself.

The question of whether and upon what conditions Congress should be permitted to delegate legislative power to other institutions is central to the theory of democratic government as well as to the effective performance of administrative agencies. The Constitution does not speak to the question explicitly, perhaps because the Framers did not consider the question a serious one. Apparently the only reference to legislative delegation in the records of the Constitutional Convention is Madison's motion that the President be given power "to execute such other powers . . . as may from time to time be delegated by the national legislature." The motion was defeated as unnecessary.[9]

The failure of the Constitutional Convention to devote any further attention to the delegation of legislative power may be explained by the Framers' belief that the legislature would be more likely to aggrandize than to delegate its powers; Madison and his contemporaries chiefly feared "legislative usurpations."[10] As Madison was to write in *The Federalist*, "[the] legislative department is everywhere extending the sphere of its activity, and drawing all power into its impetuous vortex."[11] Holding such fears, the Framers may not have regarded the prospect of voluntary legislative divestments of power as particularly worrisome.

Although the Constitution does not explicitly prohibit the delegation of legislative power, neither does it explicitly authorize it. The language most frequently relied upon to support the constitutionality of delegation is the "necessary and proper" clause – the power of Congress "to make all Laws which shall be necessary and proper for carrying into Execution the foregoing Powers, and all other Powers vested by this Constitution in the Government of the United States, or in any Department or Officer thereof."[12] This language does not, of course, explicitly support the constitutionality of delegation. But whatever the silences of the constitutional language, the propriety of delegating legislative power must now be regarded as having been settled by the practice of two centuries.

Since delegation of legislative power is permissible in some degree, the important question is in what circumstances and upon what conditions

Congress should be permitted to delegate. Although the theoretical basis of the traditional nondelegation doctrine has been eroded by the Court's inconstant practice, the philosophical and institutional issues raised by the delegation of legislative power remain of great contemporary significance. The task is to state a theory that seeks to mediate the tensions between the role that delegation to administration must play as "the dynamo of the modern social service state,"[13] and the compelling necessity of preserving the ancient democratic values of responsive, representative government.

It is a half-century since the first great scholar of American administrative law, Ernst Freund, wrote:

While it is extremely difficult to formulate a generally valid principle of legitimacy of delegation, the observation may be hazarded, that with regard to major matters the appropriate sphere of delegated authority is where there are no controverted issues of policy or of opinion. Hence a liberal delegation may be expected, and is actually found, in safety legislation, in which arrangements of a purely technical character necessarily play a conspicuous part. Even here, however, direct statutory regulation may be preferred, if the subject matter touches class interests or otherwise has a strong public appeal. . . .[14]

It is probably true, as Louis L. Jaffe has written, that Freund's observation is "demonstrably too narrow to describe legislative phenomena or to fulfill political need."[15] But it nevertheless states a major premise: Controverted issues of public policy are properly decided, as nearly as effective political and institutional arrangements will permit, in forums closest to the sources of popular representation.[16]

Strengthening the values that Freund emphasized as lying at the foundation of the nondelegation doctrine will require the Supreme Court and administrative law scholars to place greater emphasis than they have in the past upon considerations of institutional competence implicit in the structural premises of the Constitution – upon the capacity of particular institutions of government uniquely to perform certain tasks committed to them by the Constitution.

The significance of considerations of institutional competence in redefining the nondelegation doctrine can perhaps best be demonstrated by examining the relationship of the Congress, the President, and private parties to the exercise of certain constitutional powers.

The Congress

A recent decision of the Supreme Court, *National Cable Television Association v. United States*,[17] is particularly instructive in suggesting a basis for a theory of nondelegation of legislative power based upon considerations of institutional competence.

In that case, a trade association representing community antenna television (CATV) systems, which transmit television programs by cable, challenged a schedule of fees set down by the Federal Communications Commission. The fees were imposed pursuant to a statute that provided:

> It is the sense of the Congress that any work, service . . . benefit . . . license . . . or similar thing of value or utility performed, furnished, provided, granted, or issued by any Federal agency . . . to or for any person . . . shall be self-sustaining to the full extent possible, and the head of each Federal agency is authorized by regulation . . . to prescribe therefor such fee, charge, or price, if any, as he shall determine . . . to be fair and equitable taking into consideration direct and indirect cost to the Government, value to the recipient, public policy or interest served, and other pertinent facts. . . .[18]

The commission at first established only nominal filing fees, but under the prodding of Congress it later imposed an annual fee for each cable television system, calculated at the rate of thirty cents for each subscriber to the system. The commission estimated that fees set at this level would produce an annual revenue equal to the direct and indirect costs of CATV regulation. In short, the fees collected from the industry would reimburse the government for the entire cost of regulating the industry. The commission regarded the thirty-cents-per-subscriber fee as approximating, in the statutory language, the "value to the recipient" of the federal regulatory effort.

For the Court, the legality of the commission's schedule turned upon the essential difference between a fee and a tax. A fee, the Court said, is "incident to a voluntary act, e.g., a request that a public agency permit an applicant to practice law or medicine or construct a house or run a broadcast station." Congress may authorize an administrative agency to exact a fee for the services it performs in granting such requests, the Court said, because the agency thereby "bestows a benefit on the applicant, not shared by other members of society." If the statute did no more than permit the commission to impose fees measured by the "value to the recipient," no serious questions of unconstitutional delegation would be raised.

But the statute under review went further. It authorized the commission to consider the "public policy or interest served, and other pertinent facts" in imposing fees. The Court found that this language, "*if read literally*, carries an agency far from its customary orbit and puts it in search of revenue in the manner of an Appropriations Committee of the House." The implications of such a grant of authority were significant:

81

The lawmaker may, in light of the "public policy or interest served," make the assessment heavy if the lawmaker wants to discourage the activity; or it may make the levy slight if a bounty is to be bestowed; or the lawmaker may make a substantial levy to keep entrepreneurs from exploiting a semi-public cause for their own personal aggrandizement. Such assessments are in the nature of "taxes" which under our constitutional regime are traditionally levied by Congress.

In short, the statute could be taken as delegating to the commission the legislative power to levy taxes.

For the Court, this possibility presented a serious constitutional question. After invoking the authority of *Schechter Poultry Corp. v. United States*,[19] the Court decided "to read the Act narrowly to avoid constitutional problems." It held, in an opinion written by Justice Douglas, that because it "would be such a sharp break with our traditions to conclude that Congress had bestowed on a federal agency the taxing power," the statute should be read "narrowly as authorizing not a 'tax' but a 'fee.'" This construction meant that the phrase "value to the recipient" should be read as the appropriate measure of the commission's power; the nettlesome language, "public policy or interest served, and other pertinent facts," was hastily dismissed on the doubtful ground that it "would not seem relevant to the present case."

Because the fees imposed by the commission reimbursed the government for all of its direct and indirect costs in regulating community antenna television systems, those who operated such systems were paying not only for whatever special benefits they might receive from federal regulation but also for "the protective services rendered the public by the Commission" – a result beyond the commission's statutory authority to require under the "value to the recipient" language. For this reason, the Court remanded the case to the commission to set new fees in light of the narrowed reading of the statutory authorization.

The Court's reliance upon *Schechter* – long a disfavored precedent – to raise constitutional doubts about the literal meaning of the statute was at least questionable. The statutory standards that Congress prescribed for agencies to follow in setting fees were surely as intelligible and definite as those sustained by the Court in many prior decisions,[20] as Justice Marshall's dissenting opinion persuasively argued. Moreover, the legislative history gave at least some indication that Congress wanted the commission to adjust its fee structure "to fully support all its activities so the taxpayers will not be required to bear any part of the load in view of the profits regulated by this agency."[21]

By relying upon *Schechter* to confine the statutory language and avoid a constitutional adjudication that might prove premature or unnecessary, the Court sought to bring the case within the delegation principle and to warn Congress that if it intended to delegate the power to levy taxes to an administrative agency, it should do so explicitly and with full awareness that such a decision would raise serious constitutional questions.

The manner in which the Court employed the nondelegation doctrine in *National Cable Television Association* bears a strong similarity to its approach in *Kent v. Dulles*,[22] a 1958 decision also written by Justice Douglas. The issue in *Kent* was the validity of regulations promulgated by the secretary of state pursuant to a general statutory authorization to "grant and issue passports . . . under such rules as the President shall designate and prescribe. . . ."[23] The regulations required passport applicants to "subscribe, under oath or affirmation, to a statement with respect to present or past membership in the Communist Party." Kent challenged the constitutionality of this requirement. The Court found that it "would be faced with important constitutional questions" if the statute authorized the regulations; by granting the secretary "authority to withhold passports to citizens because of their beliefs or associations,"[24] Congress at least would have approached and might have trenched upon the right to travel guaranteed by the Fifth Amendment.

As in *National Cable Television Association*, the Court did not rule on the constitutionality of the substantive requirement in question. Instead, it held as a matter of statutory construction that Congress had not delegated to the secretary the authority to condition the issuance of passports upon an applicant's beliefs or associations. At least, the Court said, "Congress has made no such provision in explicit terms," and that, taken with a century of historical practice, was enough to support a narrow reading. Thus, as in *National Cable Television Association*, the effect of the Court's decision was to avoid deciding the "important constitutional questions" presented; at the same time, the decision created conditions conducive to congressional reconsideration of the substantive requirement in question.[25]

In an important sense, the Court was instructing Congress that making the underlying policy choice to require that passport applicants supply a statement as to their beliefs or associations would invite searching constitutional inquiry. The Court did not tell Congress whether to make that choice, but it did give Congress the opportunity to reconsider the choice with an awareness that an affirmation of the secretary's policy would implicate fundamental values. As Alexander M. Bickel wrote:

This was remanding to Congress for a second look – not for the necessary initial decision, but for orderly, deliberate, explicit, and formal reconsideration of a decision previously made, but made back-handedly, off-handedly, less explicitly than is desirable with respect to an issue of such grave importance.[26]

By interpreting the statute narrowly, the Court offered Congress the opportunity for what Chief Justice Stone once called a "sober second thought":[27] Was it necessary or useful or wise to grant the secretary the authority he thought he possessed if to do so would be to press substantive constitutional questions?

In straining to reach the result it did, the Court in *Kent* may well have read the prior historical practice erroneously and thereby found a narrower substantive delegation than the record warranted.[28] A more candid reading of the historical practice might have suggested that Congress had clearly expressed a choice between the policy alternatives it faced, and that the secretary had read that expression accurately.

In commenting upon the decision, Sotirios A. Barber has argued that because the substantive constitutional issue presented by Congress's action loomed so large in the Court's method of resolution, "the delegation problem was not the majority's real concern."[29] It is true, as Barber states, that the Court's resolution of the issues presented in *Kent* "did not call for greater specificity of decision or for finer legislative draftsmanship as means of holding the secretary responsible to congressional policy." But the nondelegation doctrine can and does properly serve purposes beyond holding congressional delegates responsible to legislative policy. It serves the further purpose of preventing congressional abdication of responsibility – in this case the responsibility of the legislature in a constitutional system such as ours for presenting ultimate questions of legality to the courts only when searching deliberation and thoughtful exploration of the alternatives has presented none that is acceptable and of less constitutional moment. In *Kent*, Congress may have abdicated that responsibility to the extent that it had failed to appreciate or to grapple seriously with the constitutional propriety of granting to the secretary the power he had presumed. The Court's decision allowed – if it did not indeed require – Congress to reassume that responsibility. The use of the nondelegation doctrine to enforce legislative responsibility in this manner puts at the service of the Court an additional mediating device by which it may perform its awesome responsibility of constitutional adjudication.[30]

The Court's decision in *Kent* is thus similar to its decision in *National Cable Television Association* to the extent that it admonishes Congress that when it chooses to delegate legislative power in a manner that suggests "a sharp break with our traditions," it must do so explicitly and as a matter of deliberated choice. But of the two decisions, *National Cable Television Association* may ultimately prove the more significant for the development of the nondelegation doctrine because of what it implies about the importance of institutional competence.

In *Kent* the Court began its analysis with the premise that the "right to travel is a part of the 'liberty' of which the citizen cannot be deprived without due process of law under the Fifth Amendment." The Court seemed prepared to assume that Congress could, by more precise draftsmanship, succeed in making clear its intention to delegate to the Secretary of State the authority to withhold passports from citizens because of their beliefs or associations. Such a statute would properly present the question of whether Congress may constitutionally place such restrictions upon a Fifth Amendment right. If the Court eventually were to hold that Congress may not do so, the decision would rest upon a judgment that the Fifth Amendment prohibits the federal government from restricting the right to travel in such a manner, regardless of which branch promulgates the restriction. It would not rest upon considerations of the unique institutional competence of any particular branch of government.

The decision in *National Cable Television Association*, however, does seem to address the question of institutional competence in a way that *Kent* does not. By stressing that "[t]axation is a legislative function" and that, under the Constitution, Congress "is the sole organ for levying taxes," the Court may have been seeking to hold Congress to more than merely the responsibility of presenting constitutional questions only after careful and conscious deliberation. The Court may have been seeking as well to hold Congress to the different but equally fundamental responsibility of exercising the constitutional power to impose taxes itself.

What is the basis in theory for such a responsibility? The power to tax is surely one of the most important of the legislative powers created by the Constitution. In the history of other nations, as the Framers had good reason to know, the power to tax had proved strikingly susceptible to oppressive application and abuse. "[T]he power to tax," as Chief Justice Marshall observed in *McCulloch v. Maryland*, "involves the power to destroy."[31] Rhetoric decrying taxation without representation was a part of the Framers' revolutionary heritage, affording them particular cause to construct protections against the possibility that such a momentous power might come to be exercised by small numbers of men in dark ministries. The decision of the Framers to place the power to impose taxes in the legislative branch of the government was a response to these considerations.[32]

Congress is the national institution that takes its character most directly from the political responsiveness of its members. In addition, senators and representatives, elected and subject to reelection by states or local constituencies, constitute a legislative institution of broad-based diversity. These characteristics serve to define the unique institutional competence of Congress for purposes of levying taxes. As Chief Justice Marshall went on to declare in *McCulloch*: "The only security against the abuse of this power, is found in the structure of the government itself. In imposing a tax, the legislature acts upon its constituents. This is, in general, a sufficient security against erroneous and oppressive taxation."

Because no other institution of the federal government except Congress possesses the unique characteristics that the Framers relied upon to provide citizens with an institutional security against unfair or oppressive taxation, no mere delegate of Congress could aspire to exercise the power to tax in a manner qualitatively similar to Congress. The Court in *National Cable Television Association*, familiar with the Framers' design, may have been suggesting, therefore, that considerations of institutional competence would prevent Congress from constitutionally delegating to anyone and at all the power to impose taxes.

As a more general matter, this reading of *National Cable Television Association* suggests that the Court may believe that legislative powers are not equivalent in their constitutional significance, and that the particular significance of any specific power has implications for the freedom of Congress constitutionally to delegate its exercise to others. This proposition would mean that the Constitution finally should be read to prohibit Congress from delegating certain powers no matter how clearly it proposes to speak to the policy issues involved. With respect to each of these powers the act of delegation itself would be an abdication of one of Congress's constitutional responsibilities.

How, then, does one determine whether a particular legislative power is one that Congress may not delegate? The answer must lie in the nature of the particular power involved and the intended relationship of that power to the structure of our constitutional scheme.

Consider, for example, the power of Congress to impeach and convict a President for "Treason, Bribery, or other high Crimes and Misdemeanors."[33] It was because of the extraordinary character of the charges warranting impeachment that the Framers of the Constitution assigned the function to Congress – the House to accuse and the Senate to try – rather than to the Supreme Court. The Framers regarded the institution of impeachment as "preeminently a political process, likely to agitate the passions of the whole community."[34] It was, as Hamilton wrote in *The Federalist*, "a method of NATIONAL INQUEST into the conduct of public men," best assigned to "the representatives of the nation themselves."[35] Only the Senate, in Hamilton's view, "would possess the degree of credit and authority, which might, on certain occasions, be indispensable towards reconciling the people to a decision" one way or the other. And he added another significant consideration: "The awful discretion which a court of impeachments must necessarily have, to doom to honor or to infamy the most confidential and the most distinguished characters of the community, forbids the commitment of the trust to a small number of persons."

The decision of the Framers to vest in Congress the momentous power of impeaching the President thus reflects a single judgment about the intimate relationship between the nature of the offense and the character of the tribunal. The arguments that Hamilton adduced to support the designation of Congress as the nation's impeachment tribunal indicate that the Framers believed that only a body politically responsive in the unique manner of Congress could bring the desired qualities of judgment and lend the desired lineaments of legitimacy to the uniquely political questions presented by an impeachment proceeding. The Framers' choice of Congress was thus governed significantly by considerations of institutional competence. If Congress may not delegate the power to impeach, then, it must be because no delegate, however conscientious or honorable, could replicate the qualitative dimensions of judgment that the Framers believed Congress uniquely would bring to the determination of impeachment proceedings.

There is an additional reason for concluding that any delegation of the impeachment power would be an abdication of Congress's constitutional responsibilities. As Hamilton wrote in *The Federalist*, impeachment proceedings in their nature could "never be tied down by such strict rules, either in the delineation of the offence by the prosecutors, or in the construction of it by the judges, as in common cases serve to limit the discretion of courts."[36] Hamilton's statement suggests the Framers' perception that the task of exercising judgment in an impeachment proceeding could not be principled in the usual sense. The considerations that the Framers understood would govern Congress's performance of the task, whatever they might be, would not be susceptible to formulation into directory standards

87

of the kind that Congress would traditionally seek to provide when it delegated legislative power.

When a constitutionally assigned power is by its nature peculiarly resistant to the formulation of governing principles and standards, the indications become strong that the Framers placed a deep reliance for its proper exercise upon the unique qualities – the institutional competence – of the body to which it was assigned. If Congress may not delegate the power to impeach, it must be for the further and independent reason that it is one of these powers.

Thus there are at least two classes of cases in which application of a revived nondelegation doctrine based upon considerations of institutional competence will have important consequences. The first class, represented by *Kent v. Dulles*, involves cases in which the legislature seeks to delegate a power that may be delegated constitutionally only under certain conditions. For the delegation to be constitutional, it must accurately communicate the decision that Congress actually made from among the policy alternatives that it considered.

The Supreme Court has usually invoked the delegation doctrine in cases of this kind when Congress has delegated power in such a manner as to threaten the invasion of personal constitutional rights. But there is no reason to limit application of the doctrine only to such cases. Congress should be required to meet – rather than be permitted to evade – its responsibility to make basic policy decisions before delegating legislative power, whether or not individual constitutional rights are involved.

The second class of cases, represented by *National Cable Television Association v. United States*, involves instances in which the legislature seeks to delegate a power that may not be delegated, even though the legislature itself may exercise the power constitutionally. The powers of Congress to levy taxes and to impeach the President are of this character.

In determining whether a particular legislative power falls within this second class, the Supreme Court must ask whether the structural premises of the Constitution indicate that the Farmers intended to vest the power in an institution uniquely competent to exercise it. The Court must further ask whether the power by its nature is peculiarly resistant to the formulation of governing standards for its exercise. When powers of this character are involved, the Court should hold that Congress cannot constitutionally achieve their delegation because the act would be an abdication of Congress's constitutional responsibility for decision.

The President

The possibility that certain constitutionally assigned powers may not be delegated is raised only once in *The Federalist*, but the context is revealing for purposes of this analysis. Hamilton, in discussing the power of the President "to grant Reprieves and Pardons for Offenses against the United States,"[37] writes that "it is questionable, whether, in a limited Constitution, that power could be delegated by law. . . ."[38] What is there about the unique competence of the President to perform the task of granting pardons and reprieves that casts doubt on the permissibility of its delegation?

Hamilton's principal argument for placing the power to grant pardons in the President is his special capacity for taking prompt action, particularly in comparison to Congress. Prompt action is especially to be desired, Hamilton writes, "in seasons of insurrection or rebellion . . . when a well-timed offer of pardon to the insurgents or rebels may restore the tranquility of the commonwealth." The loss of time that would result if Congress had to be convened "for the purpose of obtaining its sanction to the measure, would frequently be the occasion of letting slip the golden opportunity," perhaps forever.

To this argument he adds a further point:

As the sense of responsibility is always strongest, in proportion as it is undivided, it may be inferred that a single man would be most ready to attend to the force of those motives which might plead for a mitigation of the rigor of the law, and least apt to yield to considerations which were calculated to shelter a fit object of its vengeance. The reflection that the fate of a fellow-creature depended on his *sole fiat*, would naturally inspire scrupulousness and caution; the dread of being accused of weakness or connivance, would beget equal circumspection, though of a different kind.

Hamilton believed that vesting the power to pardon in the Congress, on the other hand, could lead to untoward consequences. Because "men generally derive confidence from their numbers," legislators if they were granted the power to pardon "might often encourage each other in an act of obduracy, and might be less sensible to the apprehension of suspicion or censure for an injudicious or affected clemency."

Hamilton's arguments forcefully support the wisdom of placing the power to pardon in a single individual. But they do not provide a rationale for reading the Constitution to restrict the President's authority to delegate that power to another. Yet the reasons that caused the Framers to select the President as the single individual with whom to entrust the "benign prerogative of mercy"[39] must reflect some sense that only a person accountable to

89

history and to the nation's traditions in the unique manner of the President could bring the desired qualities of moral strength and vision to the performance of the function. James D. Barber has noted that the President "is expected to personify our betterness in an inspiring way, to express in what he does and is (not just in what he says) a moral idealism which, in much of the public mind, is the very opposite of 'politics.'"[40]

If this is true, then the argument that the President ought not to be permitted to delegate the power to pardon to another – not even to one of Learned Hand's "twenty bishops"[41] – becomes persuasive. No other individual, however morally qualified he may appear, can ever be subject to the sobering historical forces that play upon the President and produce the special qualities of judgment that the Framers sought in selecting him as the one person who would exercise the power to pardon in the name of the nation. These qualities of judgment, representing a particular responsiveness to what is truest and best in the national character, may properly be considered a part of the institutional competence of the President.

Private parties

The Supreme Court has yet to state a satisfactory theory of the principles governing the delegation of power to private parties. In a series of decisions extending over almost a century, the Court has found some delegations to private parties constitutional[42] and others unconstitutional,[43] without enunciating persuasive reasons for differentiating the two lines of decision. The uncertain state of the law affords an opportunity to formulate a theory of delegation of legislative power to private parties that is consistent with a general theory of delegation and gives appropriate emphasis to considerations of institutional competence.

In *Carter v. Carter Coal Co.*,[44] a leading decision, the Supreme Court held that certain sections of the Bituminous Conservation Act of 1935 were unconstitutional because they permitted groups of private producers and miners to fix maximum hours and minimum wages. Because the statute "conferred upon the majority . . . the power to regulate the affairs of an unwilling minority," the Court found that it was "legislative delegation in its most obnoxious form; for it is not even delegation to an official or an official body, presumptively disinterested, but to private persons whose interests may be and often are adverse to the interests of others in the same business."

Although some commentators regard as misguided the Court's emphasis in *Carter* upon the character of the delegate rather than the quality of the legislative decision-making process, the Court's language suggests its recurrent concern with the question of whether private persons, even though they have been selected by Congress,[45] can be relied upon to exercise the sovereign power of the nation with a disinterestedness sufficient to assure that the interests of all of those subject to regulation will receive fair consideration – consideration of at least the quality and fairness they would receive in a politically accountable legislative forum. Congress abdicates its constitutional responsibility when it delegates decision-making authority to a private party lacking the capacity for such disinterested policy making.

In a nation as large and diverse as the United States, regulation if it is to be effective must depend upon a degree of voluntary cooperation between the government and those whose conduct is to be regulated. Delegations to private parties are often a useful means of securing and structuring that cooperation. Recognizing this fact, the Supreme Court has prudently refrained from regarding all such delegations as constitutionally suspect. Rather, it has proceeded on the sensible premise that delegations to private parties are constitutional when they serve important public purposes and give promise of adequately considering and protecting the interests of all of those subject to regulation – including, most particularly, minority groups.

For example, courts commonly have sustained delegations to private parties in the form of statutes that attach public consequences to decisions that the delegate has made or would be making in any event for purposes quite independent of giving content to the legislation. Typical of such statutes are those prohibiting the sale of all drugs except those recognized by the United States Pharmacopoeia and similar pharmaceutical publications. In these cases, the private party's decision to include or exclude a particular drug is invariably made according to preexisting professional standards in order to serve a particular professional need, rather than as a response to the legislation that gives such decisions a coincidental public effect.[46] Delegations of this kind carry considerable assurance that the private party's action will be guided not by self-interest but rather by extrinsic standards, usually formulated and endorsed by a professional community, designed to serve a larger social interest.

By contrast, delegations of legislative power to private parties have most commonly been held unconstitutional when the private party's "self-interest might tend to color its determination,"[47] so that a majority of the private group may come to exercise the delegated power in a manner likely to advance its own (usually economic) interests at the expense of an unwilling minority. Such delegations deprive affected individuals of the special quality of decision-making integrity promised by the legislative process, a consequence that may be objectionable on due process grounds as well.[48]

The doctrine of delegation of legislative power to private parties thus rests upon fundamental concerns for the character of the delegate and for the nature of the decision Congress has committed to the delegate. These concerns reflect considerations similar to those that govern the constitutionality of congressional delegations of legislative power to the President, a circumstance that provides an instructive analogy.

One of the reasons that delegations of legislative power to the President are so often sustained undoubtedly relates to a recognition of his special character as a delegate. He is a public official, sworn to uphold the Constitution and laws of the United States, constrained to public spiritedness by the nation's traditions and history's certain judgment, and within the reach of a number of political and finally electoral processes. Rarely are private parties exercising delegated legislative power circumscribed by such profound imperatives.

In addition, many of the Supreme Court's decisions sustaining particular delegations of legislative power to the President have clearly reflected a judgment about his institutional competence or expertise in specific areas of governance. Thus the Court's decisions in *The Brig Aurora*,[49] upholding the delegation to the President of the power to revive the Embargo Act, and in *Field v. Clark*,[50] upholding the delegation to the President of the power to impose retaliatory tariffs upon foreign nations, represent a recognition of his unique authority and position in the conduct of foreign affairs. A number of other Supreme Court decisions, particularly those sustaining the wartime delegation of powers to the President, are consistent with a recognition of the wisdom of granting to the one person who is the nation's commander in chief a wide executory flexibility in times of national exigency.[51] Private parties, on the other hand, often do not possess a similar, if not unique, competence to exercise the particular legislative powers delegated to them.

The doctrine of delegation of legislative power to private parties thus searches the fundamental question of institutional competence to perform a governmental task. The doctrine's special role is to determine whether a particular delegate is competent to perform the specific task delegated to him. That determination must take account of the fact that there is a crucial nexus between the nature of the particular legislative power being delegated and the character of the private party chosen to exercise it. The relative degree of disinterestedness that the delegate can be expected to bring to the task of decision and his relative degree of expertness in performing the task are significant criteria for estimating the institutional competence, in a constitutional sense, of a private party to whom Congress has delegated legislative power.

Although the nondelegation doctrine may currently founder in desuetude, the decision in *National Cable Television Association v. United States* suggests that the Supreme Court may yet revive the doctrine.[52] But any act of resuscitation must go beyond merely reiterating the doctrine's traditional teaching that Congress must state meaningful statutory standards for the exercise of delegated legislative power.

The new lines of the doctrine ought to be drawn to reflect the normative premise that Congress, in the act of delegating legislative power, may not abdicate its constitutional responsibility for making the nation's basic decisions of policy. This prescription would give meaning to Ernst Freund's enduring counsel that a principal office of the nondelegation doctrine is to ensure that controverted issues of policy and opinion be resolved, as nearly as effective political and institutional arrangements will permit, by those who draw their special character from a representative relationship to the people.

Whenever a court concludes that the Framers regarded the proper exercise of a specific legislative power as closely dependent upon the unique institutional competence of Congress, the nondelegation doctrine would prohibit Congress from delegating that power to another. In these circumstances, the act of delegation would so alter the manner of the power's exercise that the resulting arrangement would no longer be compatible with the Framers' reasons for vesting the power in an institution whose character and nature are defined in the special ways – of political responsiveness and broad-based diversity – that those of Congress are. The informing principle of institutional competence as a guide to the constitutionality of the delegation of legislative power thus focuses on the tension between the nature of the particular power delegated and the character of the particular institution chosen to exercise it.

There will of course be occasions when Congress cannot make wise decisions because experience with the substantive areas under consideration is too limited and the policy questions that must be answered are still too indistinct to permit responsible lawmaking. This was surely the case, for example, when Congress passed the Civil Aeronautics Act of 1938.[53] In such cases, broad delegations of legislative power to administrative agencies are essential if effective governmental action is to be taken at all.[54]

But there are many quite different cases in which Congress has not provided standards only because it could not resolve hotly controverted issues of policy, or has chosen not to do so. Delegations of this character have called into question the legitimacy of the administrative process by permitting it to exercise lawmaking powers of a kind that, as perhaps many people intuitively sense, only Congress should exercise. If courts were to insist more forcefully than they have in the past that Congress resolve the basic policy issues implicit in such legislation, the consequence might sometimes be no legislation rather than legislation without very much in the way of specific standards. But if legislation is supposed to be a democratic expression of the nation's will, that result would not always be untoward: Sometimes a nation has no will sufficiently focused or widely shared to permit present expression through a majority.[55]

A reconstruction of the nondelegation doctrine along the lines suggested here would reflect a heightened awareness of considerations of institutional competence implicit in the structural premises of the Constitution itself – of the capacity of particular institutions of government uniquely to perform certain tasks committed to them by the Framers. There is reason to hope that a nondelegation doctrine of this character, by requiring that democratic practice conform more nearly to democratic theory, would reduce the perceptions of illegitimacy that attach to those delegations that Congress must continue to make to administrative agencies.

Differences in agency performance

7

Explaining differences in agency performance: the SEC and the FTC

In a field as vast and unruly as is contemporary Administrative Law we must be wary against premature generalization and merely formal system. Administrative Law is markedly influenced by the specific interests entrusted to a particular administrative organ, as well as by the characteristics – history, structure and enveloping environment – of the particular organ of regulation.

Professor Felix Frankfurter, *Cases and Materials on Administrative Law* (1932)

Those who assert that there is a crisis in the administrative process usually do so in indiscriminately general terms. But the performance of the federal administrative agencies varies so widely that the assertion plainly fits some agencies less well than others. Certain agencies, indeed, are so highly respected for their standard of performance that critics of the administrative process typically exempt them entirely from characterizations of crisis. If we are to understand better the sources of the recurrently asserted crisis in the administrative process, we must inquire into the factors that account for the differences in agency performance. Such an inquiry might be aided initially by a comparison of the Securities and Exchange Commission (SEC), widely regarded as one of the most outstanding of the federal administrative agencies, and the Federal Trade Commission (FTC), perhaps the most consistently and severely criticized of the federal agencies.

The Securities and Exchange Commission

The Securities and Exchange Commission was created in 1934 to deal with the legacy of speculation, fraud, and knavery exposed by the Depression. During most of its history, the SEC's principal responsibilities have been the administration and enforcement of a system of full disclosure to potential investors and the policing of fraudulent and dishonest activity. Because the meaning of the statutory requirements and the thrust of the prohibitions against fraudulent activity that it enforces have always been readily susceptible of definition,[1] the work of the SEC has been greatly facilitated.

In addition, the fact that the SEC's regulatory activity is directed primarily toward a single industry – the securities industry – has permitted a more precise definition of the disclosure requirements and the antifraud prohibitions than would have been possible if these concepts were applicable to a number of different industries; were that the case, the SEC would have been required to frame definitions of greater generality and imprecision in order to take account of the divergent trade practices and customs of the various industries subject to regulation.

For these reasons, the SEC has been able to achieve a clarity of definition in the statement of its most basic policies unusual among administrative agencies; its stated policies and the rationale supporting them have not precipitously shifted direction every few years. This achievement, desirable in itself, has had the additional consequence of earning the SEC a useful reputation for steadiness of vision.

The SEC's pursuit of its goals has also been facilitated by the fact that the public and the securities industry, out of their respective self-interests, have shared a commitment to the statutory mandate. Those Americans who are the owners or beneficiaries of securities, usually estimated to be in the tens of millions of persons, have an obvious stake in the soundness of the securities market. The same is true of the millions of potential investors who require sufficient information to permit them to make a fair evaluation of the risks associated with particular purchases, and sufficient assurance that they are dealing with creditable companies and broker-dealers. The interest of the securities industry in a sound securities market – and one in which the public perceives itself to be protected by efficient regulation – is at least as great. When the health of an industry depends ultimately upon public confidence in its integrity, prudence plainly counsels that the industry support governmental regulation that sustains that confidence.

In fact, the impact of the SEC's enforcement activity falls primarily upon small, inexperienced operators, and those, such as "boiler room operators,"[2] conducting their businesses at the fringes of respectability; it rarely threatens prominent investment houses with reputable credentials and clientele. The leaders of the securities industry have widely recognized that it is in their interest to support the SEC in vigorous enforcement activity against such marginal operators, lest the public's confidence in the entire industry be dashed. For these reasons, the SEC has had the continuing encouragement of the most important members of the business community it regulates.

Because the public and the securities industry thus have supported in principle the basic goals that the SEC is charged with achieving, the agency has been spared the consequences – often destructive, sometimes immobilizing – that can follow from divisive public controversy as to the necessity or wisdom of its mission. The community of support for the *idea* of vigorous enforcement of the securities laws has permitted the SEC to avoid such controversy and thereby has contributed to the effectiveness of the SEC's performance.

The social consensus on the SEC's basic goals and the clarity with which the SEC has given definition to those goals has had the further effect of causing Congress to make clear that it will not be readily available, especially to the momentarily disgruntled, as a forum of general revision of the SEC's actions and policies. By thus granting the SEC considerable assurance that its actions are beyond the reach of casual political interference, Congress has undoubtedly strengthened the agency's resolve to take the actions it considers necessary, as well as enhanced its credibility in the marketplace.

Congress has further fortified the SEC's capacity to regulate the securities market effectively by granting it the authority to employ a full complement of enforcement techniques. The SEC may develop policy by adjudication or rule making, depending upon the nature of the question.[3] It may enforce the commands of the statutes it administers by disciplinary actions against broker-dealers,[4] stop-order proceedings against corporate issuers,[5] summary suspension of trading in registered securities,[6] and civil actions to enjoin illegal practices.[7] Congress has undoubtedly authorized the use of this wide variety of enforcement techniques because of the shared commitment of the public and the securities industry to the SEC's effective performance of its mandate. In the manner of a self-fulfilling prophecy, the flexibility and subtlety of response permitted by this array of techniques have enabled the SEC to perform more effectively than agencies less extensively equipped.

To these factors must be added the tradition that presidential appointees to the SEC almost invariably have been persons of high professional qualification. Because the securities industry and the larger financial community recognize the importance of the SEC's regulatory mission, they have supported the appointment of unusually able commissioners. More often than has been the case with members of any other agency, those appointed to the SEC have had a thorough familiarity at the time of their appointments with the area they were to regulate. Occasionally, to be sure, there have been appointments transparently referrable to political considerations, but they have occurred with less frequency than at other agencies.

Finally, the SEC's superior standard of performance may be attributable in significant part to the fact that it has not engaged in licensing or rate making during most of its existence. These two functions are the regulatory alternatives to competition in entry and competition in pricing. Because they constitute the power to create and dispense valuable "new property," they invariably have led to strong industry pressures upon agencies possessing them, the Federal Communications Commission and the Civil Aeronautics Board being notable examples. These pressures can distort, if not destroy, an agency's vitality. The absence of such pressures has been a decided advantage to the SEC, as it would be to any agency seeking to protect the integrity of its performance. But the fact that many agencies conspicuously less successful than the SEC also do not engage in licensing or rate making – the FTC is one such example – suggests that this factor alone cannot assure agency performance of high quality or account for differences in agency performance.

The SEC is unusual among federal administrative agencies in having achieved and sustained such high regard for the quality of its performance. The factors that help to account for the SEC's successful performance may also serve as useful benchmarks for inquiring into the causes underlying the comparatively less successful efforts of other administrative agencies, such as the Federal Trade Commission.

The Federal Trade Commission

The FTC is authorized, by the central provision in its statutory mandate, to address "unfair methods of competition in or affecting commerce, and unfair or deceptive acts or practices in or affecting commerce."[8] This is an extraordinarily general charge, probably as general as that of any federal agency regulating business conduct, although not one without certain common law connotations.[9] It is common, of course, for an administrative agency to be given a general charge at the time of its creation, in the hope that the agency, by the process of applying the statutory language to specific situations, will seek "to define and clarify it – to canalize the broad stream into a number of narrower ones."[10] The achievement of a fair degree of predictability of decision was, by common expectation, one of the major tasks facing the FTC in its early decades.[11] However, in the view of most commentators that expectation has not been realized.

Because of its greater generality, the FTC's statutory mandate may be less readily susceptible of precise definition than that of the SEC. But that factor accounts only partially for the differences in performance between the two agencies. The FTC's difficulties in elaborating more definite standards have been exacerbated greatly by the more extensive jurisdictional reach of its statutory mandate. Although those who created the SEC limited its jurisdiction primarily to a single industry, those who conceived the FTC, as James M. Landis enthusiastically wrote, intended that it undertake "the policing of industry as a whole, rather than being vested with supervision over the welfare of a definable line of business."[12] The FTC was thus made responsible for every consumer fraud, every retailer deception, occurring in interstate commerce,[13] as well as for standards of competition in hundreds of different lines of commerce, each with its own particular market conditions and peculiar trade practices and customs.

The enormous diversity in the various industries subject to the FTC's jurisdiction has had momentous consequences for the quality of the agency's performance. To begin with, it has presented the FTC with great substantive difficulties in devising clear and forceful standards of conduct. Prohibitions upon particular forms of conduct that are appropriate in many industries often cannot be justified as to many others. The FTC has therefore been required either to pronounce rules of sufficient generality to permit their application across-the-board, thereby risking the promulgation of mere exhortations to marketplace morality, or to devise more precise and relevant prohibitions for particular industries, thereby creating the necessity of extending such individualized treatment on an arduous, industry-by-industry basis.

The FTC's efforts to perform effectively have been complicated further by wide variations in the character of the companies it must regulate, even within a single industry. While the SEC confronts an industry composed of relatively similar companies – brokers and dealers, primarily – sharing common aspirations for respectability and a common understanding that every member of the industry benefits when administrative regulation is effective, many of the industries that the FTC confronts are composed of companies varying greatly in their character, their aspirations, and their attitudes toward regulation – from nationwide conglomerates to "mom and pop" grocery stores, from exclusive couturiers to mail-order merchandisers, from fourth-generation enterprises to fly-by-night charlatans. Far from sharing common characteristics, many members of this diverse assortment of companies are indifferent to respectability and could hardly benefit from effective administrative regulation. For these reasons, the degree of voluntary compliance or self-interested support that the FTC can typically expect from most of the industries it regulates as part of its across-the-economy jurisdiction is far less than the SEC routinely receives.

The great diversity in the industries and companies subject to its jurisdiction may also be responsible for the fact that, for most of its history, the FTC has not had strong, sustained public support of the kind that the SEC has enjoyed. The consuming public's product interests are so various, its needs for protection against deception, carelessness, and gullibility so diffuse, that it has been unable, at least until recently, to focus its concerns into a definite set of goals for the FTC to achieve.[14] The investing public, by contrast, has always been a more cohesive group with a better-defined set of substantive concerns, and it has thus been far more successful in providing the SEC with support for the achievement of its statutory goals.

The failure of consumers as a group to focus their distinctive concerns so that they might provide effective public support for the FTC has naturally had serious implications for the level of congressional support for the agency. Congress has rarely appropriated sufficient funds for the FTC to perform its responsibilities adequately. Nor has it insisted upon the appointment of highly qualified commissioners, perhaps because the existence of the Department of Justice's Antitrust Division, with its tradition of vigorous enforcement, has tended to minimize subtly the felt need for excellent appointments to the FTC. Finally, Congress too often has proved readily subservient to the protectionist demands of many of its constituent industries and of many trade associations.

Because consumers have generally not provided the FTC with significant public support, many of the industries subject to its regulatory authority, particularly those with well-placed friends in Congress, have been able to "capture" the agency in the policy areas that affect their conduct.[15] In this respect, the FTC's capacity to undertake policy initiatives has been shaped by a very different set of political forces than those that historically have influenced the SEC.

It is only in very recent years, as the consumer protection movement has gathered popular momentum, that Congress has increased the appropriations and staff of the FTC to respectable levels and enlarged the agency's statutory authority to seek injunctive relief, to promulgate substantive trade regulation rules, to bring civil actions for the benefit of consumers injured by unfair or deceptive trade practices, and to seek civil penalties against certain parties not themselves subject to outstanding commission orders.[16] These developments have created the possibility that the FTC, enjoying a measure of public support at last, may finally rise out of its historical inertia and prove the rule by translating its public support into effective action to enforce its statutory mandate.

The FTC's posture during most of its history since 1914 thus presents a marked contrast to the SEC's relative independence from industry pressures and congressional interference. In that contrast lies a partial explanation for the differences in performance between the two agencies – the one a model of excellence among administrative tribunals, the other subject to recurrent criticism as "rudderless" and "adrift in its backwater."[17]

The SEC and the FTC are thus markedly different in character. The SEC supervises a narrow segment of the economy, deals with problems that generally have proved manageable with respect to its competence and resources, has enjoyed a high degree of industry acceptance and support, has remained free from political interference, has had a broad array of enforcement techniques placed at its disposal, and consistently has attracted highly qualified personnel as well as funding sufficient to carry out its statutory mandate. In contrast, the FTC deals with an unmanageably broad spectrum of economic activity, usually has not had strong support from either the industries it regulates or the Congress, has been hampered by inadequate enforcement authority and insufficient funding, and has been less successful than the SEC in attracting well-qualified personnel. The SEC has been an uncommonly effective agency; the FTC, during most of its history, has not. It is important to observe that these characteristics are both the causes and the products of each agency's degree of effectiveness. An effective agency is more likely than an ineffective one to attract qualified personnel and adequate funding, to withstand attempts at political interference, and to gain significant public support. The implications of this interdependence of cause and effect are important considerations in evaluating the performance and prospects of an administrative agency as well as the legitimacy of the administrative process.

An agency that is effective in achieving its statutory mandate is for that

103

reason likely to be perceived by the public as a legitimate institution of government. Conversely, an agency that is perceived by the public as a legitimate institution of government is likely to engender public support, which in turn will strengthen its effectiveness. It should come as no surprise, therefore, that the public perceives the SEC as more effective and more legitimate than the FTC. Successful efforts to improve agency performance will generally contribute to reducing public uneasiness about the legitimacy of the administrative process.

8

The significance of public attitudes toward agency goals: the EEOC

Law flourishes particularly in a society in which the most fundamental questions of social values are not currently at issue or under agitation. If there is sufficiently acute value conflict, law is likely to go by the board. Similarly it flourishes in a society in which the enforcement problem is not too seriously acute.

Talcott Parsons, *Law and Sociology* (1962)

The extent to which public attitudes are a significant factor in determining the effectiveness of an administrative agency's performance – already indicated by the comparative study of the SEC and the FTC – can be illuminated further by considering the efforts of the Equal Employment Opportunity Commission (EEOC) to enforce Title VII of the Civil Rights Act of 1964.

This consideration suggests that the quality of an agency's performance is closely related to the strength of the public's support for the agency's substantive mission. When society's commitment to an agency's statutory responsibilities is ambivalent, existing uncertainly between rhetorical pronouncement and sincere determination, the indispensable element of strong public support necessary to fortify an agency's authority is likely to be missing. The absence of a general consensus in support of an agency's mission would have serious consequences for the quality of its performance in any circumstances, but those consequences become more deleterious when the agency's mandate is to reverse a pervasive pattern of private conduct rooted in more than a century of national experience.

The enactment of Title VII

Title VII of the Civil Rights Act of 1964 represents the nation's primary statutory commitment to equal employment opportunity for all of its citizens.

It prohibits specified groups of employers, labor unions, and employment agencies from discriminating against an individual – with respect to hiring, discharge, compensation, and the terms, conditions, or privileges of employment – on the basis of race, color, sex, religion, or national origin.[1] Title VII thereby seeks, as the Supreme Court said in *Griggs v. Duke Power Company*, its first decision interpreting the statute's language, "to achieve equality of employment opportunities and remove barriers that have operated in the past to favor an identifiable group of white employees over other employees."[2]

Prior to the enactment of Title VII, concern for the consequences of employment discrimination had existed for at least a generation. Many states had enacted legislation creating administrative agencies to enforce fair employment practices. President Roosevelt, in 1941, had appointed a Fair Employment Practice Committee to eliminate racial discrimination in governmental and private employment related to the war effort.[3] President Truman, in 1947, had appointed the President's Committee on Civil Rights, which reported extensively on the manner in which employment discrimination had caused black citizens to be unemployed at rates double those of their white fellow citizens.[4] But there was not yet sufficient political support for a permanent national legislative prohibition against employment discrimination.

Despite these limited state and federal efforts, the terrible consequences of employment discrimination persisted. By the time that John F. Kennedy became President, these consequences demanded a national response. They not only had a devastating economic and social impact on members of racial minority groups who could not find employment despite their willingness to work; they also deprived the national economy of the skills and energy of a significant segment of the population. As one witness poignantly testified before President Truman's Committee on Civil Rights, employment discrimination "generates insecurity, fear, resentment, division and tension in our society" – reasons more than sufficient to justify a national response by law.

The enactment of Title VII of the Civil Rights Act of 1964 thus represented an overdue national commitment of historical proportions. Alexander M. Bickel, writing shortly after passage of the Civil Rights Act, called it "a momentous statute, comparable in importance to such organic measures as the Interstate Commerce Act of 1887 and the reforms of the first Wilson administration and the first two administrations of Franklin Roosevelt" because "it commits the federal government, and particularly

Congress, which can do things neither the President nor the judiciary, despite their prior commitments, could do alone, to a set of national goals that reach beyond minimal constitutional requirements."[5]

In enacting the prohibitions against employment discrimination contained in Title VII, Congress also created a new federal administrative agency, the Equal Employment Opportunity Commission, to carry out the substantive goals of the statute.

The decision was consistent with a long legislative tradition. For almost a century, Congress has regularly chosen to create new administrative agencies to achieve newly adopted public policies, particularly when it has concluded that these policies were more likely to be achieved by a sympathetically conceived administrative approach than, for example, by a series of uncoordinated private actions brought by diverse individuals before the whole range of federal judges, some or many of whom might be thought less hospitable to the attainment of these policy objectives than newly appointed, even reform-minded, administrators would be.

The "primary purpose" of the newly created Equal Employment Opportunity Commission, as one of Title VII's supporters said during the floor debate in the House of Representatives, was "to make certain that the channels of employment are open to persons regardless of their race and that jobs in companies or membership in unions are strictly filled on the basis of qualification." The commission was thus charged with addressing "the central aspect of the major domestic social problem of our time in a context where there had been many prior laws and prior administrative efforts, all of which had failed."[6] For a country of two hundred million people, in which discriminatory employment practices were deeply embedded in a broad historical pattern of discrimination against minority groups, this would unavoidably be a major legal and social undertaking. No one at the time should have been in doubt that an administrative effort of unusual force and effectiveness would be necessary to secure its achievement.

Despite the magnitude of the task, Congress gave the commission powers that were remarkably weak and unconventionally limited. Title VII authorized the commission to investigate complaints of employment discrimination, to determine whether reasonable cause existed to believe that an unlawful employment practice had occurred, and to seek to eliminate such practices "by informal methods of conference, conciliation, and persuasion." The commission was given no authority to adjudicate claims, to impose administrative sanctions, to commence litigation in court, or otherwise to enforce Title VII on its own. When the commission was unable to secure a satisfactory resolution by the informal techniques to which it was limited, the complaining individual was authorized to bring an action in federal court seeking remedial relief and damages.

By designating conciliation and voluntary compliance rather than adjudicatory proceedings as the preferred means of enforcing Title VII, Congress rejected the traditional federal model by which an administrative agency is authorized to hold formal adjudicatory hearings, make findings of fact, and impose administrative sanctions, such as cease-and-desist orders, against those found to have violated the law.

The legislative decision to limit the commission to such "informal methods of conference, conciliation, and persuasion" had no precedent in the history of state fair employment practices legislation, and only sparse precedent in the wide range of legislation creating federal administrative agencies. The fair employment practices legislation that had been enacted in the major industrial states to deal with problems similar to those confronting the Equal Employment Opportunity Commission typically had provided for enforcement by an administrative agency with authority to hear and determine cases by adjudicatory hearings and to issue remedial orders. Many federal administrative agencies regularly engage in attempts at conciliation or settlement as part of their enforcement activities, and the Administrative Procedure Act recognizes the value of informal adjudication by requiring federal administrative agencies to give respondents an opportunity for settlement "when time, the nature of the proceeding, and the public interest permit," and to give licensees an "opportunity to demonstrate or achieve compliance with all lawful requirements" before taking adverse action against them.[7] But such attempts are rarely the limit of an agency's statutory authority and usually are followed by adjudicatory proceedings if they fail. Provisions for conciliation do no more than impose a duty upon an agency to consider offers of settlement before formal adjudicatory proceedings are instituted, a practice that most agencies follow as a matter of prudent course in any event. Moreover, the prescription of the informal process of conciliation as the commission's principal administrative technique was at least unusual in a period when the courts were increasingly stressing the value of formal trial-type hearings as a protection against arbitrary administrative action.

In light of all of this history, what motivated Congress to limit the commission's administrative authority to the "informal methods of conference, conciliation and persuasion"?

The decision to rely principally upon a program of voluntary compliance to enforce Title VII was the result of a series of legislative compromises, ''a product more of the desire for passage than the desire for a rational scheme for uprooting discrimination.''[8] Title VII as originally formulated would have granted the commission an authority to conduct formal administrative hearings and to issue cease-and-desist orders substantially similar to that of the National Labor Relations Board. But this definition of the commission's powers was stricken by the House Judiciary Committee.

The ostensible reasons for changing the original bill in this manner were a belief that court actions would lead to more rapid and more frequent settlements, a conviction that the courts would provide a fairer forum for employers to assert their defenses in, and a fear that the commission, if permitted administrative powers of remedy, would impose forced racial balance according to inflexible mathematical formulas. The action nevertheless reflected a concession to the political strength in Congress of those who were prepared to support legislation prohibiting employment discrimination only so long as its administration was not entrusted to a regulatory agency possessing significant powers of enforcement.

In place of the authority to hold formal hearings, the commission was granted the authority to act by informal means of conference, conciliation, and persuasion. In the Senate, the so-called leadership compromise – entered into in order to secure sufficient votes to obtain cloture against a filibuster – resulted in the elimination of the commission's authority to bring civil actions in its own name. The major responsibility for seeking enforcement of Title VII was thus left with private individuals who chose to bring court actions in their own names. Although Congress sought to strengthen the commission's hand when it amended Title VII in 1972, it still did not grant the commission authority to hold adjudicatory hearings or to impose administrative sanctions. Rather, it granted the commission authority to institute civil actions in federal courts against employers and unions believed to have committed unlawful employment practices, but only after it had first attempted to resolve the issue by conciliation.[9] The amendments left undisturbed the right of private individuals to institute actions of their own in federal court seeking redress for violations of Title VII. In so legislating, Congress made plain, as the Supreme Court said, that federal courts, rather than the commission, ''have been assigned plenary powers to secure compliance with Title VII.''[10] Conference, conciliation, and persuasion remain the commission's principal administrative powers.

The process by which Congress reached the decision to limit the commission's enforcement authority to informal methods designed to secure voluntary compliance with Title VII was thus the familiar one of political give-and-take. One court has described the legislative history of Title VII as "chaotic."[11] The result, in the view of a leading scholar in the field, was to leave the newly established commission "a poor enfeebled thing."[12] The resolution upon which the contending political forces in Congress came to rest in enacting Title VII hardly indicates an informed appreciation of the uses of informal administrative procedures in achieving regulatory goals, to say nothing of an appreciation of the relationship that such procedures may bear toward the elimination of discrimination in employment. Rather, it reflects the nation's incomplete commitment to the goal of equal employment opportunity.

Nevertheless, it could be argued that, in theory, Congress made a justifiable decision in emphasizing the use of informal administrative processes in the enforcement of Title VII, even if it did so in spite of itself. The reasons supporting such a view may be summarized briefly.

First, it could be argued that Congress's decision to rely upon informal processes such as conference, conciliation, and persuasion was a wise, perhaps even a necessary, encouragement to persons discriminated against in employment to bring complaints before the commission. For similar reasons, the Supreme Court held, in *Love v. Pullman Company*,[13] that filing "technicalities are particularly inappropriate in a statutory scheme in which laymen, unassisted by trained lawyers, initiate the process." Persons who found the prospect of formal administrative proceedings too intimidating, too protracted, and too expensive to pursue, might be induced to step forward if these deterrent inconveniences, which often characterize formal administrative processes, were done away with. The use of conference, conciliation, and persuasion as the means of administration gave promise of eliminating them.

Second, it could be argued that informal processes were more likely than traditional adjudicatory proceedings to induce employers to comply with the mandates of Title VII and to cooperate with the efforts of the commission. Many employers believed – whether rightly or wrongly is less important than the fact that such beliefs existed, perhaps pervasively – that Title VII represented a "government inquisition into an area of decision-making" formerly private and the "curtailment of a freedom of choice generally of far more intimate concern than [that] involved in the prevention of other forms of discrimination."[14]

It also represented an attempt to change employment practices that had been formed by generations of social experience and were likely to be highly resistant to conventional regulatory techniques. By providing that questions of employment discrimination be considered in informal proceedings, Congress reduced the possibility of inflammatory adversary confrontations and gave notice to employers of its desire to settle disputes by consent rather than coercion if at all possible. It also gave employers assurance of a substantial measure of confidentiality and freedom from damaging publicity. The prescription of informal administrative procedures in the enforcement of Title VII was thus an appropriate federal response to genuine employer concerns – a response that gave hope of increasing the acceptability of the commission's role in the business community.

Third, it could be argued that informal processes of fact finding were more likely than formal adversary proceedings to be effective in developing an understanding of the subtleties of conduct that play a significant part in the practice and motivation of employment discrimination. If discriminatory employment practices were caused primarily by isolated acts of "ill-will on the part of some identifiable individual or organization" and therefore present essentially a "human" problem, as a Senate committee report had contended,[15] then unusually sensitive methods of fact finding and of exerting federal authority might be called for. Conference, conciliation, and persuasion more nearly met this requirement than formal adjudicatory hearings, without necessarily exposing any of the participants to a greater risk of administrative arbitrariness.

Fourth, it could be argued that an administrative agency structured along the lines of the traditional model, possessing formal adjudicatory authority, eventually might be weakened by the familiar process of "industry captivity" that has compromised the initiative and effectiveness of many such traditional-model agencies. In Alfred W. Blumrosen's statement of the possibility, "a *more powerful* Commission would become the captive of those interests which were to be regulated, while the existing weak institution enabled civil rights groups to use the federal courts which are favorable to their demands."[16]

Finally, Congress's decision to limit the Equal Employment Opportunity Commission's administrative authority to conference, conciliation, and persuasion could be seen as a useful experiment in exploring the potentialities of informal administrative processes in inducing voluntary compliance with the law and achieving an accommodation of competing interests within its bounds. The decision might be seen as responsive to the concern, expressed

111

increasingly by judges and by commentators on the administrative process, that our society generally relies too greatly – perhaps too *automatically* – upon formal adversary hearings as a means of resolving disputes and of enforcing the law. There are limits to effective legal action, as Roscoe Pound reminded us many years ago, and these limits are tested most seriously "when men demand much of the law, when they seek to devolve upon it the whole burden of social control."[17] Any effort to ameliorate the consequences of generations of employment discrimination by exclusive reliance upon formal adversary hearings designed to coerce compliance with the law might well place an untoward strain upon these limits and create a society too law-ridden to be agreeable.

By combining the formal enforcement hearings of the courts with the informal conciliation efforts of the commission, Congress might be seen as having struck a sensitive balance between the need to enforce the law effectively and the limits of effective legal action. Congress's decision to employ the informal processes of conciliation as part of the enforcement processes of Title VII thus might have represented an enlightened attempt to gain general acceptance of the law, however grudging that acceptance might at first be, by the familiar combination of the carrot and the stick.

However attractive these arguments may be as a matter of theory, they do little more than make a virtue of necessity. No one seriously believes that any of them animated a majority of Congress in the decision to limit the EEOC's administrative powers to conference, conciliation, and persuasion. That decision represented a political compromise: Granting the EEOC the traditional administrative powers to hold formal adjudicatory hearings, make findings of fact, and impose administrative sanctions was simply unacceptable to a majority of Congress.

Nor does the EEOC's first decade of experience suggest that the agency has been well served by the informal methods of conference, conciliation, and persuasion in addressing its formidable regulatory responsibilities. Rather, most commentators have concluded that the EEOC will not be a fully effective administrative agency until it is granted greater enforcement powers, particularly the authority to issue cease-and-desist orders.[18] But that is not likely to occur so long as the elimination of employment discrimination remains a controversial political issue.

The consequences of public attitudes of ambivalence

The consequences of the American public's only partial commitment to the eradication of discrimination in employment is reflected in the quality of

112

the EEOC's performance, most particularly in the delay that characterizes its disposition of complaints.

When the commission opened its doors for business in 1965, it estimated that it would receive 2,000 complaints during its first year. In fact, it received 8,859 complaints, and the discrepancy was an indicator of things to come. The number of complaints filed with the commission has increased annually ever since, reaching 71,000 in the fiscal year ending June 1975. As the annual number of complaints has increased, so has the commission's backlog of unresolved cases, from 2,300 at the end of 1966 to more than 125,000 in 1976.

The appearance of such an avalanche of complaints during the commission's early years – reflecting the pressure of many decades of stored-up grievances – should hardly have been surprising. Discrimination in employment on the basis of race and sex has had a long history in the United States. Millions of persons have been subject to its unjust impact. Of the many forms that racial and sexual discrimination may take, discrimination in employment is peculiarly disabling for those aspiring to realize their full potential as wage earners and as human beings.

The inexorable growth in the commission's accumulated backlog has been accompanied by inordinately great delays in the amount of time the commission requires to resolve an individual complaint. For most of the commission's recent history, persons filing complaints typically have had to wait at least two years before the agency has been able to take up their charges of discrimination. The consequences of these delays for the commission's effectiveness are plain enough: Delay burdens the possibility of vindicating worthy complaints. When a complaint is two years old, the investigation takes longer than it would have at an earlier point and the process of establishing the facts, which might then provide a basis for persuading an employer to settle the complaint voluntarily, becomes more difficult. In addition, delay in the investigation and resolution of a complaint increases the size of the back-pay remedy that an employer potentially faces and therefore increases his inducement to resist the commission's efforts to achieve a voluntary settlement. Finally, the delays that have characterized the EEOC's administrative processes must inevitably cause those who seek the agency's assistance to become skeptical of the government's purported commitment to prohibit and redress discrimination in employment.[19]

An agency's capacity to resolve disputes without inordinate delay has been one of the traditional measures of its effectiveness.[20] During the late nineteenth century, before "administrative law" had become a part of the

113

profession's working vocabulary, judges, lawyers, and scholars were concerned with finding adequate rationalizations for the existence of administrative agencies. One of the most persuasive justifications stressed an agency's superior institutional ability to respond promptly to the conditions being regulated.[21] But an administrative agency can realize that institutional potential – which it must do if it is to achieve a substantial measure of effectiveness – only if Congress supports it with adequate appropriations for the scope of the challenge facing it.

The steady growth in the EEOC's backlog of unresolved complaints supplies a melancholy measure of Congress's failure to provide adequate fiscal support. Although it is true that Congress has regularly increased the level of appropriations made to the commission, nevertheless the agency has been chronically short of sufficient funds and staff to maintain control of its work load. This pattern of underfunding has made clear that dispute settlement processes quite uncommon to our legal system can hardly be expected to take root if they are not adequately supported in their formative years, when the normative task of persuading society to accept them as a legitimate alternative to adversary modes of dispute settlement is predictably the most demanding.

In enacting Title VII of the Civil Rights Act of 1964, the American people have declared clearly that the most pervasive forms of discrimination in employment should be prohibited as a matter of national policy. But they remain troubled and uncertain about many controversial questions raised by that declaration of moral purpose – for example, the nature of the evidence necessary to establish the existence of illegal discrimination, and the extent of the measures that should be required to remedy the consequences of such discrimination as is found to exist. The tensions created by those unresolved questions have prevented the public's commitment to ending employment discrimination from being complete and resolute. These persisting tensions have also delayed the day when a greater degree of public agreement can be attained for the formulation of more clearly stated administrative remedies.

This public ambivalence is reflected, inevitably, in the failure of Congress to grant the EEOC the traditional administrative powers to hold adjudicatory hearings, make findings of fact, and impose administrative sanctions, as well as in its failure to provide the commission with appropriations adequate to enable it to discharge its statutory mandate effectively. Only when the nation's commitment to equal employment opportunity becomes stronger and more determined, and the goals of its equal employment policy more clearly settled and widely shared, can the performance of the Equal Employ-ment Opportunity Commission as an administrative agency be expected to become more effective.

Those who seek to understand the recurring sense of crisis in the adminis-trative process must attend to the suggestion that administrative agencies achieve a high standard of performance when they enjoy strong public support for the attainment of clearly stated and socially manageable policy goals, and founder when they do not.

Too often, Americans have created administrative agencies in a burst of reforming enthusiasm, without having made a sufficient long-term commit-ment to the agencies' stated goals. In addition, Americans too often have created administrative agencies in order to provide a symbolic affirmation of political functions that are supported widely, but ambivalently. The expe-rience of the Equal Employment Opportunity Commission during its first decade provides further confirmation of the hypothesis that differences in the quality of performance among the various federal administrative agen-cies are attributable, in considerable degree, to the differentiated attitudes of the American public toward the agencies' respective responsibilities.

9

The significance of institutional capacities and limitations: meeting the needs of the elderly

A good democratic system protects the public against the demand that it do impossible things.

E. Schnattschneider, *The SemiSovereign People* (1960)

The recurrent assertions that there is a crisis in the administrative process do more than merely ignore the marked differences in performance among the federal administrative agencies that the discussion of the Securities and Exchange Commission and the Federal Trade Commission explored. They also overlook the possibility that failures of administrative performance are the result of institutional limits to the effective uses of the administrative process, of which public ambivalence of the kind associated with the Equal Employment Opportunity Commission is only one.

When Congress does not understand or respect those limits, administrative agencies may be asked to undertake tasks beyond their realistic capacities to achieve. The failures of performance that predictably follow then form the basis of adverse judgments about the effectiveness of the administrative process. These judgments contribute, in turn, to impairing the legitimacy of the administrative process.

If the performance of the administrative process is to be evaluated fairly, public expectations as to its institutional capacities must be informed and realistic. Exploration of the institutional potentialities and limitations of the administrative process could profitably focus upon any number of areas in which the federal government is now being asked to assume larger regulatory and supervisory responsibilities than it has in the past. A useful area of inquiry, as well as one of increasing social importance, concerns the proper use of the administrative process in meeting the needs of the elderly. The observations that follow concerning the administration of programs for the elderly have a potentially broad significance. A proper appreciation of the

116

institutional capacities and limitations of the administrative process in one area can contribute to the design of governmental programs in many other substantive areas.

How can the administrative process be used most creatively in achieving the nation's public policy for the elderly? Is there reason to believe that this policy can be carried out efficiently by the administrative process when administrative agencies have consistently been criticized for failures of the most fundamental kind? What, indeed, are the effective limits of the administrative process in providing programs and services for the elderly?

These questions are central to an understanding of the limitations and possibilities of reliance upon the administrative process to improve the situation of the elderly, to increase their dignity as human beings, and to enlarge the bounds of their participation in American life. The achievement of the nation's public policy goals for the elderly, whatever their substantive content, will depend in considerable degree upon whether the responses we make to these questions are realistic. Unless our responses are tempered by the skepticism that a century of significant experience with the administrative process should give, we are likely to hold improvidently optimistic expectations for the performance of administrative agencies responsible for programs concerning the elderly. When these agencies then fail to meet the unrealistic expectations set for them, as they inevitably must, the danger arises that we shall abandon the programs and indict the legitimacy of the administrative process, rather than temper our expectations to what the administrative process is more realistically capable of achieving. Inquiry into the general capacities and limitations of the administrative process may be at least as important, then, to successful implementation of public policy as any of the specific substantive programs intended to benefit the elderly.

It would be possible, of course, for Congress to develop a national policy on the problems of the elderly that does not rely primarily upon administrative agencies for its implementation. Congress might, for example, choose to rely instead upon a system of private rights enforceable in the courts, as it did in enacting the Age Discrimination in Employment Act, which authorizes private actions for violations of its terms, although the Act also retains an agency role.[1] However, Congress is quite unlikely to do so for at least two reasons.

First, the United States has a long tradition of reliance upon the administrative process to secure newly defined rights and to achieve newly endorsed goals. Since the early years of the Republic, administrative agencies have given promise of an expertise and a specialization, of an informality and an expedition, that have urgently been required in the solution of national problems. However one may assess their performance on an absolute scale, administrative agencies have been regarded throughout our history as principal instruments for the achievement of governmental programs.[2]

Second, existing programs to protect the rights and improve the situation of the elderly are already entrusted to administrative agencies to a very considerable degree. The Department of Health, Education, and Welfare, for example, administers the Older Americans Act,[3] which encourages the states to provide programs and services for the elderly, and the Social Security Act,[4] which provides benefits to the elderly under both the old age, survivors, and disability program and the medicare program. The Department of Labor administers the Age Discrimination in Employment Act,[5] which prohibits employers, labor unions, and employment agencies from discriminating on the basis of age against persons forty to sixty-five years old. The commissioner of internal revenue administers the pension plan provisions of the Internal Revenue Code,[6] which provide tax advantages to employers who create pension plans that benefit their employees in ways that Congress has prescribed.

In addition, many administrative agencies have the capacity to affect important concerns of the elderly, even though the statutes they administer are general in scope and were not enacted primarily to benefit the elderly. When the Federal Trade Commission, for example, orders a respondent to stop advertising a product in a deceptive manner – the famous *Geritol* case[7] is an illustration – the decision specifically protects prospective purchasers who are elderly, although its total impact is quite obviously more general. Similarly, when the Food and Drug Administration refuses to permit a drug to be marketed because insufficient clinical data have been collected, the decision protects the elderly along with persons of every other age group. In short, administrative agencies with authority to affect every age group will often be in a strategic position to improve significantly the quality of life of the elderly.

It may well be that the administrative process is too much with us and that historically we have relied upon it to an unwise extent. The arguments that scholars have made concerning the overuse of the criminal process – that government misuses its resources and jeopardizes public respect for law when it requires a particular form of social control to do tasks beyond its effective capacity[8] – apply as well to the administrative process. By asking administrative agencies to do tasks that are better done by courts or by pri-

118

vate groups, we pay a price in terms of efficiency and public respect for the legitimacy of the administrative process.

But given this nation's historical tendency to rely upon the administrative process to implement public policy (what might be called the normative power of history) and the fact that so many programs to improve the quality of life of the elderly have been entrusted to administrative agencies (what Thomas Reed Powell once called the normative power of the actual), it seems more than likely that the administrative process will remain the principal method for implementing public policy for the elderly. This likelihood underscores the necessity of achieving a fair estimation of the capacities and limitations of administrative agencies as institutions of government if our hopes for effective implementation of national policy are to be set realistically.

Two tendencies of administrative agencies that bear directly upon their limitations as instrumentalities of government have already been described. The first is the life cycle that characterizes many administrative agencies, an evolution from vigorous and creative enforcement of congressional policies in an agency's early years to the bureaucratic sluggishness that afflicts so many agencies in their maturity, described in Chapter 4. The second is the phenomenon of "industry captivity," described in Chapter 5.

When administrative agencies succumb to these two institutional tendencies, they obviously lose something of their will to regulate creatively and decisively. That these tendencies already exist in the administration of programs designed to carry out public policy toward the elderly seems clear. The ponderous and indifferent processes by which old age and survivors' benefits are determined by the Department of Health, Education, and Welfare is a clear example of bureaucratic routinization. The effective role that the American Nursing Home Association and the American Medical Association have been able to play in shaping the content and style of administration of the medicare program provides a ready example of the power of particular industry groups. The many organized groups with which the elderly must deal – hospitals and their professional associations, health care insurers, pharmaceutical houses – can surely be expected to seek and find similar relationships of influence with the administrative agencies responsible for regulating their conduct.

Those concerned with respecting the effective limits of the administrative process must begin by acknowledging that these two institutional tendencies exist and are not easily overcome, as more than one disillusioned agency

119

chairman, present and past, could attest. But means of reducing their force are available and merit the serious consideration of those who would make the administrative process more effectively serve the interests of the elderly.

First, careful thought should be given to placing new programs involving the elderly under the jurisdiction of newly created administrative agencies, as Congress did when it concluded that environmental spoilage required increased federal attention from an Environmental Protection Agency, rather than under the jurisdiction of existing agencies, as Congress did when it placed administration of the newly created medicare program in the Department of Health, Education, and Welfare.

Newly created agencies, freshly charged with a mandate to get a job done well, typically act with energy and imagination during their early years. The vigorous performance of the Environmental Protection Agency in its early years illustrates the capacity of newly created agencies to take decisive action in a manner quite inconsistent with patterns of bureaucratic sluggishness or industry orientation. It is not clear that the National Environmental Protection Act would have been implemented as decisively at the start had responsibility for its administration been placed in an existing agency, with its inevitable web of relationships to the industries under its jurisdiction.

By creating new administrative agencies to carry out new national programs for the elderly, Congress can avoid some of the institutional problems presented by reliance upon established agencies and can gain a heightened visibility and separate identity for these programs. The difficulty, of course, is that newly created administrative agencies eventually become established administrative agencies, and the day of reckoning has only been postponed. The test of the Environmental Protection Agency will be whether it can maintain its momentum over the long term of years, as the enthusiasm of its recently recruited staff gives way to increasing frustration, as the public inconvenience caused by efforts to improve the environment becomes greater, and as the power of the regulated industries makes itself felt politically and otherwise. Still, there may be an advantage to Congress and to the proponents of a new federal program in having a period of exemption from these problems, if only to permit the program a maximum opportunity to develop an administrative momentum.[9]

It must be recognized, however, that creating new agencies to administer programs of concern to the elderly will not always be practical. The special concerns of the elderly cannot be defined with as sharp a focus as other social problems, such as environmental spoilage.[10] The concerns of the elderly are not only much more diffuse, they are also often the subject of administrative programs that have a more extensive reach, such as tax treatment of pension plans, which itself is part of a tax structure seeking broader goals of income distribution. Frequently, then, it will be impractical to separate programs affecting the elderly from the broader regulatory context of which they are a part. In addition, a decision to create a new administrative agency rather than to rely upon an established agency may require the sacrifice of valuable regulatory experience, including an extensive knowledge of specific industries, particularly when the new legislative program is closely allied in character to programs administered by existing agencies. Finally, newly created agencies may sometimes be more vulnerable to industry "capture" than newly created programs placed in established agencies. Thus a Task Force on Medicaid and Related Programs of the Department of Health, Education, and Welfare recommended against creation of a separate Department of Health because it "would be a prime target for 'capture' by powerful special interest groups," and added that "[a]s part of a larger agency, health activities are frequently subjected to close scrutiny and countervailing forces which can act as a shield against powerful interest groups."[11]

Second, careful attention should be given to the quality of the individuals appointed by the President as chairmen of administrative agencies that have responsibilities with significant implications for the elderly. The chairman of an administrative agency can make a striking difference in the way in which the agency conceives its function, defines its ambitions, and performs its duties. As James M. Landis wrote in his report to President-elect Kennedy, "Good men can make poor laws workable; poor men will wreak havoc with good laws."[12] The impact that Chairman Kirkpatrick had upon the Federal Trade Commission during the early years of the Nixon administration suggests the way in which an individual of high competence and integrity willing to use the authority of the chairman's office can bring direction and imagination to an agency long regarded as the victim of both bureaucratic sluggishness and industry orientation.

One ought not, however, to romanticize the power of an agency chairman to lead his agency in the directions he desires. His fellow commissioners may oppose his substantive initiatives on the merits or be indifferent to his sense of urgency, and the agency's staff of career professionals may regard the current chairman as no more than a temporary policy maker who will stay for a brief period and then move on, as so many others before him have. If a chairman is to make a difference in these circumstances, he must be an individual of unusual ability and personal and intellectual force. Yet even those Presidents who have cared about such matters have found it difficult to persuade able individuals to accept administrative positions and to stay long enough to institutionalize the reforms they have initiated. The reasons underlying the reluctance of able individuals to accept such appointments are doubtless complex – although they surely relate to the low prestige of many agencies, and the fact that the opportunity to make a difference may seem small when so many others have proved unable to take advantage of it – but the existence of the situation is plain.

These, then, are some of the considerations that should guide an assessment of the effective uses of administrative agencies. The tendencies toward "bureaucratic ossification," in Chairman Cohen's phrase, and industry orientation represent significant limitations upon the institutional capacities of the administrative process. These limitations can be countered to some extent by exploiting the special strengths that newly created agencies typically bring to public administration and the reforming vigor that able administrators often inject into regulatory activity. But to the extent that these expedients finally prove inadequate in particular instances, those concerned with the legitimacy of the administrative process must accept the existential fact that there are institutional limits to its effective uses.

Finally, in considering how to make the most effective use of the administrative process in the service of public policy for the elderly, we must understand that no administrative program can succeed that does not respect the elderly as individual human beings. Here, as earlier, the importance of community attitudes toward administrative regulation and achievement is great, for these attitudes determine the degree to which administrative agencies respect the human dignity of those they serve. Lionel Trilling once wrote: "[W]e must be aware of the dangers which lie in our most generous wishes. Some paradox of our nature leads us, when once we have made our fellow men the objects of our enlightened interests, to go on to make them the objects of our pity, then of our wisdom, ultimately of our coercion."[13] An administrative process that forgets the meaning of this paradox has forfeited the aspiration to meet human needs effectively.

II

The relevance of administrative procedure

10

Administrative procedure and the nature of legitimacy

The history of American freedom is, in no small measure, the history of procedure.

Justice Felix Frankfurter, in *Malinski v. New York* (1945)

The recurrent sense of crisis in the administrative process, as the discussion so far has suggested, rests upon a number of important public perceptions that, taken together, seem to comprise a formidable indictment. The persistence of these perceptions – to a point where many have entered the nation's conventional vocabulary of political discourse – has impaired the legitimacy of the administrative process as an instrumentality of modern government.

And yet these perceptions lack the substantive weight of a successful indictment. Many of them are misconceived as conclusions of historical fact or misinformed as judgments of administrative practice. For example, those who question the legitimacy of the administrative process because administrative agencies do not conform to the constitutional theory of separation of powers forget that the Framers themselves endorsed exceptions to Montesquieu's formalistic version of the theory in order to achieve a more effective government.

Those who regret that administrative agencies represent a departure from the judicial norm ignore the possibility, long understood by European nations, that modes of procedure other than trial-type hearings are sometimes better suited to the achievement of governmental policies. They ignore as well the fact that the rights of the individual can be protected in such proceedings at least as effectively as they are protected in more traditional adversary hearings.

Similarly, those who are skeptical of administrative expertise do not always remember that a similar loss of faith colors popular attitudes toward many sources of public and social authority. Nor do they appreciate the

125

manner in which the expertise of an agency's staff can be made subject to the generalist vision and control of the agency's members. Those who criticize the federal administrative agencies for having succumbed to the evils of bureaucratization rarely consider that this development is part of a larger trend toward the growth of bureaucratic organizations (in both the public and private sectors) currently being experienced by most of the industrialized nations of the world. Skepticism of expertise and concern with the consequences of bureaucratization are each social attitudes transcending the example of the federal administrative agencies.

Still further, those who believe that administrative agencies should not decide fundamental questions of policy more appropriately settled by electorally responsive institutions of government fail to appreciate that this state of public affairs results from the failure of Congress, in delegating legislative power, to provide adequate standards or to give sufficient weight to considerations of institutional competence. It does not result from any inherent or presumptuous tendency of administrative agencies to preempt Congress's authority to decide such questions.

Finally, those who condemn the administrative process for its failures of performance fail to draw necessary distinctions among the federal administrative agencies, which in fact display distinct variations in the quality of their respective performances. Nor do such persons recognize sufficiently that the quality of an agency's performance is usually a function of the degree of public support it enjoys for the achievement of its statutory responsibilities – or the degree of public ambivalence toward its stated mission.

The recurrent sense of crisis in the administrative process also finds its source in the common belief that governmental power in a constitutional democracy can be legitimated in only two ways: Either it must be created by the Constitution or it must be exercised by officials directly accountable to the people through the political process. If these were the exclusive criteria of legitimacy, then administrative agencies could never be regarded as fully legitimate. The category of independent regulatory agency is not mentioned in the Constitution, and the appointed members of administrative agencies are not fully or directly accountable to the people through the political process.

But these unqualified criteria of legitimacy do not adequately reflect the more subtle realities, the more inventive and accommodating resiliencies, of American constitutional practice. As that practice has unfolded, it has frequently found important places for institutions, arrangements, and practices

126

not recognized by eighteenth-century political theory. Among the basic lessons that American constitutional history must be taken to teach is that institutional legitimacy is a product of consistency with values and traditions, and that governmental institutions attain legitimacy in many different ways.

A striking number of governmental institutions and practices, quite like administrative agencies, lack an explicit constitutional reference, but that circumstance has not prevented them from attaining a status of legitimacy in our constitutional practice. The Supreme Court's power of judicial review and constitutional adjudication, established in *Marbury v. Madison*,[1] the organization of the President's cabinet, and the role of political parties are only the most significant of many examples that could be summoned.

The Constitution does not speak expressly of administrative agencies, but it does confer upon Congress the power to regulate commerce among the several states. The adaptive principles by which the Supreme Court's power of constitutional adjudication was recognized and the development of the President's cabinet and the two-party system were accepted are surely broad enough to confer legitimacy upon the administrative process, an institutional arrangement created by Congress as a "necessary and proper" adjunct to the exercise of its own constitutional responsibilities.

Indeed, notwithstanding that administrative agencies are not mentioned explicitly in the Constitution, the First Congress of the United States, led by men who participated in the processes by which the Constitution was drafted and adopted, enacted legislation in 1789 creating what may be regarded as the nation's original administrative agencies. At the least, one is entitled to conclude from the decisions of that First Congress that the contemporaneous understanding of the meaning of the Constitution's broad authorizing phrases was not hostile to the theory or creation of administrative agencies.

The claim of the administrative process to a status of legitimacy rests in part upon those early understandings and practices. It rests as well upon the repeated decisions of later Congresses, throughout the nation's history, to create new federal agencies extending the dimensions of administrative government. If, as Aldous Huxley once observed, "old, established governments do not need to produce certificates of legitimacy," the same should be true of old, established institutions of government, particularly when the national legislature has regularly reaffirmed the governmental necessity of relying upon them.

The legislative practice of repeated reliance upon administrative agencies may have conferred a political legitimacy upon the administrative process in the descriptive sense that Weber emphasizes: The American people are prepared to concede that "obedience is owed to the legally established impersonal order" because of its "formal legality."[2] But that legislative practice has yet to confer a full measure of constitutional legitimacy upon the administrative process.

Would a constitutional amendment making explicit provisions for administrative agencies supply that missing measure of legitimacy? Rexford G. Tugwell, once a member of Franklin D. Roosevelt's "brain trust," has proposed that regulatory functions be elevated to a constitutional status in order to "confer a legitimacy they now lack – and badly need":

> The regulatory function, borrowing from all the branches, violating everywhere the principle of separation, and proliferating until its bureaucracy is more than half the whole, is . . . maverick. Its agencies are, indeed, established by law; but the Congress had no authorization to establish them. Their personnel are appointed, not elected, and regulatory agencies perform functions of all categories.[3]

Perhaps an explicit constitutional provision that elevated administrative agencies to the same level of dignity as the three original branches and brought them specifically within constitutional contemplation would enhance their legitimacy. Granting constitutional status to the administrative process, as Tugwell rightly points out, "would be more a matter of recognition than invention." Nevertheless, it would confirm the significant position that administrative agencies have already achieved in our governmental system and, more importantly, would lay to rest doubts about their formal constitutional legitimacy. The prospects for a constitutional amendment of this character are not promising, however, perhaps because the arguments for its necessity at this late date in the history of the administrative process are too theoretical to be phrased in terms easily grasped by the popular mind.

With respect to the second way in which it is commonly believed that governmental power is legitimated, the fact that the members of administrative agencies are not directly accountable to the people through electoral or political processes hardly means that they are freed from constraints that such accountability imposes. To a very significant degree administrative agencies are subject to influence, supervision, and sometimes control by those who have been elected by the people – that is, the President and the Congress – and bear a relationship of accountability to them. They are also subject to an extensive discipline of judicial review designed to ensure, among many goals, that the actions of agencies are consistent with the instructions of the democratically elected Congress.

128

Moreover, that administrative agencies are not directly accountable to the people in a political sense does not differentiate them from many significant institutions and practices – for example, the committee structure in Congress – that are accepted as fully legitimate elements of our constitutional system even though they are not majoritarian in character. Indeed, one of the certain strengths of American constitutional development has been its Madisonian capacity for blending majoritarian and nonmajoritarian devices into an effective system of governance.

Many of the public perceptions that have given rise to the recurrent sense of crisis in the administrative process thus prove, upon analysis, to be misconceived or based on misunderstandings. Of course, some of the concerns that these perceptions express are plausible, and some of the elements of criticism undeniable. However, most of these perceptions, when properly understood, can be refuted in their own terms or placed in a perspective less destructive of the legitimacy of the administrative process. But if the legitimacy of the administrative process is to be recognized more fully, the process of securing that recognition must involve more than merely a refutation of commonly held misconceptions and widely shared misunderstandings. The process must generate an acceptance of the legitimacy of the administrative process by arguments of a more affirmative nature.

It is surprising that more attention has not been given, in the search for sources of administrative legitimacy, to the quality of administrative justice. The procedural rules by which an institution reaches substantive decisions inevitably convey a telling indication of the fairness of its methods, the extent of its interest in protecting individual rights, and the depth of its commitment to attaining just results. In many important respects, the desire and the capacity of government to devise fair procedures for the discharge of its decision-making responsibilities are the essence of democratic practice.

The significance of procedural fairness to the integrity of the governmental institutions that exercise power over the individual has long been recognized. Justice Douglas once wrote:

It is not without significance that most of the provisions of the Bill of Rights are procedural. It is procedure that spells much of the difference between rule by law and rule by whim or caprice. Steadfast adherence to strict procedural safeguards is our main assurance that there will be equal justice under law.[4]

Justice Douglas's comments do more than merely recount a historical truth. They state a judgment that successive generations of men, reflecting on the meaning of justice, have reached over the course of centuries. For this reason, the legitimacy of the administrative process must finally rest in important part upon its dedication to decision-making procedures that are just – what Alexander M. Bickel called "the morality of process."[5]

The principal procedural authority for the federal administrative agencies is the Administrative Procedure Act,[6] enacted in 1946 after an extended period of public discussion and legislative debate. Designed to be a comprehensive code of administrative procedure, the Act prescribed minimum procedures for all federal agencies to follow in both adjudication and rule making. Passage of the Act (by unanimous votes in both the Senate and the House of Representatives) brought to a close a decade of mounting concern over the kaleidoscopic variations in administrative procedure that prevailed among the federal agencies, perhaps because so many of them had been hastily conceived in the energetic turbulence of the New Deal. It ensured that administrative agencies would be accountable to a set of legislatively drawn standards in addition to the constraints already imposed by judicial review. Reliance upon instruments of procedural regularity was, of course, a relevant response to popular charges that administrative agencies had become "a headless fourth branch of government." Finally, passage of the Act invited a new era of deliberative attention to considerations of procedural fairness and the relationship between fair procedures and effective administration.

One of the motivating impulses behind enactment of the Administrative Procedure Act, as the Supreme Court said in its first decision interpreting the Act, "was to introduce greater uniformity of procedure and standardization of administrative practice among the diverse agencies whose customs had departed so widely from each other."[7] Given such a purpose, it was necessary that the Act state procedural standards with sufficient precision that agencies might effectively implement them and with sufficient generality that agencies might creatively adapt them to the wide range of their respective regulatory responsibilities.

The Act itself is short, comprising only twelve sections. Some of its provisions are ambiguous, while others create large exemptions from its general prescriptions. But its strength, finally, lies in the fact that its provisions embody conceptions of elementary fairness quickly recognized as the basis of prevailing principles of procedural justice. The generality of the Act's major requirements has been a significant reason for its success in achieving a useful measure of procedural uniformity among agencies with very different regulatory responsibilities. It has been this generality of conception that has permitted judicial decisions applying the Act's provisions to one agency to temper and enrich decisions applying the same provisions to other agencies.

130

This achievement indicates why the Act is properly regarded as one of the most important developments in administrative law in the twentieth century. Of course, the scheme of the Administrative Procedure Act has been the subject of criticism and suggestions for revision. One area of concern has been the inflexibility of the Act's adjudicatory requirements in light of the diversity of issues that arise before the administrative agencies. Another area of concern has been the inapplicability of most of the Act's requirements to the wide range of informal decision-making processes employed by the federal agencies. But these criticisms, despite their frequent plausibility, should not obscure the Act's major strengths.

Having enacted the Administrative Procedure Act in 1946, Congress did not amend it for the first time until 1966 – and then to add the Freedom of Information Act rather than to modify any of its basic procedural provisions. Many reasons may explain Congress's prolonged reticence: the institutional difficulty of comprehensively addressing any major statute more frequently than once every several decades; the desire to emphasize to the agencies and the legal profession that the Act was a permanent part of the administrative universe and must be accepted in all of its essentials; the inability of those contending forces that would have changed the Act to agree upon a formula for amendment; the fear that a decision to permit narrow perfecting amendments would soon lead to the haphazard adoption of many broader amendments destructive of important purposes of the Act; the conviction that the Act had struck a proper balance between competing interests and did not require amendment.

Whatever the reasons for Congress's silence over two decades, the consequences have been salutary. The Act has imposed a considerable degree of procedural regularity upon the federal administrative process, and the agencies have accommodated their processes to the Act's central requirements without damage to their initiative or their effectiveness.

The importance of substantive rules to administrative regulation is obvious. But substantive rules, as Sir Henry Maine observed a century ago, rapidly become "secreted in the interstices of procedure."[8] Administrative procedure and regulatory substance always nurture each other in a kind of symbiotic tension. The design of procedural requirements is affected by the substantive goals of the legislation being enforced, just as the shape of the substantive law is influenced by the procedural setting in which it must be applied.

This means that the contribution of the Administrative Procedure Act to the legitimating forces of procedural regularity and the more perfect achievement of administrative justice can be understood only in the context of specific areas of regulation. Therefore, the discussion in Chapters 11 through 15 considers the application of the Act to the Office of Foreign Direct Investments (OFDI), an administrative agency created in 1968 to deal with the balance-of-payments crisis that the United States was then experiencing, and abolished in 1974 when its functions were no longer considered necessary. The creation of a new agency like OFDI presents an opportunity for considering the wisdom of the balance that Congress has struck between precision and generality in drafting the Administrative Procedure Act. The opportunity is particularly instructive because of the important differences in origin and function between OFDI and the older administrative agencies that provided the conception upon which the Act was modeled.

Application of the Administrative Procedure Act to OFDI is enlightening for the further reason that it requires examination of certain issues basic to fair administrative procedure: the meaning of the term "agency" with its related implications for the separation of investigative, prosecuting, and adjudicatory functions; the character of enforcement and disciplinary proceedings; the significance of an impartial hearing officer; the teachings of the Constitution with respect to the combination of inconsistent functions; and the criteria for disqualification of administrative officials for bias. Careful examination of these issues inescapably becomes a guided tour, as it were, through the terrain of the Administrative Procedure Act. The manner in which the Act resolves these basic issues of administrative procedure is an important test of its fairness, its flexibility, and its pragmatism.

The discussion of the Administrative Procedure Act's application to OFDI focuses primarily upon formal administrative proceedings. But much of the work of the federal administrative agencies is done informally, without adjudicatory or rule-making hearings of the traditional kind being held at all. About these informal decision-making processes – which potentially affect more persons, often more decisively, than formal decision-making processes – the Administrative Procedure Act says next to nothing.

Informal administrative action is typically not governed by any other prophylactic legislation. Therefore, there is a substantial possibility that it may be arbitrary or founded upon error. Chapters 16 through 19 consider the manner in which informal administrative action is taken, using summary action as the example, and discuss methods of ensuring the fairness of the informal administrative process.

The chapters that comprise Part Two of this book describe particular contexts in which the American aspiration for administrative justice has been

132

expressed. If statements concerning the nature of justice are themselves properly understood as questions inviting a continuing dialogue, then the discussion of administrative justice that follows is an invitation to renewed consideration of means for perfecting the procedural arrangements that prevail for the moment.

The nature of the formal administrative process

11

Defining the idea of "agency"

A word is not a crystal, transparent and unchanged, it is the skin of a living thought and may vary greatly in color and content according to the circumstances and the time in which it is used.

Justice Oliver Wendell Holmes, Jr., in *Towne v. Eisner* (1918)

On January 1, 1968, President Johnson created by executive order a federal program of mandatory controls limiting the amount of foreign investment that U.S. citizens and businesses would be permitted to make each year.[1] The order, relying upon the power given the President by Section 5(b) of the Trading with the Enemy Act,[2] delegated to the secretary of commerce the authority to administer the program toward the objective of "strengthening the balance of payments position of the United States during this national emergency" – that is, the national emergency declared by President Truman in 1950 during the Korean War and still in effect eighteen years later.[3] On the same day the secretary of commerce announced that he had created the Office of Foreign Direct Investments (OFDI) and had subdelegated to it the authority to administer the Foreign Direct Investment Program.[4]

The program was born of the conviction that the chronic deficit in the United States' international balance of payments threatened the nation's liquidity and must be addressed. In seventeen of the eighteen years prior to the time that President Johnson acted, the U.S. had experienced a balance-of-payments deficit. The net flow of capital out of this country in the form of investments abroad had exacerbated this payments imbalance. The administrations of Presidents Eisenhower and Kennedy had undertaken to limit government expenditures abroad and to encourage private companies to cooperate in voluntary programs of limiting their foreign investments.

By 1966, these measures, backed by tax legislation designed to discourage U.S. investment abroad, had succeeded in reducing the United States' balance-of-payments deficit to the tolerable level of $1.3 billion. But the dam did not hold. In 1967, the combination of inflation in the United States, the economic slowdown in Europe, and the escalating military expenditures required by the Vietnam War increased the nation's balance-of-payments deficit almost threefold, to $3.7 billion. It was at that point that President Johnson concluded that mandatory controls upon foreign investment were required as part of a larger economic program designed to strengthen the United States' international financial and monetary positions.[5]

The limitations that the program imposed upon foreign direct investment were embodied in the Foreign Direct Investment Regulations,[6] a complex set of substantive rules that the Office of Foreign Direct Investments administered and amended on a number of occasions as the nation's balance-of-payments position changed.[7]

The basic scheme of the regulations restricted transfers of capital between "direct investors" – both individuals and corporations – and their "affiliated foreign nationals" and limited the amount of earning that a direct investor could authorize an affiliated foreign national to reinvest. The limitations upon such transfers were expressed in terms of authorized annual maximum amounts, described as "allowables." More investment was permitted in the less-developed countries of the world than in the industrial countries.

The regulations further provided that a direct investor could apply for a "special authorization" that would permit him to exceed the amount of his annual allowables when good cause was shown. If a direct investor exceeded the amount of his annual allowables without having obtained a specific authorization, the regulations permitted OFDI to negotiate an informal voluntary settlement or to institute formal administrative proceedings, described as compliance or enforcement proceedings, which could result finally in an order requiring the direct investor to take appropriate remedial action.

The Foreign Direct Investment program remained in effect for six-and-one-half years. As the Vietnam War drew to an end, the secretary of commerce announced that the controls on foreign direct investment would be terminated on January 29, 1974, and the Office of Foreign Direct Investments abolished on June 30, 1974.[8] During those six-and-one-half years, the Office of Foreign Direct Investments played a significant role in limiting

American investment abroad, in strengthening the dollar in the world's financial markets, and in improving the nation's international balance-of-payments position. It also confronted a number of provocative and difficult questions presented by the attempt to conform the structure and activities of a new administrative agency undertaking an unusual regulatory task to the traditional conceptions of the Administrative Procedure Act.

The manner in which the Office of Foreign Direct Investments resolved those questions of structure and function makes an instructive lesson in statutory interpretation – in the fascinating interplay among legislative intention, statutory language, and wise policy results – and in the design and adaptability of the Administrative Procedure Act (APA) itself.

The first question that confronted OFDI arose from the Act's basic definition of "agency." Since the Act applied only to those parts of the federal government that were "agencies," the question was whether either the secretary of commerce or the director of the Office of Foreign Direct Investments was an agency or the agency for purposes of the Foreign Direct Investment Program. The question was of more than academic significance because only the person who was the agency would be permitted under the APA to combine investigative, prosecutorial, and adjudicative functions. If the director was the agency, he could participate in all phases of OFDI's operations, consistent with due process limitations. But if the secretary of commerce was the agency, the director would be required to circumscribe his participation so that he did not commingle functions. The question thus had significant functional importance for the way in which the Foreign Direct Investment Program would be administered.

Proliferating a legislative purpose

The Administrative Procedure Act provides that " 'agency' means each authority of the Government of the United States, whether or not it is within or subject to review by another agency. . . ." Read literally, this definition would confer agency status on persons low in the governmental hierarchy who might plausibly claim to be authorities of the United States (e.g., passport clerks, meat inspectors, and forest rangers). Congress could not have intended to confer agency status so broadly. The task that the Office of Foreign Direct Investments faced was to make functional sense of the term "agency" in a manner consistent with Congress's primary intentions in passing the Administrative Procedure Act.

Because the statutory language is unclear, the process of interpretation must begin with an examination of the legislative history. The basic legislative history of the Administrative Procedure Act resides in the reports of the Senate Judiciary Committee and the House Judiciary Committee of the Seventy-ninth Congress, which passed the Act. These reports are particularly significant because these two committees were the principal draftsmen of the Act.

The Senate Judiciary Committee, in a committee print issued in June 1945, explained why "agency" had been defined by use of the broad word "authority":

It is necessary to define agency as "authority" rather than by name or form, because of the present system of including one agency within another or of authorizing internal boards or "divisions" to have final authority. "Authority" means any officer or board, whether within another agency or not, which by law has authority to take final and binding action with or without appeal to some superior administrative authority.[9]

The final report of the Senate Judiciary Committee, issued in November 1945, also included an analysis of the defining language of the proposed statute:

The word "authority" is advisedly used as meaning whatever persons are vested with powers to act (rather than the mere form of agency organization such as department, commission, board, or bureau) because the real authorities may be some subordinate or semidependent person or persons within such form of organization.[10]

The report of the House Judiciary Committee, issued in May 1946, included a single paragraph of explanation of the use of the term "agency":

Whoever has the authority is an agency, whether within another agency or in combination with other persons. In other words agencies, necessarily, cannot be defined by mere form such as departments, boards, etc. If agencies were defined by form rather than by the criterion of authority, it might result in the unintended inclusion of mere "housekeeping" functions or the exclusion of those who have the real power to act.[11]

These few paragraphs comprise essentially all of the legislative history specifically directed to the meaning of the Administrative Procedure Act's defining language.[12] Fragmentary though they are, they suggest, in Justice Frankfurter's helpful phrase, "the known temper of legislative opinion."[13]

The theme that runs through the legislative history of the Administrative Procedure Act is that an administrative agency is a part of government that is generally independent in the exercise of its functions and that "by law has

authority to take final and binding action" affecting the rights and obligations of individuals, particularly by the characteristic procedures of rule
making and adjudication.

This theme is consistent with the general conclusion of the Attorney
General's Committee on Administrative Procedure, which "regarded as the
distinguishing feature of an 'administrative' agency the power to determine,
either by rule or by decision, private rights and obligations."[14] If the legislative history on this point can be said to reflect a dominant "temper of legislative opinion," it is a desire to use the term "agency" to identify centers of
gravity of the exercise of administrative power. Where a center of gravity
lies, where substantial "powers to act" with respect to individuals are
vested, there is an administrative agency for purposes of the APA.

The legislative materials indicate an intention to move beyond formal
designations and charts of departmental organization to assess the realities
of the exercise of administrative power. Thus the title of the authority in
question, whether it be "agency" or "board" or "bureau" or "office" or
"department," is irrelevant to assessing the power it exerts. Similarly, that
an authority of government is "within" or subject to the overall supervision
of another agency will not necessarily deprive it of the independence associated with agency status. If an authority is in complete charge of a program,
it is an agency with respect to that program, despite its subordinate position
in a larger departmental hierarchy.[15]

Perhaps more important, the legislative history of the Administrative Procedure Act indicates that although an authority's actions are subject to
appeal to and review by "some superior administrative authority," this will
not necessarily deprive them of the conclusive character associated with
agency status under the Act. Nor will the authority's exercise of its power
"in combination with other persons" necessarily deprive it of the agency
status intended by the Act. The "criterion of authority" by which the Act
measures agency status does not require that an agency exercise its power
with complete independence, either vertically (in terms of being subject to
administrative review) or horizontally (in terms of being required to act in
concert with others).

What the legislative history of the Administrative Procedure Act seems to
teach, then, is that Congress, in using the term "agency," intended the Act
to apply to authorities of government that are the center of gravity for the
exercise of substantial power against individuals – a definition that the federal courts have adopted in the course of a number of careful analyses of

141

whether an authority of government was an agency for purposes of the Administrative Procedure Act or the Freedom of Information Act.[16]

Before this definition can be applied to the administrative structure of the Department of Commerce and the Office of Foreign Direct Investments, however, several caveats must be stated. First, a definition stated as broadly as this one cannot be self-applying. It is an abstract proposition that does not neatly decide concrete cases. Its usefulness lies in the fact that it indicates a mood; it does not require a result. Second, particular sentences and phrases appearing in the legislative history cannot be read literally without doing violence to good sense and sound administrative practice. They suggest Congress's intention that "agency" be given a liberal as opposed to a restricted interpretation, but they are susceptible, if good sense and sound practice are ignored, of application in a manner that would create inappropriate and incongruous results. Third, if statutory interpretation, as Learned Hand once said, is "the art of proliferating a purpose,"[17] it would be shortsighted to draw the purpose of the Administrative Procedure Act only from its legislative history. The conclusions suggested by the legislative history must be placed in the context of the purposes underlying passage of the Act as a whole.

In *Wong Yang Sung v. McGrath*,[18] the Supreme Court pointed to two of the several purposes of the APA. The first purpose – "to introduce greater uniformity of procedure and standardization of administrative practice among the diverse agencies" of the federal government – is not relevant to the present inquiry; the APA will apply to whichever authority is determined to be the agency, whether it be the Department of Commerce or the Office of Foreign Direct Investments. But the second purpose mentioned by the Court – "to curtail and change the practice of embodying in one person or agency the duties of prosecutor and judge" – is highly relevant to interpreting the meaning of the Act's use of the term "agency."

Prior to the passage of the Administrative Procedure Act, a generation of commentators had described the unwholesome consequences that resulted from the combination of investigatory, prosecutorial, and adjudicatory functions in a single person or agency.[19] The Court in *Wong Yang Sung* devoted a major part of its opinion to reciting the consistent conclusions of those who had studied the problem that it was imperative that Congress "ameliorate the evils [resulting] from the commingling of functions."

Congress's particularized response to what was recognized by 1946 as a pervasive evil is of great significance. A central provision of the APA provides that "[a]n employee or agent engaged in the performance of investigative or prosecuting functions for an agency in a case may not, in that or a factually related case, participate or advise in the decision, recommended decision, or agency review . . . except as witness or counsel in public proceedings." As the Court noted in *Wong Yang Sung*, however, "[t]he Administrative Procedure Act did not go so far as to require a complete separation of investigating and prosecuting functions from adjudicating functions." The Act goes on to provide that the prohibition against combination of functions "does not apply . . . to the agency or a member or members of the body comprising the agency."

Thus, although Congress imposed a wide prohibition on the internal combination of functions, the practical necessity of holding members of an agency responsible for administration of a coordinated program prevented Congress from applying the prohibition against the agency itself. Of all of the members of the federal administrative establishment, only the agency, which had the ultimate responsibility for the effective exercise of administrative power, would be permitted to commingle investigatory, prosecutorial, and adjudicatory functions.

These facts suggest the importance that Congress attached to the elimination of the combination of functions generally and the necessity that Congress perceived for creating an exception limited to the agency level alone. Congress's use of the term "agency" in an early part of the Administrative Procedure Act must be read, then, in light of the resolution it made later in the Act of the combination-of-functions problem.

A definition of "agency" turning upon only the exercise of substantial authority would reach a number of second-level employees in any government office, such as division chiefs. To confer agency status on such employees would be to permit them to commingle functions, a result contrary to Congress's intention to limit the persons who may engage in that practice to those exercising authority at the highest level only. Conversely, a definition of "agency" turning upon only formal retention of supervisory authority would often confer agency status in executive departments upon cabinet members alone. To limit agency status to cabinet members would be to deny the necessary authority to commingle functions to those below cabinet level who are responsible in every real sense for the effective administration of a program.

The balance of administrative authority

By Department Order 184-A, the secretary of commerce delegated to the director of OFDI "the functions, authorities, and responsibilities" with respect to foreign direct investment that he had received by executive order from the President. The language of the department order provided that the delegation was made "subject to such policies, limitations, and directions as the Secretary may prescribe." The director was authorized to redelegate "subject to such conditions and limitations as the Secretary may deem desirable." The department order further provided that the director "report and be responsible to the Secretary," "[a]dminister the regulations issued by the Secretary," "[p]rovide advice and assistance to the Secretary," and "[p]rovide a basis for policy formulation of the Department [of Commerce] with respect to direct investment abroad and related matters."

The terms of the delegation thus reserved a degree of authority in the secretary. In estimating the relevance of that reservation to the determination of who is the agency, it was necessary to analyze carefully the nature of the authority reserved and to compare it closely with the functional realities of the Foreign Direct Investment Program.

The requirements that the director of OFDI "report and be responsible to the Secretary" and act "subject to such policies, limitations, and directions as the Secretary may prescribe" were not decisive. First, supervision by a cabinet member is common, if not implicit, in the creation of an office within the executive department that he heads. Second, the right of the delegator to take back some of his original authority is implicit in any delegation. Even absent the explicit reservations appearing in the department order, the secretary would have retained the right subsequently to impose limitations upon the director's exercise of the delegated authority.

The secretary's reservation of authority was less important than how he exercised it. The secretary did not formally prescribe any substantive policies, limitations, or conditions to govern the director's administration of the Foreign Direct Investment Program. No regulation required the director to consult with the secretary. In terms of day-to-day operations and of policy formulation, the director independently exercised "the functions, authorities, and responsibilities" that the secretary had delegated to him. The director was in charge of the staff and made almost all of the policy decisions that administration of OFDI required. It was the director who decided whether the agency should grant or deny applications for specific authorizations, one of OFDI's most important functions. It was the director who in practice exercised final responsibility for the content of OFDI's regulations. It was the director, or a person acting on his behalf, who decided whether to begin an investigation of a direct investor, whether to accept a consent settlement, and whether to bring a compliance proceeding. In these areas,

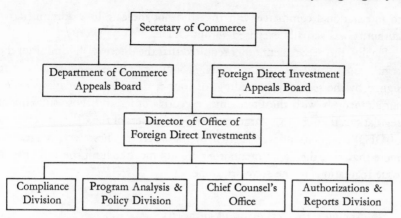

Figure 1. Organization of the Office of Foreign Direct Investments

where matters of administration and policy intersect, the director made his determinations independent of the secretary.

In some respects, however, the director lacked a similar independence. First, he did not participate directly in the fundamental determination of the amount of annual allowables – the maximum amount of direct investment that Americans could make in foreign countries in a particular year. That decision was made by the Cabinet Committee on Balance of Payments. Because the secretary was a member of the Cabinet Committee, he obviously played a greater part in this decision-making process than the director. Second, the director's decisions to deny a specific authorization were appealable to the Foreign Direct Investment Appeals Board, named by the secretary, and decisions of hearing officers in compliance cases were appealable not to the director but directly to the Department of Commerce Appeals Board, also named by the secretary. Although the power of the Department of Commerce Appeals Board to reverse the decision of a hearing officer was limited, nevertheless it did participate in adjudicatory decisions (and by authority of the department), which the director of OFDI did not.

The requirements in the secretary's Department Order 184-A that the director "[p]rovide advice and assistance to the Secretary" and "[p]rovide a basis for policy formulation of the Department with respect to direct investment abroad and related matters" imposed informational duties upon the director. They gave conventional expression to the fact that the secretary was the head of the executive department in which the Office of Foreign Direct Investments was located and that he had wide responsibilities with respect

145

to international commerce. But they did not indicate how administrative authority was actually exercised within OFDI.

Finally, the department order required that the director ''[a]dminister the regulations issued by the Secretary.'' Some of OFDI's regulations were signed by the secretary, including, of course, the initial regulations issued simultaneously with the President's executive order and those subsequent regulations thought to enlarge or clarify the powers of the director. The rest of OFDI's regulations were signed by the director. These facts suggest no more than that the department order did not mean to limit the authority to issue regulations to the secretary alone.

Applying the "criterion of authority"

Measured by the ''criterion of authority'' that the legislative history and the decided cases suggest as the test of agency status under the Administrative Procedure Act, the facts indicated a plausible basis for arguing that the director of the Office of Foreign Direct Investments was himself the agency. In terms of operational realities, the director was primarily responsible for the actual exercise of day-to-day authority in the administration of the Foreign Direct Investment Program. He acted independently in granting and denying applications for specific authorizations, in issuing substantive regulations, in authorizing investigations, and in approving consent settlements. These were actions that seriously affected the rights and obligations of individuals. The secretary's actual intervention in the director's exercise of authority was, in fact, minimal.

The argument that the director was the agency did have to take account of several considerations that seemed to cut slightly in the other direction, but none presented a serious challenge to the force of the argument.

First, the secretary had issued OFDI's initial regulations as well as some subsequent regulations. It was, of course, necessary that the secretary issue the initial regulations if substantive regulation was to begin at the time that the President announced his intention to control foreign direct investment. The subsequent regulations issued by the secretary were intended to increase the substantive authority of the director by enlarging or clarifying the secretary's original delegation. Although the subsequent regulations could be regarded as announcing rules affecting individuals, the secretary's intention seems to have been to transfer authority to the director or to confirm authority that he already possessed.

146

Second, the director's decision to deny an application for a specific authorization could be appealed to the Foreign Direct Investment Appeals Board, whose members were named by the secretary. Because a time element was so important in many applications for specific authorizations, few appeals were actually taken. Moreover, the qualifying language of the Administrative Procedure Act – "whether or not it is within or subject to review by another agency" – suggests that an authority of government may retain sufficient power and independence in the exercise of its functions to be considered an agency despite the availability of reviewing mechanisms implying a subordinate position in a larger departmental hierarchy. The power of the Foreign Direct Investment Appeals Board to reverse the director's decisions was limited to instances of "unusual hardship" or inconsistency with "the goals and objectives" of the President's executive order – grounds that did not seriously threaten the finality of the director's decisions.

Finally, the director did not participate directly in the important determination of the amount of the annual allowables, although often the secretary solicited his views and recommendations. The secretary did participate to the extent that he was a member of the Cabinet Committee on Balance of Payments, but he too lacked the authority of independent decision that characterizes agency status.

In the respects discussed so far, then, the director was the center of gravity for the exercise of governmental authority against individuals. Because he met the criterion of the "power to act" independently, set down as the dominant theme in the legislative history and affirmed by the courts, the argument that he was the agency in these respects was a persuasive one.

But the argument was difficult to sustain in every respect, particularly with regard to adjudication. Although the director participated in the negotiation and acceptance of consent settlements, he played no part in the decision of appeals in compliance proceedings. Under OFDI's regulations the Department of Commerce Appeals Board, not the director, heard appeals from the decisions of hearing officers in such proceedings. The Administrative Procedure Act provides that an authority of government may be an agency even if it is "subject to review by another agency." If the director had participated in the adjudicatory process to the extent of rendering a decision subject to review, it could have been argued that his authority was not inconsistent with agency status for purposes of adjudication. But the argument could not easily be made so long as appeals in compliance proceedings bypassed the director entirely.

The Appeals Board, whose authority derived from the secretary, was authorized to "consider appeals by persons affected by . . . administrative actions taken pursuant to law and referred to the Board by appropriate authority." The department order provided that decisions by the Appeals Board "shall be final." OFDI's regulations authorized the Appeals Board to make final administrative determinations with respect to adjudicatory appeals and made no provision for appeal to the secretary from a decision of the Appeals Board. The Appeals Board thus had authority "to take final and binding" administrative action in determining the rights of individuals.

The authority of an administrative agency to act by means of adjudication is a powerful sanction for administering its program and for enforcing its substantive regulations. Even if the negotiation and acceptance of consent settlements were regarded as part of the adjudicatory process, the heart of the process is the power to decide appeals. If the "criterion of authority" – which the legislative history of the Administrative Procedure Act suggests as the measure of agency status – is to be a meaningful standard in this area, the agency must have the power to decide adjudicatory appeals. Because the Appeals Board rather than the director had the "real power to act," it followed that the Appeals Board was the agency for purposes of adjudication.

The conclusion that the director was the agency for some purposes and the Appeals Board for others was more nearly consistent with the balance of administrative authority than any of the alternative possibilities: The director was the center of gravity for the exercise of the Foreign Direct Investment Program's rule-making authority; the Appeals Board was the center of gravity for the exercise of its final adjudicatory authority.

Other bifurcated arrangements of this kind – in which more than one agency participates in the administration of a regulatory program, each possessing authority to exercise certain functions but lacking authority to exercise others – can be found in the federal government.[20] But they are exceptions to the more usual arrangement by which a single administrative agency, with the authority to engage in both adjudication and rule making, administers a particular regulatory program.

The bifurcation of authority in the administration of the Foreign Direct Investment Program almost certainly was the result of inadvertence in the drafting of OFDI's original regulations. The conclusion that the director was not the agency for all purposes and that in fact two separate agencies were sharing the administration of the program came home to OFDI only after it had been in existence for several years. No principle of law had compelled OFDI to choose that bifurcated arrangement, nor did any principle of law compel OFDI to retain it. OFDI remained free under the Administrative Procedure Act to make the director the agency for all purposes, including adjudication, by amending its regulations to authorize him to hear adjudicatory appeals from decisions of hearing officers in compliance proceedings. As the impracticality of the bifurcated arrangement became increasingly clear – for reasons discussed in the chapters that follow – OFDI did precisely that, thereby conforming its administrative structure to that of most of the other major regulatory agencies of the federal government.

12

The Administrative Procedure Act and enforcement proceedings

Let it not be overlooked that due process of law is not for the sole benefit of an accused. It is the best insurance for the government itself against those blunders which leave lasting stains on a system of justice but which are bound to occur on *ex parte* consideration.

Justice Robert H. Jackson, in *Shaughnessy v. United States ex rel. Mezei* (1953)

The right to a hearing is one of the most important protections that an individual has against precipitate governmental action. For this reason, the hearing requirements of the Administrative Procedure Act are central to its design and to the legitimacy of the federal administrative process. The task of drafting these requirements imposed a demanding discipline, since they had to achieve a substantial measure of uniformity in the hearing processes of the federal administrative agencies while respecting the diverse character and responsibilities of these agencies.

The hearing provisions of the Administrative Procedure Act prescribe a minimum set of procedural requirements for the federal administrative agencies to follow in both adjudicatory and rule-making proceedings. But they also provide exemptions from these requirements for certain classes of cases. It is arguable that the Administrative Procedure Act should permit greater flexibility in the discriminating application of its various adjudicatory requirements to the broad spectrum of issues that arise before administrative agencies. Nevertheless, the Act has created a considerable degree of uniformity in the hearing processes of the federal administrative agencies without imposing the same requirements indiscriminately upon every decision-making process of every agency.

One of the most important questions that the Office of Foreign Direct Investments faced after promulgating its substantive regulations was whether the Administrative Procedure Act's hearing requirements for adjudication applied to compliance proceedings designed to enforce those regulations. There was little question that compliance proceedings were "adjudications" within the meaning of the Act, since they plainly were "agency process for the formulation of an order" directed at individual conduct in individual cases. The more difficult questions were whether compliance proceedings came within the Act's remaining threshhold requirements for applying the adjudication provision and, if they did, whether the Act's exemption for foreign affairs functions nevertheless applied, thereby relieving OFDI of the obligation to comply with the Act in enforcement proceedings.

After initially deciding that the Administrative Procedure Act's adjudication requirements did not apply to compliance proceedings, OFDI changed its mind. The process by which the agency eventually concluded that the Act did apply to compliance proceedings provides an instructive insight into the manner in which the most important components of the Act's hearing requirements relate to each other and to the constitutional requirements of due process.

The statutory requirement of a hearing

One of the most significant aspects of the Administrative Procedure Act's hearing requirements is that they do not apply of their own force to any federal administrative agency. Section 554 of the Act states explicitly that its provisions apply only when an adjudication is "required by statute to be determined on the record after opportunity for an agency hearing." It is only when Congress, in enacting a separate substantive statute, expressly requires that a hearing be held on the record in connection with the statute's administration that the Administrative Procedure Act's hearing provisions apply. Otherwise, the Administrative Procedure Act does not apply and an agency's hearing procedures will be governed only by the requirements of due process and of its own statute.

In interpreting the "required by statute" provisions of the Administrative Procedure Act, the Supreme Court has indicated that the separate statutory requirement of a hearing must be specific.[1] General language short of specificity – for example, statutory authorization to take particular action "after hearing" or to hold "such hearings as may be deemed necessary" – will not meet the requirement.[2] The consequence of this strict interpretation of the statutory language has been to make clear that Congress did not intend to require indiscriminate application of the Administrative Procedure Act to every agency decision-making process that might conceivably qualify as an adjudication simply by general definition. Thus Congress reserved to itself the authority to decide in each future instance whether the balance of relevant factors – such as the nature of the interests affected and of the questions in dispute, the relative costs and benefits of varying degrees of procedural formality, the imperativeness of achieving a prompt resolution of the proceeding – called for hearing procedures of the kind outlined in the Administrative Procedure Act. When it did not, Congress remained free to require different procedures suitably tailored to the character of the particular administrative hearing at issue.

For the Office of Foreign Direct Investments, then, it became necessary to determine whether any language in the Trading with the Enemy Act, or in the President's executive order, or in the secretary of commerce's department order could fairly be construed as requiring that compliance proceedings be determined on the record after opportunity for a hearing.

Section 5(b) of the Trading with the Enemy Act provides:

(1) During the time of war or during any other period of national emergency declared by the President, the President may, through any agency that he may designate, or otherwise, and under such rules and regulations as he may prescribe, by means of instructions, licenses, or otherwise –

(A) investigate, regulate, or prohibit any transactions in foreign exchange, transfers of credit or payments between, by, through, or to any banking institution, and the importing, exporting, hoarding, melting, or earmarking of gold or silver coin or bullion, currency or securities, and

(B) investigate, regulate, direct and compel, nullify, void, prevent or prohibit, any acquisition [,] holding, withholding, use, transfer, withdrawal, transportation, importation or exportation of, or dealing in, or exercising any right, power, or privilege with respect to, or transactions involving, any property in which any foreign country or a national thereof has any interest,

by any person or with respect to any property, subject to the jurisdiction of the United States. . . .

The language of Section 5(b) contains no indication, either explicit or ambiguous, of a requirement of a hearing in connection with any functions undertaken by the President pursuant to its authority. In light of the broad and unusual national emergency powers granted to the President, it would be surprising had Congress placed procedural limitations upon the manner in which he exercised them.

The executive order by which President Johnson set in motion the procedures that led to the creation of OFDI provided:

[1.] (b) The Secretary of Commerce is authorized to require, as he determines to be necessary or appropriate to strengthen the balance of payments position of the United States, that [direct investors be made subject to certain restrictions].

. . .

[3.] The Secretary of Commerce [is] authorized, under authority delegated to [him] under this Order or otherwise available to [him], to carry out the provisions of this Order, and to prescribe such definitions for any terms used herein, to issue such rules and regulations, orders, rulings, licenses and instructions, and take such other actions, as [he] determines to be necessary or appropriate to carry out the purposes of this Order. . . .

The Administrative Procedure Act speaks, of course, only of a *statutory* requirement of a hearing on the record. But even if one were to assume that the President's executive order had the legal status of a statute, there is no indication in its language that the President intended to require that a hearing be held in connection with the exercise of any of the authority it delegated. Similarly, assuming that the department order had the status of a statute, it imposed no hearing requirement upon the exercise of any authority or function it delegated to the director of OFDI.

The absence in the Trading with the Enemy Act, the President's executive order, and the secretary of commerce's department order of any explicit language requiring a hearing for the determination of compliance proceedings meant that those proceedings were not adjudications "required by statute" within the meaning of the Administrative Procedure Act, unless – as the following paragraphs explore – a hearing was constitutionally compelled.

The constitutional requirement of a hearing

Because of the decision of the Supreme Court in *Wong Yang Sung v. McGrath*,[3] the language of Section 554 governing adjudications must, in one very important respect, be given a broader interpretation than its words might literally suggest.

Wong Yang Sung involved a challenge to a deportation order resulting from a hearing that had not complied with the Administrative Procedure Act. The government sought to justify the noncompliance by arguing that because the Immigration Act contained no express requirement of a hearing, deportation orders were not "required by statute to be determined on the record after opportunity for an agency hearing." The question before the Supreme Court was whether the Immigration Act was a statute that made Section 554 (at the time denominated Section 5) of the APA applicable. After concluding that the "legislative history [of Section 5] is more conflicting than the text is ambiguous," the Court held:

But the difficulty with any argument premised on the proposition that the deportation statute does not require a hearing is that, without such hearing, there would be no constitutional authority for deportation. The constitutional requirement of procedural due process of law derives from the same source as Congress' power to legislate and, where applicable, permeates every valid enactment of that body. It was under compulsion of the Constitution that this Court long ago held that an antecedent deportation statute must provide a hearing at least for aliens who had not entered clandestinely and who had been here some time even if illegally. . . .

We think that the limitation to hearings "required by statute" in §5 of the Administrative Procedure Act exempts from that section's application only those hearings which administrative agencies may hold by regulation, rule, custom, or special dispensation; not those held by compulsion. We do not think the limiting words render the Administrative Procedure Act inapplicable to hearings, the requirement for which has been read into a statute by the Court in order to save the statute from invalidity. They exempt hearings of less than statutory authority, not those of more than statutory authority. We would hardly attribute to Congress a purpose to be less scrupulous about the fairness of a hearing necessitated by the Constitution than one granted by it as a matter of expediency.

In a number of subsequent decisions, the Supreme Court has made clear that *Wong Yang Sung* states a general statutory construction of the Administrative Procedure Act's hearing requirements, rather than an interpretation that may be limited by the fact that deportation proceedings traditionally have been an area of constitutional solicitude.[4] The decision has two important consequences. First, an adjudicatory hearing will be deemed "required by statute" in the sense necessary to make the Administrative Procedure Act applicable whenever the Constitution commands that a hearing be provided. Second, an adjudicatory hearing required by the Constitution in a *Wong Yang Sung* situation must conform to the requirements of the Administrative Procedure Act just as if an ordinary statute had required that an adjudicatory hearing be held on the record. Because the Administrative Procedure Act's procedural protections in several respects exceed those required by the Constitution, hearings compelled in this manner will provide an individual with a greater degree of procedural protection than he would have received if the Constitution had applied to his case *simpliciter*.[5]

When, then, does the Constitution require an adjudicatory hearing? The Supreme Court has most commonly announced a constitutional requirement that a trial-type hearing be held after determining that the case in issue involved adjudicative rather than legislative facts.[6] In summarizing this line of case development, Kenneth Culp Davis has written:

Adjudicative facts are the facts about the parties and their activities, businesses, and properties. Adjudicative facts usually answer the questions of who did what, where, when, how, why, with what motive or intent; adjudicative facts are roughly the kind of facts that go to a jury in a jury case. Legislative facts do not usually concern the immediate parties but are general facts which help the tribunal decide questions of law and policy and discretion.[7]

Thus, in two early and leading cases, the Supreme Court held that a "relatively small number of persons" were entitled constitutionally to a hearing on the validity of tax assessments levied against them to compensate the municipality for paving the street in front of their homes, because each case turned upon individual grounds,[8] but that taxpayers had no constitutional right to a hearing when a taxing authority raised the valuation of all taxable property generally, without regard to individual cases.[9]

More recently, the Supreme Court has seemed to narrow the occasions upon which the Constitution requires an adjudicatory hearing. The Court has stressed the centrality of the requirement that the interest in question be one of "life, liberty, or property" protected by the due process clause.[10] With respect to a property interest, the individual must demonstrate more than merely an abstract need or unilateral expectation of a governmental benefit; rather, he must be able to point to "a legitimate claim of entitlement" such as the Social Security Act's definition of eligibility for welfare assistance that was involved in *Goldberg v. Kelly*,[11] or the de facto tenure system for state university professors that was involved in *Perry v. Sindermann*.[12] Similarly, with respect to a liberty interest, the individual must demonstrate that the state action complained of did more than merely cause him inconvenience or emotional distress; rather, he must show that it stigmatized him in a constitutionally significant respect, as the dismissal of a college professor for moral turpitude would, in the language of *Board of Regents v. Roth*, foreclose "his freedom to take advantage of other employment opportunities."[13]

These principles provide a strong indication that the Constitution required the Office of Foreign Direct Investments to afford a trial-type hearing in compliance proceedings. These proceedings would be concerned with individual instances of possible violation of OFDI's regulations. In addition, they would require findings of fact on individualized issues such as willfulness and bad faith – adjudicative determinations of a kind likely to visit a stigma upon an alleged wrongdoer.

The Supreme Court once said that "consideration of what procedures due process may require under any given set of circumstances must begin with a determination of the precise nature of the government function involved as well as of the private interest that has been affected by governmental action."[14] Direct investors would have important individual interests at stake in compliance proceedings. OFDI's regulations made clear that direct investors could be subjected to orders that imposed sanctions, whether they be regarded as remedial or disciplinary. Thus an order resulting from a compliance proceeding could have required a direct investor to repatriate all or part of certain foreign earnings or balances, or to cause affiliated foreign nationals to make transfers of capital to the direct investor. Such an order also might have prohibited entirely certain kinds of foreign direct investment. Orders including such terms obviously would impose restrictions upon a direct investor. They would deny him privileges allowed to others under the Foreign Direct Investment Program. These restrictions go beyond merely enjoining one who has violated the law from violating it again, and in this respect would be more severe than the sanctions typically imposed by the Federal Trade Commission or the National Labor Relations Board. They would take from a direct investor something to which he may be said to have "a legitimate claim of entitlement" and could foreclose his opportunity to engage in direct investment. In these circumstances, a court would almost certainly have held that a direct investor was threatened at a compliance proceeding with a deprivation of property and therefore was constitutionally entitled to an adjudicatory hearing that, under the teaching of *Wong Yang Sung*, complied with the adjudication provisions of the Administrative Procedure Act.

These principles describing the constitutional requirement of a hearing apply in all but a few exceptional cases. An administrative hearing is not required when hearings are inferior as a method of inquiry to inspection, examination, or testing, or when emergency action of a temporary character is necessary to protect the public interest, as when food is unfit or drugs are mislabeled, or when the conduct of a bank's officers is under investigation.[15] But none of these exceptions would apply to compliance proceedings against direct investors. A trial-type hearing is the superior method of ascertaining the facts in these circumstances, and OFDI had no obvious need to take emergency administrative action in advance of the time required to conduct such a hearing.

The exemption for foreign affairs functions

Even though the Constitution thus required an APA hearing in compliance proceedings, there remained the question of whether compliance proceedings might nevertheless be exempted from the Administrative Procedure Act because the authority exercised by the Office of Foreign Direct Investments derived, ultimately, from the power of Congress and the President in the area of foreign affairs.

The inherent power of the President with respect to foreign affairs is obviously great. Its exercise traditionally has been subject to fewer procedural safeguards than almost any other legislative or executive power. The Supreme Court has recognized that "within the international field Congress must often accord to the President a degree of discretion and freedom from statutory restriction which would not be admissible were domestic affairs alone involved."[16]

The balance-of-payments crisis that led to the creation of the Foreign Direct Investment Program was clearly in the area of foreign affairs. The purpose of the program was to reduce the proportions of the crisis in order to strengthen the monetary position of the United States vis-à-vis other countries. One of the premises upon which the program rested was that "[h]ard currency is a weapon in the struggle between the free and the communist worlds."[17] The provision of the Trading with the Enemy Act under which the President acted applied only "[d]uring the time of war or during any other period of national emergency declared by the President." The President's executive order required the secretary of state to advise the secretary of commerce "with respect to matters under this Order involving foreign policy." Many of OFDI's substantive regulations – for example, the schedules governing the amount of direct investment permissible in particular countries – were related directly to U.S. foreign policy goals in various parts of the world. Certainly the purpose and structure of the Foreign Direct Investment Program were premised in considerable part upon foreign policy considerations. The question that OFDI faced was whether these facts were sufficient to render the Administrative Procedure Act inapplicable to compliance proceedings.

The decision in *Korematsu v. United States*,[18] permitting the enforced removal of Americans of Japanese descent from their homes, had sustained the exercise of extensive executive authority over individuals. But that decision, to the degree that it has not been discredited by the judgment of history,[19] rested finally upon the existence of a war that threatened the nation's survival. The national emergency and the balance-of-payments crisis that resulted in the creation of the Foreign Direct Investment Program could not be regarded as fair equivalents of World War II.

There is expansive language in *Chicago & Southern Air Lines, Inc. v. Waterman Steamship Corp.*[20] sustaining the unreviewability of the President's exercise of discretion in granting his approval, required by statute, of a Civil Aeronautics Board order that awarded an overseas air route. The Court denied review because "the very nature of executive decisions as to foreign policy is political, not judicial. Such decisions . . . are delicate, complex, and involve large elements of prophecy. They are and should be undertaken only by those directly responsible to the people whose welfare they advance or imperil." The decision in *Waterman* differed from OFDI's situation in two significant respects. First, the administrative decision that the Court was asked to review had been made by the President himself, rather than by an agency that he had created; the Court's reluctance to undertake such a review is understandable. Second, the decision that the Court was asked to review – whether a new airline route to a foreign country should be established – may well have depended upon foreign policy considerations; such "delicate" and "complex" considerations were hardly likely to be present in most compliance proceedings, in which the issues would be the more mundane ones of whether the direct investor had violated OFDI's regulations, and, if he had, whether his action was taken in good faith.

The argument that compliance hearings did not have to comply with the otherwise applicable constitutional requirement of a trial-type hearing because OFDI exercised the plenary power of the President and Congress over foreign affairs was doubtful. It would have been most difficult to persuade a court that the balance-of-payments crisis presented a national threat of the same order as World War II, or that a decision reached by OFDI's administrative processes was entitled to the same freedom from constitutional and statutory restraints as a decision made by the President himself, or that an order entered in a compliance proceeding raised issues of the same foreign policy sensitivity as those implicated in an order granting an overseas air route.

Moreover, Congress had recognized that foreign policy considerations could arise in administrative proceedings and that it might be inappropriate to require full compliance with the hearing requirements of the Administrative Procedure Act on such occasions. By its terms, the Act does not apply "to the extent that there is involved . . . the conduct of military or foreign affairs functions." This language has not been subject to significant judicial interpretation. But a fair reading – particularly in light of the "to the extent that" phrasing – suggests that Congress did not intend totally to exclude an agency from application of the Administrative Procedure Act merely because it may have been created to meet problems related to the conduct of foreign policy or may have been assigned tasks whose achievement has foreign policy implications.[21] Rather, Congress seems to have intended that the Act should apply to adjudications such as compliance proceedings conducted by agencies such as OFDI except "to the extent that" a particular proceeding would interfere with the conduct of foreign affairs functions and, as two congressional committees said, "clearly provoke definitely undesirable international consequences."[22]

The decision of compliance proceedings typically would not interfere with the conduct of foreign affairs functions and probably would not even implicate foreign policy considerations. Courts were most likely to regard such proceedings as presenting routine instances of the administrative necessity to regulate by sanctions and remedies. One could imagine particular cases presenting challenges to OFDI regulations that were based upon foreign policy judgments, and in such instances the exemption in the Administrative Procedure Act might become relevant. But in the generality of cases, it was difficult to argue that compliance proceedings would sufficiently implicate foreign affairs functions to justify invocation of the exemption.

Moreover, that Congress had created an exemption for proceedings that would interfere with the conduct of foreign affairs functions indicated its sensitivity to the constitutional prerogatives of the President in such matters. Because Congress had sought to supply a responsible resolution of the competing interests involved, it was particularly unlikely that a court would hold that the Office of Foreign Direct Investments's compliance proceedings were entitled to a greater immunity from the constitutional requirements of a trial-type hearing than the Administrative Procedure Act already provided.

The process by which the Office of Foreign Direct Investments concluded that the Administrative Procedure Act applied to compliance proceedings is similar in character to that which each of the federal administrative agencies must follow in determining whether the APA applies to particular functions. The process reveals the careful draftsmanship of the Act's provisions on adjudicatory hearings. Designed to avoid the indiscriminate imposition of its hearing procedures upon every adjudicatory process in every administrative agency despite their obvious differences, the Act's provisions apply only when Congress has required specifically, in an agency's enabling statute, that adjudications be determined on the record after opportunity for a hearing.

Of course, Congress cannot decline to require an adjudicatory hearing when the due process clause of the Constitution compels that one be held. The Supreme Court's decision in *Wong Yang Sung v. McGrath* responded to this circumstance by interpreting the "required by statute" language of the Administrative Procedure Act to embrace not only hearings of "less than statutory authority" but also hearings required by sources of "more than statutory authority," of which the Constitution is the most prominent example.

The Court's resourceful reading of one of the Administrative Procedure Act's central provisions did more than merely permit it to avoid declaring statutes unconstitutional whenever Congress had not met its constitutional responsibility of requiring that a particular adjudicatory proceeding be determined on the record after a hearing. It ensured that the scope of the Administrative Procedure Act's application to administrative hearings would be as broad as that of the Constitution itself. It also ensured that the Act would apply to agency adjudications even when the procedural protections it provided were more extensive than those required by the Constitution. The decision in *Wong Yang Sung*, coming only four years after the Administrative Procedure Act was passed, must thus be regarded as a timely judicial encouragement of Congress's efforts to regularize the hearing procedures of the federal administrative agencies. The success of those efforts represents an important source of legitimacy for the administrative process.

13

The significance of an impartial hearing officer

The Administrative Procedure Act was designed to give trial examiners in the various administrative agencies a new status of freedom from agency control.

Justice Hugo L. Black, in *Ramspeck v. Federal Trial Examiners Conference* (1953)

From the earliest years of the modern administrative process, the federal administrative agencies have been compelled to rely upon staff members to serve as presiding officers at adjudicatory and rule-making hearings. At least since 1906, when the Interstate Commerce Commission appointed its first hearing officers, the number of administrative proceedings at which evidence must be taken has always been far too great to permit agency members themselves to preside.

As the volume of agency hearings and business has grown, the claims and pressures upon the time of agency members have become even more intense than those that Commissioner Arpaia of the Interstate Commerce Commission described as characterizing the "typical month" of March 1953:

. . . the entire Commission disposed of 65 cases. In addition, Division 5, of which I am a member, disposed of 114 cases, including accident and safety reports, stays, revocations, temporary authorities, 212 transfers, dismissals, finance proceedings and miscellaneous orders. Added to the above, there were reviews of monthly reports, attendance at Congressional hearings, review of the weekly reports of the Bureau of Informal Cases, conferences with industry and shipper representatives, and review of many legislative proposals. I was required to read and study 8,483 pages of mimeographed reports, petitions, and memoranda. . . . This does not include research into cases and reading of briefs. Neither does it include days spent in Commission conferences at which cases are decided and listening to oral arguments.[1]

Because pressures of similar proportions customarily impinge upon the members of all the federal agencies, reliance upon staff members to preside at evidentiary hearings has long been an essential feature of the modern administrative process.

The persons who conduct administrative hearings are expected to perform a presiding function similar to that of federal district judges. Presiding employees, like trial judges, have considerable authority to regulate the order and manner in which evidence is presented, to establish the boundaries of the record, to rule upon offers of proof and objections to evidence, to propose terms of settlement, to make findings of fact, and to state their conclusions as to how the issues in the case should be decided. These are significant responsibilities.

Yet prior to the enactment of the Administrative Procedure Act, those who performed these responsibilities were rarely regarded as equivalent in any respect to federal district judges. Suspicions were prevalent that hearing officers were chosen casually and for the wrong reasons, and that they did not discharge their duties with an impartiality of the character routinely assumed in federal judges. Moreover, these suspicions were accompanied by the conviction that administrative hearing officers could not be expected to preside impartially so long as they remained no more than staff members employed by their respective agencies, subservient to the direction and discipline of their superiors in making their proposed findings of fact and recommendations for judgment.[2] It was this situation that Congress addressed in drafting the Administrative Procedure Act.

Sources of independence and status

The Act sought to increase the independence of hearing officers by a number of means, the most important of which relied upon the disinterested offices of the Civil Service Commission. The Act created within each agency a group of hearing examiners large enough to permit the agency to conduct its business efficiently. Although agencies were permitted to appoint their own examiners, they were required to make their appointments from a list of qualified persons provided by the commission.

Once appointed, hearing examiners were to be assigned to cases in rotation so far as practicable, and to be given no duties "inconsistent with their duties and responsibilities as hearing examiners." The Act also provided that the compensation of hearing examiners was to be determined by the Civil Service Commission "independently of agency recommendations or ratings" and that examiners were to be protected against removal except for good cause established and determined by the commission on the record after an opportunity for a hearing. Finally, the Act required that hearing examiners must not be subject to the supervision or direction of any agency official "engaged in the performance of investigative or prosecuting functions."

The creation of these sources of independence constituted a signal advance from the situation prevailing before the Administrative Procedure Act became law. As the Supreme Court noted in *Ramspeck v. Federal Trial Examiners Conference*, the most important decision on the revised status of hearing examiners, the Act makes clear that "Congress intended to make hearing examiners 'a special class of semi-independent subordinate hearing officers' by vesting control of their compensation, promotion and tenure in the Civil Service Commission to a much greater extent than in the case of other federal employees."[3]

In addition to increasing the independence and professionalism of hearing examiners, the Administrative Procedure Act sought to elevate their status, again by a number of means that are central to understanding the Act's basic purposes. The Act provided that hearing examiners should initially decide all cases at which they had presided and that their decisions would become a part of the record. The implications of these requirements for the status of hearing examiners became clear when the Supreme Court held, in *Universal Camera Corporation v. NLRB*,[4] that an examiner's decision must be given an appropriate weight in determining whether an agency decision that disagreed with his conclusions was supported by substantial evidence on the record as a whole. The Court stressed, however, that although the APA elevated the status of hearing examiners by comparison to their prior station, nevertheless examiners remained in a subordinate position with respect to agency members, who retained "all the powers" they would have in making the initial decision. In addition, the Act provided that a hearing examiner's decision would become the decision of the agency itself whenever the agency chose not to review the case on appeal.

By enlarging the responsibilities of hearing examiners and attaching force to their judgments, these statutory provisions confirmed, as Justice Frankfurter stated in *Universal Camera*, that "enhancement of the status and function of the trial examiner was one of the important purposes of the movement for administrative reform" that culminated in enactment of the Administrative Procedure Act. It remained for the Civil Service Commission, in 1972, to accomplish the final step in the enhancement of the dignity of hearing examiners: By regulation it granted them the title of administrative law judge that Congress had specifically declined to grant them by statute.[5]

By increasing the independence and elevating the status of hearing examiners, the Administrative Procedure Act moved a considerable distance toward professionalizing the position of hearing examiners and meeting due process objections to the nature of their role in the American system of administrative justice. Although it did not confer upon hearing examiners quite the degree of security that Article III of the Constitution confers upon federal judges, the Act did grant them sufficient independence from agency control and pressure to create confidence in the integrity of their institutional position. The disinterested commitment and the capacity of hearing examiners to reach just decisions were no longer the subject of public suspicion. And the manner in which the Act accorded greater significance to the decisions of hearing examiners suggested that Congress had settled upon a formulation that gave new content in the administrative context to the ancient, if simplistic, maxim that "he who decides must hear," and yet at the same time preserved the ultimate authority of agency members over administrative decision making.

The requirement that a hearing examiner preside

Having thus increased the independence and elevated the status of hearing examiners, the Administrative Procedure Act went on to require that hearing examiners must "preside at the taking of evidence" in all "case[s] of adjudication required by statute to be determined on the record after opportunity for an agency hearing" unless – and these were intended to be the rare exceptions to the general rule – the "agency" or one of its members chose to preside.

The applicability of these requirements to the Office of Foreign Direct Investments was plain, since compliance proceedings were concededly cases of adjudication within the meaning of the Act. This conclusion may not have been apparent to OFDI in its early months, however, for shortly after it was created, the office adopted a regulation providing that compliance proceedings "shall be presided over by an individual designated by the Director of the Office." Even though the regulation went on to provide that the individual named "shall not be employed by the Office in any investigative or prosecuting function, and shall not be subject to the supervision of the Director of the Compliance Division in any way,"[6] it nevertheless would have permitted the designation as a hearing officer of a person who was neither the agency, nor a member of the agency, nor a hearing examiner. In this respect, the regulation obviously was inconsistent with the more restrictive language of the APA and would have been held invalid had it been challenged before a court.

Perhaps coming to recognize the invalidity of this original regulation, OFDI subsequently undertook to draft a revised regulation governing the designation of hearing officers at compliance proceedings. Three choices were possible. First, if the Department of Commerce Appeals Board were the agency for purposes of adjudication, the APA would permit OFDI to designate one of its members to preside at compliance hearings. But given the significant department-wide responsibilities that members of the Appeals Board already carried, this alternative was probably never a practical possibility.

Second, if OFDI were to amend its regulations to place adjudicatory appeals in the director – as it eventually did – then the director, having become the agency for purposes of adjudication, would himself be entitled to preside at compliance hearings. Although it might be valuable to preserve this alternative for a narrow range of particular cases, its wisdom as a regular practice was doubtful. Serving as the presiding officer in compliance proceedings could well turn out to be a time-consuming job. A presiding officer must participate in the conference stages preceding the hearing, conduct the hearing itself, perhaps over an extended period of time, and prepare a report embodying his findings of fact and conclusions of law. If the volume of adjudications proved great, the director could be required to spend a significant part of his time on compliance hearings. Furthermore, by tradition and necessity, the presiding officer at adjudicatory hearings should be a lawyer, and there was no requirement that the director of OFDI be a person trained in law.

Moreover, the person who is the agency usually does not serve as the presiding officer at adjudicatory hearings; the use of independent impartial hearing examiners, trained by the Civil Service Commission, is overwhelmingly the norm in federal administrative proceedings. For the director to serve as the presiding officer would create substantial doubts as to the fairness of the proceedings – for example, with respect to his ability to consider objectively challenges to the validity of OFDI regulations that he had earlier approved.

Perhaps for reasons of this nature, OFDI's revised regulation chose the third alternative: designation of an APA hearing examiner.[7] The choice of this alternative made OFDI's practice consistent with that of the greatest number of federal administrative agencies.

Waiver of the requirement of a hearing examiner

Despite the clarity of the Administrative Procedure Act's requirements of hearing examiners, at one point OFDI considered the possibility of granting the director the authority in a few narrowly defined sets of circumstances to designate a senior attorney in the chief counsel's office to serve as the presiding officer at compliance hearings in place of an APA hearing examiner.

Such authority might have been given to the director, for example, whenever a direct investor had not formally requested the designation of an APA hearing examiner within a specified period of days, perhaps twenty or thirty, after being informed that his failure to make such a request would result in a waiver of the right. Or it might have been given whenever the director and the direct investor stipulated to the substitution of an OFDI attorney for an APA hearing examiner as the presiding officer. These proposed courses of action are worth careful examination because resolution of the legal questions they pose illuminates the significance of the APA's requirement of an impartial hearing officer.

The possibility that an administrative agency might provide for the waiver of an APA hearing examiner was raised by the Supreme Court's decision in *United States v. L. A. Tucker Truck Lines, Inc.*[8] In that case the Interstate Commerce Commission had granted a certificate of public convenience and necessity to a trucker, over the objection of competitors, after a hearing conducted by a trial examiner who had not been appointed pursuant to the Administrative Procedure Act. The commission took the position that the hearing was not one of those made subject to the formal hearing requirements of the APA. Subsequent to the hearing, in *Riss & Co. v. United States*,[9] the Supreme Court held that such hearings were indeed governed by the APA and that an agency's failure to appoint a hearing examiner constituted reversible error. However, the contention in *Tucker* that the ICC's action was invalid because a hearing examiner had not been appointed pursuant to the APA was raised for the first time in the district court, no objection having been taken at the administrative hearing.

The Supreme Court dismissed the contention on the ground that no objection had been made in the administrative proceeding. The decision in *Riss & Co.*, it said, had "established only that a litigant in such a case as this who does make such demand at the time of hearing is entitled to an examiner chosen as the Act prescribes." The decision in *Tucker* thus reflects the orthodox rule that a court will not consider objections to the validity of an administrative proceeding if the objections were not raised at the proceeding itself.

The decision also is tied closely to the facts of the case. In considering the competing truck line's failure to object to the status of the hearing officer, the Court noted:

The apparent reason for complacency was that it was not actually prejudiced by the conduct or manner of appointment of the examiner. There is no suggestion that he exhibited bias, favoritism or unfairness. Nor is there ground for assuming it from the relationships in the proceeding. He did not act and was not expected to act both as prosecutor and judge. The Commission, which appointed him, did not institute or become a party in interest to the proceeding. Neither it nor its examiner had any function except to decide justly between contestants in an adversary proceeding.

In addition, the commission's omission of an APA hearing examiner was in the nature of a good faith judgment that happened to be in error. Finally, the Court noted that "in about five thousand cases commenced after the effective date of the Administrative Procedure Act, orders are for an indefinite period vulnerable to attack if no timely objection during the administrative process is required."[10]

Because of the special factual context in which it arose, the decision in *Tucker* could not be read as authorizing OFDI to provide for the routine substitution, by intentional design, of its own employees for properly qualified APA hearing examiners. The decision gives no indication that the Court intended to compromise the view, expressed in *Wong Yang Sung v. McGrath*, that perhaps the primary motivating impulse behind passage of the APA was the desire to ensure that hearings be conducted by "examiners whose independence and tenure are so guarded by the Act as to give the assurances of neutrality which Congress thought would guarantee the impartiality of the administrative process."[11]

To these concerns – which properly gave OFDI pause in considering provisions for the waiver of a hearing examiner – were added the Administrative Procedure Act's requirement that a "subsequent statute may not be held to supersede or modify [the APA] . . . except to the extent that it does so expressly." In *Borg-Johnson Electronics, Inc v. Christenberry*,[12] the court held invalid an attempt by the postmaster general to delegate his hearing functions to the judicial officer of the department pursuant to a statutory provision authorizing him to delegate to subordinates "such of his functions as he deems appropriate." "The provisions for the appointment of impartial, independent Hearing Examiners are the very heart and soul of the Administrative Procedure Act," the court said, "and variations therefrom should not be countenanced except where a statute provides for a Hearing Examiner appointed in another manner." The court found that the statutory language upon which the postmaster general had relied was inadequate to meet the "express exception" requirement of the APA.[13]

On the basis of this body of case law, OFDI concluded that it could not validly provide that a direct investor who did not request the designation of an APA hearing examiner would be deemed to have waived his right to the appointment of such an examiner. When one considers the premises underlying the case law, the conclusion seems almost inescapable.

First, the use of independent, impartial hearing examiners is a fundamental aspect of the Administrative Procedure Act. It is designed to provide individuals against whom an agency proceeds the substance and the appearance of fairness and to assure the public of the integrity of the administrative process. Nothing in the APA – which uses mandatory language in providing that hearing examiners "shall preside at the taking of evidence" – suggests that the right to a hearing examiner can be waived or made dependent upon the timely request of the party involved. In this respect, the APA's provision for hearing examiners is different from the historical practices governing waiver of jury trial in criminal cases. A regulation that placed the burden of requesting the appointment of a hearing examiner upon a direct investor, as the court noted in *Borg-Johnson*, easily "could provide the vehicle by which [an agency] might avoid entirely the Hearing Examiner provisions of the Administrative Procedure Act."

Second, the director, assuming he is the agency, has the authority himself to serve as the presiding officer at compliance proceedings. But his right to delegate this authority to a subordinate who is not a hearing examiner depends upon the existence of statutory language "expressly" indicating an intention of thus modifying the hearing examiner requirement of the APA. There was no suggestion that the Trading with the Enemy Act, the President's executive order, or the secretary of commerce's department order contained such express language.

Third, a regulation providing as a matter of routine procedure that a direct investor bear the burden of formally requesting the appointment of a hearing examiner too readily would have suggested that OFDI was attempting to gain an unfair advantage in a proceeding in which it was the direct investor's adversary. It is unrealistic to believe that a presiding officer who was an employee of OFDI would not have been more committed to the achievement of OFDI's substantive goals, and therefore less capable of objective assessment of the direct investor's arguments, than a hearing examiner. The decision in *Tucker* refused to set aside an administrative proceeding in which an Interstate Commerce Commission employee improperly presided, but the Court noted that the case involved a dispute between private parties, and that the commission "did not institute or become a party in interest to the proceeding." Any attempt to formalize the possibility of substituting an OFDI employee for an APA hearing examiner almost certainly would have struck a court as unfair and inconsistent with the narrow exception tolerated in *Tucker*.

It was perhaps a closer question whether OFDI could have authorized the direct investor and the director to agree by stipulation to the substitution of an OFDI attorney for a hearing examiner as the presiding officer. Such a regulation would not have imposed upon the direct investor the burden of requesting what the APA appears to give him as of right. In addition, such a regulation, when it was invoked, could often be expected to result in the designation of a presiding officer with a greater competence in the substantive issues presented by compliance proceedings than might be possessed by an APA hearing examiner, perhaps newly recruited to the area of international investment. Moreover, no decided case appeared to prohibit the use of such stipulations. Such a regulation would thus avoid some of the obvious difficulties that waiver provisions typically present.

Nevertheless, OFDI's decision not to authorize the use of such stipulations was a wise one. Had OFDI chosen to permit the director to enter into stipulations of this character, the decision would properly have raised serious judicial concern. To begin with, the selection of a presiding officer by stipulation of the parties has the appearance of the selection of an arbitrator. The process may well result in the selection of a presiding officer acceptable to the parties for any number of reasons – for example, because he would be available to hear the case at a much earlier date than would a hearing examiner. But the process gives no assurance that it will result in the selection of a presiding officer possessing the qualities of independence and impartiality that were of primary concern to the Congress that enacted the Administrative Procedure Act. Moreover, no statute expressly authorized OFDI to modify the general requirement of the APA that hearing examiners preside at adjudicatory hearings.

In addition, in most cases it would be OFDI rather than the direct investor that would be most interested in stipulating to the substitution of an OFDI employee for a hearing examiner, a fact that would not escape the notice of direct investors. At the same time, direct investors, knowing that they must continue to deal with OFDI after the compliance proceeding was completed, would have an interest in remaining on good terms with OFDI. The coincidence of these interests means that a regulation permitting the parties to stipulate to the selection of an OFDI employee as presiding officer could have had a coercive effect upon a direct investor's decision to forego his right to an APA hearing examiner. Indeed, the possibility that a direct investor might believe that OFDI would refuse in the future to grant discretionary relief to those who did not stipulate to the waiver of an APA hearing examiner heightened the coercive potential of such a regulation.

In light of the purposes of the Administrative Procedure Act, then, it seems clear that the Office of Foreign Direct Investments could not have properly adopted a regulation requiring a direct investor to request the designation of an APA hearing examiner upon penalty of waiver. Nor could it properly have adopted a regulation permitting the director and a direct investor to stipulate to the substitution of an OFDI employee for a hearing examiner as the presiding officer at compliance proceedings.

One of the most significant departures that the administrative process makes from judicial norms is its reliance upon hearing examiners to preside at adjudicatory proceedings. Doubts about the competence and the impartiality of hearing examiners, particularly in comparison with federal judges, were one of the factors that impaired the legitimacy of the administrative process during much of the first half of the twentieth century.

The enactment of the Administrative Procedure Act in 1946 met many of these doubts by increasing the independence and enhancing the status of hearing examiners. The Act made clear that its requirement that a hearing examiner selected by the Civil Service Commission must preside at administrative hearings could not readily be evaded by agency regulations providing either for waiver of a hearing examiner or for the substitution of an agency employee for a hearing examiner. These conclusions emphasize the achievement of the Administrative Procedure Act in regularizing the use of impartial hearing officers in the federal administrative process.

Of course questions about the role of hearing examiners in the federal administrative process have continued to arise. These questions tend to focus upon whether hearing examiners should be granted a larger role in the process of institutional decision making, particularly to the extent of permitting them to consult with technical experts on the agency's staff, rather than upon their capacity to perform their role with the necessary assurance of procedural fairness. But since the time of the enactment of the Administrative Procedure Act, the healthy exploration of functional questions such as these no longer need call into question the legitimacy of the administrative process because of the departures it makes from the judicial norm in relying upon hearing examiners for the conduct of its proceedings.

14

Separation of functions and the Constitution

> No one can fail to recognize that there are dangers implicit in this combination of functions in an administrative agency. The curious fact remains, however, that the tendency toward this combination has been notably upon the increase.
>
> James M. Landis, *The Administrative Process* (1938)

The combination of functions has long been one of the distinguishing features of the federal administrative process. With some few exceptions, Congress has traditionally authorized the major regulatory agencies to investigate, to prosecute, and finally to judge. No aspect of American administrative law has proved so disturbing in theory or aroused such anxiety in practice. The combination of functions has been one of the principal sources of the recurrent sense of crisis attending the federal administrative process. Proposals for placing the adjudicatory functions of administrative agencies in administrative courts and for converting independent administrative agencies into executive departments have regularly been revived by sophisticated and experienced observers of the administrative process.[1] Although the prospect of combining the function of adjudicating with any other functions, and particularly those of investigating and prosecuting, seems thus to run against something resistant in the American grain, nevertheless the combination of functions remains one of the most characteristic and enduring aspects of the modern administrative process.

The reasons for permitting administrating agencies to combine functions that would be regarded as inconsistent in most other contexts have always been the simple ones of necessity and efficiency. James M. Landis, in his classic justification of the administrative process, put the argument plainly: "If in private life we were to organize a unit for the operation of an industry, it would scarcely follow Montesquieu's lines."[2] Still it is hardly arguable that the impartiality required for the proper performance of adjudicatory

172

functions is not always consistent with the performance of investigating and prosecuting functions.

Section 554(d) of the Administrative Procedure Act represents the balance that Congress struck between its desire for efficiency and its aspiration for impartiality, between those circumstances in which the combination of inconsistent administrative functions will be permitted and those in which they must be separated in order to protect the judicial function from an inappropriate contamination. The Act provides that a hearing examiner may neither "consult a person or party on a fact in issue, unless on notice and opportunity for all parties to participate" nor "be responsible to or subject to the supervision or direction of an employee or agent engaged in the performance of investigative or prosecuting functions for an agency." In addition, it prohibits an employee "engaged in the performance of investigative or prosecuting functions" in a particular case from participating or advising in the decision in that case or in a factually related case. Finally, the Act provides that these constraints upon the combination of functions shall not apply to the members of the agency themselves, who alone among administrative officials are permitted to exercise inconsistent functions.

By considering the implications of these provisions for the Office of Foreign Direct Investments, one can form an estimate of how effectively the Administrative Procedure Act's reliance upon an internal separation of functions meets the plausible concerns of those who are uneasy in the presence of a combination of functions. In addition, one can gain an understanding of the limits of statutory language in resolving procedural questions of fundamental social and substantive significance.

Applying the Act to OFDI's administrative structures

Under the administrative structure that the Office of Foreign Direct Investments created originally, the Department of Commerce Appeals Board was the agency for purposes of adjudication and the director was the agency for purposes of rule making. As long as OFDI undertook to employ a hearing examiner as the presiding officer at compliance proceedings, this structure presented no problems with respect to the separation of functions. Appeals in compliance proceedings would go directly from the hearing examiner to the Appeals Board, whose only function would be to adjudicate; it would have no part in investigating, prosecuting, or negotiating settlements.

Had those arrangements been retained, OFDI's procedures for deciding adjudicatory appeals would have been in compliance with the separation of functions provisions of the Administrative Procedure Act. The difficulty was that those arrangements were highly impractical. They placed the power of decision in compliance proceedings entirely in the hands of persons – a hearing examiner and the members of the Department of Commerce Appeals Board – not subject in any substantive manner to the authority of the director. Thus the director, who bore the primary responsibility for administering the Foreign Direct Investment Program, was denied the opportunity to participate in the performance of OFDI's adjudicatory functions. From the standpoint of the development of substantive rules of law by effective and flexible means of administrative action, there was little to recommend an arrangement that deprived a person with the director's responsibilities of any significant part in the adjudicatory process.

It might be argued that the director need not have been totally excluded from the adjudicatory process under that original administrative structure. The argument would be that the Appeals Board was free to consult the director during the process of exercising its adjudicatory authority, although nothing in OFDI's regulations suggested that such consultation was contemplated. Even assuming that such an optional consultative role for the director was better than no role at all, the argument is subject to certain limitations. By the terms of the Administrative Procedure Act, the Appeals Board could consult only agency employees who had not been "engaged in the performance of investigative or prosecuting functions" in the adjudication before it. The Appeals Board's freedom to consult the director was thus limited to adjudicatory proceedings in which the director had played no investigatory or prosecutory part. This limitation would almost certainly have proved disabling because it would have permitted the director a consultative role in the adjudicatory process at the price of denying him any role at all in the investigative and prosecutory processes. An arrangement that precluded the director from exercising decisive authority over any part of the compliance process hardly was wise.

The impracticality of that original administrative structure suggested the wisdom of making the director the agency for purposes of adjudication, and OFDI eventually amended its regulations in order to place appeals in compliance proceedings directly in the director. This meant that the director as the agency would have the authority – which the Administrative Procedure Act recognizes as necessary if agencies are to achieve their substantive goals – to combine investigative, prosecuting, negotiating, and adjudicatory functions, subject only to such limitations as the Constitution or the APA might impose. The question, then, was whether separation-of-functions problems were presented by OFDI's revised administrative structure which made the director the agency for purposes of both adjudication and rule making.

The Supreme Court has made clear on several occasions that the combination of investigative, prosecuting, and adjudicatory functions does not, without more, constitute a violation of due process. The most recent major decision is *Withrow v. Larkin*,[3] in which the Court sustained the authority of a state medical board to initiate a medical license suspension proceeding even though the board had conducted an investigative hearing into the facts of the case only two months earlier. Taking note of the "presumption of honesty and integrity in those serving as adjudicators," the Court found that the risk of prejudgment did not "raise a sufficiently great possibility that the adjudicators would be so psychologically wedded to their complaints that they would consciously or unconsciously avoid the appearance of having erred or changed position." Rather, the Court said, "there is no incompatability between the agency filing a complaint based on probable cause and a subsequent decision, when all the evidence is in, that there has been no violation of the statute."

Indeed, the Supreme Court had indicated in an earlier decision that a combination of functions that would be prohibited by the Administrative Procedure Act did not constitute a denial of due process. In its first major decision interpreting the Administrative Procedure Act, *Wong Yang Sung v. McGrath*,[4] the Court remarked, in the course of holding the Act applicable to the Immigration and Naturalization Service, that it "might be difficult to justify as measuring up to constitutional standards of impartiality a hearing tribunal for deportation proceedings the like of which has been condemned by Congress as unfair even where less vital matters of property rights are at stake."[5] Congress responded to the decision in *Wong Yang Sung* by expressly exempting deportation proceedings from the Administrative Procedure Act.[6] Under the new procedure, deportation proceedings were to be held before special inquiry officers with powers of the kind that the Court had described in *Wong Yang Sung* as "a perfect exemplification of the [concentration of functions] practices so unanimously condemned" by Congress in enacting the APA. But in the subsequent decision of *Marcello v. Bonds*,[7] the Court rejected an argument that these new hearing procedures denied due process because the special inquiry officers were subject to the supervision and control of officials charged with investigative and prosecuting functions. The Court did not follow up its remark in *Wong Yang Sung*, which had virtually no support in the previous case law, and has not returned to it since. Taken together, these two decisions indicate that the prohibitions on the combination of functions found in the Administrative Procedure Act are more restrictive than the Constitution requires.

The Supreme Court stated in *Wong Yang Sung* that one of the central ·purposes behind passage of the APA was "to curtail and change the practice of embodying in one person or agency the duties of prosecutor and judge," and "to ameliorate the evils [resulting] from the commingling of functions." Section 554(d) represents Congress's attempt to achieve those goals. But it is important to remember, as the Court noted in *Wong Yang Sung*, that the Administrative Procedure Act "did not go so far as to require a complete separation of investigating and prosecuting functions from adjudicating functions." The Act concludes its prohibition against certain forms of combination of functions by providing that it does not apply "to the agency or a member or members of the body comprising the agency." By this exception Congress recognized that those who bear ultimate responsibility for the administration of a substantive program must necessarily be involved in all phases of its implementation.

Because Section 554(d) does not apply to the agency, the director of the Office of Foreign Direct Investments was not prohibited from combining functions. He was entitled to participate in every phase of OFDI's administrative procedures – investigating, prosecuting, negotiating settlements, and adjudicating – without challenge under the Administrative Procedure Act, no matter how provocative the combination of inconsistent functions might be. The clarity of the statutory language may explain the absence of even a single case raising a question about its meaning. (Of course, the particular nature of the director's participation in the investigatory or prosecutory stages of a proceeding might compromise his capacity to serve as an impartial adjudicator – an issue to be discussed in Chapter 15 in terms of bias rather than of separation of functions.)

One provision of Section 554(d) however, did apply to the administrative procedures of OFDI and required an internal separation of functions:

An employee or agent engaged in the performance of investigative or prosecuting functions for an agency in a case may not, in that or a factually related case, participate or advise in the decision, recommended decision, or agency review pursuant to section 557 of this title, except as witness or counsel in public proceedings.

The language of Section 554(d) makes clear that any OFDI employee who had "engaged in the performance of investigative or prosecuting functions . . . in a case" could not "participate or advise in the [director's] decision"

176

of the case. This language – designed to prevent the director from consulting certain persons in the course of the performance of his adjudicatory functions – presents a number of difficult and instructive questions of interpretation.

"Investigative or prosecuting functions"

The Administrative Procedure Act did not require that the director be insulated from the advice of every OFDI employee in the performance of his adjudicatory functions. It only required that he be insulated from the advice of those employees who had engaged in the performance of "investigative" or "prosecuting" functions in the case that the director had under consideration. The first question that OFDI faced in establishing its internal organization concerned the meaning and reach of "investigative" and "prosecuting."

Read literally, Section 554(d) would have prohibited the director from consulting the director of the compliance division, since he would typically have been involved in investigating and prosecuting functions in every compliance proceeding, as well as those employees of the compliance division who had participated in investigating, preparing, or presenting the case against the direct investor. Such activity – within the division of OFDI directly responsible for prosecuting individuals – would fall most obviously within the literal meaning of "investigative" and "prosecuting" functions.

The difficulty lay in determining when OFDI employees who were *not* a part of the compliance division had performed "investigative" or "prosecuting" functions that would disqualify them from participating or advising in the director's decision. Three questions may help to expose the difficulty.

First, did Section 554(d) prohibit the director from asking the judgment of the chief counsel (or any other OFDI employee) if the chief counsel had participated in granting an interpretation or determining an application for a specific authorization, particularly if the meaning or validity of one or the other were at issue? Such participation by the chief counsel would plausibly be part of neither an "investigative" nor a "prosecuting" function.

Second, did Section 554(d) prohibit the director from asking the judgment of the chief counsel if the chief counsel had advised the director of the compliance division that this was an appropriate case for prosecution or had urged him to bring the prosecution? We have it on the authority of Professor Davis that "[t]hose who determine that proceedings should be instituted may participate in judging"[8] because the language of the Act speaks only of

177

"prosecuting" and "says nothing about combination of instituting proceedings with judging. Under the Act the same individual may 'accuse' in the sense of deciding that proceedings should be instituted, and may also judge. This is true whether the individual is a head of an agency or a subordinate,"[9] because what a person does in "approving the institution of proceedings is much like what judges do in ruling on demurrers or motions to dismiss."[10]

Third, did Section 554(d) prohibit the director from asking the judgment of the chief counsel if the chief counsel had taken part in unsuccessful attempts to negotiate a settlement? Because the language speaks only of "investigative" and "prosecuting" functions, Davis concludes that the "same individual may attempt to negotiate a settlement and later serve as judge."[11]

However plausible these conclusions may seem in terms of a literal reading of "investigative" and "prosecuting," they are not wholly satisfying in terms of the purpose of Section 554(d). The premise underlying Section 554(d) is that the integrity of the adjudicatory process will best be protected by excluding participation by agency employees the nature of whose participation in prior stages of a case suggests that their contribution might not be sufficiently disinterested. The adjudicator should be insulated from one who has performed investigative functions because "an investigator's functions may in part be that of a detective, whose purpose is to ferret out and establish a case. Of course, this may produce a state of mind incompatible with the objective impartiality which must be brought to bear in the process of deciding."[12] The adjudicator should be insulated from one who has performed prosecutory functions because "[a] man who has buried himself in one side of an issue is disabled from bringing to its decision that dispassionate judgment which Anglo-American tradition demands of officials who decide questions."[13]

Section 554(d) thus represents the language chosen by Congress to ensure that the adjudicatory process is not contaminated by the participation of those whose state of mind may be that of the advocate rather than the impartial judge. Once this premise is accepted, it becomes clear that a literal reading of "investigative" and "prosecuting" is inadequate to serve the purposes underlying the section. Such a reading would permit some employees with an advocate's state of mind to participate in adjudicatory functions and would exclude others from participating even though their state of mind is unlikely to be that of an advocate.

For example, it is fairly clear upon a literal reading of Section 554(d) that the chief counsel could participate and advise in the director's decision of a compliance proceeding directly challenging the validity of an interpretation that the chief counsel had issued, although one might think that the chief counsel's natural commitment to sustaining the interpretation would make his cast of mind that of an advocate. Similarly, it is fairly clear upon a literal reading of Section 554(d) that the chief counsel could participate and advise in the director's decision of a compliance proceeding after having attempted to negotiate a settlement that failed when the direct investor would not accept terms that the chief counsel regarded as absolute minima in light of the direct investor's conduct and after having urged that a prosecution be brought, although here too one might think that the chief counsel would hold an advocate's sincere belief in the justice of his cause.

Yet the chief counsel might be barred by a literal reading of Section 554(d) from participating and advising in the director's decision in a compliance case under circumstances in which it was quite unlikely that his prior participation had given him an advocate's cast of mind. For example, it might be argued that the chief counsel had engaged in an "investigative" function by advising the director of the compliance division on the appropriate reach and limits of the subpeona power and on the necessary language that a particular subpoena must contain to be valid, although one might think that the chief counsel would make such routine judgments without especially noticing the merits of the case involved.

Paradoxes of these kinds suggest the necessity of working out a solution that takes account of the literal meaning of the language as well as the underlying purposes of Section 554(d). The task is difficult because of the dearth of relevant legislative history and of cases on point.[14] Moreover, resolution of the appropriate adjudicatory role of agency employees involves subtleties of human motivation and behavior that are difficult to assess in particular cases and unamenable to generalization beyond them.

Professor Davis – whose views are likely to be relied upon by courts because of the paucity of decided cases – has suggested that "[f]rom the standpoint of accomplishing the basic purpose [of Section 554(d)] without undue harm to other interests, the need may be for giving a narrow interpretation to the term 'investigative' and a broad interpretation to the term 'prosecuting.'" At a later point Davis argues that "[i]f the agencies follow the broad intent as distinguished from the literal words, they will interpret the term 'prosecuting' to cover all advocating, whether or not any accusation is made. Whatever the Act provides or fails to provide, reviewing courts should not allow an advocate to participate in judging."[15] It should be recognized, however, that courts are more likely to accept Davis's contention that a narrow reading be given to "investigative" with respect to a claims agency, such as the Railroad Retirement Board, than to a prosecuting agency, such as the Office of Foreign Direct Investments. Perhaps one can be no more precise than to suggest that an agency must ensure that the adjudicatory process is not seriously contaminated by the participation of employees whose prior association with a case raises the possibility that their contribution will be shaped by an advocate's state of mind.

Investigators and prosecutors as supervisors and subordinates

As the discussion to this point has indicated, Section 554(d) excludes from participation in the adjudicatory process agency employees who have "engaged in the performance of investigative or prosecuting functions" in the case under decision. The language does not explicitly exclude the participation of agency employees whose prior activity does not fairly constitute "the performance of investigative or prosecuting functions."

Thus it might be thought that, in the course of performing his adjudicatory functions, the director could appropriately have sought the advice of (1) agency employees who were the subordinates of investigators and prosecutors, so long as they had not themselves performed investigative or prosecuting functions in the case under decision, and (2) agency employees who supervised investigators and prosecutors, again so long as they had not themselves performed investigative or prosecuting functions in the case under decision.

This would mean, for example, that the director would have been permitted to consult employees of the chief counsel's office and of the compliance division on occasions when Section 554(d) would have prohibited consultation with the chief counsel and the director of the compliance division themselves. It would also mean that the director would have been permitted to consult the chief counsel or the director of the compliance division on occasions when Section 554(d) would have prohibited consultation with their subordinates.

Although a reading of Section 554(d) permitting such results would appear plausible in terms of its language alone, it is not clear that such a reading is correct, since even a small degree of contamination of the adjudicator by those who investigate or prosecute might subvert the purposes of the Act. Unless there are prohibitions beyond those stated in the language of Section 554(d) upon the persons whom the director may consult in the course of adjudication, it is possible that Section 554(d) could be read to permit some results that seem questionable in light of the premises underlying the Administrative Procedure Act.

The separation-of-functions provisions of the Act are based on the premise that the impartiality of the adjudicatory process will be protected significantly by excluding the participation of those whose contribution is not likely to be sufficiently disinterested. The purpose of Section 554(d) – put with only something of an oversimplification – is to prevent the advocate from advising the judge and thereby to preclude a biased input in the adjudicatory process.

The first question facing the Office of Foreign Direct Investments, then, was whether agency employees who were the subordinate of investigators or prosecutors could advise and participate in the director's performance of his adjudicatory functions. Many subordinates – when asked their advice at the adjudicatory stage of a proceeding in which their supervisor had played an investigative or prosecuting role that has disqualified him from advising the adjudicator – will at least be inclined to support their superior's position. Subordinates understand the wisdom of justifying the public commitments made by their superiors. To permit a subordinate of the chief counsel to advise the director in an adjudication in which the chief counsel himself was precluded from doing so because he had performed investigative or prosecuting functions would be to risk that the subordinate's contribution was other than dispassionate – precisely a result Section 554(d) was designed to prevent.

In a provision of Section 554(d) different from that under discussion, Congress recognized the possibilities of personal self-interest inherent in a supervisor-subordinate relationship. It provided that the employee presiding at the reception of evidence may not "be responsible to or subject to the supervision or direction of an employee or agent engaged in the performance of investigative or prosecuting functions for an agency." The use of an impartial and independent hearing examiner appointed by the Civil Service Commission, of course, satisfies this provision. Yet it is curious that, having perceived the risk in this context, Congress did not go further and prohibit any subordinate from participating in an adjudication that almost necessarily will pass upon judgments that his supervisor made as an investigator or prosecutor. Perhaps Congress regarded the risks beyond the one it provided for insufficiently serious to warrant a legislative prohibition.

The second question facing OFDI was whether agency employees supervising investigators and prosecutors could advise and participate in the director's performance of his adjudicatory functions. This question was perhaps easier than the first. The risk that a supervisor would feel inclined out of professional self-interest to support a position taken by a subordinate, while perhaps not improbable, would seem less than the risk created when the roles are reversed. A supervisor's career (the chief counsel's, for example) depends most directly upon his superior's estimate of the quality of his work; he has small incentive in terms of self-interest to support automatically positions taken by subordinates. Moreover, Section 554(d) contains no provision expressing a concern in this area comparable to the concern reflected in its provision that a hearing officer may not be supervised by an investigator or a prosecutor. In short, neither the policy nor the language of Section 554(d) would seem to have precluded the director from seeking the judgment of those who had supervised investigators and prosecutors during the performance of his adjudicatory functions.

In responding to these two questions, it would have been helpful if one could have relied upon judicial decisions rather than upon only an abstract analysis of the premises underlying Section 554(d) and hypotheses about the ways in which reciprocal loyalties are likely to make supervisors and subordinates behave. Unfortunately, there are not more than a handful of relevant decisions.[16] They do suggest, however, that courts may be prepared to move beyond the literal language of Section 554(d) in order to effectuate the spirit of its prohibitions against a combination of functions.

Three decisions involving the Post Office Department are particularly instructive. In *Glanzman v. Schaffer*,[17] an action to enjoin an order of the Post Office Department, the question was whether "the administrative proceedings [that had resulted in the order] were invalid because of . . . lack of proper separation of judicial and prosecutive functions in the administrative forum." The case was heard by a hearing examiner whose initial decision was sustained on appeal by the solicitor for the department, to whom, as the court held, the postmaster general had validly delegated his adjudicatory functions pursuant to a specific statutory authorization. The matter was presented to the hearing examiner by the assistant solicitor of the department. The court stated the following facts as central to its consideration:

The affidavit of [the] Assistant Solicitor for the Post Office Department . . . states that in the handling of these proceedings no officer or employee who presided at the reception of evidence or who made the initial or final agency decisions for the Post

Office Department is subject to or responsible to, or subject to the supervision or direction of any officer, employee or agent engaged in the performance of investigative or prosecuting functions for the Post Office Department and that neither [the assistant solicitor] nor any other officer, employee or agent engaged in the performance of investigative or prosecuting functions in this case participated or advised in the initial decision by the hearing examiner or the agency decision by . . . the Solicitor for the Post Office Department.

On the basis of the affidavit, the court held, without any discussion, that "there has been no violation of the principle of separation of prosecutive and judicial functions in this department. Actually, there has been a separation of such functions as required by the Administrative Procedure Act. . . ."

The affidavit upon which the decision in *Glanzman* relies made clear that no employee engaged in the performance of investigative or prosecuting functions in the case had participated or advised in the solicitor's decision except as counsel in public proceedings; such facts state compliance with Section 554(d). The adjudicator, the solicitor, was the supervisor of the investigator and prosecutor, the assistant solicitor, but no language in Section 554(d) forbids such a relationship.

That the court could sustain the validity of this relationship without discussion – the court of appeals did not discuss the issue either, because it had been "adequately disposed of in the opinion" below – suggests that it could find no issue raised under the literal language of Section 554(d). It seems unlikely that the court considered whether an adjudicator, by virtue of his position as supervisor of an investigator and prosecutor, might have a self-interested inclination, inconsistent with the impartiality expected of judges, to support the position taken by his subordinate. Therefore, one should be circumspect in asserting claims about the necessary implications of the court's decision. The result the court announced, however, appears consistent with the conclusion suggested earlier that Section 554(d) does not seem to preclude participation in the adjudicatory process by supervisors of investigators and prosecutors.

The second decision involving the Post Office Department, *Pinkus v. Reilly*,[18] reversed a postal fraud order in part on the ground that the department had failed to comply with the Administrative Procedure Act's requirement that it publish its rules of organization and procedure. But the decision rests as well on the second ground that the administrative procedures of the department violated the combination-of-functions provisions of the Act.

The court in *Pinkus* examined the department's regulations far more carefully than the court had in *Glanzman*. It noted that the regulations in effect when *Glanzman* was decided "vested [the solicitor] with prosecuting authority generally, including both the supervision of prosecutions, and, as a matter of procedure, the filing of complaints," as well as adjudicating authority. "This," the court said, "indubitably constituted a violation of the above separation of functions provisions of the Administrative Procedure Act, as it was then, and is now, in effect."

By the time that the proceeding in *Pinkus* arose, the department had changed the title of the solicitor to general counsel and of the assistant solicitor to assistant general counsel. It had also amended its regulations slightly "to vest in the Assistant General Counsel the duty to file complaints similar to that here involved against Pinkus." The court found the amendment wanting. "But the violation continued," it said, "since the General Counsel continued to have the general supervisory power over such prosecutions and over his assistant . . . together with the sole adjudicating authority in such cases. . . ."

The court then spoke to the argument made successfully by the department in *Glanzman:*

> Of course, the Department's claim is immaterial that in this case in fact the General Counsel did not tell the Assistant General Counsel what to do in prosecuting Pinkus. For the purpose of the Act is not only to see that such commingling of the judicial and prosecuting authority does not occur in fact in a single case, but to see that it can never occur, and that the public should know, by publication, that it can never occur, in order to insure their confidence in the fairness of their government.

What explains the difference in result between *Glanzman* and *Pinkus?* The court in *Glanzman* held that the adjudicator was not an employee who had engaged in the performance of investigative or prosecuting functions, even though he possessed investigative and prosecuting authority, because an affidavit indicated that he had not in fact performed such functions in the present case; therefore, read literally, Section 554(d) did not prohibit him from participating and advising in the decision. The court in *Pinkus* came to a contrary conclusion on the same procedural facts because it feared the potential for commingling of functions that the Post Office Department's administrative structure appeared to permit; it did not seem to feel constrained by the fact that Section 554(d) is limited to circumstances in which the adjudicator has participated in investigative or prosecuting functions in the present case. The prohibition announced in *Pinkus* may be recommended by the purpose of Section 554(d) but it cannot be found in its language.

It may be suggested that the court's discussion in *Pinkus* of the separation-of-functions issue was at most an alternative holding, which the court itself qualified by a subsequent passage:

It is a further interesting question whether the Administrative Procedure Act as adopted prevents all such harmful commingling of the functions of adjudication and prosecution or only certain harmful commingling, leaving certain commingling of prosecuting and adjudicating authority still lawful. This question is raised now by the parties since, as seen above, in this case it is not the prosecuting authority which is alleged to be the superior of the adjudicating authority, which *Wong Yang Sung* holds to be prohibited, but rather it is the adjudicating authority which is alleged to be the superior of the prosecuting authority. . . . [I]t is clear that in either aspect such commingling may have harmful results, and so is contrary to the spirit of the Act itself. Now the Department claims that in fact, according to its plan of "organization" (unpublished as above), its "General Counsel" is not the superior of this particular "Assistant General Counsel," when the latter prosecutes fraud cases, despite these titles, and despite the fact that its General Counsel is the superior of any or all other Assistant General Counsel in charge of all the Department's other legal proceedings – a rather unusual situation. However, assuming this to be correct in fact, it is unnecessary to pursue this point through the lengthy legislative history of the statute, in view of the clear invalidity of the present procedure [because it was not published].

Judge Learned Hand adopted this suggestion in adverting to *Pinkus* in his opinion in *Columbia Research Corp. v. Schaffer*,[19] the third and most important of the decisions involving combination of functions in the Post Office Department.

Columbia Research involved the same procedural facts as *Pinkus*, except that the department had by now published regulations that sought to describe its internal organization with respect to hearings: The assistant general counsel was the prosecutor and the general counsel decided appeals from the hearing examiner's decisions. As in *Glanzman* and *Pinkus*, the department submitted an affidavit asserting that

. . . there has been and there is a complete and actual separation of investigative and judicial functions . . . and no officer or employee who presides at the reception of evidence or who makes either initial or final agency decisions . . . is subject to or responsible to or subject to [*sic*] the supervision or direction of any officer, employee or agent engaged in the performance of prosecuting functions for said Post Office Department.

The terms of the affidavit thus presented again the question whether Section 554(d) permits an employee who hears administrative appeals, thereby performing an adjudicatory function, to supervise employees who perform investigative or prosecuting functions. The court did not decide that question on the merits because it found the department's regulations inadequate in their description of the supervisory authority that the general counsel had over the assistant general counsel. But the court did consider whether the relationship between the general counsel and the assistant general counsel could be made consistent with the theory of Section 554(d):

[W]e are not satisfied that it is enough that the Assistant General Counsel, on whom §201.4 of the Regulations imposes the duty of preparing complaints, has in fact no part in the final decision of the General Counsel himself. It would be plainly contrary to the purpose of the section, if the General Counsel prepared the complaint and the Assistant Counsel made the final decision; for the subordinate would then be passing upon the success of what his superior had undertaken. True, the reverse, which is the actual situation, does not present so obvious a fusion of prosecutor and judge; nevertheless, when the subordinate is prosecutor and his superior is judge, it appears to us reasonable to suppose that the prosecutor will be disposed to select such cases as he believes will meet with his superior's approval, and that his discretion may be exercised otherwise than if each was responsible to the Postmaster only by a separate chain of authority. It is of course true that under any possible system of administration in the end there will be the fusion of prosecutor and judge, subject only to the supervision of the courts; but it makes much difference whether it be reserved to the highest level of authority: i.e., to the "agency" itself and it is fairly obvious that Congress had just this in mind when . . . it provided that the subsection should not apply to the "agency" or to any of its "members." There alone was the fusion to be permissible.

Having spoken at such length to the merits, the court added a further comment during the course of reversing the department's order because the regulation failed to comply with the Administrative Procedure Act:

However, if, contrary to what appears to us its very probable purpose, the section does not forbid the powers of the prosecutor and the judge to interpenetrate: that is, if the prosecutor may be subject to the judge in some specifically declared circumstances, nevertheless, we think that §1002(a) (1) and (2) require that any such relation, to be valid at all, must be spelled out and published as a regulation. . . .

Finally, the court noted that neither *Glanzman* nor *Pinkus* could fairly be said to have decided the question whether Section 554(d) permits an adjudicator to supervise an investigator or prosecutor. In *Glanzman* the court did not "give any reasons for [its] conclusion" that "an affidavit like that filed in the case at bar was enough to comply with the statute" and "neither in the notice of appeal nor in the briefs on appeal was the question raised or discussed." In *Pinkus* the court "reserved the added question, which we have discussed here, whether by a published regulation the 'agency' could make an investigating or prosecuting officer subordinate to the deciding officer.'' Judge Hand concluded by a further reference to the merits:

As has already appeared we too reserve any final decision as to that, although it seems to us indeed difficult in the situation here presented to forecast how a regulation could be so drafted as to avoid the objection if the Assistant General Counsel remains a subordinate of the General Counsel.

Judge Hand's thoughtful analysis of the purposes of Section 554(d) makes *Columbia Research* the most important of the three decisions discussed, even though it does not formally decide the separation-of-functions question. Several observations may be relevant.

First, the decision in *Columbia Research* is consistent with the conclusion that courts sensitive to the premises underlying the APA's prohibition against the combination of functions will not regard the literal language of Section 554(d) as the end of the matter. The administrative structure created by the Post Office Department was in compliance with Section 554(d) in the sense that no explicit language prohibited it, but that was insufficient to persuade Judge Hand that he was estopped from inquiring further. That Judge Hand found justification for looking beyond the literal language – indeed, for strongly suggesting that the Post Office Department's administrative structure was invalid – almost certainly means that other courts will, too.

Second, the decision in *Columbia Research* confirms the suggestion that courts that look beyond the literal language of Section 554(d) are likely to focus on the psychological tendencies that may be created by a relationship involving supervisors who adjudicate and subordinates who investigate or prosecute. Judge Hand was concerned that a prosecutor in such a relationship ''will be disposed to select such cases as he believes will meet with his superior's approval, and that his discretion will be exercised otherwise'' than if he were independent of the adjudicator's supervision. Assuming that a prosecutor supervised by an adjudicator may be so disposed, Judge Hand does not indicate why this consequence would conflict with the purposes underlying Section 554(d). Prosecutors generally tend to bring cases they expect an adjudicator to sustain. Although a concern that forum shopping be minimized – perhaps particularly by a prosecutor – finds expression at some points in our law, it does not seem to be a concern of Section 554(d). The language Judge Hand chose to make his point suggests that he read Section 554(d) as condemning any relationship between the adjudicator and the prosecutor, short of complete separation, that might conceivably appear to open up the psychological possibility of partiality. (Judge Hand does not mention the possibility that an adjudicator who supervises a prosecutor may feel a self-interested inclination to support a position taken by a subordinate.)

Third, the decision in *Columbia Research* would have a limited application to OFDI because it rests upon a factual pattern significantly different from the pattern that was likely to exist at OFDI during the course of adjudication. At the Post Office Department, the general counsel who exercised final adjudicatory authority was not the agency for purposes of the Administrative Procedure Act. At OFDI, the director in whom final adjudicatory authority resided was the agency. That the Act permits the agency (for example, the director of OFDI) alone among administrative employees to adjudicate as well as to supervise prosecutors while denying a combination of functions to all other employees (for example, the general counsel of the Post Office Department) suggests the possibility that *Columbia Research* did not control the facts at OFDI.

The difference in the factual patterns may be put still another way. At the Post Office Department, the adjudicator supervised the prosecutor. At OFDI, the adjudicator might have sought the advice of employees such as the chief counsel who supervised employees who had performed investigative or prosecuting functions, but the chief counsel was not the adjudicator and, as it may happen, might not have been consulted by the adjudicator at all. The relationship at OFDI between the adjudicator and employees supervising prosecutors was thus more attenuated than the same relationship was at the Post Office Department. Judge Hand's fear that the prosecutor might be disposed to select cases with knowledge of the adjudicator's predilections seemed unlikely to result at OFDI merely because the director might have asked the chief counsel's advice during the course of adjudications. This conclusion is strengthened by the fact that the authority to bring compliance proceedings formally rested with the chief of the compliance division rather than with the chief counsel.

Because the Post Office Department responded to Judge Hand's opinion by vesting adjudicatory authority in a judicial officer with no supervisory power over employees who prosecuted,[20] and because other agencies have not created relationships in which adjudicators have supervised prosecutors, the theory of *Columbia Research* has not been put to subsequent judicial testing. The paucity of decided cases involving separation-of-functions issues suggests that violations of Section 554(d) either rarely occur or rarely come to light. It was only because the Post Office Department's published rules seemed on their face to raise the possibility that inconsistent functions would not be kept separate that the decisions resulted in *Glanzman*, *Pinkus*, and *Columbia Research*.

In the absence of published rules obviously presenting such questions on their face, separation-of-functions issues are unlikely to be raised, if only because members of the public will not typically have an opportunity to learn the identity of agency employees whom agency members may have consulted during the course of any particular adjudication. This cannot be the end of the matter, however, for an agency conscientiously interested in complying with Section 554(d) no matter how small the chances that a violation may be discovered. Some concluding observations may therefore be appropriate.

Despite the evident ambiguities of Section 554(d), it was clear the director of OFDI ought not to consult the chief of the compliance division or any of his subordinates during the course of performing his adjudicatory functions. The chief of the compliance division almost certainly would have performed "investigative or prosecuting functions" in every compliance proceeding reaching the director for decision. Although subordinates of the chief of the compliance division might not have actually performed "investigative or prosecuting functions" in particular cases, the likelihood that they would be motivated by a self-interested inclination to support the position their superior had taken would bring them within the interdiction of *Columbia Research*. Moreover, that OFDI was a relatively small administrative agency probably increased the likelihood that a court would be concerned over participation by members of the compliance division, even if literal compliance with Section 554(d) might plausibly be argued.

Conversely, the director could properly consult members of the authorizations and policy divisions during the course of performing his adjudicatory functions. Neither of these divisions performed "investigative or prosecuting functions." Routine consultation between these divisions and the compliance division – for example, as to the intended meaning or proper construction of the language used in a particular specific authorization – would not have implicated them in the performance of "investigative or prosecuting functions" and would not have disabled the director from consulting them if he had so chosen.

The question whether the director could properly consult the chief counsel during the course of performing his adjudicatory functions cannot be answered categorically. The answer would depend upon a case-by-case analysis of whether the chief counsel's prior participation in the proceeding

189

- most likely as a consultant to the compliance division – was sufficiently intensive to make his cast of mind that of an advocate. Routine consultation with the compliance division, particularly upon questions of law or agency policy, ought not have been regarded as barring the director from seeking the judgment of the chief counsel during the decision-making process. Prudence cautioned, however, against permitting the compliance division to consult the chief counsel about the merits of particular compliance proceedings unless the director was willing to risk being disabled from consulting the chief counsel during the performance of his adjudicatory functions.

The risk hardly seemed worth running. It was plainly to the director's advantage to be able to receive legal advice from the man who was the agency's chief legal officer and who might be required to support the director's decision in court. The chief of the compliance division, of course, might need access to legal advice, but he had lawyers on his own staff to whom he could turn. If the chief counsel were held to have engaged in "investigative or prosecuting functions," he could not present his views to the director. The chief of the compliance division, on the other hand, could always present his views to the director as witness or counsel in the public proceedings, including the filing of briefs. Thus it seemed wiser for OFDI to ensure that the director, rather than the chief of the compliance division, remained free to consult with the chief counsel when the choice was mutually exclusive.

Throughout the twentieth century, Congress has regularly expressed the judgment that most administrative agencies must be permitted a combination of functions – investigative, prosecuting, and adjudicatory – in order to perform their regulatory responsibilities effectively. The Supreme Court, in holding that the combination of functions does not, without more, constitute a denial of due process, has respected that repeatedly affirmed legislative judgment. At the same time, however, the Court has made clear that a particular combination of functions may constitute a denial of due process when the risk of unfairness from bias or prejudgment becomes intolerably high.

Public concern that administrative agencies are permitted to combine inconsistent functions has contributed to sustaining the recurrent sense of crisis attending the administrative process. That concern is not implausible as an abstract matter, but it does not take adequate account of the specific manner in which the Administrative Procedure Act has required virtually a complete internal separation of functions in every administrative agency subject to its provisions.

The Act permits a combination of functions only in the members of the agency themselves – a significant exception designed to ensure that the ultimate authority over the development of agency policy and the control of agency initiatives remains in the highest agency officials, persons who typically are nominated by the President and confirmed by the Senate. Apart from that exception, justified by principles of efficient management and democratic control, no agency employee who engaged in investigative or prosecuting functions in a case may also participate in its adjudication.

Despite the fact that Congress used particular care in drafting the separation-of-functions provisions of the Act, a number of important questions of statutory interpretation remain. These questions focus upon the proper meaning of "investigative or prosecuting functions" and upon the appropriate role of investigators and prosecutors as supervisors and subordinates. Exploration of the reach of these statutory provisions illuminates the intentions and philosophy of a theory of separation of functions. It also supplies an illustration of the inevitable limitations of language in expressing legislative intentions, even when such intentions seem to be as clear as those that Congress had in mandating an internal separation of inconsistent administrative functions.

The formal procedural protections that the Administrative Procedure Act has created against the risks of bias that might otherwise find expression in the process of institutional decision making are thus substantial. Indeed, as the decisions in *Wong Yang Sung v. McGrath* and *Marcello v. Bonds* indicate, they place greater restrictions upon the combination of functions than the due process clause requires. The existence of these protections, properly understood, supplies the federal administrative process with a significant contemporary source of legitimacy.

15

Disqualification for bias

[A] fair trial by an unbiased and non-partisan trier of the facts is of the essence of the adjudicatory process as well when the judging is done in an administrative proceeding by an administrative functionary as when it is done in a court by a judge.

Judge Joseph C. Hutcheson, Jr., in *NLRB v. Phelps* (1943)

In settling upon the terms of the Administrative Procedure Act, Congress concluded that members of administrative agencies should be permitted to combine the performance of investigative, prosecuting, and adjudicatory functions. But the legislative history of the Act indicates that Congress understood that this combination of functions could give rise to the possibility of bias. It sought to meet this possibility by permitting the combination of functions only to the extent necessary to serve its essential purposes[1] and by making available a procedure by which agency employees could disqualify themselves and claims of bias could be passed upon by the administrative agencies themselves, subject to judicial review.[2]

The possibility of bias often has seemed to lie near the heart of public uneasiness over the departures that the administrative process has made from judicial norms. It is important, therefore, in constructing a theory of the legitimacy of the administrative process to inquire into how well the administrative process has been insulated against the influence of bias, particularly when it arises from the combination of functions.

But what is bias? The Administrative Procedure Act includes no definition of the concept. In undertaking to describe the kinds of bias that will disqualify an administrator from deciding an adjudicatory proceeding, the courts have drawn upon Supreme Court decisions involving allegations of judicial bias.[3] In so doing, they have declared that a combination of functions that creates the possibility of bias in administrative adjudication gives rise to serious questions of due process. A number of cases make clear that an agency decision rendered in compliance with the Administrative Procedure Act's strictures on separation of functions may nevertheless be set aside as a denial of due process because the adjudicator was biased.

The possibility that an agency member may bring judgments about law and policy – as opposed to judgments about facts – to the adjudication of particular disputes has never been thought to present a substantial constitutional question of bias. Indeed, Congress often has created new administrative agencies, as it did in the case of the National Labor Relations Board, precisely because it hoped that such agencies would be more sympathetic than the tradition-bound federal courts – if not more committed, as well – to the substantive goals of the controversial social legislation it was enacting into law. That members of administrative agencies have an intellectual obligation to develop coherent philosophies of regulatory law and policy is now widely accepted.[4]

In its most conventional sense, bias has been condemned by the courts in two basic classes of cases. The first class has involved bias resulting from an adjudicator's personal, usually pecuniary, interest in the outcome of a proceeding.[5] Cases involving bias of this kind in the federal administrative agencies have been rare, although the 1973 decision of the Supreme Court in *Gibson v. Berryhill*[6] seems to indicate that state agencies regulating professional conduct may now be vulnerable on this ground if their membership is drawn from the profession being regulated. The second class has involved bias resulting from an adjudicator's personal prejudice, hostility, or favoritism toward a party to a proceeding. Cases involving bias of this kind typically have seen an adjudicator create the appearance that impartial adjudication could not be had by publicly announcing his conclusion, before an administrative proceeding was held, that a person was guilty of agency charges pending against him.[7] These conventional forms of bias are not instructive for present purposes. Each derives from personal attributes or attitudes of an administrator; neither is the consequence of permitting agency members to combine functions.

When prior involvement becomes bias

It is, of course, a truism that a fair hearing presupposes an impartial trier of fact and that prior involvement with the facts of a proceeding may compromise an adjudicator's capacity to render judgment impartially. But the question of when prior involvement becomes bias is often a subtle one. The Supreme Court has made clear that many forms of prior official involvement in a case will not result in an adjudicator's disqualification for bias. A contention that the combination of functions in an administrative official has created an unconstitutional attitude of bias must do more than merely demonstrate the official's familiarity with the facts of the case. Rather, as the Supreme Court held unanimously in *Withrow v. Larkin*, "it must convince that, under a realistic appraisal of psychological tendencies and human weaknesses, conferring investigative and adjudicative powers on the same individuals poses such a risk of actual bias or prejudgment that the practice must be forbidden if the guarantee of due process is to be adequately implemented."[8]

The leading Supreme Court decision involving the risk of bias in the federal administrative process is *NLRB v. Donnelly Garment Co.*,[9] decided a year after the Administrative Procedure Act became law. The question was whether a hearing examiner who had rejected the proffer of certain evidence as valueless should have been disqualified as biased from hearing the case on remand after a court of appeals had held that exclusion of the evidence had resulted in denial of a fair hearing. Although it could be argued that the examiner had prejudged the value of the proffered evidence – the argument might seem strengthened by the fact that at the second hearing the examiner heard the previously excluded evidence and then made the same findings as he had at the first hearing – the Supreme Court held that he was not disqualified. "Certainly it is not the rule of judicial administration that, statutory requirements apart . . . a judge is disqualified from sitting in a retrial because he was reversed on earlier rulings," the Court said. "We find no warrant for imposing upon administrative agencies a stiffer rule, whereby examiners would be disentitled to sit because they ruled strongly against a party in the first hearing."

The decision in *Donnelly Garment* thus stands for the proposition that an adjudicator will not automatically be held disqualified for bias merely because he previously has announced an appraisal of certain issues of fact that he subsequently is called upon to decide again during the course of an adjudication. By comparing the role of the hearing examiner to that of a federal judge, the Supreme Court gave an important demonstration of support for the Administrative Procedure Act's aspiration to elevate the status of hearing examiners in the federal administrative process.

The conclusion that a hearing examiner is not biased in a constitutional sense simply because he previously has ruled against one of the parties to a proceeding is reflected in a consistent line of decisions. For example, in

MacKay v. McAlexander[10] the court held that a hearing officer who presided at a deportation hearing in which he issued an order that effectively rejected appellant's central factual claim was not disqualified from presiding at a subsequent hearing on appellant's application for a suspension of deportation. The court stated:

The unfavorable opinion of a party or witness which a hearing officer or a trial judge may entertain as a result of evidence received in a prior and connected hearing involving that individual is not "bias" in the invidious sense. It is in effect a judicially-determined finding which may properly influence such officer or judge in a supplemental proceeding involving the penalty or punishment to be assessed, or the grace to be extended. No unfairness or lack of due process was inherent in the fact that the same hearing officer presided in both proceedings.

Because of the factual context in which *MacKay* arose, it seems a fair conclusion that the application of *Donnelly Garment* is not limited to circumstances involving remand of an administrative proceeding to an adjudicator; it extends as well to successive proceedings on related matters involving the same adjudicator. It also seems a fair conclusion that the principle of *Donnelly Garment* applies to adjudicators who are members of an agency with at least as much force as it does to hearing examiners; indeed, because of the premises underlying the Administrative Procedure Act's decision to permit a combination of functions, it may apply to members of an agency with even greater force.

These conclusions are supported by the decision in *Pangburn v. CAB*,[11] which involved two successive administrative determinations by members of the Civil Aeronautics Board. In the first proceeding, the board determined that the probable cause of an accident involving a plane piloted by Pangburn was pilot error; the board issued its accident report as part of its statutory duty to investigate airplane crashes and make public reports as to their circumstances and probable cause. Shortly thereafter, in the second proceeding, the board issued an order suspending Pangburn's pilot license for ninety days; the record upon which this order was based did not include the accident report from the first proceeding.

The Court of Appeals for the First Circuit rejected Pangburn's contention that the board should be disqualified for bias from deciding the second proceeding because of the "concrete and specific factual determination" it had made in the first. "It is well settled," the court said, "that a combination of investigative and judicial functions within an agency does not violate due process." The court noted that the Administrative Procedure Act's strictures with respect to combination of functions do not apply to the agency and that *Donnelly Garment* had found no violation of due process when an adjudicator presided at a second hearing after having formed judgments of fact at a first. The court also noted that the Supreme Court had sustained the right of judges to try contempt proceedings that they had initiated, even when the contempt was personal to themselves. The court concluded that ''we cannot say that the mere fact that a tribunal has had contact with a particular factual complex in a prior hearing, or indeed has taken a public position on the facts, is enough to place that tribunal under a constitutional inhibition to pass upon the facts in a subsequent hearing. We believe that more is required.''

The decision in *Pangburn* is not beyond criticism. Because the board had made a public commitment to a finding of pilot error in the first proceeding, it is not unlikely that its members felt an incentive in the second proceeding to avoid the appearance of inconsistency. It is fair to respond to such criticism by pointing out that the decision in *Pangburn* is supported by the existing case law. In addition, if all the members of the board had been disqualified, the case could not have been decided at all. But the response is incomplete because the thrust of the criticism is that in some circumstances not currently reached by the case law an adjudicator should be disqualified because he has prejudged certain issues of fact. Perhaps the decision should be understood as representing a particular instance of judicial deference to a deliberative judgment of Congress – that the risk of bias from a combination of functions was properly to be tolerated because (1) accident reports must be issued promptly in order to inform and reassure the public, and (2) the Civil Aeronautics Board is the agency best qualified both to issue accident reports on the causes of crashes and to determine whether a pilot's license should be suspended.

However, the decision of the Court of Appeals for the District of Columbia Circuit in *Amos Treat & Co. v. SEC*[12] suggests that courts are prepared to look beyond existing case law in determining when to limit participation by an adjudicator who has formed judgments in prior proceedings about factual issues presented by the proceedings currently before him.

The court in *Amos Treat* held that Commissioner Cohen was disqualified for bias, under principles of due process, from participating in an adjudicatory proceeding. Before becoming a member of the SEC, Cohen had served as director of the commission's Division of Corporate Finance. In that capacity he had ordered an informal investigation of a company that had filed a registration statement. He reported the results of that investigation to the full commission, which ordered the institution of a formal examination and investigation. Within a month after Cohen had become a commissioner, the SEC acted upon the recommendation of the Division of Corporate Finance and instituted administrative proceedings to suspend the effectiveness of the company's registration statement. Relying solely on due process grounds, the court held:

We are unable to accept the view that a member of an investigative or prosecuting staff may initiate an investigation, weigh its results, perhaps then recommend the filing of charges, and thereafter become a member of that commission or agency, participate in adjudicatory proceedings, join in commission or agency rulings and ultimately pass upon the possible amenability of the respondents to the administrative orders of the commission or agency. So to hold, in our view, would be tantamount to that denial of administrative due process against which both the Congress and the courts have inveighed.

The facts in *Amos Treat* presented a circumstance in which a member of an agency changed his function completely during the course of an adjudicatory proceeding. Commissioner Cohen began the proceeding entirely as a prosecutor; by its conclusion, he had become entirely an adjudicator. The case thus presented a question of a succession – not a combination – of functions.

There is no reason to believe that the section of the Administrative Procedure Act exempting members of the agency from the proscription against combining functions was intended to apply to such a situation. First, the facts do not present the necessity for a combination of functions that Congress concluded existed at the agency level alone; in this respect, the case is distinguishable from *Pangburn*. Second, the facts are inconsistent with the hypothesis, implicit in the Administrative Procedure Act, that an adjudicator who is a member of an agency may be expected to exercise his prosecuting function with a self-restraint unnecessary and inappropriate in a person (such as the director of the SEC's Division of Corporate Finance) whose function is to make the case as strong as possible, not to preserve a cast of mind capable of subsequently rendering impartial judgment.

It seems clear, then, that the decision in *Amos Treat* could properly have been rested upon the court's conclusion that the separation-of-functions provisions of the Administrative Procedure Act ''applied to Commissioner Cohen as director of the Division of Corporate Finance. Its prohibitory impact followed him and attended when he became a member of the Commission.'' Even when the decision in *Amos Treat* is accepted as resting upon constitutional grounds, the result is still dependent upon the fact that the case presented a question of a succession, rather than a combination, of functions.

The principal authority upon which the court relied, *Trans World Airlines v. CAB*,[13] closely resembled the facts before the court. The solicitor of the Post Office Department had signed a brief to the board on behalf of the postmaster general before becoming a member of the board and casting the deciding vote in favor of the postmaster general. The court vacated the board's order on the ground that fundamental fairness in the performance of quasi-judicial functions requires "at least that one who participates in a case on behalf of any party, whether actively or merely formally by being on pleadings or brief, take no part in the decision of that case by any tribunal on which he may thereafter sit."

A similar result was reached in *American Cyanamid Co. v. FTC*,[14] in which Chairman Dixon was held disqualified for bias from participating in the adjudication of a proceeding involving the same companies and the same facts that had been investigated by a Senate subcommittee of which he had been chief counsel. Chairman Dixon – like Commissioner Cohen in *Amos Treat* and the former solicitor of the Post Office Department in *Trans World Airlines* – had engaged in a succession, rather than a combination, of functions.

This conclusion – that *Amos Treat* is relevant primarily to circumstances involving a succession of functions – is supported by the court's explanation of the inapplicability of the provision of the Administrative Procedure Act excluding the agency from the proscription against the combination of functions:

It is our view that the exclusionary sentence relied upon was intended to permit one who is a Commissioner to participate in a decision of the Commission that an investigation go forward and even that charges be filed to the end that an adjudicatory proceeding might be initiated. In such circumstances, it was the purpose of Congress as we construe the section, to permit a Commissioner to participate in the ultimate decisional process, and not otherwise.

The court thus makes clear that it did not intend to disturb on constitutional grounds of bias the combination of functions that the Administrative Procedure Act permits to members of the agency. The decision has been described by one court of appeals as "the exceptional case"[15] and has been considerably limited by another.[16] Nevertheless, *Amos Treat* may have implications beyond questions presenting a succession of functions because of the court's willingness to invoke the due process clause to disqualify an agency member even though statutory means were at hand.

Applying the principles of bias

Of what relevance were these general principles of administrative bias to the Office of Foreign Direct Investments? It was obvious that the director, having been made the agency for purposes of adjudication, would sometimes have gained knowledge of the facts (and may also have formed some judgments as to the policy issues) in most compliance proceedings before being required to perform his adjudicatory functions. The director's knowledge of the facts would derive from his participation in prior stages of the proceedings. The director might gain such knowledge, for example, when he approved the decision to initiate an investigation or issue a complaint against a direct investor on the basis of a presentation made by the compliance division. He might gain such knowledge when he approved the terms upon which OFDI would be prepared to accept a consent settlement as the result of prehearing negotiation with the direct investor. He might gain such knowledge when he determined a direct investor's application for a specific authorization.

Yet none of these possibilities was particularly worrisome. The Administrative Procedure Act permitted the director to commingle functions because of his status as the agency. Disqualification for bias remains an exception to the unusual grant of authority in the Administrative Procedure Act to combine otherwise inconsistent functions. And the Office of Foreign Direct Investments could find support in the fact that no judicial decision had held a member of an agency disqualified by bias when the process of adjudication had been carried out in a regularized setting that complied with the separation-of-functions requirements of the APA.

This meant that in the generality of cases the director of OFDI could safely perform routine supervisory functions in the investigative and prosecuting stages of a compliance proceeding to the same extent as members of other federal administrative agencies – such as the Federal Trade Commission or the Securities and Exchange Commission – without running the risk of disqualification for bias. It also meant that the director could become acquainted with the facts in a compliance proceeding during the course of exercising his preadjudicatory responsibilities without risking disqualification for bias. Indeed, he might even make judgments as to factual issues that were later presented to him for adjudicatory determination.

Thus allegations of bias would probably have failed so long as the director's exposure to the merits of compliance cases was not greater than was necessary to enable him to meet his larger responsibilities of supervising

OFDI's operations and personnel, setting the agenda of cases appropriate for investigation, prosecution, and settlement, and protecting direct investors from the excessive zeal or disproportionate severity of staff members. This meant that the director ought not "bury himself in one side of an issue"[17] or take a greater interest in the progress of a particular case than his basic duties required; he ought not, in short, develop a psychological stance or commitment inconsistent with the reality or the appearance of impartial adjudication, however appropriate it might be in a member of the compliance division.

The importance of circumspection by the director with respect to bias is emphasized by the disabling limitations of the two most obvious alternatives available in the event that the director was disqualified in a particular case.

The first alternative would be the designation of another employee of OFDI as the adjudicator for cases in which the director had voluntarily disqualified himself or had been held disqualified by a court. The most appropriate employee probably would be the deputy director because, more than any other senior official of OFDI, he would tend to bring an officewide perspective to the decision of adjudicatory proceedings.

The limitations of this alternative are similar to those Judge Hand spoke to in *Columbia Research v. Schaffer*. The deputy director (or any other OFDI employee designated to substitute for the director) would be asked to decide a case in which his immediate superior had been disqualified because of bias, a circumstance that in some instances might give rise to an impression in the mind of the deputy director as to whom the director would prefer to see prevail. *Columbia Research* was precisely concerned with the fairness of an administrative structure in which an adjudicator might be constrained by professional self-interest to make decisions that would please his biased superior. Although it is not impossible to seek to distinguish *Columbia Research*, the central fact remains that the designation of the deputy director would have meant that a biased superior would have been supervising an adjudicator.

The second alternative would be invocation of the so-called doctrine of necessity, a principle with roots that reach back at least as far as Chancellor Kent.[18] The doctrine provides that when the only tribunal that has authority to act in a proceeding allegedly is biased, it will be permitted to act nevertheless because the alternative would mean nonenforcement of the law entirely. In a famous case testing the constitutionality of taxing the income of federal judges, the Supreme Court made an important statement of the doctrine:

Because of the individual relation of the members of this court to the question, thus broadly stated, we cannot but regret that its solution falls to us. . . . The plaintiff was entitled by law to invoke our decision . . . and there was no other appellate tribunal to which under the law he could go. . . . In this situation, the only course open to us is to consider and decide the cause, – a conclusion supported by precedents reaching back many years.[19]

Cases presenting the question of the appropriate invocation of the doctrine of necessity do not frequently reach the Supreme Court. The most important decision involving the federal administrative process is *FTC v. Cement Institute*.[20] The issue was whether the entire membership of the Federal Trade Commission should be disqualified for bias. The court of appeals had rejected such a contention on the ground that since the FTC was "the only tribunal clothed with the power and charged with the responsibility of protecting the public against unfair methods of competition and price discrimination," the doctrine of necessity required that it be permitted to hear the case.[21]

Although the Supreme Court found that the members of the FTC were not in fact biased, it did affirm the appropriateness of invoking the doctrine:

Moreover, Marquette's position, if sustained, would to a large extent defeat the congressional purposes which promoted passage of the Trade Commission Act. Had the entire membership of the Commission been disqualified in the proceedings against these respondents, this complaint could not have been acted upon by the Commission or by any other government agency. Congress has provided for no such contingency. It has not directed that the Commission disqualify itself under any circumstances, has not provided for substitute commissioners should any of its members disqualify, and has not authorized any other government agency to hold hearings, make findings, and issue cease and desist orders in proceedings against unfair trade practices. Yet if Marquette is right, the Commission . . . [by its alleged bias] completely immunized the practices investigated, even though they are "unfair," from any cease and desist order by the Commission or any other governmental agency.

Although the doctrine of necessity was, of course, applicable to OFDI, a court would probably not have permitted the director to invoke it in the generality of cases. Courts can be expected to be sensitive to the perception that the "easy and seemingly automatic application of the rule of necessity is more dangerous than is [typically] recognized . . . for grave injustice may result from allowing disqualified officers to adjudicate cases."[22] Because of this possibility, the doctrine of necessity is subject to two important conditions that indicate that OFDI could not prudently have relied on the possibility that the director could invoke the doctrine.

First, courts would not permit an agency to invoke the doctrine when the agency had failed, in designing its administrative structure, to provide for an impartial tribunal for occasions upon which the adjudicator is disqualified for bias. OFDI was not in the position of the FTC in the *Cement Institute* proceeding; it had the authority to provide that another employee of the agency should perform the director's adjudicatory functions when the director was disqualified. Moreover, a court would have been unlikely to permit OFDI to invoke the doctrine of necessity if it appeared that OFDI had not attempted to ensure that the director's participation in the early stages of proceedings had kept him free from the possibilities of bias.

Second, courts would be likely to review administrative decisions in which the doctrine of necessity had been invoked with a greater intensity than they would ordinarily exercise, precisely because the acknowledged presence of bias would present the due process issue with such clarity. A court exercising such extraordinary scrutiny might well have concluded that there was no overriding necessity to enforce an OFDI order against any particular direct investor – the adverse consequences to the public of nonenforcement probably would appear as less severe than in *Cement Institute* – when the decision underlying the order might have been contaminated by the director's bias.

The rules describing when an adjudicator should be disqualified for bias from participating in an administrative proceeding seek to ensure that the administrative process provides the substance as well as the appearance of justice. By requiring the use of an impartial and independent hearing examiner in all agency adjudications ''required by statute to be determined on the record after opportunity for an agency hearing,'' by limiting the right to combine functions to agency members alone, and by imposing a strict separation of powers on all other agency personnel, the Administrative Procedure Act eliminates the most obvious opportunities for the occurrence of institutional bias.

But the courts have remained properly alert to the possibility that bias constituting a denial of due process can sometimes result despite the existence of these statutory safeguards. By acting upon the assumption that claims of administrative bias should be measured against the same standards as claims of judicial bias, the courts have enhanced the legitimacy of administrative agencies as instruments of impartial adjudication.

The cases in which the courts have found that administrative bias has constituted a denial of due process typically have involved either specific instances of insensitivity to an obvious impropriety or exceptional situations in which an agency employee has exercised a succession of functions by virtue of a change in his responsibilities during the course of a particular adjudication. Significantly, the courts have rarely found bias when administrative authority has been exercised routinely according to regularized institutional arrangements that complied with the separation-of-functions provisions of the Administrative Procedure Act.

The pattern of the decided cases suggests that the Administrative Procedure Act has responded effectively to public reservations about the legitimacy of the administrative process based upon the possibilities of bias inherent in the institutional decision-making processes of the federal administrative agencies. That response should be counted as one of Congress's most important contributions to reducing a source of the recurrent sense of crisis attending the administrative process.

The nature of the informal administrative process

16

The meaning of summary action

Of course there cannot be a trial by jury before killing an animal supposed to have a contagious disease, and we assume that a legislature may authorize its destruction in such emergencies without a hearing beforehand. But it does not follow that it can throw the loss on the owner without a hearing.

Justice Oliver Wendell Holmes, Jr., in *Miller v. Horton* (1891)

More than 80 percent of the work of the federal administrative agencies is done informally, without an adjudicatory hearing. If one is to appreciate the special strengths and peculiar limitations of administrative agencies as instrumentalities of modern government, one must gain an understanding of the nature of the informal administrative process. Such an understanding is perhaps best achieved by carefully examining the factors that shape and give force to a typical form of informal administrative action. This chapter and the three that follow attempt to achieve that understanding by examining one of the most important and least studied of the informal procedures used by administrative agencies, both federal and state: summary action pending an adjudicatory hearing, sometimes called emergency action or temporary action.

The justification for summary action lies in the necessity for the government to act immediately – against an epidemic of a contagious disease, against the distribution of putrid meat or adulterated drugs, against the sale of worthless securities, against bank officers whose conduct is jeopardizing the interests of depositors – if public policy is to be enforced at all. If an administrative agency were to provide a hearing before acting in such circumstances, the attendant delay would often render any eventual action or order ineffective to protect the public interest. Yet the asserted factual basis for a particular exercise of summary authority may be quite in error, as a prior hearing might have revealed, and the person against whom summary action has been taken may never completely recover from the drastic impact it may have.

In weighing the need for effective administrative action against the possibility of error in the administrative determination to act, the law has struck the balance in favor of permitting summary action in certain circumstances. This balance may be the only one consistent with effective public administration. But it unavoidably raises questions as to the permissible uses and limits of summary action – as a matter of history, as a matter of the Constitution, and as a matter of wise policy.

The use of summary procedures by the states has its roots in the common law of nuisance. The Supreme Court, in tracing the history of summary action, noted that "the summary abatement of nuisances without judicial process or proceeding was well known to the common law long prior to the adoption of the Constitution."[1] By placing this common law authority to act against nuisances at the service of the police power, the states were able to reach any circumstance that could plausibly be related to the public health, safety, or morals. The result, given the deference that nineteenth-century courts paid to state exercises of the police power, was to extend summary authority to conduct and conditions that earlier generations of common lawyers could hardly have foreseen.

What kinds of conduct and conditions did the states' summary authority reach? Statutes permitting the seizure and destruction of unwholesome food, particularly meat and milk, were common,[2] as were statutes permitting the destruction of diseased animals,[3] diseased trees,[4] and goods whose use was illegal, such as liquor.[5] States also enacted statutes permitting the seizure of banks thought to be at the brink of insolvency,[6] the suspension of proposed utility rates and the entry of temporary rate orders,[7] and the demolition of houses falling to decay or standing in the path of a conflagration.[8]

Although the states continue to act under these and similar statutes, the most important state uses of summary action today probably involve matters of licensing. State agencies typically have the authority to suspend a license summarily, pending a hearing on the merits, when it appears that the licensee has acted in a manner that threatens the public health or safety. Because of the many occupations and activities subject to state licensing requirements, this authority potentially affects a large number of citizens.

The authority of the states to act summarily thus has been as extensive as the substantive reach of the law of nuisance and of the police power. The federal government, on the other hand, has exercised its authority to act summarily in fewer substantive areas, primarily those of economic regulation. Nonetheless, because of the decisive position of federal administrative agencies in regulating the national economy, summary action by the federal government has been at least as significant as that of the states. Various federal agencies have summary authority to seize adulterated or misbranded foods, drugs, cosmetics, and hazardous substances;[9] to appoint conservators to take possession of banks whose financial structures are thought to be precarious;[10] to halt trading in certain securities;[11] and to suspend many of the various licenses that the federal government requires to engage in particular activities.[12] A number of federal agencies have the authority to suspend summarily the effective date of proposed tariff schedules submitted by carriers,[13] an authority that has been described as ''one of the most useful and important powers in the entire field of administrative regulation.''[14] Finally, the commissioner of internal revenue may summarily impose a jeopardy assessment, thereby permitting the government to levy against a taxpayer's property in advance of any adjudicatory determination that a tax is owing.[15]

The Constitution requires that whenever the government must provide an adjudicatory hearing for the determination of an issue, the hearing must ''be granted at a meaningful time and in a meaningful manner.''[16] Whether the constitutional standard of meaningfulness requires that the hearing be held before the government takes any action is a proper subject for case-by-case determination. A number of important Supreme Court decisions indicate that in most circumstances the due process requirement of a hearing can be satisfied only by a prior hearing.[17] They suggest that many of the Court's earlier decisions sustaining summary procedures against due process challenges rested upon the existence of ''extraordinary'' or ''emergency'' circumstances in which summary action was ''essential to protect a vital governmental interest.''[18] But several more recent decisions of the Court have emphasized that due process does not always require a prior administrative hearing when the government's interests in efficiency and economy are substantial.[19] These decisions rest upon what the Court has called ''the ordinary principle . . . that something less than an evidentiary hearing is sufficient prior to adverse administrative action.''[20] Chapter 17 examines the decisions sustaining the constitutionality of summary action as well as those holding particular exercises of summary authority unconstitutional, in an effort to identify the contemporary constitutional limits to the government's right to act without a prior administrative hearing.

209

Informal administrative process

Although the courts have the power to define the constitutional limitations upon the use of summary action, the legislatures – and particularly the Congress of the United States, with its power to occupy many regulatory fields – have the initial responsibility to decide whether to authorize particular agencies to act summarily in particular circumstances; and the agencies have the initial responsibility to determine whether to exercise their summary authority in specific situations. Chapters 18 and 19 examine the performance of the federal administrative agencies in exercising summary authority and analyze particular proposals by which Congress and the agencies can improve that performance. They address the problem of controlling the use of summary authority without sacrificing its effectiveness. The fairness with which summary authority is exercised will rest, finally, in at least as great a degree upon the quality of decisions made by Congress and the administrative agencies as it will upon decisions of the Supreme Court. And those decisions, in turn, can go far toward removing the causes of the recurrent sense of crisis attending the federal administrative process by establishing the procedural regularity that must inform a theory of administrative legitimacy.

17

Summary action and the Constitution

Expressing as it does in its ultimate analysis respect enforced by law for that feeling of just treatment which has been evolved through centuries of Anglo-American constitutional history and civilization, "due process" cannot be imprisoned within the treacherous limits of any formula. Representing a profound attitude of fairness between man and man, and more particularly between the individual and government, "due process" is compounded of history, reason, the past course of decisions, and stout confidence in the strength of the democratic faith which we profess. Due process is not a mechanical instrument. It is not a yardstick. It is a process. It is a delicate process of adjustment inescapably involving the exercise of judgment by those whom the Constitution entrusted with the unfolding of the process.

> Justice Felix Frankfurter, in *Joint Anti-Fascist Refugee Committee v. McGrath* (1951)

In determining when the Constitution should be read to permit an administrative agency to act summarily pending an adjudicatory hearing, the courts have engaged in the intellectual process, often employed in constitutional adjudication, of balancing one competing interest against another, one value against another with which it conflicts. The Supreme Court has addressed this problem in about a score of decisions, extending over a century and touching a wide range of substantive concerns. Taken together, these decisions have been a significant force in shaping one of the most important of informal administrative processes. Although here as elsewhere generalizations are hazardous, the factors that the Court has taken into account in the process of creating the constitutional law of summary action can be analyzed systematically.

The logic of statutory authorization

The question of when the Constitution should be interpreted to permit an administrative agency to act summarily can perhaps be put with a more use-

211

ful precision: When should the Constitution be interpreted to permit the legislature to authorize an administrative agency to act summarily? This formulation directs attention to two important threshold considerations.

First, in considering challenges to summary action, courts properly begin by assuring themselves that the legislature has given the agency statutory authority to act summarily.[1] Administrative agencies exercise delegated powers. The question of what powers the legislature has delegated to an agency is never a matter of indifference, either to the legislature, the agency, or those subject to the agency's regulatory jurisdiction, particularly when the powers in issue are significant. The power to act summarily is a drastic and sensitive one, akin to the injunctive power of a court; it is granted to agencies, usually those having the confidence of the legislature, only for the performance of a limited number of tasks. Given the political process by which administrative agencies are brought to birth and the drastic nature of the power to act summarily, it is justifiable to assume that a legislature's failure to delegate summary authority has not been inadvertent. Whatever arguments can be made in favor of implying the existence in an agency of particular powers not expressly or precisely delegated, they are not appropriate to the power to act summarily.

Moreover, any assertion of authority to act summarily potentially presents questions of constitutional dimension, particularly with respect to the limitations summary action may impose on the right to a hearing. By enforcing a requirement of statutory authorization, courts ensure that they will confront these questions only when the legislature has focused upon them as a matter of policy and thus has unambiguously elected to present them. Courts thereby avoid imputing to the legislature the intention to enact laws presenting serious constitutional questions when the legislature's intention is far from clear.[2] The requirements of statutory authorization thus allows the courts both to respect the legislature's prerogative and to enforce its responsibility of initial decision in matters likely to have a constitutional dimension. It also serves to maintain the integrity of the judicial process by avoiding premature adjudication of constitutional questions.

Second, the fact that the legislature, after weighing the need for prompt action against the protections afforded by a prior hearing, has authorized an administrative agency to act summarily often seems itself to be a persuasive element in the judicial determination that the authorization is constitutional.[3] For example, in *North American Cold Storage Co. v. Chicago*,[4] the Supreme Court said:

212

What is the emergency which would render a hearing unnecessary? We think when the question is one regarding the destruction of food which is not fit for human use the emergency must be one which would fairly appeal to the reasonable discretion of the legislature as to the necessity for a prior hearing, and in that case its decision would not be a subject for review by the courts.

It is clearly appropriate for courts to respect a legislative judgment that, on the balance of risks, summary action is necessary for effective administrative regulation, if only because the legislature is more likely to be informed adequately on such matters than a court. At the same time, however, reliance on the legislature's judgment would have too much the quality of bootstrapping if it were permitted to do service by itself. A number of decisions of the past decade in which the Supreme Court has held certain summary procedures unconstitutional suggest that statutory authorization, taken alone, is not dispositive of the question of constitutionality. That question requires reference to standards that are in the ultimate keeping of courts; there remains the eminently judicial task of inquiring into the asserted justification for each statutory grant of summary authority.

Situations justifying summary action

An understanding of the circumstances in which summary action is constitutionally permissible must begin by recognizing the historical role in our legal system of adversary hearings in resolving factual disputes. Adversary hearings, held on the record after notice and opportunity for participation by all interested parties, permit intensive examination of the factual assertions of the parties, particularly by the classic means of confrontation and cross-examination, and are plainly superior to *ex parte* proceedings in their capacity for ascertaining truth and reducing the possibility of error. This at least has been our faith, particularly when the protection of important interests has been at stake. That faith – based, too, on the desire that justice should *appear* to have been done – has found expression in statutes requiring administrative hearings and in a steady line of judicial decisions requiring administrative agencies to provide adversary hearings with respect to a widening range of governmental actions.[5]

There is, however, no rule of constitutional law requiring in absolute terms that a constitutionally compelled hearing always be a prior hearing. Language in several Supreme Court decisions can arguably be read to suggest that whenever due process requires a hearing, it requires a prior hearing.[6]

The context of that language, however, indicates that, almost certainly, it was not intended to carry such weight, and, in any event, the language is inconsistent with the holdings of a number of important decisions.[7] Rather, what the Constitution does require, as *Armstrong v. Manzo* held, is that a constitutionally compelled hearing "be granted at a meaningful time and in a meaningful manner," a standard that counsels a prudential inquiry case by case.[8]

Although the constitutional requirement of a prior hearing is not absolute, it is no less clear that prior hearings have usually been regarded as the norm. Speaking for a unanimous Court in *Bell v. Burson*, Justice Brennan asserted as "fundamental" that "except in emergency situations . . . due process requires that when a State seeks to terminate an interest such as that here involved, it must afford 'notice and opportunity for hearing appropriate to the nature of the case' *before* the termination becomes effective."[9] It is fair to say, therefore, that when the Constitution requires a hearing, an administrative agency generally may be authorized to act summarily in advance of that hearing only in "emergency situations" that are themselves constitutionally defined. The question, then, becomes what constitutes an "emergency situation" within the constitutional meaning of the term.[10]

Protecting the national security during wartime

War is the clearest example of an emergency situation in the life of a nation. When the United States has faced the extremity of war, Congress has enacted laws providing for summary procedures in the regulation of significant areas of the economy, and the Supreme Court – perhaps mindful of Hamilton's ironic vision of "the most extraordinary spectacle which the world has yet seen – that of a nation incapacitated by its Constitution to prepare for defence"[11] – has sustained them.

Thus, in *Stoehr v. Wallace*,[12] a case involving World War I legislation, the Court upheld the constitutional authority of Congress to permit the summary siezure of "property believed to be enemy-owned" so long as provision was made for an eventual hearing. The provision for a subsequent hearing was found constitutionally adequate because it reserved to the claimant the right to establish his claim at a full judicial hearing, "unembarrassed by the precedent executive determination."

A generation later, in *Bowles v. Willingham*,[13] the Court considered the constitutionality of a provision in the Emergency Price Control Act of 1942

214

authorizing the price administrator to establish maximum rents by order and without a hearing. The Court rejected the constitutional challenge in strong terms:

Congress was dealing here with the exigencies of wartime conditions and the insistent demands of inflation control. . . . National security might not be able to afford the luxuries of litigation and the long delays which preliminary hearings traditionally have entailed. . . . [W]here Congress has provided for judicial review after the regulations or orders have been made effective it has done all that due process under the war emergency requires.

One of the central considerations in the Court's reasoning was that the 1942 Act allowed the landlord to seek a subsequent judicial determination of his claim. The Act, however, permitted the courts to review the price administrator's decision only for arbitrariness; it did not provide a plenary judicial hearing of the kind approved in *Stoehr v. Wallace*. Although the judicial review provided by the 1942 Act was thus more restricted than that available in earlier cases sustaining summary procedures, a fact that would seem relevant to the constitutional adequacy of the legislative scheme, the Court took no note of the distinction.

That Congress has acted pursuant to the war power, the Supreme Court once said, "does not remove constitutional limitations safeguarding essential liberties."[14] But it inevitably conditions the attitude that the Court takes in deciding whether the balance that Congress has struck on an issue such as the substitution of summary for plenary administrative hearings is constitutional.[15] In *Stoehr* and in *Willingham*, the Court doubtless realized that the exigencies of wartime conditions were bound to infect many summary seizures of property and many summary establishments of maximum rents with serious error, but it was not prepared to interfere with Congress's discharge of its responsibilities during a grave national emergency.

Perhaps one cannot expect a court to undertake a skeptical balancing of the gains and losses from the use of summary procedures when Congress and the President, answerable to history for preserving the safety of the nation, have deemed them necessary to the successful conduct of the war effort. This suggests that decisions of the Supreme Court sustaining the constitutionality of summary administrative procedures enacted pursuant to the war powers should not be taken to mean that the same result would follow in time of peace. Justice Holmes made the point with characteristic felicity: "A limit in time, to tide over a passing trouble, well may justify a law that could not be upheld as a permanent change."[16]

Protecting the federal government's revenues

The tax laws of the United States have long permitted the collection of the internal revenue by the summary administrative method of jeopardy assessments.[17] Because the usual methods of tax assessment and collection are deliberate, the delay attendant to their use may sometimes result in frustration of the government's proper claim, particularly when a taxpayer is wasting or concealing his assets or otherwise engaging in fraud. The jeopardy assessment ensures that if the government's claim is sustained, there will be assets from which it can be paid: unless the assessed taxpayer makes payment of the alleged deficiency or stays collection by filing a bond to ensure payment, the government may proceed to collect the tax by distraint.

The jeopardy assessment is a drastic remedy, capable of imposing hardships that might have been demonstrated, had a hearing been held, to be unnecessary or disproportionate to the apparent exigencies of the moment. In order to make a jeopardy assessment, the commissioner need only "believe" that collection of the tax will be jeopardized by delay – a judgment not subject to judicial review. Yet a taxpayer whose assets are frozen because he is unable to furnish a bond may be disabled from carrying on his business and enjoying his ordinary style of life. The impact of a jeopardy assessment is intensified by the fact that the commissioner often determines the amount of the assessment in haste and has a tendency to overassess in order to protect the government against all possible losses.[18]

By what reasoning does the Constitution permit the use of procedures that have such harsh results? In the leading case of *Phillips v. Commissioner,*[19] the Supreme Court sustained the constitutionality of summary tax collection procedures as both long accepted and necessary. The Court's assertion, documented extensively in the margins of Justice Brandeis's opinion, that the government's right to use summary administrative procedures in the collection of tax revenues "has long been settled" and "consistently sustained" was not an overstatement. The constitutionality of such procedures had been sustained as early as 1856 in *Murray's Lessee v. Hoboken Land & Improvement Co.*[20] But although summary tax collection procedures may make legitimate claim to a historical standing, and the result in *Phillips v. Commissioner* may be explained in part by the Supreme Court's willingness to honor that claim, the Court sought to rely on more than the normative power of history. The result was plainly intended to rest in considerable part upon what the Court called "the need of the government promptly to secure its revenues."

The government's need to collect tax revenues promptly, however, even when coupled with an appeal to history, is not adequate to support the result the Court reached. The question is not whether such a governmental need exists and is significant. Rather, it is whether the governmental need is of a character and weight sufficient to justify in constitutional terms the severe injury that summary administrative procedures can impose upon the taxpayer. The Court did not undertake to answer that question. Instead, it simply observed that "[d]elay in the judicial determination of property rights is not uncommon where it is essential that governmental needs be immediately satisfied." Yet the cases cited by the Court to support this observation – cases involving hazards to the public health, wartime threats to national security, and the power of eminent domain – are not obviously apposite. Public health hazards and wartime threats to national security are among the most serious perils a society faces, and the power of eminent domain is itself the product of a special historical development. That "only property rights" may be involved – although that is hardly the most sympathetic characterization of the values asserted by the taxpayer – does not distinguish summary tax collection procedures from others involving property rights in which summary process would not be constitutional. Nor would the fact that the taxpayer is allowed a subsequent judicial determination of his rights by itself usually justify summary procedures, although it would doubtless be entitled to weight in a reasoned inquiry into the balance of competing claims.

Perhaps after a more careful inquiry, marked by a systematic attempt to balance the government's need to act summarily against the impact that jeopardy assessments can have on taxpayers, the Court in *Phillips* would have reached the same result. The Court might have concluded, for example, that effective administration of a tax system in a nation this large depends upon a norm of voluntary and prompt payment by the overwhelming number of taxpayers, and that use of the jeopardy assessment is essential if that norm is to be fostered and maintained. On the other hand, the court might have concluded that alternative methods of enforcement could achieve the same result without such drastic consequences for the taxpayer. In either event, a systematic inquiry would have exposed the reasoning that led to the result and thereby served better to illuminate the constitutional law of summary action. Perhaps summary procedures have become so traditional in the collection of tax revenues that their consistency with due process is not seen as presenting a difficult question. However, as Justice Holmes once commented: "Everywhere the basis of principle is tradition, to

217

such an extent that we even are in danger of making the role of history more important than it is.''[21]

Protecting the public against economic injury

When the government acts summarily in tax matters, it does so to protect its own position as collector of the internal revenue. Constitutional questions are presented as well when the government acts summarily to protect the public against imminent economic injury, as when the Federal Home Loan Bank Board, without notice or hearing, appoints a conservator to enter into possession of a bank whose management it believes to be ''pursuing a course injurious to, and jeopardizing the interests of, its members, creditors and the public.''[22]

The arguments supporting a constitutional right to a prior hearing in these circumstances are straightforward. The board's decision to appoint a conservator tenders factual issues – about the character and quality of the bank's management and the potential for harm to the banking public – of a kind that traditionally have required an adversary hearing for their resolution. Moreover, the seizure of a bank and ouster of its management have such serious consequences for all concerned that a prior hearing might reasonably be required as an essential safeguard against error, especially since the board's determination to appoint a conservator is not subject to an anticipatory injunction and may not be reviewed for abuse of discretion until an administrative hearing on the merits has been concluded.[23]

These arguments in favor of a constitutional right to a prior hearing, persuasive as they may be in other contexts, did not prevail in *Fahey v. Mallonee*,[24] in which the Court held that the summary authority given to the board in 1933 was constitutional ''in the light of the history and customs of banking.''[25] Congress was obviously aware that incompetence and malfeasance in the administration of a bank could precipitate its collapse, which in turn could present grave dangers to a community. The solvency of perhaps scores of creditors and the life savings of tens of thousands of depositors could be destroyed by what the Court called ''problems of insecurity and mismanagement.'' By empowering the board to appoint a conservator when substantial questions of malfeasance or incompetence were raised about a bank's management, Congress sought to avert real and serious dangers.

In acting to protect the public interest against the threat of a bank's collapse, Congress also attempted to accommodate the banking community's interest in the continued functioning of the bank until final disposition of the charges. When the Federal Home Loan Bank Board appoints a conservator, it does so not to put a banking institution out of business, but rather to permit it to continue in business under a management whose competence and honesty are free from doubt. As one court said, "this temporary supersession involves no liquidation, no alteration of existing interests, and no discontinuity in the business of the [bank], but only a substitution pendente lite of the Board's representative for the directors and officers of the [bank] in the control and management of its affairs."[26] Appointment of a conservator, although a "drastic procedure," may thus be the most appropriate way in which to protect the interests of both the public and the bank.

The question remains, however, why the administrative hearing on the issues of incompetence and malfeasance should not come before, rather than after, appointment of a conservator. The answer lies in the realities of the situation. The bank might well be insolvent long before a prior hearing could be concluded. This is doubtless what the Court had in mind when it referred to "the delicate nature of the institution and the impossibility of preserving credit during an investigation." If the hearing were held in private, depositors and creditors would continue to entrust their money to a bank that the federal authorities believed might be unable to meet its obligations. A prior hearing would thus be of small value. On the other hand, the delay and publicity that would accompany a public hearing could be fatal to preservation of the banking institution as a going business and destructive of the position of depositors and creditors for whose protection the board is responsible. The summary action upheld in *Fahey v. Mallonee* was, therefore, truly a response to an emergency situation: Appointment of a conservator can effectively protect the interests of depositors and creditors and of the banking institution only if it can be done summarily.[27]

Protecting the public health against impure foods and drugs

Protection of the public health against the dangers posed by impure foods and drugs has in this century become an accepted governmental responsibility, and summary procedures have become one of the standard means by which to carry it out. In the early case of *North American Cold Storage Co. v. Chicago*,[28] the Court sustained the constitutionality of an Illinois statute permitting health inspectors to enter cold storage houses and "forthwith seize, condemn and destroy any such putrid, decayed, poisoned and

219

infected food, which any such inspector may find in and upon such premises.'' The decision relied heavily on the state's authority to abate a nuisance:

> We are of opinion, however, that provision for a hearing before seizure and condemnation and destruction of food which is unwholesome and unfit for use, is not necessary. . . . Food that is in such a condition, if kept for sale or in danger of being sold, is in itself a nuisance, and a nuisance of the most dangerous kind, involving, as it does, the health, if not the lives, of persons who may eat it.

The state clearly has a significant interest in protecting "the lives and health of its inhabitants,'' and summary destruction of food unfit for human consumption is plainly an effective means of doing so. But what if the inspector errs, and orders the destruction of food that in fact is not unfit for human consumption? The Court in *North American Cold Storage* found that the possibility of such error did not affect the constitutionality of the statute because a party whose property was mistakenly destroyed could recover in an action at law. The adequacy of a subsequent remedy in damages was, however, questionable. As the cold storage company argued, when the state destroyed the food it had seized, it also destroyed the only possible evidence of wholesomeness. The difficult question, therefore, is not whether summary seizure is supportable as an emergency measure – surely it is when one considers the serious injury that putrid food can inflict on large numbers of persons – but whether summary destruction is warranted.

The problem created by summary destruction for an owner who asserts the fitness of his food could be avoided in some cases by requiring that, whenever possible, the food be preserved until a hearing can be held or at least until the owner's experts can examine it. (Indeed, in *North American Cold Storage*, the owner maintained that the condemned poultry would have continued in the same condition, if properly stored, for three months.) That procedure would protect the public health and, at the same time, preserve the property owner's right to make a meaningful presentation on the merits and to regain his property if successful.[29] Given the possibility of thus accommodating both parties' interests, what emergency remained to justify the constitutionality of summary destruction?

The Court's response indicated its concern that preservation of the seized food, although less drastic than destruction, might also be less effective. The food might be tampered with or distributed to the public by accident or by intentional evasion. Therefore, as the Court concluded, the legislature might plausibly believe that preservation itself constituted a serious threat to public health. The Court in *North American Cold Storage* thus deferred to the legislature's judgment that, in the particular emergency confronting health inspectors, no remedy less drastic than destruction can be an effective means of protecting the public health.[30]

The degree to which the Court remains prepared to defer to legislative judgments authorizing summary action arguably concerned with public health is illustrated by the leading case of *Ewing v. Mytinger & Casselberry, Inc.*[31] The Food and Drug Administration, with the approval of the attorney general, had made eleven summary seizures of a food supplement that it believed to be misbranded. In sharp contrast to the state's rationale for acting summarily in *North American Cold Storage*, no claim was made that the product was dangerous or in any way harmful to health. As the trial court found, the supplement, described as "an encapsulated concentrate of alfalfa, water cress, parsley, and synthetic vitamins combined in a package with mineral tablets," was "at worst, harmless" and would do the public no good.

The distributor of the product, seeking to enjoin the seizures as unconstitutional, argued that no emergency existed to justify the hardship and destructive publicity caused by the multiple summary seizures. Although the Court recognized that multiple seizures "can cause irreparable damage to a business" and that the preparation in question "may be relatively innocuous," it nevertheless sustained the constitutionality of the summary seizure provision:

[Congress] may conclude, as it did here, that public damage may result even from harmless articles if they are allowed to be sold as panaceas for man's ills. A requirement for a hearing, as a matter of constitutional right, does not arise merely because the danger of injury may be more apparent or immediate in the one case than in the other. For all we know, the most damage may come from misleading or fraudulent labels. That is a decision for Congress, not for us.

Because the food supplement presented no apparent threat to the public health, the Court's readiness to sustain the constitutionality of summary seizure on public health grounds is difficult to accept. Nonetheless, the Court has continued to point to the decision as an example of an emergency situation in which summary action is permissible.[32] In doing so, the Court may be looking to the consumer protection rather than the public health aspects of the case. On that basis, *Mytinger & Casselberry* can be thought to go beyond *North American Cold Storage* in the deference shown the legislature, since, without analyzing the nature of the consumer protection emergency to which Congress might have been responding, the Court said that "[t]here is no constitutional reason why Congress in the interests of consumer protection may not extend [the] area'' in which summary seizure may be taken. Because of the apparent casualness with which the result was reached, it may be incautious to impute to the decision the broad holding that this statement suggests.

The Court in *Mytinger & Casselberry* did not indicate that the legislature is required to select the least drastic remedy consistent with an effective response to the emergency confronting it. But the decision should not be read to extend the constitutionally permissible scope of summary action. For as the Court noted, the Food, Drug, and Cosmetic Act authorizes summary seizure only with the approval of the attorney general.[33] The Court may well have been persuaded that, by building this procedural safeguard into the administrative process by which summary authority may be exercised, Congress had satisfied the requirements of due process.

Protecting the integrity and efficiency of the civil service

As the regulatory responsibilities of the federal government have grown, the number of persons employed by the government also has grown. As a result, the administration of the civil service – including the maintenance of high standards of performance and integrity and the development of fair procedures for discharging employees who do not meet those standards – has itself become an important responsibility of the federal government. Because so many Americans are government employees, the questions of what procedural protections the due process clause mandates for the discharge of federal employees and whether it permits the use of summary action are important ones. In *Arnett v. Kennedy*,[34] the Supreme Court held that the Constitution does not require the federal government to grant a nonprobationary civil service employee a trial-type hearing prior to discharging him.

Arnett was a field representative in the Chicago office of the Office of Economic Opportunity. He was discharged for allegedly falsely stating that his supervisor had attempted to bribe a community action organization with which the office had dealings. The process by which the discharge was effected was governed by the Lloyd-LaFollette Act,[35] which since 1912 had protected civil service employees from arbitrary discharge and permitted their removal ''only for such cause as will promote the efficiency of the service.''

Taken with a number of regulations that enlarge its procedural protections, the Act requires that a federal agency give an employee thirty days'

222

written notice of the charges against him, as well as copies of the material on which the notice is based; an opportunity to submit a written answer to the charges, together with affidavits; the right to appear personally before the official vested with the authority to make the removal decision; and a written statement of the reasons for the removal. An employee can secure a full evidentiary hearing with cross-examination by appealing the adverse decision to a reviewing authority within his own agency or to the Civil Service Commission itself, but this hearing is typically held after the removal has occurred. Thus the provisions of law that governed Arnett's employment situation did require the federal government to observe a number of procedural requirements before discharging an employee, but they did not require it to provide a predetermination trial-type hearing.

The arguments that Arnett advanced to support his claim to a prior hearing were drawn along standard due process lines. Adversary proceedings, with the opportunity for confrontation and cross-examination, are the traditional method for resolving factual issues of the kind typically implicated in dismissals for cause: mistakes of identity, faulty perceptions of the facts, uncertain and subjective memories, clashes of personality, and fabrications born of personal antagonism. Such proceedings provide a particularly meaningful protection for the individual when the possibility of administrative error is great – a consideration of specific pertinence to Arnett's situation, since almost one-fourth of all appeals by discharged employees result in a reversal of the decision. The protection provided by such proceedings also is important when the injury inflicted upon the individual by an erroneous decision is substantial – a consideration relevant to discharged federal employees, since, during the period of months before an evidentiary hearing can be held, they must bear an unjustified stigma, be burdened by uncertainty, and suffer financial losses for which the statutory provision for reinstatement and back pay does not fully compensate.

Arnett thus argued (1) that the necessity to discharge a federal employee does not constitute an emergency situation or a threat to a significant interest of the commonweal sufficient to justify an exception to the constitutional norm of a prior hearing; and (2) that even if a balancing approach were appropriate, the government's interest in being free to act expeditiously to remove an unsatisfactory employee does not outweigh the interests of federal employees that prior hearings would protect.

In light of the Supreme Court's prior decisions involving summary action, one would have expected these arguments to prevail. The government's need to discharge civil service employees prior to an evidentiary hearing is hardly comparable to the emergency situations created by the government's need to protect the national security in time of war, to protect the public against the collapse of a bank, or to protect consumers against impure food and drugs. In addition, the government's assertion of urgency is called into doubt by the fact that at least nine federal agencies, although they are not required by law to do so, regularly provide evidentiary hearings prior to the dismissal of tenured employees.[36] Despite their force, these arguments did not prevail.

The nine justices of the Supreme Court filed five separate opinions. Only three members of the Court – Justices Marshall, Brennan, and Douglas – accepted Arnett's argument that due process required an evidentiary hearing before the government deprived a civil service employee of his position, and that the government's interest in discharging an employee in advance of such a hearing did not constitute an emergency sufficient constitutionally to justify an exception to that established requirement.

Five members of the Court concluded that the procedures prescribed by the Lloyd-LaFollette Act satisfied the requirements of due process, but they reached that conclusion by fundamentally disparate routes. Justice Rehnquist, in an opinion for the three members of the plurality, found that federal employees enjoyed a property interest in their positions only because the Lloyd-LaFollette Act prohibited their removal except for cause. Building upon the rationale of *Board of Regents v. Roth*,[37] which had held that procedural due process protects only those interests to which an individual has a "legitimate claim of entitlement," Justice Rehnquist noted that "the very section of the statute" granting a federal employee protection against discharge without cause "expressly provided also for the procedure by which 'cause' was to be determined, and expressly omitted the procedural guarantees which appellee insists are mandated by the Constitution." If the government may place substantive limitations upon the employment interests that it creates, so, he concluded, may it place procedural limitations upon the enforcement of those interests – and the federal employee "must take the bitter with the sweet."

Since the Office of Economic Opportunity had complied with the procedural requirements of the Lloyd-LaFollette Act in discharging Arnett, Justice Rehnquist held that no further process was constitutionally due. Under this reasoning, which is darkly reminiscent of what the Court has repeatedly termed the discredited distinction between rights and privileges, there would seem to be few constitutional limits on the power of Congress to authorize summary action with respect to any property interests created by positive law.[38]

Justice Powell, in an opinion joined by Justice Blackmun, rejected the plurality's premise that an individual's procedural protections under the due process clause were limited to those provided by Congress in creating the substantive interest in question. But the two justices joined the plurality in voting to sustain the constitutionality of the Lloyd-LaFollette Act because they found that the procedures it prescribed satisfied the independent requirements of due process.

Justice Powell's opinion does not mention the requirement of an emergency that the Court's earlier decisions had made central, but it does take account of many of the considerations traditionally found relevant to assessing the constitutionality of summary action. Justice Powell recognizes that a civil service employee's interest in avoiding the deprivations that an erroneous discharge can cause is substantial, but he concludes that the procedures set forth in the Lloyd-LaFollette Act achieve a reasonable accommodation of that interest with the government's interest in protecting discipline and morale in the workplace by being able to remove an inefficient employee with dispatch. Justice White, accepting the same analytic premises, also found that the due process clause did not require a full evidentiary hearing prior to discharge; he found Arnett's discharge improper, however, because his superior, who was the object of the alleged false accusation, was permitted to make the discharge decision despite the possibility that he could not be impartial.

Perhaps Justices Powell, Blackmun, and White were correct in stressing that, in view of the procedural safeguards that the Lloyd-LaFollette Act made available to federal employees before discharge, the case did not present a question of summary action in its typical form, in which no protective formalities designed to reduce the risk of error or permit an opportunity for informal response had been observed. But under the balancing approach that these justices followed, the circumstances in which Congress could authorize summary action without a prior evidentiary hearing would almost certainly be widened by comparison to the narrow limits permitted by the traditional requirement of an emergency situation.

The inability of the Supreme Court to agree upon a rationale for deciding the constitutionality of discharging federal employees without a prior evidentiary hearing is disquieting. The decision in *Arnett v. Kennedy* not only seems dubious on its facts; it also suggests a failure of coherence in the

Court's understanding of the precedents that govern the constitutionality of summary action.

Situations not justifying summary action

The classic decisions sustaining the constitutionality of summary action suggest the significance that the Supreme Court has attached to legislative decisions that summary procedures are necessary for effective governmental action. In a number of decisions, however, the Court has shown its willingness to override a legislative decision authorizing summary procedures when the facts do not make out an "emergency" or "extraordinary" situation in the sense required by the Constitution.

The most important of these decisions is *Goldberg v. Kelly*,[39] which held unconstitutional the summary termination or suspension of welfare benefits under the federally assisted program of Aid to Families with Dependent Children. Because the administrative scheme challenged in that case provided for a "fair hearing" after the termination of benefits, the question whether due process required a prior hearing was squarely presented.

The Court recognized at the outset the impact that summary termination of benefits has on an eligible recipient: "Termination of aid pending resolution of a controversy over eligibility may deprive an eligible recipient of the very means by which to live while he waits. Since he lacks independent resources, his situation becomes immediately desperate." The Court went on to find two other factors basic to its decision.

First, in cases in which subsequent hearings were held, decisions to terminate benefits were reversed with great frequency – according to one study, in over half the cases.[40] It may be that those persons who persevered to the conclusion of the hearing process were not a representative group. Nonetheless, the incidence of error was sufficiently high to warrant the Court's concern with the use of summary procedures, given "the welfare bureaucracy's difficulties in reaching correct decisions on eligibility."

Second, very few decisions to terminate welfare payments – perhaps 1 percent – were, in fact, appealed to subsequent hearings. As the Court suggested, this may have been in part because the recipient's "need to concentrate upon finding the means for daily subsistence" after his benefits have been terminated "adversely affects his ability to seek redress from the welfare bureaucracy."

In light of the sobering import of these figures – that posttermination hearings cannot be expected to protect eligible welfare recipients against erroneous terminations – what countervailing governmental interests could justify the use of summary action? The government's argument that summary action "conserves both the fisc and administrative time and energy" was properly rejected. The government's interest in protecting its purse, although a legitimate one, is hardly comparable to those that the Court has found adequate to sustain summary action in the true emergency cases. The payment of welfare benefits to persons subsequently found ineligible threatens no harm to the public health or safety or to national security, inflicts no economic injury on a specific group, and does not compromise the performance of a vital governmental function. In addition, in a humane scheme of constitutional values, conservation of the government's resources surely is not entitled to as much weight as "the individual's overpowering need in this unique situation not to be wrongfully deprived of assistance"[41] until a hearing can be completed, particularly when no adequate remedy exists to correct the high incidence of error in termination decisions. In these circumstances, the rule of *Armstrong v. Manzo* that constitutionally required hearings must "be granted at a meaningful time and in a meaningful manner" could be met only by a pretermination hearing.[42]

In another significant decision, *Sniadach v. Family Finance Corp.*,[43] the Court held Wisconsin's summary garnishment procedure unconstitutional because it did not provide a hearing prior to the in rem seizure of an individual's wages. Wages, the Court said, are "a specialized type of property," distinctive in the hardship that their deprivation can cause. Thus the Court implicitly recognized that prejudgment garnishment inflicts social costs similar to those that, in *Goldberg v. Kelly*, it found imposed by termination of welfare benefits.

The factors that the Court weighed in *Sniadach* and in *Goldberg* are similar in other respects. There is a considerable possibility that a creditor would garnish wages erroneously or fraudulently and could not sustain his position at a judicial hearing. Moreover, once a person's wages are garnished, he typically is disabled from persevering to an eventual hearing on the merits. These two characteristics, like their analogues in *Goldberg*, suggest that a subsequent judicial hearing is not an effective protection for the wage earner against a garnishment that he could defeat on the merits – if he were able to persevere until a hearing.

In *Goldberg* the Court did not doubt that the state's asserted fiscal interest was a legitimate one, but found that it was not of sufficient weight to justify the injury inflicted by summary termination of welfare benefits. In *Sniadach* the Court found no state interest that rose to the level of the

227

"extraordinary situations" that it said had existed in earlier decisions sustaining the constitutionality of summary action. The state merely had made available to creditors a procedural device giving their private interest an advantage over that of their alleged debtors.[44] It is reasonable that a court should demand an especially compelling justification for summary action that is designed to protect the interests of one individual at the expense of the interests of another, but it would be hazardous to assert that state protection of a private interest never would be entitled to the same degree of constitutional respect as state protection of a governmental interest – there is an obvious state interest in protecting important private interests. In *Sniadach*, however, the state made no attempt to justify the importance of the particular private interest protected by the summary garnishment procedure at issue.

The concerns that motivated the Court in *Goldberg* and *Sniadach* appear again in two later decisions. In *Wisconsin v. Constantineau*,[45] the Court held unconstitutional a state statute authorizing certain persons to post a public notice in retail liquor outlets prohibiting the sale or gift of liquor to named individuals with excessive drinking habits. Despite the "degrading" impact that posting might have on an individual, there was no provision in the law for notice or prior hearing. The statute gave the power of posting to a wide array of persons, including "the wife of such person" and a number of minor local officials. It is not surprising, therefore, that the Court was concerned that a posted individual "may have been the victim of an official's caprice," especially since injury to reputation by error, as the melancholy history of defamation litigation suggests, is never wholly reversible.[46]

In *Bell v. Burson*,[47] the Court again applied the principles of *Goldberg* and *Sniadach*, holding unconstitutional a state statute requiring summary suspension of the driver's license of an uninsured motorist who was unable after an accident to post security for the amount of damages claimed against him. The Court found that the statute's failure to provide for a prior determination "whether there is a reasonable possibility of a judgment being rendered against [the motorist] as a result of the accident" was a denial of due process. The Court assigned great weight, as it had in *Goldberg, Sniadach*, and *Constantineau*, to the impact of summary action on the individual. Bell, a clergyman whose ministry required him to travel by car to cover three rural Georgia communities, was "severely handicapped in the performance of his ministerial duties by a suspension of his licenses."

Moreover, the likelihood of error meant, as it had in the earlier cases, that the impact would be entirely unjustified in some instances.

The ultimate question in *Burson* was the nature of the governmental interest justifying the use of summary authority in the suspension of drivers' licenses. The Court found that "the only purpose" of summary suspension was to help private individuals to secure any judgment they might recover from the uninsured motorist. It may well be that such a use of summary authority serves a legitimate governmental purpose, especially since accident victims who do not receive compensation from those who have caused their injuries may require public assistance. But the legitimacy of the government's interest does not necessarily justify protecting it by summary action. If there was, in *Burson*, an emergency necessitating summary action, the state made no attempt to demonstrate it.

The decisions in these four cases – *Goldberg v. Kelly*, *Sniadach v. Family Finance Corp.*, *Wisconsin v. Constantineau*, and *Bell v. Burson* – indicate that the Supreme Court has been prepared, after weighing certain factors, to override a legislative determination that summary action is necessary or permissible. The factors to be considered include the severity of the impact of summary action on the individual's means for survival, his livelihood, and his reputation; the likelihood that the summary action will be taken erroneously; the degree to which it will disable the individual from participating in a subsequent hearing; the adequacy of the subsequent hearing to protect his interests; and the importance of the societal interest furthered by the summary procedure.

It may be suggested that these decisions are primarily a special response to poverty, and do not illuminate generally the constitutional law of summary action. There is no question that in *Goldberg, Sniadach*, and perhaps *Bell*, poverty served to intensify the impact of summary action on the individual. In each case, however, the state had the opportunity to demonstrate a countervailing governmental interest adequate to justify that impact. Indeed, the significance of these decisions lies in the states' inability to persuade the Court that such an interest existed.

The line of decisions that *Goldberg* initiated now seems, however, to have been a peak in the range of recent precedents announced by the Supreme Court in the area of summary action. At least three significant decisions since *Goldberg* represent a retreat from its implications.

The first decision is *Arnett v. Kennedy*. The statutory schemes in *Goldberg* and *Arnett* were similar. Each provided for a claim of entitlement

229

based on a statutory scheme permitting termination of a benefit through summary proceedings, followed by a trial-type hearing after termination. The economic hardship caused to the wrongfully discharged federal employee was analogous to that caused to the wrongfully terminated welfare recipient. Yet the Court, having held the use of summary procedures unconstitutional in *Goldberg*, sustained their use in *Arnett*.

The plurality opinion in *Arnett* made no serious attempt to make its approach consistent with *Goldberg* or the decisions following it. Justice Rehnquist simply observed that those cases involved "areas of the law dissimilar to one another and dissimilar to the area of governmental employer-employee relationships with which we deal here." Justice Powell, in seeking to distinguish *Goldberg*, did properly note that not every wrongfully discharged federal employee will be exposed to "brutal need" while awaiting a subsequent hearing, but his opinion also placed far greater weight upon the government's interests in administrative convenience and efficiency than the Court had found permissible in *Goldberg*.

The second decision representing a retreat from the implications of *Goldberg* is *Mathews v. Eldridge*.[48] The Court there held that a recipient of Social Security disability benefits was not constitutionally entitled to an evidentiary hearing prior to termination of payments. In finding that the requirements of due process had been met by an informal hearing process, the Court distinguished *Goldberg* on the grounds that the adverse impact of an erroneous decision was likely to be less severe because eligibility for disability benefits was not based on financial need or a lack of other supportive resources; an evidentiary hearing would be of less potential value to a recipient because issues of credibility and veracity do not play an important role in administrative decisions to discontinue benefits, which typically rest upon reliable and unbiased medical reports; and the additional financial costs and administrative burdens that more elaborate pretermination procedures would impose would not be insubstantial. The Court thus found less reason than in *Goldberg* to depart from what it called, surprisingly, "the ordinary principle" that "something less than an evidentiary hearing is sufficient prior to adverse administrative action."

Finally, in *Goss v. Lopez*,[49] the Supreme Court held that summary action may not constitutionally be employed in the suspension of high school students for disciplinary reasons, but it stopped short of finding a requirement of a trial-type hearing. Rather, it held that due process only requires school officials to give a student prior notice of the grounds for the proposed suspension, an explanation of the evidence the authorities have, and an opportunity to explain his conduct before ordering the suspension, provided it is for less than ten days. This prescription for "an informal give-and-take between student and disciplinarian" plainly impressed the Court as more appropriate in the context of an educational institution than a trial-type hearing of a more adversary character would be. Although the decision emphasizes many of the concerns traditionally addressed in summary action cases – it stresses, for example, that charges of misconduct can damage a student's reputation and seriously interfere with his later educational and occupational opportunities, and makes clear that summary suspension of a student remains justified in emergency situations – still it must be counted as further evidence of a retreat from the implications of *Goldberg*.

The decisions in *Arnett v. Kennedy*, *Mathews v. Eldridge*, and *Goss v. Lopez* suggest that the Supreme Court has become more willing to credit governmental interests in administrative efficiency and economy than it was at the time that *Goldberg* was decided. The consequence is that the *Goldberg* requirement of prior evidentiary hearings has been eroded.

Although summary action remains an exception to the traditional due process requirement of a prior hearing, the Supreme Court had indicated that the state is justified in acting summarily, and hence does so without denying due process, when the state's interest in acting promptly to protect the public against a serious threat to its safety, health, or economic well-being outweighs the individual's interest in having an opportunity to be heard before the state acts, perhaps in error, in ways that may cause him significant injury. The Court has sustained the traditional uses of summary action in areas of long-standing governmental primacy – the waging of war, tax collection, the regulation of banking, and protection of the public health – because of the authenticity and urgency of the state's interest in meeting an emergency. Yet few of these decisions attempt to define an emergency by careful analysis of the facts that were before the legislature or the administrative agency.

More difficult cases – in which the gravity of the state's interest was less convincing and the impact of summary action on the individual more obvious – have made greater intellectual demands on the Court and caused it to refine its approach to the balancing process. These cases have arisen in contexts, such as the termination of welfare payments, quite removed from traditional areas of summary governmental action. The Court in these cases has examined factual situations skeptically and intensively, inquiring into both the precise nature of the state's asserted interest in acting summarily

231

and the impact of summary process on the individual. As the state's interest in summary action has become more attenuated and the severity of its impact correspondingly less justifiable, the Court has declined to defer to particular legislative judgments. Rather, it has enforced stricter constitutional requirements as to what properly constitutes an "emergency" or "extraordinary" situation warranting the use of the summary procedures.

Several recent decisions suggest that the Court may be prepared to relax the traditional due process requirement that summary action may be taken only in emergency situations. In permitting the government to act against the individual in advance of an evidentiary hearing, the Court has indicated an increased sympathy toward the state's interests in administrative efficiency and economy and an increased readiness to recognize a more flexible definition of due process in the exercise of summary authority. Such a redefinition would require "some kind of hearing,"[50] although not necessarily a trial-type hearing, before the state could take adverse action against an individual. But the dimensions of the required hearing would be tailored to achieve a fair balance between the state's interest in acting effectively and the individual's interest in avoiding the impact of erroneous administrative action. In a period in which the administration of comprehensive public welfare programs involves periodic adjustments in the entitlements of millions of American citizens, the Court may have come to believe that reliance upon procedures less burdensome than prior trial-type hearings is necessary if the administrative process is to retain its effectiveness.

18

Summary action as an administrative process

Yet the powers that are committed to these regulating agencies, and which they must have to do their work, carry with them great and dangerous opportunities for oppression and wrong.

Elihu Root, *Public Service by the Bar* (1916)

The Supreme Court's decisions illuminating the theory of summary action and the constitutional principles to which it is subject are clearly important to understanding summary action as an informal administrative process. But the legitimacy of the process of government by which summary action is authorized and invoked depends on more than the decisions of the Supreme Court. It is the responsibility of the legislature in the first instance to determine whether to authorize an administrative agency to act summarily. The courts' insistence on statutory authorization seeks to ensure that the legislature will authorize divergence from the constitutional norm of a prior hearing only after it has considered the implications of doing so.

The question whether Congress should authorize an administrative agency to act summarily – on what terms and under what restrictions – is thus a prudential one. A prior administrative hearing has become the constitutional norm because of the fundamental values that deliberative hearings are believed to serve: reducing the possibility of error and protecting the individual against precipitate use of governmental authority. When Congress grants an administrative agency the power to act summarily, it subordinates these values to others deemed more important.

What considerations should Congress take into account when it makes so significant a judgment? The inquiry is perhaps best approached by exploring how summary action works in practice, which is the subject of this chapter, and how administrative procedures can be structured to ensure careful exercise of summary authority, which is the subject of the next chapter.

233

The risk of error

Summary authority is designed to be exercised in emergency situations. To be effective, it must often be exercised quickly, under the pressures of the moment. When an administrative agency acts in such exigent circumstances, it is likely to be acting upon incomplete information. Even when an agency has several weeks, or even months, to decide whether to act, as agencies empowered to suspend proposed rates usually do, the decision to take summary action is not always based upon adequate information. This is scarcely a description of the Weberian ideal in the exercise of bureaucratic competence.

When an administrative agency acts on incomplete information, untested by the adversary process and untempered by an opportunity for deliberation, it is far more likely to err. The bounds of the resulting error may be extended by an agency's tendency – perhaps a proper one in the premises of an emergency – to ensure that the public interest is adequately protected by entering summary orders that prove, in retrospect, unnecessarily broad. The tendency of the commissioner of internal revenue to overassess in making jeopardy assessments and the practice of the Food and Drug Administration of condemning entire shipments of goods on the basis of representative samples are familiar examples. More complete information and an opportunity for greater deliberation would undoubtedly result in more precisely calibrated orders.

In addition, the risk of arbitrary action almost surely is increased when an administrative agency is permitted to act without the moderating constraint that the prospect of a prior hearing typically imposes on administrative initiatives. The existence of this risk was the subject of Judge Pell's vigorous dissent in *Nor-Am Agricultural Products, Inc. v. Hardin*.[1] A national news program had reported that three young children were "rendered virtually vegetables" as the result of mercury poisoning allegedly caused by a fungicide. The next morning, the secretary of agriculture summarily suspended the registration of the fungicide as an "economic poison"[2] pending a hearing on its permanent cancellation. The district court enjoined the suspension preliminarily, but the court of appeals ultimately reversed en banc, holding that the secretary's action was not subject to judicial review.

Judge Pell's dissent argued that the secretary's decision to take summary action, reached on the basis of no more than undocumented and uninvestigated allegations, exemplified the danger that emotional charges would increase the likelihood of administrative arbitrariness and error:

When a product has been used on the market for more than twenty years and is essential for agriculture and when there has been no other recorded incident that the use of the product has been detrimental to the public health, I can reach no conclusion other than that the suspension was, in a technical and legal sense, an arbitrary and capricious one.

The most deliberative administrative action may, of course, prove erroneous or arbitrary. The relevant question is the extent to which summary action results in a higher incidence of error than that resulting from formal adjudication. The few studies of summary termination of welfare payments undertaken prior to *Goldberg v. Kelly* found a disturbingly high incidence. In the absence of judicial review of summary action, however, empirical studies are possible only when a formal adjudicatory hearing is held after summary action has been taken, and such subsequent hearings are relatively infrequent. For example, more than 80 percent of the proposed tariffs summarily suspended by the Interstate Commerce Commission and more than 90 percent of those suspended by the Civil Aeronautics Board are either voluntarily withdrawn by the filing carrier or canceled because of the carrier's failure to defend at a hearing.[3] The percentage of summary seizures made by the Food and Drug Administration that are never contested at a subsequent hearing is almost certainly as high.

Although it is difficult to measure the incidence of error accompanying summary action, the hypothesis that summary action results in a higher incidence of error than formal adjudicatory hearings remains convincing. The infrequency with which those affected by summary action contest its merits at a subsequent hearing does not obviously make the hypothesis less plausible. It does not necessarily indicate that those affected by summary action are prepared to concede the correctness of the agency's judgment; rather, it more likely suggests that the costs of contesting, in terms of resources, adverse publicity, and agency disfavor, often are prohibitive. In deciding whether to grant summary authority to a particular agency, Congress should therefore determine in each case whether the higher incidence of uncorrected error likely to result is acceptable in light of that agency's responsibilities.

The role of the staff

Commentators have long been concerned with the significant role that an agency's staff plays in the determination of administrative proceedings. The staff's role is accentuated when informal administrative decisions, such as the determination to invoke summary authority, are made. The staff's power to decide which matters to present to the members of the agency is itself of considerable significance. And once the staff elects to present a particular matter, the pressures of time and events that almost always surround a decision whether to act summarily make independent consideration by the agency's members difficult. They inevitably must rely heavily on the staff – to investigate the facts, to create a record, to assess the seriousness of the threat to the public, to analyze the likely consequences of acting or declining to act summarily, to give legal advice, and to recommend what action should be taken. These circumstances give the staff's recommendation an especial momentum for acceptance.[4]

The Hoover Commission noted the possibility that the staff may "extend or curtail the policies" of an agency in informal matters; it pointed to claims that the staff of the Securities and Exchange Commission, in enforcing the agency's registration requirements, "has insisted on more onerous requirements for disclosure than the Commission would demand."[5] Others have argued that years of enforcement effort unconsciously bias the staff, and that the staff often is permitted to enforce its bias without adequate supervision or correction by the members of the agency.

It would be surprising if an agency's staff, as a result of its investigation in a particular case, did not become convinced of the desirability of taking decisive administrative action. Indeed, because of its professional dedication and its regular exposure to an industry's marginal conduct, the staff may well become increasingly less sensitive to the individual problems of those whom the agency regulates and develop a propensity for strong regulation. It may believe that its proper role is to recommend that the agency act in borderline cases in order to encourage a toughened regulatory stance and to expose the members of the agency to the difficulties of controlling conduct at the extremity of its regulatory authority. The consequence may be that the members of the agency will approve staff recommendations that the staff thought would be rejected.

Care must be exercised, however, in drawing conclusions from these observations. Agency members are likely to be more sensitive than the staff to the unfavorable repercussions that can result from the injudicious use of summary power. Moreover, they are usually aware of the staff's desire to exert influence and its possible bias in pressing its recommendations. The Securities and Exchange Commission, for example, requires the staff to submit a memorandum as detailed as possible whenever it recommends that summary action be taken; if time does not permit, the agency members may be apprised of the basis for the staff's recommendation by an oral presentation, but the staff must submit a memorandum supporting its recommendation as soon as possible thereafter. Similarly, the Internal Revenue Service has designed an elaborate system of internal administrative review, including a progression of audits at the regional and national levels, to guard against unreasonable staff recommendations to make use of jeopardy assessments.

Still, the question remains whether the staff is likely to have greater influence on decisions to exercise summary authority than it has on agency decisions made in the fullness of time. A categorical answer cannot be given because administrative agencies respond with varying degrees of urgency and success to the recurrently expressed concern that staff influence is too great. The concern, however, remains – it reflects tendencies that have been commented on for a generation and it corresponds with widely held views of how bureaucracies tend to make decisions under the pressure of time.

The possibility of prejudgment

Whenever the members of an agency participate in a decision to institute administrative proceedings, they run the risk – contemplated by the permissive provisions of the Administrative Procedure Act on commingling of functions – of becoming committed to a position on the merits. Philip Elman, reflecting on his service as a federal trade commissioner, has said that "when Commission members, prior to issuing a complaint, review investigative files for evidence of violations of the law, the burden of persuasion is subtly shifted to the respondent once the complaint does issue."[6]

In order to minimize the risk that members of an agency will become biased by participation in the decision to institute proceedings, many commentators have suggested that greater authority to act be delegated to the agency staff.[7] Other commentators have been less alarmed by the risk; they have argued that the determination to issue a complaint "calls for mental activity like that involved in a judge's action on a demurrer or on an application for a temporary restraining order, and wholly unlike that involved in a prosecutor's efforts to compile an impressive record of convictions."[8] This argument may be valid with respect to the "mental activity" demanded in deciding to issue a complaint, but it does not deal adequately with the peculiar impetus to partiality that a decision to authorize summary action may create.

237

The decision to act summarily differs from other decisions to institute administrative proceedings. Because it typically has immediate and severe consequences for the respondent, the decision is quite properly exposed to closer public examination and the pressure on the agency to demonstrate the necessity and propriety of its action is increased. A decision in favor of the respondent at the ultimate hearing on the merits may be construed as an admission that the original action was arbitrary. The agency may therefore approach the hearing with a greater institutional self-interest in justifying its initial decision than it does in proceedings instituted by a complaint.

Even when self-interest of this kind does not affect the ultimate decision, the appearance of prejudgment is likely to remain. This situation may have serious consequences: it may place a cloud over the perceived fairness of the subsequent proceeding and may induce some respondents to forego their statutory right to a hearing. Both Congress and the agencies should therefore give careful thought to the development of means by which to avoid the possibility, as well as the appearance, that the decision to act summarily will influence the ultimate decision on the merits of the case, although the goal is concededly difficult of achievement.

The capacity to injure wrongfully

Summary action has a particular capacity to injure those against whom it is wrongfully invoked. In addition to its immediate effects, which may themselves be harsh, summary action often generates publicity that causes damage more enduring and extensive than do the terms of the summary order itself. When Secretary Flemming of Health, Education, and Welfare warned the public two weeks before Thanksgiving in 1959 that a dangerous residue of pesticide chemicals remained on many cranberries in that year's crop, and the Food and Drug Administration summarily seized several shipments, substantially all of the crop remained unsold, although more than 99 percent of all the cranberries produced that year were subsequently found fit for consumption.[9] Similarly, when the Securities and Exchange Commission summarily suspends trading in a security, the resulting publicity can destroy the marketability of the stock.

The capacity to generate publicity damaging to an individual is one that summary action shares, of course, with other forms of prehearing administrative action, particularly the issuance of press releases announcing the initiation of agency proceedings against an individual. The commissioner of internal revenue, for example, has the capacity to inflict substantial damage

238

upon an organization by use of a press release pending an administrative determination, as the Sierra Club found out in 1966. At that time, the commissioner announced that the Internal Revenue Service was instituting a proceeding to determine whether the club should be disqualified from receiving charitable contributions, deductible to the donor, because it had engaged in activities designed to influence legislation. Charitable contributions made to the Sierra Club after the date of the commissioner's announcement would not be deductible if the Internal Revenue Service ultimately concluded that the club was not a charitable organization for purposes of the Internal Revenue Code. That the commissioner's press release severely hurt the Sierra Club cannot be doubted. By issuing the press release, the commissioner prevented the Sierra Club from assuring potential contributors that contributions made during the period of the investigation would be deductible.

Because of the peculiar sensitivity of the securities market, the capacity of the Securities and Exchange Commission to cause substantial injury by announcing that a public proceeding will be commenced is perhaps as great as that of any federal agency. The commission is authorized to issue a stop order suspending the effectiveness of a registration statement only after notice and hearing. But the very announcement that such a hearing will be held, usually given widespread publicity, can have grave consequences. Similarly, serious injury typically follows the public announcement that the commission has given a broker-dealer notice of a hearing to suspend his registration pending a final determination at a hearing on revocation. ''The moment you bring a public proceeding against a broker-dealer who depends upon public confidence in his reputation,'' an experienced lawyer in this area has written, ''he is to all intents and purposes out of business. His business is destroyed before he has a chance to defend himself and before the Commission has had a chance to hear his side of the case and to decide whether he is guilty of the matters charged, or whether, in fact, he is innocent.''[10]

The capacity wrongfully to impose serious injury significantly distinguishes summary action from administrative action taken after a formal adjudicatory hearing. The damaging impact of summary action is a cause for particular concern because, in the absence of an administrative hearing, the risk of error is probably greater; the unfavorable publicity rests wholly on the agency's *ex parte* assertion; the order may be broader than necessary; and judicial review is typically unavailable.

Moreover, the injury inflicted by summary action is sometimes so great that, in effect, the availability of a subsequent hearing is meaningless. In

Aquavella v. Richardson,[11] the secretary of health, education, and welfare's summary suspension of medicare payments to a nursing home, which depended almost entirely on such payments for its revenue, quickly forced it out of business. For the businessman whose market wrongfully has been destroyed by a summary order, for the college student who wrongfully has been expelled on the eve of graduation, the prospect of achieving ultimate vindication on the merits has little appeal: The damage and disruption already imposed are irremediable.

In other instances, including many in which a favorable decision at a subsequent hearing would be meaningful, summary action has such a devastating impact that the affected party is disabled from effectively contesting the merits. Thus, as the Court noted in *Goldberg v. Kelly*, the termination of welfare benefits "adversely affects [a recipient's] ability to seek redress from the welfare bureaucracy."[12] As a consequence, the injury caused by wrongful invocation of summary authority may never be cured.

Increased reliance on informal processes

The capacity of summary action to render a subsequent hearing meaningless or to disable an individual from participating in it effectively has important implications for an agency's relationship with those whom it regulates. Whenever the impact of summary action is likely to be severe, the power to threaten its invocation may be as significant as actually invoking it. The power of the Food and Drug Administration, for example, to threaten the seizure of goods is so great that the owner may acquiesce in the agency's objections even though he believes them unfounded. Exercise of a rate-regulating agency's power summarily to suspend proposed rates can have such costly consequences that a carrier may be prepared to consent to a specific rate structure whose approval has been foreshadowed by the agency simply because it cannot absorb the financial loss that suspension would impose.[13] The power of the Federal Home Loan Bank Board to appoint a conservator is so momentous that few banks can resist the agency's recommendation that they sign proposed consent decrees agreeing to changes in challenged practices, even though the bank may be convinced that the practices are proper.[14]

The extent to which the mere availability of summary authority is sufficient to coerce compliance with an agency's demands, typically by means of an informal settlement, cannot readily be measured. But the existence of the phenomenon – what Commissioner Goddard of the Food and Drug Administration called "the somber gun of enforcement"[15] – can hardly be doubted. Indeed, it sometimes is argued that administrative agencies need credible reserves of power precisely because of their usefulness in encouraging informal settlements, without which effective regulation would be considerably more difficult to achieve.

The power to act summarily is doubtless a forceful bargaining weapon in strengthening an agency's capacity to secure settlements: It lessens an individual's incentive to assert unrealistic positions and to employ delaying tactics. But when the powers possessed by the administrator are great, he may be inclined to take advantage of their coercive potential by demanding changes in behavior that, however much they conform to an enlightened conception of equity or justice, are beyond his statutory authority to exact. An administrator who can back his demands with the threat of summary action may also be tempted to seek concessions to which he would not be entitled on the evidence, were it fully developed at an adjudicatory hearing. Some commentators have charged, for example, that the Securities and Exchange Commission sometimes succumbs to these temptations in exercising its discretionary power to accelerate the effective date of a registration statement (which is requested by virtually every registrant). As Kenneth C. Davis has noted, "Business reasons usually make acceleration . . . so compelling that the registrant is willing to yield to onerous conditions,"[16] particularly with respect to the extent of disclosure of information, even though he is convinced that a court would find that the commission had exceeded its proper authority. Similarly, prior to *Goldberg v. Kelly* it was said that because of the power to terminate public assistance without a hearing, caseworkers were able to enforce standards of personal behavior that were not required by law.

Whatever the validity of these particular objections, the inclination of an agency to seek informal settlements as a substitute for the use of summary authority is probably explained more by a reluctance to invoke such awesome powers than by a temptation to coerce illegitimate results. Indeed, this reluctance to risk imposing the severe injuries of which summary action is capable often leads an agency to devise mechanisms that eventually supplant summary action as the usual method for achieving the agency's legislative mandate. Examples of these mechanisms include the Food and Drug Administration's elaborate recall procedures, described in the regulations as "an alternative to multiple seizures"[17] and regarded, in the words of former

Commissioner Goddard, as "less punitive"[18] than summary action; the Federal Communications Commission's technique of "constant surveillance" in regulating the rates of common carriers; the Federal Home Loan Bank Board's reliance on consent orders to end questionable banking practices; and the "speaking" rate suspension order of the Civil Aeronautics Board, condemned in *Moss v. CAB*[19] as subversive of the statutory scheme.

The consequence of administrative innovations such as these is that governmental challenges to private conduct are more often resolved informally than by the hearing processes that Congress has provided as part of the legislative scheme authorizing summary action. This has serious implications for administrative regulation. When an agency prefers informal negotiations to the more formal process that moves from summary action to the conclusion of a subsequent evidentiary hearing, its actions are shielded from judicial review and public scrutiny alike.

If granting summary authority to an agency can thus lead to increased reliance on informal processes, then a responsible legislative decision to grant that authority cannot be made without considering whether this is a desirable result. Congress undoubtedly understood that administrative agencies would rely in some measure on informal processes, but it did provide for formal, more public procedures in areas made subject to summary action. The question in each instance, therefore, must be whether an agency has struck a proper balance between the use of summary action and the negotiation of informal settlements.

As an exception to the general constitutional norm that government may not act against an individual before it has granted him a hearing, summary action has the competence to permit effective governmental action in emergency situations as well as the capacity wrongfully to inflict serious injury. Yet its exercise is almost wholly free of administrative regulations or formalized agency practices. The task of devising procedural safeguards for the informal administrative processes such as summary action must begin with particularized studies of how these processes actually work in practice. Only after such studies have been made can students of the administrative process begin to inquire how informal administrative procedures might be structured to enhance their fairness and effectiveness. Because procedural fairness is related so intimately to administrative legitimacy, these inquiries are indispensable steps in responding to the recurrent sense of crisis attending the federal administrative process.

19

Structuring the use of summary action

In framing a government which is to be administered by men over men, the great difficulty lies in this: you must first enable the government to control the governed; and in the next place oblige it to control itself.

James Madison, *The Federalist*, No. 51 (1788)

Lawyers have long understood as a general proposition what James Willard Hurst has called the substantive importance of procedure. But the relevance of procedure to informal administrative action has only begun to receive serious scholarly attention. It is necessary to move tentatively, therefore, in considering whether procedures commonly used to structure formal administrative processes have appropriate application to the informal process of summary action. The extent to which a specific procedure can serve to increase the fairness of an agency's performance in acting summarily depends, of course, on whether it is adapted to the agency's particular responsibilities and circumstances. The task of Congress is to determine, after individualized inquiry, the specific procedures appropriate for a particular agency and whether such procedures should be imposed by legislation. The most appropriate response for Congress in many regulatory contexts may be to encourage agencies to devise their own procedures and to permit them to modify these procedures as experience recommends. Regardless of whether Congress acts, administrative agencies have a continuing responsibility to consider whether particular procedural devices would achieve greater fairness in the exercise of summary authority.

A number of requirements and procedures – some drawn from formal administrative processes, some suggested by the general features of summary action – are worthy of serious examination. They do not, of course, exhaust the possibilities.

Statutory standards

One way in which Congress could structure the use of the summary authority would be to enact statutory standards for its exercise. It would be possible to formulate standards in a variety of terms. Congress could follow the language of constitutional requirement appearing in Supreme Court decisions, for example, in order to stress the exceptional nature of summary action. It could borrow from the criteria that equity courts enforce in granting and denying preliminary injunctions. Or it could use new formulations defining the degree of exigency or emergency required, or the quantum of evidence that an agency must possess, before summary action could be taken. One such definition might provide that an agency could take summary action only if no less drastic means gave promise of being equally effective in achieving substantially the same result.

In framing statutory standards, the stringency of the requirements would necessarily vary from one agency to another, depending, for example, on the severity of the impact that the summary actions of each agency typically would have. In addition, different evidentiary standards might be appropriate when an agency took summary action on its own initiative than when it did so in response to the request of an interested private citizen.

Although Congress has not always undertaken to provide statutory standards for the exercise of summary authority, it has done so occasionally with apparent success. The Federal Insecticide, Fungicide, and Rodenticide Act, for example, provides that the administrator of the Environmental Protection Agency may suspend the federal registration of an "economic poison" only if it presents "an imminent hazard to the public."[1] Although Congress chose language sufficiently precise to convey its intention that "this authority . . . should only be exercised under the most extreme conditions and with the utmost care,"[2] it also chose language sufficiently general to allow the administrator to exercise discretion on issues of substantive significance: for example, whether a hazard may be considered "imminent" if its impact will not be felt for many years, and whether the preservation of fish and wildlife is among the interests of the "public" that the statute is designed to protect.

Because statutory standards for the exercise of summary authority typically are framed in general terms, it might be argued that they would be regarded as no more than hortatory and have little influence on the actual behavior of administrators. One cannot be certain that there is not some truth to this argument. Nonetheless, when Congress enacts a statute imposing standards,

244

even general ones, on the exercise of administrative authority, it "expresse[s] a mood," as Justice Frankfurter wrote in a relevant connection. "As legislation that mood must be respected, even though it can serve only as a standard for judgment and not as a body of rigid rules assuring sameness of application."[3] It cannot fairly be assumed that conscientious administrators would remain indifferent to the mood that Congress has expressed in limiting their discretion to exercise summary authority. But if there is reason to doubt in particular instances that agencies would comply with the statutory standards Congress has enacted, procedures to give greater assurance of agency compliance might be adopted. Congress might require, for example, that the members of the agency personally approve the decision to act summarily, as the securities and exchange commissioners do; or that an agency secure the prior certification of the attorney general that the statutory standards have been met, as the Food and Drug Administration must do before instituting summary seizures; or that administrative decisions to take summary action be subject to judicial review, a question considered later in this chapter. Because the cost of each of these procedures – in terms of delay, the possibility of prejudgment, the consumption of agency resources – would vary for each type of summary action, selection must be made on a function-by-function basis.

Rules and reasons

Two procedures commonly used to structure formal administrative processes are the promulgation of rules for the exercise of a particular discretionary power and the provision of a statement explaining the agency's reasons in each instance for its discretionary acts. The existence of a body of standards tends to encourage greater deliberation, self-consciousness, and consistency in the exercise of administrative discretion and thereby reduces the likelihood that an agency will act arbitrarily. By promulgating rules and providing statements of reasons, an administrative agency creates a body of standards against which its performance can be measured by Congress, the courts, and the public, and thereby tends to make the law more democratic and accountable.

These arguments have found renewed expression in scholarly criticism and judicial decisions urging administrative agencies to make greater use of rules and reasons.[4] The immediate question, however, is whether the promulgation of rules and guidelines and the provision of statements of reasons – practices growing out of formal administrative processes – would be effective in structuring an agency's exercise of its discretion to invoke summary authority.

The Administrative Procedure Act requires agencies to "publish in the Federal Register for the guidance of the public . . . statements of general policy or interpretations of general applicability formulated and adopted by the agency."[5] Despite this requirement, the policies that administrative agencies have developed for exercising their discretion to take summary action generally have not been published as rules or regulations or in any other form. In many instances, these policies appear only in internal memorandums prepared for the guidance of the agency's staff. The fact that these memorandums are unpublished increases the possibility of unequal treatment; knowledge of their substance is likely to be limited to an elite group of agency specialists, many of them former members of the agency's legal staff, who alone can assert them on behalf of their clients. It also prevents any effective inquiry into whether the agency's enforcement policies are applied unequally in practice, particularly when a degree of autonomy has been granted to the agency's regional offices.

The explanation most often given by agency officials for not publishing rules for the exercise of summary authority is the difficulty of framing them. Most decisions to take summary action, it is said, are based on a highly developed expertise that gives the agency confidence in the refined quality of what are, essentially, educated guesses and hunches. To articulate criteria for taking summary action – the type of harm, the magnitude of the violation, the seriousness of the threat to the public interest, the substantiality of the agency's evidence, the availability of alternative relief, and the special characteristics of the individual involved, including his prior record of violations, his degree of culpability, and his vulnerability to successful action – would be, in the view of many administrators, to do no more than announce obvious generalities that would neither standardize an agency's decision-making processes nor provide the public with reliable information on how future cases, each of them turning on individual facts, would be decided.[6]

Although this explanation has some validity, it is not wholly persuasive. Some administrative agencies have managed to formulate and publish rules defining the circumstances in which they will take summary action. The Federal Home Loan Bank Board, for example, has promulgated rules governing the appointment of conservators.[7] In addition many agencies have published rules governing the circumstances in which they will initiate adjudicatory proceedings, even though the criteria are as numerous and the facts as individually diverse as those involved when summary action is contemplated. Even when an administrative agency is reluctant to formalize its criteria for summary action in published rules, a useful purpose could still be served by making these criteria available in other forms, such as summaries of prior practices, illustrations of real or hypothetical situations at the extremes of enforcement and nonenforcement, digests of prior decisions to take summary action, and advisory interpretations. In considering whether to require a particular agency to promulgate rules governing its discretion in this area, Congress might wisely permit the agency some freedom to explore the utility of these other forms and methods.

A practical method by which an administrative agency could lay a foundation for the eventual promulgation of rules or guidelines would be to provide a statement of reasons whenever it took summary action. This would permit an agency gradually to develop generalized criteria out of particular fact situations and to refine them as experience recommends. Once an agency has promulgated rules, it would be possible to discern any discrepancy between the agency's stated criteria for acting and the reasons given for acting in a particular case.

There is no general requirement, either constitutional or deriving from the Administrative Procedure Act, that administrative agencies give reasons for the actions they take informally, as the Supreme Court's decision in *Citizens To Preserve Overton Park, Inc. v. Volpe*[8] confirms. Congress remains free, however, to require that an administrative agency provide a statement of reasons whenever it takes summary action, but it has done so only occasionally. The Interstate Commerce Act and the various rate suspension statutes modeled after it are notable examples of statutes requiring explanations for each use of summary administrative authority.[9] In most instances the requirement that administrative agencies state the reasons for their decisions has been of judicial origin, based both on the desirability of refining the exercise of administrative discretion and on the necessity of facilitating judicial review.[10]

The substantial number of judicial decisions requiring administrative agencies to state the reasons for their decisions are, however, limited almost entirely to formal agency proceedings. Although the purposes underlying the requirement of reasons – improvement of the exercise of discretion and prevention of arbitrary administrative action – are probably more in need of vindication when an agency acts informally than when it uses the formal hearing process, courts have only begun to require administrative agencies to provide a statement of reasons when they act informally.[11]

247

In *Environmental Defense Fund, Inc. v. Ruckelshaus*,[12] the court remanded the case to the administrator of the Environmental Protection Agency because it found that he had "not yet provided an adequate explanation for his decision to deny interim relief" to environmentalist groups seeking the summary suspension of the federal registration of DDT. The court explicitly instructed the administrator to identify the factors he had considered in reaching his decision and to relate them to the evidence before him. In *Environmental Defense Fund, Inc. v. EPA*,[13] the same court remanded a similar case to the administrator because of his failure to provide an adequate statement of reasons. The court regarded the interests at stake in the case as "too important to permit the decision to be sustained on the basis of speculative inference as to what the Administrator's findings and conclusions might have been" regarding a central issue in the case.

The possibility that the courts might extend the two *Environmental Defense Fund* decisions by requiring other administrative agencies to provide a statement of reasons when they take summary action does not relieve Congress or the individual administrative agencies of their respective obligations to address the question of when a statement of reasons should accompany particular exercises of summary power. The general usefulness of statements of reasons is so plain that they probably should be required in most instances of summary action, as they already are in formal agency adjudication. In some circumstances, of course, the pressures of time will not permit an agency to prepare a statement of reasons before taking summary action.[14] When preparation of a statement would be impractical at the time summary action is taken, the agency should still be required to provide the statement within a specified time subsequent to the action.[15]

Once the decision has been made to require an administrative agency to provide a statement of reasons when it acts summarily, it is important that the statement be sufficiently detailed to permit the respondent to know the actual basis for the agency's decision and to plan his subsequent strategy realistically. Statements of reasons that merely recite statutory phrases ritualistically do not serve this function, nor do they seek to exploit the possibility of making the agency's decision to act summarily acceptable in at least some degree to the person against whom the action was taken. When the Interstate Commerce Commission suspends a proposed rate schedule, it gives one of six standard reasons – for example, that the proposed schedule is "unjust and unreasonable in violation of the Interstate Commerce Act" – each of which merely paraphrases a broad statutory requirement. If the agency issued a statement giving some sense of its reasoning rather than merely its conclusion, then, as Ralph Spritzer has written, "the proponent obviously would be in a much better position to respond: to abandon the proposal, or particular features of it; to withdraw the pending proposal and submit an appropriately modified version that might pass muster; or to go forward with an awareness of the issue or issues that would have to be litigated to the agency's satisfaction."[16]

By promulgating rules describing generally the criteria that guide its discretion in taking summary action and by providing an informative statement of reasons whenever it does act summarily, an administrative agency could make one of its most significant informal processes more visible. These reforms would be an important step toward strengthening the fairness of the process by which summary action is taken. Sunlight, as Justice Brandeis said, is the best of disinfectants.

Prior informal discussions

A fundamental problem of summary action is the risk of error created when an administrative agency must act quickly, often on incomplete information, always on information untested by the adversary process of a hearing. This risk is tolerated because formal adjudicatory hearings, with their careful, deliberative consideration of the evidence, are inconsistent with effective governmental action in emergency situations. Informal procedures preceding the final decision to take summary action can, however, be effective in reducing the risk of error in what may be a decision with drastic consequences for the individual involved.

Requiring an administrative agency to inform an individual that it is contemplating summary action against him, to describe the general nature of its information and the tenor of its reasoning, and to permit him a brief opportunity to discuss the matter with the agency's staff and advance arguments why summary action should not be taken could be most helpful in reducing the risk of error. Warner Gardner, in proposing in 1972 an "Informal Procedure Act of 1980," would provide that before an administrative agency initiates action that "might impose a penalty or detriment or deny a benefit" – a formulation broad enough to embrace summary action – it must, "to the extent practicable," advise the persons affected that such action is under consideration and "give them a reasonable opportunity to supply relevant facts and the reasons why such agency action should or should not be taken."[17]

Despite the absence of any explicit requirement of law, several administrative agencies follow a general practice of engaging in informal discussions before taking summary action. The Suspension Board of the Interstate Commerce Commission, for example, often holds informal discussions, usually by telephone, with carriers or their representatives before deciding whether to suspend proposed tariffs summarily. Prior to instituting summary seizures, the Food and Drug Administration often enters into informal recall discussions initiated by firms that have either been informed in writing as the statute requires that an inspector has found violations of law on their premises, or have seen the results, routinely referred to them, of sample analyses indicating violations of law. The Securities and Exchange Commission, before summarily suspending trading in a security, often discusses the matter informally with the company involved and its counsel, and seeks their cooperation in working out a less drastic method for protecting the public.

These practices indicate that it would be feasible in some contexts for administrative agencies to inform an individual that summary action is contemplated and permit him an opportunity for informal discussion before action is taken. The sound identification of these contexts is crucial; if prior informal notice is required or given in inappropriate contexts – for example, to a taxpayer suspected of engaging in fraud – the social consequences may be more severe than the risk of error that notice is designed to reduce. Whether prior notice would be appropriate in a particular context is a function of the degree to which the decision to act summarily depends on an understanding of the facts that may be mistaken, the degree to which the time required to conduct an informal prior discussion would reduce the effectiveness of any summary action eventually taken, and the volume of business and amount of staff time that a practice of prior notice and informal discussion would involve. Quite plainly, these considerations could not be applied at large, but they could be applied on a particularized basis, agency by agency and function by function.

Similarly, the specific shape that informal discussions should take – how complete a description of its evidence and outline of its reasons the agency should provide, whether the individual may submit documentary evidence, affidavits, or a written statement in the nature of a brief, for how long a period the discussions should be permitted – will necessarily vary with the particular agency and the particular summary power involved. Resolution of these questions may have to reflect the varying degree to which informal discussions between the staff and the individual against whom summary action is contemplated may become a process of detailed negotiation into which

250

the members of the agency, who have the ultimate power of decision, will be improperly drawn.[18] Again, the seriousness of that danger and its implications for a practice of informal discussions prior to taking summary action must be assessed individually by and for each agency exercising summary authority.

The evident desirability of particularized adaptations to a norm of informal discussion prior to taking summary action indicates caution in enacting legislation. For many agencies, statutory prescription would be premature, particularly if they have not employed informal procedures of prior discussion in the past. These agencies should first – or should first be required to – devise and adopt informal discussion procedures tailored to reducing the risk of error created by the specific type of summary authority that they exercise. Experience with the varying procedures that doubtless can be devised might then supply a basis for informed legislative action.

Expedited hearings

The prolonged delay that sometimes occurs between the time an agency takes summary action and the time an adjudicatory hearing is held is one of the most egregious consequences of the failure to structure the use of summary authority. In *Gonzalez v. Freeman*,[19] for example, the secretary of agriculture's summary order debarring a businessman from eligibility for certain government contracts on account of alleged misuse of official inspection certificates remained in effect for twenty-eight months without a hearing being held. In *Aquavella v. Richardson*,[20] the secretary of health, education, and welfare's summary order suspending medicare payments to a nursing home remained in effect for eighteen months without a hearing being held. In *Beacon Federal Savings & Loan Association v. FHLBB*,[21] the board's summary order appointing a supervisory representative in charge of a banking institution remained in effect for five months before a hearing was held and fourteen months before the board adopted the hearing examiner's recommended decision.

The justification for summary action, as an exception to the general rule that an administrative agency may act against an individual only after granting him a hearing, lies in the necessity for the government to act immediately if public policy is to be enforced at all. Having invoked the exception to achieve its immediate objectives, an administrative agency in fairness has an obligation to hold an adjudicatory hearing promptly so that the adverse impact of its summary order on the individual will be confined to the shortest possible period. Congress should take steps to ensure that this obligation is met.

One step Congress could take would be to require that all federal agencies taking summary action expedite the subsequent adjudicatory hearing in every way consistent with sound administrative resolution of the issues presented. Some federal statutes already contain provisions mandating expedited administrative hearings after summary action has been taken.[22] Institutional considerations, however, may stand in the path of their effectiveness. Once an administrative agency has taken summary action, it is no longer under immediate pressure to resolve the matter in dispute. Summary action places the pressure for an expedited adjudicatory hearing on the individual; he must persuade the agency to grant him a prompt hearing, whereas the agency is probably content with the status quo. A statutory requirement of expedition may not be sufficient to alter this balance of pressures. Moreover, even when an agency is prepared to grant an expedited hearing, whether or not it is required by statute to do so, the individual will often be unable to take advantage of it because of the disabling injury that the agency's exercise of summary authority will have inflicted and the limitations that expedition imposes on the development of complex issues.

As an alternative to requiring an expedited hearing following summary action, Congress could provide that summary orders would be effective for only limited periods of time. Such provisions obviously must be tailored on an agency-by-agency, function-by-function basis. Congress has already demonstrated the capacity to make individualized judgments of this sort. Summary orders of the Securities and Exchange Commission suspending trading in a security, for example, are limited by the Securities Exchange Act to ten days' duration.[23] Summary orders of the Interstate Commerce Commission suspending proposed tariffs are effective for seven months; if the commission has not ruled upon the validity of the proposed tariffs by the expiration of that period, the carrier is free to put them into effect.[24]

By giving an agency an incentive to move forward to the completion of an adjudicatory hearing, statutory provisions limiting the effective periods of summary orders may be more effective than statutory requirements of expedition would be in reducing the incidence of prolonged delays. Limitation provisions would distribute the pressures to proceed to an adjudicatory hearing more equally between the agency and the individual, creating a common interest in expedition that might not exist if the statute simply directed an expedited hearing.

The effectiveness of limitation provisions in reducing prolonged delays might sometimes be secured, however, at the expense of other values. When an administrative agency would be unable to hold an adjudicatory hearing promptly because it lacked the staff and resources to complete its investigation and prepare its case adequately in the limited time available, a difficult choice would confront it. It might then choose not to act summarily, even though it was convinced that the public interest so required. Provisions limiting the effective periods of summary orders might thus compel an agency to make more selective use of a remedy already restricted to emergency situations.[25] Or, in order to protect the public interest for the limited period that its order could have effect, an agency might choose to act summarily anyway, inflicting injury on an individual whom it knew would not receive an opportunity to contest the merits before the order expired. Even if not prohibited by statutory provisions limiting the effective periods of summary orders, the latter course would consist uneasily with the constitutional theory allowing summary action on the condition that the individual has an adequate opportunity for a subsequent adjudicatory hearing. It also would permit the individual, when the statutory period of limitation expires, to resume the very conduct that threatened the public interest sufficiently to require summary action in the first place.

These considerations suggest that Congress should impose statutory limitations on the effective periods of summary orders – rather than limiting itself to requiring expedited hearings – only after a particularized examination of the agency and function involved. Congress need not, of course, prescribe the specific period of limitation in order to adopt the principle that particular summary orders should be of limited duration. But it should at least require the agencies to provide by rule for reasonable but specific periods of limitation, just as some agencies, for example, have promulgated rules requiring hearing examiners to file their initial decisions within a specified number of days after the record is completed. Engaging the responsibility of agencies on matters of this kind is almost always a wise and practical course.

Judicial review

In addition to considering the four methods of structuring the use of summary action just discussed, Congress should also consider whether judicial review would enhance the fairness of an agency's performance in acting summarily.

Only rarely has Congress exercised its power to permit or preclude judicial review of summary administrative action.[26] The absence from most statutes of a clear expression of Congress's intention has compelled the courts to decide the question of the availability of judicial review for themselves, to strike a careful balance between the need for adequate protection of individual interests and the need for effective and responsible administrative action. In so doing, they have sought guidance from various sources and considerations, including the common law presumption of the reviewability of administrative action; inferences, drawn from the statutory scheme, of a legislative intention to preclude judicial review; the relevant provisions of the Administrative Procedure Act; the appropriateness of the issues for judicial resolution; the seriousness of the impact of the agency's action on the individual; and the disruption and interference that judicial review would create in the administrative process.[27]

Because Congress does have the power to legislate in this area, however, the fact that courts have heretofore played a prominent role in determining the availability of judicial review does not conclude the matter. Congress has an independent obligation to consider the role that judicial review should play in ensuring that summary authority is fairly exercised.

The specific contexts in which summary powers are exercised are so various that a single, undifferentiated response – for example, enactment of a statute of general application or amendment of the Administrative Procedure Act to permit or preclude judicial review of all summary action – would be impractical. Permitting judicial review of all summary action might interfere slightly, if at all, with some administrative processes but seriously disrupt others; precluding any judicial review might expose individuals to injuries harsh and senseless in some contexts but quite tolerable in others. Legislative decisions concerning judicial review of summary action can be made wisely only on an agency-by-agency, function-by-function basis.

In making these decisions, Congress should take into account not only the factors that courts have considered relevant in determining the availability of judicial review but also other considerations that, although not often expressed in judicial opinions, have probably influenced the results courts have reached. First among these is the confidence that Congress has in an agency's competence and sensitivity when the agency exercises summary authority. If Congress is uncertain about a particular agency's capacity to exercise summary authority fairly, it should consider whether the availability of judicial review would motivate the agency to a higher standard of performance. Second, the probable effectiveness of judicial review in preventing unnecessary injury to an individual against whom summary action has been taken must be weighed realistically when evaluating the advisability of providing for review of particular types of summary action. Judicial review might not be effective, for example, where summary action wrongfully inflicts irremediable damage, or where the court gives great deference to administrative expertise, as it often does in scientific and technical areas. If judicial review would not be effective in protecting the individual, it might as well be precluded and judicial resources conserved.

There is much to be said for leaving the entire question of judicial review of summary action to the courts, particularly if agencies adopt effective administrative procedures for protecting the individual. Certain decisions of the Supreme Court have focused on the role of summary action and the timing of judicial review in our legal system,[28] stimulating reconsideration of problems the relevant dimensions of which may not yet have fully been perceived. Codification of existing principles of judicial review of summary action might prematurely restrict the courts' resourcefulness in fashioning wise solutions to these problems. In addition, the courts are probably better situated institutionally than Congress to appreciate the factors relevant to a decision to review specific forms of summary action and to see those factors in the larger context of social values that a system of judicial review is designed to serve.

Structuring the use of informal administrative action in order to increase its fairness is one of the great challenges facing those who would seek to enhance the legitimacy of the contemporary administrative process. Many of the procedures commonly used to structure formal administrative processes have an appropriate application to informal administrative processes, as the discussion of summary action suggests.

But none of these procedures, including statutory standards, rules and reasons, prior informal discussions, expedited hearings, and judicial review, will be sufficient, finally, to prevent abuses in the exercise of informal administrative authority. Of course these procedures will sometimes prevent an administrative agency from carrying out unwise decisions, but they cannot ensure that agency decisions to act informally will invariably be made wisely. Conscientious administrators who appreciate the responsibilities of their power will be likely to serve that ideal better than any set of administrative procedures. "Constitute government how you please," wrote Edmund Burke, "infinitely the greater part of it must depend upon . . . the prudence and uprightness of ministers of state."[29]

255

Conclusion

20

The challenge of administrative legitimacy

> The mere existence of a real and substantial doubt as to the legitimacy of a government must surely enfeeble it and strip it of moral force, even while the lack of anything better keeps it going a while longer.
>
> Charles L. Black, Jr., *The People and the Court* (1960)

Although the roots of the American administrative process reach back to the First Congress of the United States, recognition of the profound implications that the growth of the administrative process has had for the nation's legal and political institutions came remarkably late. The significance of administrative law in the United States emerged clearly only when three remarkable scholars – Frank Goodnow at Columbia, Ernst Freund at Chicago, and Felix Frankfurter at Harvard – began to publish their pioneering work in the early decades of the twentieth century. That work laid the foundation for a systematic exploration of the administrative process as a distinctive development in American law.

Perhaps the nineteenth century's delay in recognizing the implications of administrative law reflected a reluctance to acknowledge the apparently anomalous fact that the administrative process had become so important in a nation whose Constitution made no reference to it. But the American reluctance to acknowledge the emerging significance of administrative law must have reflected other factors as well because it ran parallel historically to the experience in Great Britain, a nation without a written constitution. There, Dicey denied as late as 1915 that a system of administrative law existed in either England or the United States, even though Maitland, lecturing in 1887–88, had reported that half the cases decided by the Queen's Bench Division involved the rules of administrative law.[1]

Such denials became increasingly untenable in the years immediately after Dicey wrote, particularly during the administration of Franklin D.

Roosevelt, when reliance upon the administrative process as a principal instrumentality for the achievement of national policies increased extensively. In the decades since the New Deal, what Professor Frankfurter described in 1932 as "a vast congeries of agencies"[2] has grown apace with the enlarged responsibilities of modern government. In virtually every relevant respect, the administrative has become a fourth branch of government, comparable in the scope of its authority and the impact of its decision making to the three more familiar constitutional branches.

The growth of the administrative process has raised troubling questions concerning its implications for the character of American democracy, the nature of American justice, and the quality of American life. These questions have almost always been based upon the premise that there is a crisis in the administrative process. That successive generations of lawyers, judges, political scientists, and citizens have failed to still the recurrent sense of crisis attending the federal administrative process, even though each has made important efforts to do so, suggests that the sources of the sense of crisis are more fundamental than the dominant concerns of any particular historical moment would indicate.

The sense of crisis attending the administrative process has, by its persistence, impaired the legitimacy of the federal administrative agencies. Because institutional legitimacy is an essential condition for institutional effectiveness, the sources of the recurrent sense of crisis must be understood if the administrative process is to fulfill the promise that has animated the nation's repeated decisions to rely upon it for the achievement of public purposes.

The recurrent sense of crisis attending the federal administrative process derives from many factors. Perhaps the most prominent is the fact that administrative agencies do not conform to three of the most powerful conceptions of the American imagination: the inviolability of the constitutional prescription of a separation of governmental powers, the importance of the judicial norm of trial-type hearings for the fair determination of disputed questions, and the insistence that policy-making officials of government be directly accountable to the people through political and electoral processes. In each of these respects, the legitimacy of the administrative process has been called into question unfairly.

The belief that the administrative agencies of the federal government are not entirely legitimate because they do not conform to the constitutional requirement of the separation of powers is misguided. The Constitution requires that the legislative, executive, and judicial powers be separated to the extent necessary to prevent the emergence of tyranny from the concentration of too much power in a single person or institution. But the lines that the Framers drew between the exercise of the respective powers are not rigid ones, and in a number of notable instances the Constitution permits one branch of government to participate in functions assigned primarily to another branch. The conventional understanding of the separation of powers that informs the American imaginations is simplistic by comparison to the flexible and pragmatic vision that Madison and his contemporaries expressed in the Constitution itself.

The procedural departures that the administrative process makes from judicial norms have also impaired the legitimacy of administrative regulation, primarily because of the uncritical faith that Americans have traditionally placed in trial-type proceedings of the kind employed by the courts. Yet those departures have resulted in a system of fact finding and decision making that, for many substantive issues, is better suited to the attainment of justice than trial-type proceedings would be. In a period when the efficacy of adversary hearings is being widely questioned, increasing adoption of the less formal methods that characterize the administrative process seems likely. Perhaps that development will finally persuade Americans of what Europeans learned long ago, that the fair and expeditious resolution of disputed questions can sometimes be achieved better by procedural methods that depart from judicial norms.

The claim that administrative agencies lack a democratic legitimacy because they are not directly accountable to the people through the political process is similarly dubious. Although many administrative agencies are independent of the political branches in theory, they are subject in fact to a considerable measure of control and influence by the President and the Congress. Moreover, the circumstance that administrative agencies are not majoritarian in character does not distinguish them from some of the most significant and necessary institutions in our governmental system, institutions whose legitimacy is seldom questioned on that account. Indeed, a considerable part of the genius of American government lies in the fact that public policy has always been formed by a complicated, Madisonian interplay between institutions of a majoritarian character and those of a non-majoritarian character.

The legitimacy of the administrative process cannot turn, then, upon its nonconformity to a simplistic version of the separation of powers, the departures it makes from judicial norms, or the formal independence of many agencies from direct political accountability. Rather, it must be tested pragmatically, by the responsiveness of administrative institutions to the most fundamental principles of a democratic society and by the degree to which administrative institutions meet the nation's highest aspirations for justice and effective government.

Beyond the three factors just discussed, the recurrent sense of crisis attending the administrative process derives from two related public attitudes: skepticism of administrative expertise and concern with bureaucratization. There is an undoubted element of validity in both attitudes. Administrative expertise, burdened with unrealistic expectations, has not been translated into sound public policy as frequently as the New Deal's idealized conception of its role anticipated. And administrative bureaucracy, as Weber foresaw and feared, has often been impersonal, coercive, and dehumanizing in its manner of dealing with the lives and fortunes of those it was created to serve. These public attitudes toward expertise and bureaucracy have been important factors in impairing the legitimacy of the administrative process.

Yet the concerns that these attitudes express are hardly limited in their application to the federal administrative process. Public skepticism of administrative expertise is part of a larger loss of faith in many traditional sources of public and social authority. And public concern with bureaucratization is part of a larger pattern of social uneasiness over the impact upon American life of large organizations, within both the public and private sectors. The administrative agencies of the federal government, in short, are not the exclusive focus of these concerns; they are merely prominent examples of wider social trends that Americans understandably find disturbing.

Reliance upon administrative expertise and administrative bureaucracy is likely to remain essential to the difficult and imperfect enterprise of governing a continental nation of two hundred million people. The important task facing those concerned with this prospect is to devise means of subjecting administrative expertise to democratic and generalist control and of limiting the undesirable influences of bureaucracy upon the quality of American life.

Finally, the recurrent sense of crisis attending the federal administrative process reflects our society's basic ambivalence toward the idea of economic regulation. During the years when the New Deal was enlarging the role of administrative agencies as instrumentalities of modern government, the people of the United States shared a common commitment to the need for national recovery and economic growth. The social consensus that supported that commitment was sufficiently pervasive that philosophical differences over governmental intervention in the economy were, for the moment, put to the side.

But the reality of those differences as matters of public policy and democratic strategy inevitably became more pronounced as society's shared objectives of national recovery and economic growth were achieved. It now seems clear that the New Deal's apparent success in achieving economic recovery by placing extensive reliance upon the administrative process merely served temporarily to obscure the fact that Americans have not developed a coherent ideology of when, and to what extent, governmental intervention in the economy is appropriate. To this day the United States has failed to resolve its basic ambivalence toward the concept of governmental regulation of economic activity.

The persistence of that ambivalence has had adverse consequences for the legitimacy of the administrative process. When the propriety of economic regulation is subject to philosophical as well as pragmatic question, the legitimacy of the administrative institutions created by Congress to perform specific regulatory responsibilities will also be open to challenges of the same fundamental kind.

The ambivalence that has frustrated society's attempts to formulate a coherent ideology of governmental intervention in the economy has also caused Congress to legislate economic regulation in evasive generalities, delegating to the respective administrative agencies the essential tasks of resolving the fundamental political and social questions that it has not been able to resolve itself. The freedom of Congress to delegate legislative power without instructive standards has been nurtured by the Supreme Court's permissive interpretation of the doctrine of the delegation of legislative power.

That most administrative agencies have finally been unable to resolve satisfactorily questions that Congress itself could not resolve is hardly surprising. Nevertheless, the failures of the administrative agencies to develop coherent policies in the course of their regulatory activities has been a continuing source of criticism. That criticism has had distressing implications for the legitimacy and effectiveness of the administrative process. It is important to recognize that these implications are a result of society's ambivalence toward economic regulation and of the delegation doctrine that permits Congress to make the administrative process the focus of that ambivalence; they are not the result of any inherent qualities of the administrative process itself.

Conclusion

The sources of the recurrent sense of crisis attending the federal administrative process thus prove, upon analysis, to be less forceful than at first they seem. Many are based upon perceptions that are misconceived as conclusions of historical fact or misinformed as judgments of administrative practice. Although there is a measure of validity in some of these perceptions, the cumulative effect is far from sufficient to support an indictment of the legitimacy of the administrative process.

Still a further difficulty with the assertion that there is a crisis in the administrative process arises from the fact that it is usually phrased in indiscriminately general terms. The performance of the federal administrative agencies varies so widely that generalizations of that kind are quite impossible. Some agencies are highly respected for their standard of performance; others are generally regarded as chronic failures.

These differences in the quality of agency performance are attributable to many factors, of which perhaps the most decisive is the strength of the public's support for an agency's substantive responsibilities. When public support for an agency's statutory mandate is strong, the agency is likely to perform effectively, as the history of the Securities and Exchange Commission indicates. But when public support for an agency's substantive mission is ambivalent, the agency is likely to perform much less effectively, as the experience of the Equal Employment Opportunity Commission suggests. In short, there are limits to the effective uses of the administrative process, and these limits tend to coincide with the bounds of the social consensus on an agency's statutory responsibilities. When society does not respect these limits – when it requires administrative agencies to achieve more than public opinion is ready to support unambivalently – it condemns agencies to undertake tasks beyond their institutional capacity to perform effectively.

Indiscriminately general assertions that there is a crisis in the administrative process obscure the facts that variations in agency performance do exist and that there are limits to the effective uses of the administrative process. It would be more accurate, and less destructive of the legitimacy of the administrative process as a whole, to speak of failures in the performance of particular agencies. And it would be more useful, in inquiring into the factors that account for these failures, to consider the possibility that, here as elsewhere, the fault may lie not in the stars but in ourselves.

But however much reformers deride the administrative process for its failures of effectiveness, political accountability, and fairness, they seem invariably to fall back upon administrative regulation as the institutional method for implementing their own programs of reform. The nation's repeated reliance upon administrative agencies to meet the emerging problems of successive generations provides a historical basis for believing that the United States is likely to have more, rather than less, administrative regulation in the future. This likelihood heightens the importance of understanding the fundamental sources of the recurrent sense of crisis attending the federal administrative process. It also lends urgency to the related task of constructing a theory of legitimacy for the role of the administrative process in modern government.

It was Weber who described most powerfully the impulse that motivates ordinary citizens to seek a measure of legitimacy in the state's power to coerce them. He regarded that impulse as a universal human characteristic: the need to find meaning and justification in the social and political arrangements by which daily life is authoritatively bound. The quest for understanding the implications of the American administrative process is finally a search for the sources and definition of its legitimacy.

The search is more than conventionally difficult because administrative agencies can point to neither of the two principal methods by which governmental power is typically legitimated in a democracy, either creation by the Constitution or exercise by officials directly accountable to the people through the political process. Yet neither method is invariably exclusive, and efforts to legitimate the exercise of administrative power properly have stressed other factors as well, including the need for new institutional forms of authority and decision making to complement the legislature and the courts, the responsiveness of the administrative process to democratic constraints, the opportunities that administrative agencies permit for effective public participation, and the availability of judicial review.

The relationship of procedural fairness to the integrity of governmental institutions has, of course, long been recognized. But too little attention has been given to the ways in which the quality of administrative justice supplies an important source of administrative legitimacy. The procedural rules by which a government agency reaches substantive decisions are significant evidences of the nature of its commitment to protecting individual rights and attaining just results. For these reasons, the desire and capacity of government to devise fair administrative procedures for the discharge of its decision-making responsibilities is the essence of democratic practice.

Fair administrative procedure most often results when Congress and the administrative agencies share with the courts the responsibility for creating it. The Administrative Procedure Act has been successful in achieving greater fairness in the formal processes of adjudication and rule making because Congress, in drafting its central provisions, struck a workable balance between prescribing fundamental principles of fair procedure and permitting administrative agencies the freedom to adapt these principles to the disparate patterns of their regulatory responsibilities. The case study of the Office of Foreign Direct Investments suggests the creative possibilities inherent in that balance.

An opportunity of the character that the draftsmen of the Administrative Procedure Act grasped in 1946 now confronts those concerned with the fairness of the informal, discretionary processes of administrative agencies. Although the importance of informal agency action has been recognized for a generation, only recently have students of the administrative process begun to suggest systematic approaches to understanding its nature. The study of the procedures by which a large number of administrative agencies and the courts have sought to govern the exercise of summary authority suggests that society can limit the risks of unfairness associated with discretionary administrative action without sacrificing the special competence to act effectively that informal procedures typically permit.

The task of devising an effective theory of the legitimacy of the administrative process is one of the most important challenges facing those concerned with American administrative law and institutions. That challenge requires that the recurrent sense of crisis attending the federal administrative process be examined candidly, and that effective administrative procedures be devised, for formal and informal proceedings, that give promise of being fair, efficient, and responsive to democratic values and constitutional restraints.

As the role of the administrative process in American government grows in scope and authority, systematic reconsideration of administrative procedure becomes a philosophic and practical necessity. One can hope, as Professor Frankfurter wrote of his generation's quest to understand the administrative process, that "efforts at systematization may themselves be creative forces."[3]

Excerpts from the Administrative Procedure Act

60 Stat. 237 (1946), as amended by 80 Stat. 378 (1966), as amended by 81 Stat. 54 (1967), 88 Stat. 1561, 88 Stat. 1897 (1974), 89 Stat. 1057 (1975), 90 Stat. 1241, 90 Stat. 2721 (1976), 5 U.S.C. §§ 551-59, 701-06, 1305, 3105, 3344, 5362, 7521. [Freedom of Information Act, P.L. 93-502, 88 Stat. 1561 (§ 552); Privacy Act of 1974, P.L. 93-579, 88 Stat. 1897 (§ 552a); and Government in the Sunshine Act, P.L. 94-409, 90 Stat. 1241 (§ 552b) have been omitted.]

§ 551. Definitions

For the purpose of this subchapter—

(1) "agency" means each authority of the Government of the United States, whether or not it is within or subject to review by another agency, but does not include—

(A) the Congress;

(B) the courts of the United States;

(C) the governments of the territories or possessions of the United States;

(D) the government of the District of Columbia;

or except as to the requirements of section 552 of this title—

(E) agencies composed of representatives of the parties or of representatives of organizations of the parties to the disputes determined by them;

(F) courts martial and military commissions;

(G) military authority exercised in the field in time of war or in occupied territory; or

(H) functions conferred by sections 1738, 1739, 1743, and 1744 of title 12; chapter 2 of title 41; or sections 1622, 1884, 1891-1902, and former section 1641(b) (2), of title 50, appendix;

(2) "person" includes an individual, partnership, corporation, association, or public or private organization other than an agency;

(3) "party" includes a person or agency named or admitted as a party, or properly seeking and entitled as of right to be admitted as a party, in an agency proceeding, and a person or agency admitted by an agency as a party for limited purposes;

(4) "rule" means the whole or a part of an agency statement of general or particular applicability and future effect designed to implement, interpret, or prescribe law or policy or describing the organization, procedure, or practice requirements of an

agency and includes the approval or prescription for the future of rates, wages, corporate or financial structures or reorganization thereof, prices, facilities, appliances, services or allowances therefor or of valuations, costs, or accounting, or practices bearing on any of the foregoing;

(5) "rule making" means agency process for formulating, amending, or repealing a rule;

(6) "order" means the whole or a part of a final disposition, whether affirmative, negative, injunctive, or declaratory in form, of an agency in a matter other than rule making but including licensing;

(7) "adjudication" means agency process for the formulation of an order;

(8) "license" includes the whole or a part of an agency permit, certificate, approval, registration, charter, membership, statutory exemption or other form of permission;

(9) "licensing" includes agency process respecting the grant, renewal, denial, revocation, suspension, annulment, withdrawal, limitation, amendment, modification, or conditioning of a license;

(10) "sanction" includes the whole or a part of an agency—

(A) prohibition, requirement, limitation, or other condition affecting the freedom of a person;

(B) withholding of relief;

(C) imposition of penalty or fine;

(D) destruction, taking, seizure, or withholding of property;

(E) assessment of damages, reimbursement, restitution, compensation, costs, charges, or fees;

(F) requirement, revocation, or suspension of a license; or

(G) taking other compulsory restrictive action;

(11) "relief" includes the whole or a part of an agency—

(A) grant of money, assistance, license, authority, exemption, exception, privilege, or remedy;

(B) recognition of a claim, right, immunity, privilege, exemption, or exception; or

(C) taking of other action on the application or petition of, and beneficial to, a person;

(12) "agency proceeding" means an agency process as defined by paragraphs (5), (7), and (9) of this section;

(13) "agency action" includes the whole or a part of an agency rule, order, license, sanction, relief, or the equivalent or denial thereof, or failure to act; and

(14) "ex parte communication" means an oral or written communication not on the public record with respect to which reasonable prior notice to all parties is not given, but it shall not include requests for status reports on any matter or proceeding covered by this subchapter.

§ 553. Rule making

(a) This section applies, according to the provisions thereof, except to the extent that there is involved—

(1) a military or foreign affairs function of the United States; or

(2) a matter relating to agency management or personnel or to public property, loans, grants, benefits, or contracts.

(b) General notice of proposed rule making shall be published in the Federal Register, unless persons subject thereto are named and either personally served or otherwise have actual notice thereof in accordance with law. The notice shall include—

(1) a statement of the time, place, and nature of public rule making proceedings;

(2) reference to the legal authority under which the rule is proposed; and

(3) either the terms or substance of the proposed rule or a description of the subjects and issues involved.

Except when notice or hearing is required by statute, this subsection does not apply—

(A) to interpretative rules, general statements of policy, or rules of agency organization, procedure, or practice; or

(B) when the agency for good cause finds (and incorporates the finding and a brief statement of reasons therefor in the rules issued) that notice and public procedure thereon are impracticable, unnecessary, or contrary to the public interest.

(c) After notice required by this section, the agency shall give interested persons an opportunity to participate in the rule making through submission of written data, views, or arguments with or without opportunity for oral presentation. After consideration of the relevant matter presented, the agency shall incorporate in the rules adopted a concise general statement of their basis and purpose. When rules are required by statute to be made on the record after opportunity for an agency hearing, sections 556 and 557 of this title apply instead of this subsection.

(d) The required publication or service of a substantive rule shall be made not less than 30 days before its effective date, except—

(1) a substantive rule which grants or recognizes an exemption or relieves a restriction;

(2) interpretative rules and statements of policy; or

(3) as otherwise provided by the agency for good cause found and published with the rule.

(e) Each agency shall give an interested person the right to petition for the issuance, amendment, or repeal of a rule.

§ 554. Adjudications

(a) This section applies, according to the provisions thereof, in every case of adjudication required by statute to be determined on the record after opportunity for an agency hearing, except to the extent that there is involved—

(1) a matter subject to a subsequent trial of the law and the facts de novo in a court;

(2) the selection or tenure of an employee, except a hearing examiner appointed under section 3105 of this title;

(3) proceedings in which decisions rest solely on inspections, tests, or elections;

(4) the conduct of military or foreign affairs functions;

(5) cases in which an agency is acting as an agent for a court; or

(6) the certification of worker representatives.

(b) Persons entitled to notice of an agency hearing shall be timely informed of—

(1) the time, place, and nature of the hearing;

(2) the legal authority and jurisdiction under which the hearing is to be held; and

(3) the matters of fact and law asserted.

When private persons are the moving parties, other parties to the proceeding shall give prompt notice of issues controverted in fact or law; and in other instances agencies may by rule require responsive pleading. In fixing the time and place for hearings, due regard shall be had for the convenience and necessity of the parties or their representatives.

(c) The agency shall give all interested parties opportunity for—

(1) the submission and consideration of facts, arguments, offers of settlement, or proposals of adjustment when time, the nature of the proceeding, and the public interest permit; and

(2) to the extent that the parties are unable so to determine a controversy by consent, hearing and decision on notice and in accordance with sections 556 and 557 of this title.

(d) The employee who presides at the reception of evidence pursuant to section 556 of this title shall make the recommended decision or initial decision required by section 557 of this title, unless he becomes unavailable to the agency. Except to the extent required for the disposition of ex parte matters as authorized by law, such an employee may not—

(1) consult a person or party on a fact in issue, unless on notice and opportunity for all parties to participate; or

(2) be responsible to or subject to the supervision or direction of an employee or agent engaged in the performance of investigative or prosecuting functions for an agency.

An employee or agent engaged in the performance of investigative or prosecuting functions for an agency in a case may not, in that or a factually related case, participate or advise in the decision, recommended decision, or agency review pursuant to section 557 of this title, except as witness or counsel in public proceedings. This subsection does not apply—

(A) in determining applications for initial licenses;

(B) to proceedings involving the validity or application of rates, facilities, or practices of public utilities or carriers; or

(C) to the agency or a member or members of the body comprising the agency.

(e) The agency, with like effect as in the case of other orders, and in its sound discretion, may issue a declaratory order to terminate a controversy or remove uncertainty.

§ 555. Ancillary matters

(a) This section applies, according to the provisions thereof, except as otherwise provided by this subchapter.

(b) A person compelled to appear in person before an agency or representative thereof is entitled to be accompanied, represented, and advised by counsel or, if permitted by the agency, by other qualified representative. A party is entitled to appear in person or by or with counsel or other duly qualified representative in an agency proceeding. So far as the orderly conduct of public business permits, an interested person may appear before an agency or its responsible employees for the presentation, adjustment, or determination of an issue, request, or controversy in a proceeding, whether interlocutory, summary, or otherwise, or in connection with an agency function. With due regard for the convenience and necessity of the parties or their representatives and within a reasonable time, each agency shall proceed to conclude a matter presented to it. This subsection does not grant or deny a person who is not a lawyer the right to appear for or represent others before an agency or in an agency proceeding.

(c) Process, requirement of a report, inspection, or other investigative act or demand may not be issued, made, or enforced except as authorized by law. A person compelled to submit data or evidence is entitled to retain or, on payment of lawfully prescribed costs, procure a copy or transcript thereof, except that in a nonpublic investigatory proceeding the witness may for good cause be limited to inspection of the official transcript of his testimony.

(d) Agency subpenas authorized by law shall be issued to a party on request and, when required by rules of procedure, on a statement or showing of general relevance and reasonable scope of the evidence sought. On contest, the court shall sustain the subpena or similar process or demand to the extent that it is found to be in accordance with law. In a proceeding for enforcement, the court shall issue an order requiring the appearance of the witness or the production of the evidence or data within a reasonable time under penalty of punishment for contempt in cases of contumacious failure to comply.

(e) Prompt notice shall be given of the denial in whole or in part of a written application, petition, or other request of an interested person made in connection with any agency proceeding. Except in affirming a prior denial or when the denial is self-explanatory, the notice shall be accompanied by a brief statement of the grounds for denial.

§ 556. Hearings; presiding employees; powers and duties; burden of proof; evidence; record as basis of decision

(a) This section applies, according to the provisions thereof, to hearings required by section 553 or 554 of this title to be conducted in accordance with this section.

(b) There shall preside at the taking of evidence—

    (1) the agency;

    (2) one or more members of the body which comprises the agency; or

    (3) one or more hearing examiners appointed under section 3105 of this title.

This subchapter does not supersede the conduct of specified classes of proceedings, in whole or in part, by or before boards or other employees specially provided for by or designated under statute. The functions of presiding employees and of employees participating in decisions in accordance with section 557 of this title shall be conducted in an impartial manner. A presiding or participating employee may at any time disqualify himself. On the filing in good faith of a timely and sufficient affidavit of personal bias or other disqualification of a presiding or participating employee, the agency shall determine the matters as a part of the record and decision in the case.

(c) Subject to published rules of the agency and within its powers, employees presiding at hearings may—

(1) administer oaths and affirmations;

(2) issue subpenas authorized by law;

(3) rule on offers of proof and receive relevant evidence;

(4) take depositions or have depositions taken when the ends of justice would be served;

(5) regulate the course of the hearing;

(6) hold conferences for the settlement or simplification of the issues by consent of the parties;

(7) dispose of procedural requests or similar matters;

(8) make or recommend decisions in accordance with section 557 of this title; and

(9) take other action authorized by agency rule consistent with this subchapter.

(d) Except as otherwise provided by statute, the proponent of a rule or order has the burden of proof. Any oral or documentary evidence may be received, but the agency as a matter of policy shall provide for the exclusion of irrelevant, immaterial, or unduly repetitious evidence. A sanction may not be imposed or rule or order issued except on consideration of the whole record or those parts thereof cited by a party and supported by and in accordance with the reliable, probative, and substantial evidence. The agency may, to the extent consistent with the interests of justice and the policy of the underlying statutes administered by the agency, consider a violation of section 557(d) of this title sufficient grounds for a decision adverse to a party who has knowingly committed such violation or knowingly caused such violation to occur. A party is entitled to present his case or defense by oral or documentary evidence, to submit rebuttal evidence, and to conduct such cross-examination as may be required for a full and true disclosure of the facts. In rule making or determining claims for money or benefits or applications for initial licenses an agency may, when a party will not be prejudiced thereby, adopt procedures for the submission of all or part of the evidence in written form.

(e) The transcript of testimony and exhibits, together with all papers and requests filed in the proceeding, constitutes the exclusive record for decision in accordance with section 557 of this title and, on payment of lawfully prescribed costs, shall be made available to the parties. When an agency decision rests on official notice of a material fact not appearing in the evidence in the record, a party is entitled, on timely request, to an opportunity to show the contrary.

§ 557. Initial decisions; conclusiveness; review by agency; submissions by parties; contents of decisions; record

(a) This section applies, according to the provisions thereof, when a hearing is requried to be conducted in accordance with section 556 of this title.

(b) When the agency did not preside at the reception of the evidence, the presiding employee or, in cases not subject to section 554(d) of this title, an employee qualified to preside at hearings pursuant to section 556 of this title, shall initially decide the case unless the agency requires, either in specific cases or by general rule, the entire record to be certified to it for decision. When the presiding employee makes an initial decision, that decision then becomes the decision of the agency without further proceedings unless there is an appeal to, or review on motion of, the agency within time provided by rule. On appeal from or review of the initial decision, the agency has all the powers which it would have in making the initial decision except as it may limit the issues on notice or by rule. When the agency makes the decision without having presided at the reception of the evidence, the presiding employee or an employee qualified to preside at hearings pursuant to section 556 of this title shall first recommend a decision, except that in rule making or determining application for initial licenses—

(1) instead thereof the agency may issue a tentative decision or one of its responsible employees may recommend a decision; or

(2) this procedure may be omitted in a case in which the agency finds on the record that due and timely execution of its functions imperatively and unavoidably so requires.

(c) Before a recommended, initial, or tentative decision, or a decision on agency review of the decision of subordinate employees, the parties are entitled to a reasonable opportunity to submit for the consideration of the employees participating in the decisions—

(1) proposed findings and conclusions; or

(2) exceptions to the decisions or recommended decisions of subordinate employees or to tentative agency decisions; and

(3) supporting reasons for the exceptions or proposed findings or conclusions.
The record shall show the ruling on each finding, conclusion, or exception presented. All decisions, including initial, recommended, and tentative decisions, are a part of the record and shall include a statement of—

(A) findings and conclusions, and the reasons or basis therefor, on all the material issues of fact, law, or discretion presented on the record; and

(B) the appropriate rule, order, sanction, relief, or denial thereof.

(d)(1) In any agency proceeding which is subject to subsection (a) of this section, except to the extent required for the disposition of ex parte matters as authorized by law—

(A) no interested person outside the agency shall make or knowingly cause to be made to any member of the body comprising the agency, administrative law judge, or other employee who is or may reasonably be expected to be involved in the decisional process of the proceeding, an ex parte communication relevant to the merits of the proceeding;

(B) no member of the body comprising the agency, administrative law judge, or other employee who is or may reasonably be expected to be involved in the decisional process of the proceeding, shall make or knowingly cause to be made to any interested person outside the agency an ex parte communication relevant to the merits of the proceeding;

(C) a member of the body comprising the agency, administrative law judge, or other employee who is or may reasonably be expected to be involved in the decisional process of such proceeding who receives, or who makes or knowingly causes to be made, a communication prohibited by this subsection shall place on the public record of the proceeding: (i) all such written communications; (ii) memoranda stating the substance of all such oral communications; and (iii) all written responses, and memoranda stating the substance of all oral responses, to the materials described in clauses (i) and (ii) of this subparagraph;

(D) upon receipt of a communication knowingly made or knowingly caused to be made by a party in violation of this subsection, the agency, administrative law judge, or other employee presiding at the hearing may, to the extent consistent with the interests of justice and the policy of the underlying statutes, require the party to show cause why his claim or interest in the proceeding should not be dismissed, denied, disregarded, or otherwise adversely affected on account of such violation; and

(E) the prohibitions of this subsection shall apply beginning at such time as the agency may designate, but in no case shall they begin to apply later than the time at which a proceeding is noticed for hearing unless the person responsible for the communication has knowledge that it will be noticed, in which case the prohibitions shall apply beginning at the time of his acquisition of such knowledge.

(2) This subsection does not constitute authority to withhold information from Congress.

§ 558. Imposition of sanctions; determination of applications for licenses; suspension, revocation, and expiration of licenses

(a) This section applies, according to the provisions thereof, to the exercise of a power or authority.

(b) A sanction may not be imposed or a substantive rule or order issued except within jurisdiction delegated to the agency and as authorized by law.

(c) When application is made for a license required by law, the agency, with due regard for the rights and privileges of all the interested parties or adversely affected persons and within a reasonable time, shall set and complete proceedings required to be conducted in accordance with sections 556 and 557 of this title or other proceedings required by law and shall make its decision. Except in cases of willfulness or those in which public health, interest, or safety requires otherwise, the withdrawal, suspension, revocation, or annulment of a license is lawful only if, before the institution of agency proceedings therefor, the licensee has been given—

(1) notice by the agency in writing of the facts or conduct which may warrant the action; and

(2) opportunity to demonstrate or achieve compliance with all lawful requirements.

When the licensee has made timely and sufficient application for a renewal or a new license in accordance with agency rules, a license with reference to an activity of a continuing nature does not expire until the application has been finally determined by the agency.

§ 559. Effect on other laws; effect of subsequent statute

This subchapter, chapter 7, and sections 1305, 3105, 3344, 4301(2)(E), 5362, and 7521 of this title, and the provisions of section 5335(a)(B) of this title that relate to hearing examiners, do not limit or repeal additional requirements imposed by statute or otherwise recognized by law. Except as otherwise required by law, requirements or privileges relating to evidence or procedure apply equally to agencies and persons. Each agency is granted the authority necessary to comply with the requirements of this subchapter through the issuance of rules or otherwise. Subsequent statute may not be held to supersede or modify this subchapter, chapter 7, sections 1305, 3105, 3344, 4301(2)(E), 5362, or 7521, or the provisions of section 5335(a)(B) of this title that relate to hearing examiners, except to the extent that it does so expressly.

§ 701. Application; definitions

(a) This chapter applies, according to the provisions thereof, except to the extent that—

(1) statutes preclude judicial review; or

(2) agency action is committed to agency discretion by law.

(b) For the purpose of this chapter—

(1) "agency" means each authority of the Government of the United States, whether or not it is within or subject to review by another agency, but does not include—

(A) the Congress;

(B) the courts of the United States;

(C) the governments of the territories or possessions of the United States;

(D) the government of the District of Columbia;

(E) agencies composed of representatives of the parties or of representatives of organizations of the parties to the disputes determined by them;

(F) courts martial and military commissions;

(G) military authority exercised in the field in time of war or in occupied territory; or

(H) functions conferred by sections 1738, 1739, 1743, and 1744 of title 12; chapter 2 of title 41; or sections 1622, 1884, 1891–1902, and former section 1641(b)(2), of title 50, appendix; and

(2) "person", "rule", "order", "license", "sanction", "relief", and "agency action" have the meanings given them by section 551 of this title.

§ 702. Right of review

A person suffering legal wrong because of agency action, or adversely affected or aggrieved by agency action within the meaning of a relevant statute, is entitled to judicial review thereof. An action in a court of the United States seeking relief other than money damages and stating a claim that an agency or an officer or employee thereof acted or failed to act in an official capacity or under color of legal authority shall not be dismissed nor relief therein be denied on the ground that it is against the

United States or that the United States is an indispensable party. The United States may be named as a defendant in any such action, and a judgment or decree may be entered against the United States: *Provided*, That any mandatory or injunctive decree shall specify the Federal officer or officers (by name or by title), and their successors in office, personally responsible for compliance. Nothing herein (1) affects other limitations on judicial review or the power or duty of the court to dismiss any action or deny relief on any other appropriate legal or equitable ground; or (2) confers authority to grant relief if any other statute that grants consent to suit expressly or impliedly forbids the relief which is sought.

§ 703. Form and venue of proceeding

The form of proceeding for judicial review is the special statutory review proceeding relevant to the subject matter in a court specified by statute or, in the absence or inadequacy thereof, any applicable form of legal action, including actions for declaratory judgments or writs of prohibitory or mandatory injunction or habeas corpus, in a court of competent jurisdiction. If no special statutory review proceeding is applicable, the action for judicial review may be brought against the United States, the agency by its official title, or the appropriate officer. Except to the extent that prior, adequate, and exclusive opportunity for judicial review is provided by law, agency action is subject to judicial review in civil or criminal proceedings for judicial enforcement.

§ 704. Actions reviewable

Agency action made reviewable by statute and final agency action for which there is no other adequate remedy in a court are subject to judicial review. A preliminary, procedural, or intermediate agency action or ruling not direcly reviewable is subject to review on the review of the final agency action. Except as otherwise expressly required by statute, agency action otherwise final is final for the purposes of this section whether or not there has been presented or determined an application for a declaratory order, for any form of reconsideration, or, unless the agency otherwise requires by rule and provides that the action meanwhile is inoperative, for an appeal to superior agency authority.

§ 705. Relief pending review

When an agency finds that justice so requires, it may postpone the effective date of action taken by it, pending judicial review. On such conditions as may be required and to the extent necessary to prevent irreparable injury, the reviewing court, including the court to which a case may be taken on appeal from or on application for certiorari or other writ to a reviewing court, may issue all necessary and appropriate process to postpone the effective date of an agency action or to preserve status or rights pending conclusion of the review proceedings.

§ 706. Scope of review

To the extent necessary to decision and when presented, the reviewing court shall decide all relevant questions of law, interpret constitutional and statutory provisions, and determine the meaning or applicability of the terms of an agency action. The reviewing court shall—

(1) compel agency action unlawfully withheld or unreasonably delayed; and

(2) hold unlawful and set aside agency action, findings, and conclusions found to be—

(A) arbitrary, capricious, an abuse of discretion, or otherwise not in accordance with law;

(B) contrary to constitutional right, power, privilege, or immunity;

(C) in excess of statutory jurisdiction, authority, or limitations, or short of statutory right;

(D) without observance of procedure required by law;

(E) unsupported by substantial evidence in a case subject to section 556 and 557 of this title or otherwise reviewed on the record of an agency hearing provided by statute; or

(F) unwarranted by the facts to the extent that the facts are subject to trial de novo by the reviewing court.

In making the foregoing determinations, the court shall review the whole record or those parts of it cited by a party, and due account shall be taken of the rule of prejudicial error . . .

§ 3105. Appointment of hearing examiners

Each agency shall appoint as many hearing examiners as are necessary for proceedings required to be conducted in accordance with sections 556 and 557 of this title. Hearing examiners shall be assigned to cases in rotation so far as practicable, and may not perform duties inconsistent with their duties and responsibilities as hearing examiners.

§ 7521. Removal

A hearing examiner appointed under section 3105 of this title may be removed by the agency in which he is employed only for good cause established and determined by the Civil Service Commission on the record after opportunity for hearing.

§ 5362. Hearing examiners

Hearing examiners appointed under section 3105 of this title are entitled to pay prescribed by the Civil Service Commission independently of agency recommendations or ratings and in accordance with subchapter III of this chapter and chapter 51 of this title.

Appendix

§ 3344. Details; hearing examiners

An agency as defined by section 551 of this title which occasionally or temporarily is insufficiently staffed with hearing examiners appointed under section 3105 of this title may use hearing examiners selected by the Civil Service Commission from and with the consent of other agencies.

§ 1305. Hearing examiners

For the purpose of sections 3105, 3344, 4301(2) (E), 5362, and 7521 and the provisions of section 5335(a) (B) of this title that relate to hearing examiners, the Civil Service Commission may investigate, require reports by agencies, issue reports, including an annual report to Congress, prescribe regulations, appoint advisory committees as necessary, recommend legislation, subpena witnesses and records, and pay witness fees as established for the courts of the United States.

Notes

Chapter 1: Crisis and legitimacy in the administrative process: a historical perspective

1 See L. White, The Republican Era, 1869–1901, at 211–14 (1958).
2 Report of the President's Comm. on Administrative Management 41 (1937).
3 11 U.S. (7 Cranch) 382 (1813).
4 Frankfurter, The Supreme Court in the Mirror of Justices, 105 U. Pa. L. Rev. 781, 793 (1957)
5 E. Erikson, Childhood and Society 23 (2d ed. 1963).
6 See L. Jaffe, Judicial Control of Administrative Action 28–86 (1965).
7 J. Dickinson, Administrative Justice and the Supremacy of Law in the United States (1927).
8 5 U.S.C. § 551 *et seq.* (1970).
9 H. Friendly, The Federal Administrative Agencies: The Need for Better Definition of Standards 5–6 (1962).
10 FTC v. Ruberoid Co., 343 U.S. 470 (1952) (Jackson, J., dissenting).
11 Report of the President's Committee on Administrative Management (1937); Final Report of the Attorney General's Committee on Administrative Procedure, S. Doc. No. 8, 77th Cong., 1st Sess. (1941).
12 Commission on Organization of the Executive Branch of the Government, Report on Legal Services and Procedure 61–62 (1955).
13 Report on Regulatory Agencies to the President-Elect, Submitted by the Chairman of the Subcomm. on Administrative Practice and Procedure of the Senate Comm. on the Judiciary, 86th Cong., 2d Sess. (Comm. Print 1960).
14 A New Regulatory Framework: Report on Selected Independent Regulatory Agencies (1971).
15 Elman, Administrative Reform of the Federal Trade Commission, 59 Geo. L.J. 777 (1971); Elman, A Modest Proposal for Radical Reform, 56 A.B.A.J. 1045 (1970); Elman, The Regulatory Process: A Personal View, BNA Antitrust & Trade Reg. No. 475 at D-1-D-5 (1970); Hector, Problems of the CAB and the Independent Regulatory Commissions, 69 Yale L.J. 931 (1960); Minow, Suggestions for Improvement of the Administrative Process: Letter to President Kennedy from Newton N. Minow, Chairman, Federal Communications Commission, 15 Ad. L. Rev. #146 (1963).
16 Perhaps the most notable recent example was the failure of several Southern states, after the decision in *Brown v. Board of Education*, 347 U.S. 483 (1954), to establish a theory of interposition of state sovereignty as a qualification upon the authority of the Supreme

279

Court. See Cooper v. Aaron, 358 U.S. 1 (1958); Bush v. Orleans Parish School Board, 188 F. Supp. 916 (E.D. La. 1960).

17 See, e.g., J. Beck, Our Wonderland of Bureaucracy (1932); M. Bernstein, Regulating Business by Independent Commission (1955); J. Sax, Defending the Environment (1971); H. Vreeland, Jr., Twilight of Individual Liberty (1944); The Politics of Regulation (S. Krislov & L. Muslof eds. 1964); The Crisis of the Regulatory Commissions (P. MacAvoy ed. 1970).

18 M. Weber, The Theory of Social and Economic Organization 130–32 (T. Parsons ed. 1947). See R. Bendix, Max Weber: An Intellectual Portrait 412–17 (1960).

19 C. Black, Jr., The People and the Court 42 (1960).

Chapter 2: Separation of powers and the American imagination

1 Montesquieu, The Spirit of the Laws, 38 Great Books of the Western World 70 (Hutchins ed. 1952).

2 See Constitution of the Commonwealth of Massachusetts, Declaration of Rights, art. XXX (1780); Constitution of the State of New Hampshire, Part First, art. 37 of the Bill of Rights (1784).

3 A. Schlesinger, Jr., The Imperial Presidency vii (1973).

4 The Federalist No. 47, at 336 (B. Wright ed. 1961).

5 The Federalist No. 48, at 343 (B. Wright ed. 1961).

6 The Federalist No. 51, at 356 (B. Wright ed. 1961).

7 The Federalist No. 51, at 356 (B. Wright ed. 1961). See A. Bickel, The Morality of Consent 86 (1975).

8 103 U.S. 168, 191 (1881).

9 272 U.S. 52, 293 (1926).

10 Youngstown Sheet & Tube Co. v. Sawyer, 343 U.S. 579, 593 (1952) (Frankfurter, J., concurring).

11 Report of the President's Comm. on Administrative Management 39 (1937).

12 Report of the President's Comm. on Administrative Management 40–41 (1937). Similar rhetorical flourishes characterize other documents of the period arguing that the existence of administrative agencies is inconsistent with the constitutional scheme of separation of powers. J. Beck, Our Wonderland of Bureaucracy (1932); G. Hewart, The New Despotism (1929); See also E. Corwin, The President, Office and Powers 95–97 (4th rev. ed. 1957); Jaffe, Invective and Investigation in Administrative Law, 52 Harv. L. Rev. 1201 (1939).

13 1 K. Davis, Administrative Law Treatise § 1.09, at 64 (1958).

14 The Federalist Nos. 47 & 48 (B. Wright ed. 1961).

15 The Federalist No. 47, at 342 (B. Wright ed. 1961).

16 See O. Holmes, Jr., Collected Legal Papers 263 (1920) ("His [Montesquieu's] England – the England of the threefold division of power into legislative, executive and judicial – was a fiction invented by him. . . ."); 2 J. Story, Commentaries on the Constitution 8 (1833) ("The slightest examination of the British Constitution will at once convince us, that the legislative, executive and judiciary departments are by no means totally distinct, and separate from each other."). See also Maitland, *The Shallows and Silences of Real Life*, in I Collected Legal Papers 478 (1888).

17 The Federalist No. 47, at 339 (B. Wright ed. 1961).

18 Quoted in The Federalist No. 47, at 339 (B. Wright ed. 1961) (emphasis in original). The pragmatic philosophic temper of those who formed the founding American generation is discussed in M. Kammen, People of Paradox: An Inquiry Concerning the Origins of American Civilization (1972).

19 The Federalist No. 47, at 336 (B. Wright ed. 1961).
20 See The Works of James Wilson (R. McCloskey ed. 1967).
21 Frankfurter & Landis, Powers of Congress over Procedure in Criminal Contempts in "Inferior" Federal Courts – A Study in Separation of Powers, 37 Harv. L. Rev. 1010, 1013 (1924).
22 424 U.S. 1, 121 (1976).
23 See Jaffe, An Essay on Delegation of Legislative Power, 47 Colum. L. Rev. 369, 560 (1947).
24 W. Wilson, Constitutional Government in the United States 56–57 (1908). Charles M. Wiltse, in a perceptive article written in 1941, commented that administrative agencies have become "the instrument through which the close fusion of executive and legislative functions required by the complex nature of modern government may be brought about under a constitution committed to the eighteenth-century doctrine of separation of powers." Wiltse, The Representative Function of Bureaucracy, 35 Am. Pol. Rev. 510, 511 (1941).

Chapter 3: The departure from judicial norms

1 Letter written in 1832 to James A. G. Davis, 4 Letters and Writings of James Madison 259 (1865), quoted in A. Koch, Madison's "Advice to My Country" 115 (1966).
2 L. Fuller, The Morality of Law 170–77 (1964); Fuller, The Forms and Limits of Adjudication (1959) (unpublished paper prepared for the Roundtable on Jurisprudence, Association of American Law Schools, 1959).
3 See M. Bernstein, Regulating Business by Independent Commission 179–82 (1955).
4 Pound, The Causes of Popular Dissatisfaction with the Administration of Justice, 40 Am. L. Rev. 729, 738 (1906).
5 See, e.g., Scenic Hudson Preservation Conf. v. FPC, 354 F.2d 608 (2d Cir. 1965), *cert. denied*, 384 U.S. 941 (1966).
6 Richardson v. Perales, 402 U.S. 389, 410 (1971).
7 Sherrer v. Sherrer, 334 U.S. 343, 366 (1948) (dissenting opinion).
8 FMB v. Isbrandtsen Co., 356 U.S. 481, 519 (1958) (dissenting opinion).
9 United States v. Morgan, 313 U.S. 409, 422 (1941). See also Nathanson, Mr. Justice Frankfurter and Administrative Law, 67 Yale L.J. 240 (1957).
10 Frankfurter, Foreword – The Final Report of the Attorney General's Committee on Administrative Procedure, 41 Colum. L. Rev. 585, 586 (1941).
11 See J. Auerbach, Unequal Justice 221–30 (1975); W. Gellhorn, Individual Freedom and Governmental Restraints (1956); Jaffe, Invective and Investigation in Administrative Law, 52 Harv. L. Rev. 1201 (1939).
12 Root, Public Service by the Bar, 41 A.B.A. Rep. 355, 368 (1916).
13 O'Brian, The Menace of Administrative Law, in Proceedings of the Twenty-Fifth Annual Meeting of the Maryland State Bar Association (1920), reprinted in John Lord O'Brian, 1874–1973, A Commemorative Issue of the Buffalo Law Review 65 (1974).
14 Report of the Special Committee on Administrative Law, 57 A.B.A. Rep. 542–43 (1934).
15 Report of the Special Committee on Administrative Law, 63 A.B.A. Rep. 339–40 (1938). Dean Pound's hostile attitude toward the administrative process also appears in Pound, The Challenge of the Administrative Process, 30 A.B.A.J. 121 (1944); Pound, For the "Minority Report," 27 A.B.A.J. 664 (1941).
16 285 U.S. 22 (1932).
17 253 U.S. 287 (1920).
18 St. Joseph Stockyards Co. v. United States, 298 U.S. 38, 52 (1936).
19 259 U.S. 276, 285 (1922).

20 FCC v. Pottsville Broadcasting Co., 309 U.S. 134, 143 (1940).

21 The Court's decisions are outlined and criticized in Friendly, "Some Kind of Hearing," 123 U. Pa. L. Rev. 1267 (1975).

22 See Wright, The Courts and the Rulemaking Process: The Limits of Judicial Review, 59 Corn. L. Rev. 375 (1974).

23 See, e.g., NLRB v. Phelps, 136 F.2d 562 (5th Cir. 1943); Given v. Weinberger, 380 F. Supp. 150 (S.D.W.Va. 1974).

24 See J. Landis, Report on Regulatory Agencies to the President-Elect, Submitted by the Chairman of the Subcomm. on Administrative Practice and Procedure of the Senate Comm. on the Judiciary, 86th Cong., 2d Sess. (Comm. Print. 1960).

25 The relationship between distrust of government officials and reliance upon adversary procedures is splendidly argued at a number of points in the work of Karl N. Llewellyn. See, e.g., K. Llewellyn, Jurisprudence 44–50 (1962).

26 See J. Frank, Courts on Trial (1949).

27 Frankel, The Search for Truth: An Umpireal View, 123 U. Pa. L. Rev. 1031, 1034, 1036 (1975).

28 Fuller, *The Adversary System*, in Talks on American Law 30 (H. Berman ed. 1961).

Chapter 4: Public perceptions and administrative performance

1 C. Dole, The American Citizen 146 (1891).

2 An influential book of the period, arguing that the era of laissez faire had passed, was J. Clark, Social Control of Business (1926).

3 A. Schlesinger, Jr., The Crisis of the Old Order 1–8 (1957).

4 See Minnesota *ex rel.* Railroad & Warehouse Comm'n v. Chicago, M., & St. P. Ry., 38 Minn. 281, 301, 37 N.W. 782, 788 (1888), *rev'd*, 134 U.S. 418 (1890); Freedman, The Uses and Limits of Remand in Administrative Law: Staleness of the Record, 115 U. Pa. L. Rev. 145, 146 (1966).

5 Dicey had noticed this phenomena in Great Britain. Speaking of the strict construction given by English judges to the Common Law Procedure Act of 1854, he wrote: "However this may be, we may, at any rate as regards the nineteenth century, lay it down as a rule that judge-made law has, owing to the training and age of our judges, tended at any given moment to represent the convictions of an earlier era than the ideas represented by parliamentary legislation. If a statute, as already stated, is apt to reproduce the public opinion not so much of today as of yesterday, judge-made law occasionally represents the opinion of the day before yesterday." A. Dicey, Law and Opinion in England 369 (2d ed. 1926).

6 Compare Report of the President's Comm. on Administrative Management 39 (1937): "Beginning with the Interstate Commerce Commission in 1887, the Congress has set up more than a dozen independent regulatory commissions to exercise the control over commerce and business necessary to the orderly conduct of the Nation's economic life. These commissions have been the result of legislative groping rather than the pursuit of a consistent policy."

7 See E. Hawley, The New Deal and the Problem of Monopoly: A Study in Economic Ambivalence (1966); W. Leuchtenburg, Franklin D. Roosevelt and the New Deal (1963).

8 Something of the tone and nature of President Roosevelt's philosophy of governmental intervention in the economy – his prophetic optimism, his sense of destiny, his willingness to experiment on a large scale – is captured in Justice Brandeis's stirring summons of 1932, "If we would guide by the light of reason, we must let our minds be bold." New State Ice Co. v. Liebmann, 285 U.S. 262, 311 (1932) (dissenting opinion).

9 See E. Goldman, Rendezvous with Destiny 326–28, 333–42, 361–67 (1952); A. Schlesinger, Jr., The Coming of the New Deal 179–94 (1959); A. Schlesinger, Jr., The Politics of Upheaval 385–408 (1960).

10 Compare M. Friedman, Capitalism and Freedom (1962), with J. Galbraith, The Affluent Society (1958).

11 Federal Communications Act of 1934 § 307(a), 47 U.S.C. § 307(a) (1970).

12 Lionel Trilling once noted that it is "one of the tendencies of liberalism to simplify" and that "the ideas that can survive delegation, that can be passed on to agencies and bureaus and technicians, incline to be ideas of a certain kind and of a certain simplicity; they give up something of their largeness and modulation and complexity in order to survive." L. Trilling, The Liberal Imagination xiv–xv (1950).

13 See, e.g., H. Friendly, The Federal Administrative Agencies: The Need for Better Definition of Standards (1962).

14 See, e.g., Federal Trade Comm'n Cigarette Rule, 29 Fed. Reg. 8325 (1964), overruled by Congress in Cigarette Labelling Advertising Act of 1965, 15 U.S.C.A. § 1333 (1970); 29 Fed. Reg. 503 (1964), giving notice of abandonment of proposed rule making of 28 Fed. Reg. 5158 (1963) because of pressure and disapproval from House of Representatives. See also L. Kohlmeier, Jr., The Regulators 55–57 (1969).

15 The most felicitous judicial statement of this imperative is perhaps that of Justice Cardozo: "When the task that is set before one is that of cleaning house, it is prudent as well as usual to take counsel of the dwellers." Schechter Poultry Corp. v. United States, 295 U.S. 495, 552 (1935) (concurring opinion).

16 See M. Bernstein, Regulating Business by Independent Commission (1955).

17 Louis L. Jaffe has summarized the phenomenon cogently: "When the evil which gives rise to a reform has been somewhat alleviated, the initial dynamism is dispersed. There is a newly evolved status quo. It requires an exceptional effort of concern and attention to maintain human energies at high pitch, to keep courage screwed to the sticking point." Jaffe, The Effective Limits of the Administrative Process: A Reevaluation, 67 Harv. L. Rev. 1105, 1109 (1954).

18 G. Stigler & M. Cohen, Can Regulatory Agencies Protect the Consumer? 54 (1971).

19 Laski, Bureaucracy, 3 Encyc. Soc. Sci. 70 (E. Seligman ed. 1930).

20 M. Weber, The Theory of Social and Economic Organization 324–423 (T. Parsons ed. 1947). See J. Jowell, Law and Bureaucracy 20 (1975).

21 M. Weber, The Theory of Social and Economic Organization 337 (T. Parsons ed. 1947).

22 R. Merton, Social Theory and Social Structure 253 (rev. ed. 1968) (footnotes omitted). See K. Mannheim, Ideology and Utopia 106 (1954); Merton, The Unanticipated Consequences of Purposive Social Action, 1 Am. Soc. Rev. 894 (1936).

23 See, e.g., W. Whyte, The Organization Man (1956).

24 "Specifically," as Stanley Milgram has written in a related context, "the person entering an authority system no longer views himself as acting out of his own purposes but rather comes to see himself as an agent for executing the wishes of another person. Once an individual conceives his action in this light, profound alterations occur in his behavior and his internal functioning." S. Milgram, Obedience to Authority 133 (1974).

25 G. Henderson, The Federal Trade Commission 328 (1924).

26 A brilliant analysis appears in H. Kissinger, The Necessity for Choice 340–58 (1961).

27 Power in federal bureaucracies, as Charles Frankel, a Columbia University philosopher. learned during a tour of duty at the Department of State, belongs to "team players, to bargainers, to the gregarious, to men who like to get together with other people more than they like to see ideas clean and neat." C. Frankel, High on Foggy Bottom 57 (1969). See generally E. Weisband & T. Franck, Resignation in Protest (1975).

28 S. Lipset, Political Man 389–94 (Anchor ed. 1963). Compare Shils, Faith, Utility, and the Legitimacy of Science, Daedalus, Summer 1974, at 1.

29 The changes in Justice Douglas's views can be seen by comparing his early book, Democracy and Finance (1940), with two later books, We the Judges (1956), and Points of Rebellion (1969). An excellent discussion appears in B. Wolfman, J. Silver, & M. Silver, Dissent Without Opinion: The Behavior of Justice William O. Douglas in Federal Tax Cases (1975).

30 400 U.S. 309, 335 (1971). Other illustrative opinions include Arnett v. Kennedy, 416 U.S. 134, 203 (1974) (Douglas, J., dissenting); Richardson v. Perales, 402 U.S. 389, 411 (1971) (Douglas, J., dissenting); United States v. Powell, 379 U.S. 48, 59 (1964) (Douglas, J., dissenting); Public Util. Comm'n v. Pollak, 343 U.S. 451, 467–69 (1952) (Douglas, J., dissenting); United States v. Wunderlich, 342 U.S. 98, 101 (1951) (Douglas, J., dissenting).

31 Reich, The New Property, 73 Yale L.J. 733 (1964).

32 A. de Tocqueville, The Old Regime and the French Revolution 61 (Anchor ed. 1955).

33 H. Jacoby, The Bureaucratization of the World (1974); W. Robson, The Governors and the Governed 17–21 (1964).

34 See A. Okun, Equality and Efficiency, The Big Tradeoff 39–40, 60–62 (1975).

35 H. Gerth & C. Mills, From Max Weber: Essays in Sociology 214 (1946).

36 E. Erikson, Dimensions of a New Identity 123 (1974).

37 J. Landis, The Administrative Process 23–24 (1938).

38 Letter from Felix Frankfurter to Learned Hand, Sept. 23, 1912, quoted in Note, The Democratic Faith of Felix Frankfurter, 25 Stan. L. Rev. 430, 433 n.16 (1973).

39 F. Frankfurter, The Public and Its Government 145 (1930).

40 NLRB v. Seven-Up Bottling Co., 344 U.S. 344, 349 (1953).

41 F. Frankfurter, The Public and Its Government 157 (1930).

42 F. Frankfurter, The Public and Its Government 160 (1930).

43 W. Douglas, Democracy and Finance 246 (1940). Jerome Frank, another important intellectual figure of the New Deal, held views similar to those of Douglas. J. Frank, If Men Were Angels 19–20 (1941).

44 Joint Anti-Fascist Refugee Comm. v. McGrath, 341 U.S. 123, 163 (1951) (Frankfurter, J., concurring). See, as to the termination of welfare benefits, Goldberg v. Kelly, 297 U.S. 254 (1970); Wheeler v. Montgomery, 397 U.S. 280 (1970); the determination of alleged violations of parole and probation, Morrissey v. Brewer, 408 U.S. 471 (1972); Gagnon v. Scarpelli, 411 U.S. 778 (1973); the denial of tenure to professors in public institutions, Board of Regents v. Roth, 408 U.S. 564 (1972); Perry v. Sindermann, 408 U.S. 593 (1972); and the suspension of children from school, Goss v. Lopez, 419 U.S. 565 (1975).

45 W. Wilson, A Crossroads of Freedom: The 1912 Campaign Speeches of Woodrow Wilson 83–84 (J. Davidson ed. 1956).

46 Carter Mountain Transmission Corp., 32 F.C.C. 459, 462 (1962).

47 In a perceptive passage, Herbert A. Simon has written: "Democratic institutions find their principal justification as a procedure for the validation of value judgments. There is no 'scientific' or 'expert' way of making such judgments, hence expertise of whatever kind is no qualification for the performance of this function. If the factual elements in decision could be strictly separated, in practice, from the ethical, the proper roles of representative and expert in a democratic decision-making process would be simple. [But] this is not possible." H. Simon, Administrative Behavior 56–57 (2d ed. 1957).

48 L. Hand, The Bill of Rights 73 (1958).

49 J. Landis, The Administrative Process 50 (1938).

50 See A. Link, Woodrow Wilson and the Progressive Era (1954).

51 Laski, The Limitations of the Expert, 162 Harper's Monthly Magazine 101 (1930) (Fabian

Tract No. 235). It is interesting to note that Laski's careful elaboration of the limitations of the expert appeared in the same year as Frankfurter's most important work in praise of expertise in government. See F. Frankfurter, The Public and Its Government (1930).

52 K. Llewellyn, The Common Law Tradition: Deciding Appeals 263 (1960).

53 See, e.g., A. Bickel, The Supreme Court and the Idea of Progress (1970); R. Dahl, After the Revolution? (1970); H. Finer, The Presidency: Crisis and Regeneration (1960); R. Goodwin, The American Condition (1974); T. Lowi, The End of Liberalism (1969); R. Nisbet, Twilight of Authority (1975); G. Reedy, The Twilight of the Presidency (1970); A. Schlesinger, Jr., The Imperial Presidency (1973).

54 R. Dahl, A Preface to Democratic Theory (1956); Choper, The Supreme Court and the Political Branches: Democratic Theory and Practice, 122 U. Pa. L. Rev. 810 (1974). Compare Finer, Administrative Responsibility in Democratic Government, 1 Pub. Admin. Rev. 335 (1941), with Friedrich, Public Policy and the Nature of Administrative Responsibility, in Public Policy 3 (C. Friedrich & E. Mason eds. 1940).

55 See A. Bentley, The Process of Government (1908); T. Lowi, The End of Liberalism (1969); D. Truman, The Governmental Process (1950).

56 M. Weber, The Theory of Social and Economic Organization 338 (T. Parsons ed. 1947).

Chapter 5: Agency independence and political accountability

1 Jaffe, The Effective Limits of the Administrative Process: A Reevaluation, 67 Harv. L. Rev. 1105, 1107 (1954).

2 Quoted in R. Hofstadter, The American Political Tradition 176 (1948); M. Josephson, The Politicos 526 (1938). The letter was sent to Charles E. Perkins, President of the Chicago, Burlington, and Quincy Railroad.

3 Ring Lardner perhaps came closest when he quipped, "Prohibition is better than no liquor at all." The remark is quoted in Rehnquist, Civility and Freedom of Speech, 49 Ind. L.J. 1 (1973).

4 Robert MacGregor Dawson, writing in 1922, had argued that "independence supplies the moral inducement to do well" and "calls forth a host of qualities that otherwise might have remained dormant – the official's vanity, his conscience, his desire for applause, his zeal for the public good, his feeling of special fitness for his post, his craftsman's delight in his skill – any one or all of these are given freer play." R. Dawson, The Principle of Official Independence 7 (1922).

5 J. Landis, The Administrative Process 111 (1938).

6 J. Eastman, Selected Papers and Addresses of Joseph B. Eastman, 1942–44, at 375 (G. Wilson ed. 1948).

7 272 U.S. 52 (1926).

8 295 U.S. 602 (1935).

9 See also Wiener v. United States, 357 U.S. 349 (1958); Morgan v. TVA, 115 F.2d 990 (6th Cir. 1940), *cert. denied*, 312 U.S. 701 (1941).

10 See, e.g., WKAT Inc., 29 F.C.C. 216 (1958), *rehearing denied*, 29 F.C.C. 983 (1960), *enforced*, 296 F.2d 375 (D.C. Cir. 1960), *cert. denied sub nom.* Public Serv. Television v. FCC, 368 U.S. 841 (1961). See generally P. Douglas, Ethics in Government 85–92 (1952).

11 See, e.g., MacIntyre, The Status of Regulatory Independence, 29 Fed. B.J. 1 (1969); Carrow, Dean Landis and the Regulatory Process, 29 Geo. Wash. L. Rev. 718 (1961).

12 See DixonenThe Independent Commissions and Political Responsibility, 27 Ad. L. Rev. 1, 8 n. 30 (1975).

13 28 U.S.C. §§516–19 (1970).

14 President's Message to Congress on the Regulatory Agencies, 107 Cong. Rec. 5356 (1961), reprinted as H.R. Doc. 135, 87th Cong., 1st Sess. (1961).
15 See United States v. George S. Bush & Co., 310 U.S. 371 (1940); Chicago & Southern Air Lines, Inc. v. Waterman S.S. Co., 333 U.S. 103 (1948).
16 See H. Seidman, Politics, Position, & Power: The Dynamics of Federal Organization 224 (1970).
17 W. Cary, Politics and the Regulatory Agencies 12 (1967).
18 E. Corwin, The President: Office and Powers 98 (4th ed. 1957).
19 A. Wildavsky, The Politics of the Budgetary Process (2d ed. 1974).
20 R. Fenno, Congressmen in Committees (1973).
21 R. Fenno, The Power of the Purse (1966); R. Wallace, Congressional Control of Federal Spending (1960).
22 R. Harris, Congressional Control of Administration 249–78 (1964); M. Kirst, Government Without Passing Laws (1969); D.C. Federation of Civic Ass'ns v. Volpe, 459 F.2d 1231 (D.C. Cir. 1971), *cert. denied*, 405 U.S. 1030 (1972); Pillsbury Co. v. FTC, 354 F.2d 952 (5th Cir. 1966).
23 Elman, The Regulatory Process: A Personal View, BNA, Antitrust and Trade Reg. Rep. No. 475, D1, at D5 (1970).
24 L. Jaffe, Judicial Control of Administrative Action 23–24 (1965).
25 Bi-Metallic Inv. Co. v. State Bd. of Equalization, 239 U.S. 441, 445 (1915).
26 Report of the President's Committee on Administrative Management 40 (1937).
27 A New Regulatory Framework: Report on Selected Independent Regulatory Agencies 40 (1971).
28 M. Bernstein, Regulating Business by Independent Commission 293 (1955).
29 A. Bickel, The Least Dangerous Branch 19 (1962).
30 Stewart, The Reformation of American Administrative Law, 88 Harv. L. Rev. 1669, 1791–93 (1975).
31 See, e.g., Cutler & Johnson, Regulation and the Political Process, 84 Yale L.J. 1395 (1975).
32 See W. Lippmann, The Public Philosophy (1955); A. Lowell, Public Opinion and Popular Government (1913); D. Truman, The Governmental Process (1951).
33 W. Wilson, Congressional Government xxiv (1885).
34 See, e.g., A. Bickel, The Least Dangerous Branch (1962); C. Black, Jr., The People and the Court (1960); L. Hand, The Bill of Rights (1958); H. Wechsler, *Toward Neutral Principles of Constitutional Law*, in Principles, Politics, and Fundamental Law (1961).
35 R. Dahl, A Preface to Democratic Theory 46 (1956). In the view of some scholars, the asserted antithesis between the majoritarian institutions of government, which are assumed to be responsive to the popular will, and the nonmajoritarian institutions, which are regarded as centers of political irresponsibility in a democratic polity, is at most an attractive literary convention; it does not accurately describe the subtle and complicated ways in which either set of institutions actually functions. These scholars argue that there are so many elements of political irresponsibility in the majoritarian institutions and so many currents of democratic responsiveness in the nonmajoritarian institutions as to discredit the asserted antithesis almost entirely. See M. Shapiro, Freedom of Speech: The Supreme Court and Judicial Review (1966); Dahl, Decision-Making in a Democracy: The Supreme Court as a National Policy-Maker, 6 J. Pub. L. 279 (1957); Deutsch, Neutrality, Legitimacy, and the Supreme Court: Some Intersections Between Law and Political Science, 20 Stan. L. Rev. 169 (1968). These arguments further weaken the validity of attacks upon the legitimacy of the independent administrative agencies as nonmajoritarian institutions.
36 Eastman, The Place of the Independent Commission, 12 Constitutional Rev. 95 (1928).

Chapter 6: Delegation of power and institutional competence

1 U.S. Const. art. I, § 1.
2 143 U.S. 649, 692 (1892).
3 Everson v. Board of Educ., 330 U.S. 1, 19 (1947) (dissenting opinion).
4 The most important judicial attempt in recent years to rationalize the doctrine is Judge Leventhal's opinion in Amalgamated Meat Cutters & Butcher Workers v. Connally, 337 F. Supp. 737 (D.D.C. 1971); see also Federal Energy Administration v. Algonquin SNG, Inc., 426 U.S. 548 (1976).
5 T. Lowi, The End of Liberalism 145 (1969).
6 Lowi, The Public Philosophy: Interest-Group Liberalism, 61 Am. Pol. Sci. Rev. 5, 18 (1967); see Jaffe, The Illusion of the Ideal Administration, 86 Harv. L. Rev. 1183 (1973); Wright, Beyond Discretionary Justice, 81 Yale L.J. 575 (1972).
7 K. Davis, Administrative Law Treatise § 2.00, at 40 (Supp. 1970); Davis, A New Approach to Delegation, 36 U. Chi. L. Rev. 713 (1969). A British commentator has written that the requirement of a standard has become "hardly more than a ceremonial incantation handed down from an earlier constitutional era." Wade, Anglo-American Administrative Law: Some Reflections, 81 Law. Q. Rev. 357, 372 (1965).
8 H. Friendly, The Federal Administrative Agencies: The Need for Better Definition of Standards 6, 22–23 (1962); L. Jaffe, Judicial Control of Administrative Action 48–51 (1965).
9 1 The Records of the Federal Convention of 1787, at 67 (M. Farrand ed. 1911). The only reference to delegation in *The Federalist* relates to the President's pardoning power. The Federalist No. 74, at 473–75 (B. Wright ed. 1961) (A. Hamilton).
10 The Federalist No. 48, at 344 (B. Wright ed. 1961) (J. Madison); see The Federalist No. 73, at 468–69 (B. Wright ed. 1961) (A. Hamilton) (discussing the "propensity of the legislative department to intrude upon the rights, and to absorb the powers, of the other departments").
11 The Federalist No. 48, at 343 (B. Wright ed. 1961).
12 U.S. Const. art. I, § 8; see McCulloch v. Maryland, 17 U.S. (4 Wheat.) 316 (1819).
13 L. Jaffe, Judicial Control of Administrative Action 85 (1965).
14 E. Freund, Administrative Powers over Persons and Property 218 (1928). See also Freund, The Substitution of Rule for Discretion in Public Law, 9 Am. Pol. Sci. Rev. 666 (1915); Allen, *Ernst Freund and the New Age of Legislation*, in E. Freund, Standards of American Legislation vii (1965).
15 L. Jaffe, Judicial Control of Administrative Action 34 (1965).
16 Alexander M. Bickel, in arguing that "the doctrine that delegation without standards is unconstitutional is no mere technical teaching," wrote: "It is concerned with the sources of policy, with the crucial joinder between power and broadly based democratic responsibility, bestowed and discharged after the fashion of representative government. Delegation without standards shortcircuits the lines of responsibility that make the political process meaningful." Bickel, The Constitution and the War, Commentary, July 1972, at 49, 52.
17 415 U.S. 336 (1974). A related issue was decided according to similar principles in a companion case, FPC v. New England Power Co., 415 U.S. 345 (1974). Justice Marshall, with whom Justice Brennan joined, wrote a separate opinion dissenting in the *FCC* case and concurring in the result of the *FPC* case. Justices Blackmun and Powell took no part in either decision.
18 Independent Offices Appropriation Act of 1952, 31 U.S.C. § 483a (1970).
19 295 U.S. 495 (1935).
20 See, e.g., Lichter v. United States, 334 U.S. 742 (1948); Yakus v. United States, 321 U.S. 414, 423–27 (1944); 1 K. Davis, Administrative Law Treatise § 2.03 (1958).

21 H.R. Rep. No. 316, 91st Cong., 1st Sess. 7–8 (1967); H.R. Conf. Rep. No. 649, 91st Cong., 1st Sess. 6 (1969). The passage is quoted by the Court.

22 357 U.S. 116 (1958).

23 22 U.S.C. § 211(a) (1970). The Court quotes the relevant sections of the statute in its opinion.

24 The legitimacy of granting the State Department almost unrestricted authority to deny passports had been questioned for at least a generation. See E. Freund, Administrative Powers over Persons and Property 97 (1928).

25 See also Hampton v. Mow Sun Wong, 426 U.S. 88 (1976).

26 A Bickel, The Least Dangerous Branch 165–66 (1962).

27 Stone, The Common Law in the United States, 50 Harv. L. Rev. 4, 25 (1936).

28 The Court's reading of the prior historical practice was sharply disputed by the dissenting opinion and elsewhere has been characterized as "fictive." A. Bickel, The Least Dangerous Branch 201 (1962); see Zemel v. Rusk, 381 U.S. 1 (1965); Jaffe, The Right to Travel: The Passport Problem, 35 Foreign Affairs 17, 22–23 (1956).

29 S. Barber, The Constitution and the Delegation of Congressional Power 98 (1975).

30 See Bickel, Foreword: The Passive Virtues, 75 Harv. L. Rev. 40 (1961).

31 17 U.S. (4 Wheat.) 316, 431 (1819). The Court in *National Cable Television Association* quoted Justice Holmes's rejoinder: "The power to tax is not the power to destroy while this Court sits."

32 This may explain, too, why the Constitution, in an unusually explicit provision, requires that "[a]ll bills for raising Revenue shall originate in the House of Representatives," the most broadly representative of our legislative institutions. U.S. Const. art. I, § 7.

33 U.S. Const. art. II, § 4. See generally R. Berger, Impeachment: The Constitutional Problems (1973); Pollak, The Constitution as an Experiment, 123 U. Pa. L. 1318 (1975).

34 A. Schlesinger, Jr., The Imperial Presidency 11 (1973).

35 The Federalist No. 65, at 427 (B. Wright ed. 1961).

36 The Federalist No. 65, at 428 (B. Wright ed. 1961).

37 U.S. Const. art. I, § 5; see Schick v. Reed, 419 U.S. 256 (1974); Biddle v. Perovich, 274 U.S. 480 (1927); *Ex parte* Grossman, 267 U.S. 87 (1925); E. Corwin, The President: Office and Powers 158–68 (4th rev. ed. 1957); W. Humbert, The Pardoning Power of the President (1941).

38 The Federalist No. 74, at 475 (B. Wright ed. 1961).

39 *Ex parte* Garland, 71 U.S. (4 Wall.) 333, 380 (1866).

40 J. Barber, The Presidential Character 9 (1972). See M. Novak, Choosing Our King (1974).

41 Hotchkiss v. National City Bank, 200 F. 287, 293 (S.D.N.Y. 1911), *aff'd*, 201 F. 664 (2d Cir. 1912), *aff'd*, 231 U.S. 50 (1913).

42 City of Eastlake v. Forest City Enterprises, Inc., 426 U.S. 668 (1976); Parker v. Brown, 317 U.S. 341 (1943); Sunshine Anthracite Coal Co. v. Adkins, 310 U.S. 381 (1940); United States v. Rock Royal Co-operative, Inc., 308 U.S. 533 (1939); Currin v. Wallace, 306 U.S. 1 (1939); Thomas Cusack Co. v. Chicago, 242 U.S. 526 (1917); St. Louis, I. Mt. & S. Ry. v. Taylor, 210 U.S. 281 (1908); Jackson v. Roby, 109 U.S. 440 (1883).

43 Carter v. Carter Coal Co., 298 U.S. 238 (1936); Washington *ex rel.* Seattle Title Trust Co. v. Roberge, 278 U.S. 116 (1928); Eubank v. City of Richmond, 226 U.S. 137 (1912).

44 298 U.S. 238 (1936); see R. Jackson, The Struggle for Judicial Supremacy 153–65 (1941).

45 It could be argued that Congress is most likely to evade its constitutional responsibilities when pressure from private groups is greatest, particularly when the groups are economically or socially powerful. Delegations of legislative power to private parties would then appear as one class of statutory enactments that should alert courts to the possibility that an abdication of congressional responsibility has occurred.

288

46 See, e.g., State v. Wakeen, 263 Wis. 401, 57 N.W.2d 364 (1953); Liebmann, Delegation to Private Parties in American Constitutional Law, 50 Ind. L. Rev. 650, 680-83 (1975).

47 Group Health Ins. v. Howell, 40 N.J. 436, 447, 193 A.2d 103, 109 (1963), *supplemented*, 43 N.J. 104, 202 A.2d 689 (1964). See also State Bd. of Dry Cleaners v. Thrift-D-Lux Cleaners, 40 Cal. 2d 436, 254 P.2d 29 (1953).

48 See Berryhill v. Gibson, 331 F. Supp. 122 (M.D. Ala. 1971), *vacated and remanded on other grounds*, 411 U.S. 564 (1973); Jaffe, Law Making by Private Groups, 51 Harv. L. Rev. 201 (1937).

49 11 U.S. (7 Cranch.) 382 (1813).

50 143 U.S. 649 (1892). See also J. W. Hampton, Jr. & Co. v. United States, 276 U.S. 394 (1928).

51 See, e.g., Lichter v. United States, 334 U.S. 742 (1948); Bowles v. Willingham, 321 U.S. 503 (1944); Yakus v. United States, 321 U.S. 414 (1944); United States v. Curtiss-Wright Export Corp., 299 U.S. 304 (1936); United States v. Yoshida Int'l, Inc., 526 F.2d 560 (C.C.P.A. 1975).

52 Several Justices of the Supreme Court have expressed their belief in the vitality of the doctrine. See United States v. Robel, 389 U.S. 258, 272-73 (1967) (Brennan, J., concurring); Arizona v. California, 373 U.S. 546, 626 (1963) (Harlan, J., with Stewart and Douglas, JJ., dissenting).

53 See K. Davis, Discretionary Justice: A Preliminary Inquiry 39-41 (1969).

54 Congress should be encouraged to build upon the agency's exercises of discretion in resolving basic policy questions by eventually enacting its own policy choices into law. One mechanism to accomplish this purpose is outlined in S. Barber, The Constitution and the Delegation of Congressional Power 123-27 (1975).

55 It is often suggested that the failure of Congress to resolve basic policy issues is an inevitable fact of legislative life that courts must tolerate if there is to be any legislation at all. But it is possible that Congress's failure to prescribe standards results from its awareness that it can consitutionally avoid such politically difficult judgments under the prevailing decisions of the courts.

Chapter 7: Explaining differences in agency performance: the SEC and the FTC

1 The core of the disclosure requirements is set out in § 5 of the Securities Act of 1933, 15 U.S.C. § 77e (1970). The antifraud prohibitions of both the 1933 and 1934 Acts – see Securities Act of 1933, § 17, 15 U.S.C. § 77g (1970), and Securities Exchange Act of 1934, § 10(b), 15 U.S.C. § 78j(b) – draw upon centuries of common law development of the doctrines of deceit, false pretenses, and misrepresentation. See Shulman, Civil Liability and the Securities Act, 43 Yale L.J. 227 (1933).

2 See, e.g., Berko v. SEC, 316 F.2d 137 (2d Cir. 1963).

3 Securities Act of 1933, §§ 8, 19(a), 15 U.S.C. §§ 77h, 77s(a) (1970); Securities Exchange Act of 1934, §§ 19, 23, 15 U.S.C. §§ 78s, 78w (1970). See SEC v. Chenery Corp., 332 U.S. 194 (1947).

4 Securities Exchange Act of 1934, § 15(b)(6), 15 U.S.C. § 78o(b)(7) (1970).

5 Securities Act of 1933, § 8(d), 15 U.S.C. § 77h(d) (1970). See Jones v. SEC, 298 U.S. 1 (1936).

6 Securities Exchange Act of 1934, §§ 15(c)(5), 19(a)(4), 15 U.S.C. 78o(c)(5), 78s(a)(4) (1970). See R. A. Holman & Co. v. SEC, 299 F.2d 127 (D.C. Cir.), *cert. denied*, 370 U.S. 911 (1962).

7 Securities Act of 1933, § 20(b), 15 U.S.C. § 77t(b) (1970); Securities Exchange Act of 1934, § 21(e), 15 U.S.C. § 78u(e) (1970). See SEC v. Jones, 85 F.2d 17 (2d Cir.), *cert. denied,* 299 U.S. 581 (1936).

8 Federal Trade Commission Act § 5(a)(1), 15 U.S.C.A. § 45(a)(1) (1975).

9 See Schechter Poultry Corp. v. United States, 295 U.S. 495 (1935); FTC v. R. F. Keppel & Bros., 291 U.S. 304 (1934); FTC v. Raladam Co., 283 U.S. 643 (1931); FTC v. Gratz, 253 U.S. 421 (1920).

10 H. Friendly, The Federal Administrative Agencies: The Need for Better Definition of Standards 14 (1962).

11 John Dickinson, writing in 1927, expressed the hope that the "run of decisions may, however, in time cause standardized competitive methods to be pronounced once and for all as either 'fair' or 'unfair'. . . ." J. Dickinson, Administrative Justice and the Supremacy of Law in the United States 237 (1927).

12 J. Landis, The Administrative Process 17 (1938).

13 The Supreme Court, however, has limited the reach of the statute by requiring the FTC to find that the prosecution of specific actions will serve the "public interest." Compare FTC v. Klesner, 280 U.S. 19 (1929), with Exposition Press, Inc. v. FTC, 295 F.2d 869 (2d Cir. 1961).

14 See generally S. Lazarus, The Genteel Populists 53–62 (1974); M. Olsen, The Logic of Collective Action 165–66 (1965).

15 A commission established to study the FTC took note of this problem in recommending that the agency's chairman be a person of "sufficient strength and independence to resist pressures from Congress, the Executive Branch, or the business community that tend to cripple effective performance by the FTC." Report of the ABA Comm'n to Study the Federal Trade Commission 35 (1969).

16 See Magnuson-Moss Warranty-Federal Trade Commission Improvement Act, Pub. L. No. 93–637, 88 Stat. 2183 (1975).

17 Posner, The Federal Trade Commission, 37 U. Chi. L. Rev. 47, 88 (1969). It is interesting to note that the SEC and the FTC employ essentially the same organizational structure. Although there is undoubtedly a relationship between an agency's organizational structure and its effectiveness in meeting its assigned responsibilities, there is considerable reason to believe that an agency's structure is less important than the factors discussed in the text in determining the standard of performance that an agency achieves.

Chapter 8: The significance of public attitudes toward agency goals: the EEOC

1 Civil Rights Act of 1964 §§ 701–16, 42 U.S.C. §§ 2000e to 2000e-15 (1970).

2 401 U.S. 424, 429–30 (1971).

3 Executive Order No. 8802, 6 Fed. Reg. 3109 (1941).

4 President's Committee on Civil Rights, To Secure These Rights (1947).

5 A. Bickel, Politics and the Warren Court 104–05 (1965).

6 A. Blumrosen, Black Employment and the Law 52 (1971).

7 5 U.S.C. §§ 554(c), 558(c) (1970).

8 Note, Discrimination in Employment and in Housing: Private Enforcement Provisions of the Civil Rights Acts of 1964 and 1968, 82 Harv. L. Rev. 834, 835 (1969).

9 Equal Employment Opportunity Act of 1972, § 706(f)(1), 42 U.S.C. § 2000e (f) (1) (Supp. 1972). See Sape & Hart, Title VII Reconsidered: The Equal Employment Opportunity Act of 1972, 40 Geo. Wash. L. Rev. 824 (1972).

10 Alexander v. Gardner-Denver Co., 415 U.S. 36, 45 (1974).

11 Hall v. Werthan Bag Corp., 251 F. Supp. 184, 186 (M.D. Tenn. 1966).

12 M. Sovern, Legal Restraints on Racial Discrimination in Employment 205 (1966).

13 404 U.S. 522, 527 (1972).

14 Berg, Equal Employment Opportunity Under the Civil Rights Act of 1964, 31 Bklyn. L. Rev. 62, 63 (1964).

15 Senate Comm. on Labor and Pub. Welfare, S. Rep. No. 415, 92d Cong., 1st Sess. 5 (1971).

16 A. Blumrosen, Black Employment and the Law 59 (1971) (emphasis in original).

17 Pound, The Limits of Effective Legal Action, 22 Pa. B. Ass'n Rep. 221, 222 (1916); see also Parsons, *The Law and Social Control*, in Law and Sociology 56 (Evan ed. 1962); Freund, Civil Rights and the Limits of Law, 14 Buff. L. Rev. 199 (1964).

18 See, e.g., H. Friendly, Federal Jurisdiction: A General View 85–87 (1973); Notes, Developments in the Law – Employment Discrimination and Title VII of the Civil Rights Act of 1964, 84 Harv. L. Rev. 1109, 1245–46 (1971).

19 The commission has sought to do the best it could under the straitened circumstances. It has issued an extensive set of guidelines and persuaded the courts to sustain many of its most crucial interpretations of Title VII, thereby playing a significant part in shaping the meaning of a developing body of law. See Blumrosen, Strangers in Paradise: Griggs v. Duke Power Co. and the Concept of Employment Discrimination, 71 Mich. L. Rev. 59 (1972). It has concluded settlement agreements with a number of major corporations for alleged discrimination against members of racial minorities and women, thereby ensuring fair treatment for thousands of employees and prospective employees at a single stroke. And it has regularly refined its internal procedures, thereby permitting it to process an increasing number of complaints each year, even though the backlog has continued to grow because of the even greater increase in the number of complaints filed annually.

20 See Freedman, Review Boards in the Administrative Process, 117 U. Pa. L. Rev. 546 (1969).

21 Minnesota *ex. rel.* Railroad & Warehouse Comm'n v. Chicago, M., & P. Ry., 38 Minn. 281, 37 N.W. 782 (1888), *rev'd*, 134 U.S. 418 (1890); see Freedman, The Uses and Limits of Remand in Administrative Law: Staleness of the Record, 115 U. Pa. L. Rev. 145 (1966).

Chapter 9: The significance of institutional capacities and limitations: meeting the needs of the elderly

1 Age Discrimination in Employment Act of 1967, 29 U.S.C. § 621 *et seq.* (1970), *as amended*, Pub. L. No. 93–259, § 28 (1974).

2 See L. Friedman, A History of American Law 384–87 (1973). Recent illustrations of congressional reliance upon the administrative process for the implementation of new programs include Federal Insecticide, Fungicide and Rodenticide Act, 7 U.S.C. § 135 *et seq.* (1970); Food, Drug and Cosmetic Act, 21 U.S.C. § 301 *et seq.* (1970); Highway Safety Act of 1966, 23 U.S.C. § 401 *et seq.* (1970); Water Quality Act of 1965, 33 U.S.C. § 1151 *et seq.* (1970); Clean Air Act of 1970, 42 U.S.C. § 1857 *et seq.* (1970), *as amended*, 42 U.S.C.A. § 1857 (Supp. 1973); National Environmental Policy Act of 1969, 42 U.S.C. § 4321 *et seq.* (1970); Consumer Product Safety Act, 15 U.S.C.A. § 2051 *et seq.* (Supp. 1973).

3 Older Americans Act of 1965, 42 U.S.C. § 3001 *et seq.* (1970), *as amended*, 42 U.S.C.A. § 3001 *et seq.* (Supp. 1973).

4 Social Security Act of 1935, 42 U.S.C. § 301 *et seq.* (1970), *as amended*, 42 U.S.C.A. § 301 *et seq.* (Supp. 1973).

5 Age Discrimination in Employment Act of 1967, 29 U.S.C. § 621 *et seq.* (1970), *as amended*, Pub. L. No. 93–259, § 28 (1974).

6 Int. Rev. Code of 1954, §§ 401–05.

7 J. B. Williams Co., 68 F.T.C. 481, *rehearing denied*, 68 F.T.C. 1225 (1965), *enforced*, 381 F.2d 884 (6th Cir. 1967).

8 N. Morris & G. Hawkins, The Honest Politician's Guide to Crime Control 4 (1970); H. Packer, The Limits of the Criminal Sanction 266 (1968); Kadish, The Crisis of Overcriminalization, 374 Annals 157 (1967).

9 Professor Lowi has suggested the wisdom of tenure-of-statutes acts, by which Congress would "[set] a Jeffersonian limit of from five to ten years on the life of every organic act." T. Lowi, The End of Liberalism 309 (1969). At the end of the statutory period, Congress would be required to evaluate an agency's performance and to decide whether to take affirmative action to renew the agency's life, to create a new and perhaps differently structured administrative agency, or to move to a different form of social control entirely.

10 Wilson, The Dead Hand of Regulation, 25 Public Interest 29, 58 (1971).

11 Department of Health, Education, and Welfare, Recommendations of the Task Force on Medicaid and Related Programs 95 (1970).

12 J. Landis, Report on Regulatory Agencies to the President-Elect 66, Submitted by the Chairman of the Subcomm. on Administrative Practice and Procedure to the Senate Comm. on the Judiciary, 86th Cong., 2d Sess. (Comm. Print 1960).

13 L. Trilling, The Liberal Imagination 221 (1950).

Chapter 10: Administrative procedure and the nature of legitimacy

1 5 U.S. (1 Cranch) 137 (1803).

2 M. Weber, The Theory of Social and Economic Organization 328 (T. Parsons ed. 1947). See also R. Bendix, Max Weber: An Intellectual Portrait 412–17 (1960).

3 R. Tugwell, The Emerging Constitution 573, 574 (1974).

4 Joint Anti-Fascist Refugee Comm. v. McGrath, 341 U.S. 123, 179 (1951) (Douglas, J., concurring).

5 A. Bickel, The Morality of Consent 123 (1975).

6 5 U.S.C. § 551 *et seq.* (1970).

7 Wong Yang Sung v. McGrath, 339 U.S. 33, 41 (1950).

8 H. Maine, Early Law and Custom 389 (1886).

Chapter 11: Defining the idea of "agency"

1 Exec. Order No. 11,387, 3 C.F.R. 433 (1970), 12 U.S.C. §95a (Supp. V, 1970).

2 Section 5(b) of the Trading with the Enemy Act, originally enacted as the Act of Oct. 6, 1917, ch. 106, §5(b), 40 Stat. 966, has been amended several times and is now codified at both 12 U.S.C. § 95a (1970) and 50 U.S.C. App. 85(b) (1970),

3 Proclamation No. 2914, Dec. 16, 1950, 3 C.F.R. 99 (Comp. 1949–53), 50 U.S.C. App. § 1 (1964).

4 Dep't of Commerce Order 184-A, 33 Fed. Reg. 54 (1968).

5 When the Foreign Direct Investment Program was created, the attorney general gave his opinion that it was "a valid exercise of the authority conferred on the President by section 5(b) [of the Trading with the Enemy Act]." Letter from Attorney General Ramsey Clark to Secretary of Commerce Alexander B. Trowbridge, Feb. 3, 1968, in CCH Bal. Paym. Rep. ¶9031. The only legal challenge to the validity of the program ended inconclusively when OFDI settled the case. See International Legal Materials, Vol. XII, No. 5, p. 1165 (1973).

6 15 C.F.R. §§ 1000.101–1000.1303 (1970).
7 See, e.g., 34 Fed. Reg. 9564 (1969); Ellicott, United States Controls on Foreign Direct Investment: The 1969 Program, 34 Law & Contemp. Prob. 47 (1969).
8 Department of Commerce Organization Order 25-3A, 39 Fed. Reg. 25677 (1974).
9 Staff of Senate Comm. on the Judiciary, 79th Cong., 1st Sess., Report on the Administrative Procedure Act 13 (Comm. Print 1945).
10 S. Rep. No. 752, 79th Cong., 1st Sess. 10 (1945).
11 H. Rep. No. 1980, 79th Cong., 2d Sess. 19 (1946).
12 See also Attorney General's Manual on the Administrative Procedure Act 9–10 (1947); Attorney General's Memorandum on the Public Information Section of the Administrative Procedure Act 4 (1967).
13 F. Frankfurter, *The Reading of Statutes*, in Of Law and Men 44, 61 (P. Elman ed. 1956).
14 Final Report of the Attorney General's Committee on Administrative Procedure, S. Doc. No. 8, 77th Cong., 1st Sess. 7 (1941).
15 Final Report of the Attorney General's Committee on Administrative Procedure, S. Doc. No. 8, 77th Cong., 1st Sess. 7 (1941).
16 See, e.g., Renegotiation Board v. Bannercraft Clothing Co., 415 U.S. 1 (1974); Soucie v. David, 448 F.2d 1067 (D.C. Cir. 1971). Cf. Hannah v. Larche, 363 U.S. 420 (1960).
17 Brooklyn Nat'l Corp. v. Commissioner, 157 F.2d 450, 451 (2d Cir.), *cert. denied*, 329 U.S. 733 (1946).
18 339 U.S. 33 (1950).
19 See, e.g., Report of the President's Committee on Administrative Management 40 (1937); Nathanson, Separation of Functions Within Federal Administrative Agencies, 35 Ill. L. Rev. 901 (1941).
20 Separate agencies participate in the administration of the tax laws, the Treasury Department and the Internal Revenue Service having only rule-making authority, the Tax Court having only adjudicatory authority. The same is true for the administration of the Occupational Safety and Health Act of 1970, 29 U.S.C. § 651 *et seq.* (1970), under which the secretary of labor has the authority to issue citations for violations of safety and health standards and the Occupational Safety and Health Review Commission has the authority to adjudicate contested claims of violation.

Chapter 12: The Administrative Procedure Act and enforcement proceedings

1 United States v. Florida East Coast Ry., 410 U.S. 224 (1973). Although that decision involved the rule-making section of the Administrative Procedure Act, the language of that section is identical to that of the adjudication provisions in Section 554.
2 See Attorney General's Manual on the Administrative Procedure Act 14 (1947); United States v. Allegheny-Ludlum Steel Corp., 406 U.S. 742 (1972); First Nat'l Bank of Smithfield v. Saxon, 352 F.2d 267 (4th Cir. 1965).
3 339 U.S. 33 (1950).
4 Cf. Marcello v. Bonds, 349 U.S. 302 (1955); United States v. L. A. Tucker Truck Lines, Inc., 344 U.S. 33 (1952); Riss & Co. v. United States, 341 U.S. 907 (1951), *rev'g per curiam* 96 F. Supp. 452 (W.D. Mo. 1950).
5 The decision in *United States v. Florida East Coast Ry.*, 410 U.S. 224 (1973), does not mention that a constitutional requirement of a hearing can trigger the "required by statute" provision of the Administrative Procedure Act. But nothing in the opinion indicates an intention to call into question the reasoning of *Wong Yang Sung*. See Friendly, "Some Kind of Hearing," 123 U. Pa. L. Rev. 1267, 1310 (1975).

6 See, e.g., Goldberg v. Kelly, 397 U.S. 254 (1970); Cafeteria Workers Local 473 v. McElroy, 367 U.S. 886 (1961); Southern Ry. v. Virginia, 290 U.S. 190 (1933).

7 1 K. Davis, Administrative Law Treatise § 7.02, at 413 (1958). See H. Wade, Towards Administrative Justice 120 (1963).

8 Londoner v. City of Denver, 210 U.S. 373 (1908).

9 Bi-Metallic Inv. Co. v. State Bd. of Equalization, 239 U.S. 441 (1915).

10 Perry v. Sindermann, 408 U.S. 593 (1972); Board of Regents v. Roth, 408 U.S. 564 (1972).

11 397 U.S. 254 (1970).

12 408 U.S. 593 (1972).

13 408 U.S. 564, 573 (1972). See Gellhorn & Hornby, Constitutional Limitations on Admissions Procedures and Standards – Beyond Affirmative Action, 60 Va. L. Rev. 975 (1974).

14 Cafeteria Workers Local 473 v. McElroy, 367 U.S. 886, 895 (1961).

15 See North Am. Cold Storage Co. v. City of Chicago, 211 U.S. 306 (1908); Ewing v. Mytinger & Casselberry, Inc., 339 U.S. 594 (1950); Fahey v. Mallonee, 332 U.S. 245 (1947).

16 United States v. Curtiss-Wright Export Corp., 299 U.S. 304, 320 (1936). See Zemel v. Rusk, 381 U.S. 1 (1965); United States v. Pink, 315 U.S. 203 (1942).

17 Sardino v. Federal Reserve Bank, 361 F.2d 106, 112 (2d Cir.), *cert. denied*, 385 U.S. 898 (1966).

18 319 U.S. 432 (1943).

19 See Rostow, The Japanese American Cases – A Disaster, 54 Yale L.J. 489 (1945), reprinted in E. Rostow, The Sovereign Prerogative 193 (1962).

20 333 U.S. 103 (1948).

21 See United States *ex rel.* Schonbrun v. Commanding Officer, 403 F.2d 371, 375 n.2 (2d Cir. 1968); Bonfield, Military and Foreign Affairs Rule-Making Under the APA, 71 Mich. L. Rev. 221 (1972).

22 S. Rep. No. 752, 79th Cong., 1st Sess. 13 (1945); H.R. Rep. No. 1980, 79th Cong., 2d Sess. 23 (1946).

Chapter 13: The significance of an impartial hearing officer

1 Quoted in W. Gellhorn & C. Byse, Administrative Law, Cases and Comments 1077 (4th ed. 1960). See also Johnson, A Day in the Life: The Federal Communications Commission, 82 Yale L.J. 1575 (1973).

2 Final Report of the Attorney General's Committee on Administrative Procedure, S. Doc. No. 8, 77th Cong., 1st Sess. 43–46 (1941); Pound, For the "Minority Report," 27 A.B.A.J. 664 (1941).

3 345 U.S. 128, 132 (1953).

4 340 U.S. 474 (1951).

5 37 Fed. Reg. 16787 (1972), now 5 C.F.R. § 930.203a (1975).

6 15 C.F.R. § 1030.431(a) (1970).

7 15 C.F.R. § 1030.431(a) (1975).

8 344 U.S. 33 (1952).

9 341 U.S. 907 (1951), *rev'g per curiam* 96 F. Supp. 452 (W.D. Mo. 1950).

10 See also L. Jaffe, Judicial Control of Administrative Action 457 (1967).

11 339 U.S. 33, 52 (1950).

12 169 F. Supp. 746 (S.D.N.Y. 1959).

13 In 1962, an express statutory provision was enacted authorizing the judicial officer to become the agency for purposes of the Administrative Procedure Act, to the extent that

such functions are delegated to him by the postmaster general. 39 U.S.C. § 308a (1964). Cf. Grove Press, Inc. v. Christenberry, 175 F. Supp. 488 (S.D.N.Y. 1959).

Chapter 14: Separation of functions and the Constitution

1 Report of the President's Committee on Administrative Management (1937); Commission on Organization of the Executive Branch of the Government, Report on Legal Services and Procedure 61–62 (1955) (Second Hoover Commission); Hector, Problems of the CAB and the Independent Regulatory Commissions, 69 Yale L.J. 931 (1960).
2 J. Landis, The Administrative Process 10 (1938).
3 421 U.S. 35 (1975). See also Hortonville Joint School Dist. No. 1 v. Hortonville Educ. Ass'n, 426 U.S. 482 (1976); Richardson v. Perales, 402 U.S. 389 (1971).
4 339 U.S. 33 (1950).
5 339 U.S. at 50–51.
6 Immigration and Naturalization Act of 1952, 8 U.S.C. § 1252(b) (1970). See W. Gellhorn, Individual Freedom and Governmental Restraints 11–4 (1956).
7 349 U.S. 302 (1955).
8 2 K. Davis, Administrative Law Treatise § 13.06, at 215 (1958).
9 2 K. Davis, Administrative Law Treatise § 13.10, at 237 (1958).
10 2 K. Davis, Administrative Law Treatise § 13.11, at 249 (1958).
11 2 K. Davis, Administrative Law Treatise § 13.06, at 215 (1958).
12 Final Report of the Attorney General's Committee on Administrative Procedure, S. Doc. No. 8, 77th Cong., 1st Sess. 56 (1941).
13 Final Report of the Attorney General's Committee on Administrative Procedure, S. Doc. No. 8, 77th Cong., 1st Sess. 56 (1941).
14 See S. Rep. No. 752, 79th Cong., 1st Sess. 17–18 (1945); H.R. Rep. No. 1980, 79th Cong., 2d Sess. 30–31 (1946).
15 2 K. Davis, Administrative Law Treatise § 13.07, at 216; § 13.11, at 249 (1958).
16 In addition to the decisions discussed in the text, see ITT v. Local 134, Int'l Bhd. Elec. Wkrs., 419 U.S. 428 (1975); Camero v. United States, 375 F.2d 777 (Ct. Cl. 1967).
17 143 F. Supp. 243 (S.D.N.Y. 1956), *aff'd*, 252 F.2d 333 (2d Cir. 1958).
18 157 F. Supp. 548 (D.N.J. 1957).
19 256 F.2d 677 (2d Cir. 1958).
20 See United States Bio-Genics Corp. v. Christenberry, 173 F. Supp. 645 (S.D.N.Y. 1959); Greene v. Kern, 178 F. Supp. 201 (D.N.J.), *aff'd per curiam*, 269 F.2d 344 (3d Cir. 1959).

Chapter 15: Disqualification for bias

1 See S. Rep. No. 752, 79th Cong., 1st Sess. 18 (1945); H.R. Rep. No. 1980, 79th Cong. 2d Sess. 31 (1946).
2 Section 556(b) of the Administrative Procedure Act provides: "On the filing in good faith of a timely and sufficient affidavit of personal bias or other disqualification of a presiding or participating employee, the agency shall determine the matters as a part of the record and decision in the case."
3 Nilva v. United States, 352 U.S. 385 (1957); *In re* Murchison, 349 U.S. 133 (1955); Sacher v. United States, 343 U.S. 1 (1952).
4 2 K. Davis, Administrative Law Treatise § 12.01, at 131 (1958).

5 Tumey v. Ohio, 273 U.S. 510 (1927); Ward v. Village of Monroeville, 409 U.S. 57 (1973).
6 411 U.S. 564 (1973).
7 See Cinderella Career & Finishing Schools, Inc. v. FTC. 425 F.2d 583 (D.C. Cir. 1970); Texaco, Inc. v. FTC, 336 F.2d 754 (D.C. Cir. 1964), *vacated and remanded on other grounds*, 381 U.S. 739 (1965); cf. American Cyanamid Co. v. FTC, 363 F.2d 757 (6th Cir. 1966); Pillsbury Co. v. FTC, 354 F.2d 952 (5th Cir. 1966); Bufalino v. Kennedy, 322 F.2d 1016 (D.C. Cir. 1963).
8 421 U.S. 35 (1975). See Hortonville Joint School Dist. No. 1 v. Hortonville Educ. Ass'n, 426 U.S. 482 (1976).
9 330 U.S. 219 (1947).
10 268 F.2d 35 (9th Cir. 1959), *cert. denied*, 362 U.S. 961 (1960).
11 311 F.2d 349 (1st Cir. 1962).
12 306 F.2d 260 (D.C. Cir. 1962).
13 254 F.2d 90 (D.C. Cir. 1958).
14 363 F.2d 757 (6th Cir. 1966).
15 SEC v. R. A. Holman & Co., 323 F.2d 284, 286 (D.C. Cir. 1963), *cert. denied*, 375 U.S. 943 (1964).
16 R. A. Holman & Co. v. SEC, 366 F.2d 446 (2d Cir. 1966).
17 Final Report of the Attorney General's Committee on Administrative Procedure, S. Doc. 8, 77th Cong., 1st Sess. 56 (1941).
18 See *In re* Leffe, 2 Barb. 39 (N.Y. 1846).
19 Evans v. Gore, 253 U.S. 245, 247–48 (1920). See also Loughran v. FTC, 143 F.2d 431 (8th Cir. 1944); Brinkley v. Hassig, 83 F.2d 351 (10th Cir. 1936).
20 333 U.S. 683 (1948).
21 Marquette Cement Mfg. Co. v. FTC, 147 F.2d 589, 594 (7th Cir. 1945).
22 2 K. Davis, Administrative Law Treatise § 12.04, at 164 (1958).

Chapter 16: The meaning of summary action

1 Lawton v. Steele, 152 U.S. 133, 142 (1894). See generally Powell, Administrative Exercise of the Police Power, 24 Harv. L. Rev. 333, 336–38 (1911).
2 See, e.g., Adams v. Milwaukee, 228 U.S. 572 (1913); North Am. Cold Storage Co. v. Chicago, 211 U.S. 306 (1908).
3 See, e.g., State v. Schriber, 185 Ore. 615, 205 P.2d 149 (1949). It was a Massachusetts statute declaring horses with the glanders to be a nuisance that gave rise to Justice Holmes's celebrated opinion in Miller v. Horton, 152 Mass. 540, 26 N.E. 100 (1891).
4 See, e.g., Miller v. Schoene, 276 U.S. 272 (1928).
5 See, e.g., Samuels v. McCurdy, 267 U.S. 188 (1925).
6 See, e.g., State Sav. & Commercial Bank v. Anderson, 165 Cal. 437, 132 P. 755 (1913), *aff'd*, 238 U.S. 611 (1915).
7 See, e.g., Driscoll v. Edison Light & Power Co., 307 U.S. 104 (1939).
8 See, e.g., Jackson v. Bell, 143 Tenn. 452, 266 S.W. 207 (1920); Genesse Recreation Co. v. Edgerton, 172 App. Div. 464, 158 N.Y.S. 421 (1916).
9 Federal Hazardous Substances Labeling Act § 6, 15 U.S.C. § 1265 (1964), *as amended*, 15 U.S.C. § 1265 (1970); Food, Drug, and Cosmetic Act § 304, 21 U.S.C. § 334 (1970), *amending* 21 U.S.C. § 334 (1964); Drug Abuse Control Amendments of 1965 § 8(a), 21 U.S.C. § 372(e) (1970); Federal Meat Inspection Act §§ 3–6, 7(e), 21 U.S.C. §§ 603–06, 607(e) (1970).

10 Home Owners' Loan Act of 1933 § 5(d), 12 U.S.C. § 1464(d) (1970), *as amended by* Pub. L. No. 89-695 (Oct. 16, 1966) (appointment of a conservator or receiver subject to judicial removal within thirty days on petition of the savings association).

11 Securities Exchange Act of 1934 §§ 15(c)(5), 19(a)(4), 15 U.S.C. §§ 78*o*(c)(5), 78s(a)(4) (1970). The SEC's authority to enter "stop orders" against misleading registration statements may be exercised only after a hearing, Securities Act of 1933 § 8(d), 15 U.S.C. § 77h(d) (1970), but the impact of the announcement that such a hearing will be held has so great an effect in the marketplace that the authority is often regarded as summary. See Jones v. SEC, 298 U.S. 1 (1936); J. Landis, The Administrative Process 107–09 (1938).

12 E.g., United States Cotton Standards Act § 3, 7 U.S.C. § 53 (1970); United States Grain Standards Act § 7, 7 U.S.C. § 85 (1970); Federal Aviation Act §§ 609, 1005(a), 49 U.S.C. §§ 1429, 1485(a) (1970); 21 C.F.R. § 8.28 (1971).

13 E.g., Natural Gas Act § 4(e), 15 U.S.C. § 717c(e) (1970); Federal Power Act § 205(e), 16 U.S.C. § 824d(e) (1970); Federal Communications Act § 204, 47 U.S.C. § 204 (1970); Interstate Commerce Act §§ 15(7), 216(g), 218(c), 406(e), 907(g), 49 U.S.C. §§ 15(7), 316(g), 318(c), 1006(e), 907(g) (1970); Federal Aviation Act § 1002, 49 U.S.C. § 1482(g) (1970).

14 Report on Practices and Procedures of Governmental Control of Transportation, H.R. Doc. No. 678, 78th Cong., 2d Sess. 96 (1944).

15 Int. Rev. Code of 1954, § 6861.

16 Armstrong v. Manzo, 380 U.S. 545, 552 (1965). See also Mullane v. Central Hanover Trust Co., 339 U.S. 306, 313 (1950); Grannis v. Ordean, 234 U.S. 385, 394 (1914).

17 Goss v. Lopez, 419 U.S. 565 (1975); Fuentes v. Shevin, 407 U.S. 67 (1972); Bell v. Burson, 402 U.S. 535 (1971); Wheeler v. Montgomery, 397 U.S. 280 (1970); Goldberg v. Kelly, 397 U.S. 254 (1970); cf. Morrissey v. Brewer, 408 U.S. 471 (1972); Wisconsin v. Constantineau, 400 U.S. 433 (1971).

18 Sniadach v. Family Finance Corp., 395 U.S. 337, 343 n.* (1969) (Harlan, J., concurring); see Boddie v. Connecticut, 401 U.S. 371, 379 (1971).

19 Arnett v. Kennedy, 416 U.S. 134 (1974); see Perry v. Sindermann, 408 U.S. 593 (1972); Board of Regents v. Roth, 408 U.S. 564 (1972).

20 Mathews v. Eldridge, 424 U.S. 319, 343 (1976).

Chapter 17: Summary action and the Constitution

1 See, e.g., National Airlines, Inc. v. CAB, 306 F.2d 753, 758 (D.C. Cir. 1962); Nebraska Dep't of Aeronautics v. CAB, 298 F.2d 286 (8th Cir. 1962). Agencies asserting the power to act summarily without statutory authorization have been rebuffed by the courts. See, e.g., Kirby v. Shaw, 358 F.2d 446 (9th Cir. 1966); Standard Airlines, Inc. v. CAB, 177 F.2d 18 (D.C. Cir. 1949).

2 See, e.g., Stanard v. Olesen, 74 S. Ct. 768 (Douglas, Circuit Justice, 1954) (refusal to infer Post Office authority to impound mail summarily pending a hearing on mail fraud charges in light of the "constitutional implications" of such authority).

3 See, e.g., Phillips v. Commissioner, 283 U.S. 589, 594 (1931); R. A. Holman & Co. v. SEC, 299 F.2d 127, 132–33 (D.C. Cir.), *cert. denied*, 370 U.S. 911 (1962).

4 211 U.S. 306 (1908).

5 See, e.g., Jenkins v. McKeithen, 395 U.S. 411 (1969); Willner v. Committee on Character & Fitness, 373 U.S. 96 (1963); Goldsmith v. Board of Tax Appeals, 270 U.S. 117 (1926); Londoner v. Denver, 210 U.S. 373 (1908).

6 See, e.g., Morgan v. United States, 304 U.S. 1, 18–19 (1938); Garfield v. United States *ex rel.* Goldsby, 211 U.S. 249, 262 (1908); cf. Londoner v. Denver, 210 U.S. 373, 385 (1908).

7 See, e.g., Bowles v. Willingham, 321 U.S. 503, 519–21 (1944); Yakus v. United States, 321 U.S. 414, 436 (1944).

8 380 U.S. 545, 552 (1965). The "meaningful time" standard indicates some qualification of Chief Justice Stone's declaration that "[t]he demands of due process do not require a hearing, at the initial stage or at any particular point or at more than one point in an administrative proceeding so long as the requisite hearing is held before the final order becomes effective." Opp Cotton Mills, Inc. v. Administrator, 312 U.S. 126, 152 (1941). The Chief Justice's statement has usually been taken to mean that it is not of constitutional significance whether the constitutionally required hearing is given at the administrative level, Brown v. United States, 367 F.2d 907 (10th Cir. 1966), *cert. denied*, 387 U.S. 917 (1967), or by de novo review in court, Lichter v. United States, 334 U.S. 742 (1948); Jordan v. American Eagle Fire Ins. Co., 169 F.2d 281 (D.C. Cir. 1948).

9 408 U.S. 535, 542 (1971) (emphasis in original).

10 Analogies to commonplace stages of the criminal process, such as the return of an indictment, Ewing v. Mytinger & Casselberry, Inc., 339 U.S. 594, 599 (1950), or the denial of bail Oestereich v. Selective Serv. Sys. Local Bd. No. 11, 393 U.S. 233, 250 n.10 (1968) (Stewart, J., dissenting), are misleading insofar as they suggest that "emergency situations" may be of an equally commonplace character. Those analogies draw upon practices with distinctive historical roots, Jenkins v. McKeithen, 395 U.S. 411, 430 (1969); they are not helpful in assessing the constitutional meaning of words drawn from a different historical context.

11 The Federalist No. 25, at 211 (B. Wright ed. 1961).

12 255 U.S. 239 (1921).

13 321 U.S. 503 (1944).

14 Home Bldg. & Loan Ass'n v. Blaisdell, 290 U.S. 398, 426 (1934) (footnote omitted).

15 Legislation enacted under the war power "is executed in a time of patriotic fervor that makes moderation unpopular. And, worst of all, it is interpreted by the judges under the influence of the same passions and pressures." Woods v. Cloyd W. Miller Co., 333 U.S. 138, 146 (1948) (Jackson, J., concurring).

   With respect to the Emergency Price Control Act, Congress's concern that prior hearings might hamper the rent control program seems to have been borne out by subsequent developments: in the first four years of the program, landlords filed 1,340,955 petitions for rent adjustments, each seeking an individual determination. W. Gellhorn & C. Byse, Administrative Law, Cases and Comments 495 n.7 (5th ed. 1970). In light of the volume of cases, the administrative appeals machinery made available by OPA, and the opportunity for judicial review, the Court might well have held summary determination of maximum rents constitutional even in the absence of war.

16 Block v. Hirsh, 256 U.S. 135, 157 (1921).

17 The present provision permits the commissioner to assess a deficiency against a taxpayer and make demand for payment whenever he "believes that the assessment or collection of a deficiency . . . will be jeopardized by delay. . . ." Int. Rev. Code of 1954, § 6861(a).

18 See B. Bittker & L. Stone, Federal Income Estate and Gift Taxation 935 (4th ed. 1972).

19 283 U.S. 589 (1931). See also Laing v. United States, 423 U.S. 161 (1976).

20 59 U.S. (18 How.) 272 (1856).

21 O. W. Holmes, *The Path of the Law*, in Collected Legal Papers 191 (1920).

22 Fahey v. Mallonee, 332 U.S. 245, 247 (1947). See Home Owner's Loan Act of 1933 § 5(d), *as amended*, 12 U.S.C. § 1464(d) (1946).

23 Hykel v. Federal Sav. & Loan Ins. Corp., 317 F. Supp. 332 (E.D. Pa. 1970); Beacon Fed.

Sav. & Loan Ass'n v. FHLBB, 162 F. Supp. 350 (E.D. Wis. 1958), *appeal dismissed*, 266 F.2d 246 (7th Cir.), *cert. denied*, 361 U.S. 823 (1959).

24 332 U.S. 245 (1947).

25 The quoted phrase brings to mind the Court's reliance on tradition in *Phillips v. Commissioner*. The importance of long usage as a factor in the reasoning by which the constitutionality of summary action has been upheld was made express in an earlier decision that sustained a summary procedure by which the state took custody of abandoned bank deposits: "The fact that a procedure is so old as to have become customary and well known in the community is of great weight in determining whether it conforms to due process, for 'Not lightly vacated is the verdict of quiescent years.'" Anderson Nat'l Bank v. Luckett, 321 U.S. 233, 244 (1944), *quoting from* Coler v. Corn Exch. Bank, 250 N.Y. 136, 141, 164 N.E. 882, 884 (1928) (Cardozo, J.), *aff'd*, 280 U.S. 218 (1930).

26 Greater Del. Valley Fed. Sav. & Loan Ass'n v. FHLBB, 262 F.2d 371, 374 (3d Cir. 1958).

27 In the related context of summary suspension of a broker-dealer's exemption from the full registration requirements of the federal securities laws, the District of Columbia Circuit cited *Fahey v. Mallonee* for the proposition that summary action may be taken where the public harm from failure so to act will exceed the private harm that summary action may inflict. R. A. Holman & Co. v. SEC, 299 F.2d 127, 131 (D.C. Cir.), *cert. denied*, 370 U.S. 911 (1962).

28 211 U.S. 306 (1908).

29 See J. Dickinson, Administrative Justice and the Supremacy of Law in the United States 255–56 (1927). The Court dismissed the company's argument that destruction was improper because decayed foods have value for certain purposes.

30 Cf. Adams v. Milwaukee, 228 U.S. 572 (1913), sustaining the constitutionality of an ordinance providing for the summary destruction of milk brought into the city without having been tested for tuberculosis and other contagious diseases. The Court concluded that the legislature could properly believe that preservation of uninspected milk until it could be inspected was impractical, but it did so only after evaluating the alternatives itself. Similar demonstrations of the limited scope of extraordinary governmental action are often required, under various rhetorical formulas, even as courts are upholding the action. See, e.g., Miller v. Schoene, 276 U.S. 272, 278–79 (1928) ("the only practicable method of controlling the disease"); Anderson v. Dunn, 19 U.S. (6 Wheat.) 204, 231 (1821) ("least possible power adequate to the end proposed"); Miller v. Horton, 152 Mass. 540, 547, 26 N.E. 100, 102 (1891) (Holmes, J., would require "actual necessity").

31 339 U.S. 594 (1950).

32 See, e.g., Bell v. Burson, 402 U.S. 535, 545 n.5 (1971); Goldberg v. Kelly, 397 U.S. 254, 263 n.10 (1970).

33 21 U.S.C. § 337 (1946), *as amended*, 21 U.S.C. § 337 (1970).

34 416 U.S. 134 (1974). See Bishop v. Wood, 426 U.S. 341 (1976).

35 5 U.S.C. § 7501 (1970).

36 Merrill, Procedures for Adverse Actions Against Federal Employees, 59 Va. L. Rev. 196, 236 n.215 (1973).

37 408 U.S. 564 (1972). See Perry v. Sindermann, 408 U.S. 593 (1972).

38 See Tribe, Structural Due Process, 10 Harv. Civ. Rights–Civ. Lib. L. Rev. 269, 277 (1975).

39 397 U.S. 254 (1970); see Wheeler v. Montgomery, 397 U.S. 280 (1970).

40 See Handler, Justice for the Welfare Recipient: Fair Hearings in AFDC – The Wisconsin Experience, 43 Soc. Serv. Rev. 12, 22 (1969); cf. Richardson v. Wright, 405 U.S. 208, 221 (1972) (Brennan, J., dissenting) (official figures of a similar magnitude for reversals of suspensions of disability benefits under the Social Security Act).

41 Kelly v. Wyman, 294 F. Supp. 893, 901 (S.D.N.Y. 1968).

42 The Court sought to buttress its holding by reference to the social goals that animate the public assistance system: providing opportunities to the poor, avoiding the consequences of widespread frustration and insecurity. Achievement of those goals depends not only on termination procedures but also on the procedures by which initial eligibility is established. The Court, however, did not consider the possibility raised by Justice Black that if pretermination hearings are required, "the government will not put a claimant on the rolls initially until it has made an exhaustive investigation to determine his eligibility," thereby "insur[ing] that many will never get on the rolls, or at least that they will remain destitute during the lengthy proceedings followed to determine eligibility."

43 395 U.S. 337 (1969).

44 Although the impact of a jeopardy assessment may be as severe as the impact of a garnishment, it is doubtful whether *Sniadach* undermines the constitutionality of the jeopardy assessment, which rests on the more substantial state interest that it serves.

45 400 U.S. 433 (1971). See Paul v. Davis, 424 U.S. 693 (1976).

46 A statute that lodges the authority to initiate summary action in relatively minor officials, as in *Constantineau*, or in private citizens, as in both *Constantineau* and *Sniadach*, greatly increases the likelihood of its ill-considered use. An administrative agency exercising summary authority is more likely to be cognizant of the legal implications of acting summarily, to have an informed basis for action, and to be compelled by its limited resources to restrict its use of summary action to the most egregious instances.

47 402 U.S. 535 (1971).

48 424 U.S. 319 (1976). See also Fusari v. Steinberg, 419 U.S. 379 (1975); Carleson v. Yee-Litt, 412 U.S. 924 (1973); Daniel v. Goliday, 398 U.S. 73 (1970).

49 419 U.S. 565 (1975).

50 Wolff v. McDonnell, 418 U.S. 539, 557–58 (1974). See Friendly, "Some Kind of Hearing," 123 U. Pa. L. Rev. 1267 (1975).

Chapter 18: Summary action as an administrative process

1 435 F.2d 1151, 1161, *rev'g on rehearing en banc* 435 F.2d 1133 (7th Cir. 1970), *petition for cert. dismissed*, 402 U.S. 935 (1971). The case is described in B. Roueche, The Orange Man 116–37 (1971).

2 Federal Insecticide, Fungicide, and Rodenticide Act § 4(c), 7 U.S.C. § 135b(c) (1970).

3 Spritzer, Uses of Summary Power to Suspend Rates: An Examination of Federal Regulatory Agency Practices, 120 U. Pa. L. Rev. 39, 53, 57 & 76 (1971).

4 The Interstate Commerce Commission formalized the reality of the staff's preponderant role in the determination of whether to act summarily: The commissioners delegated to a board of five employees the authority to decide initially whether to suspend proposed tariffs, subject to review by a division of the commission. 26 Fed. Reg. 5167 (1961).

5 Commission on Organization of the Executive Branch of the Government, The Independent Regulatory Commissions 146 (1949) (Apendix N).

6 Elman, Administrative Reform of the Federal Trade Commission, 59 Geo. L.J. 777, 810 (1971). See Withrow v. Larkin, 421 U.S. 35 (1975).

7 See, e.g., Final Report of the Attorney General's Comm. on Administrative Procedure, S. Doc. No. 8, 77th Cong. 1st Sess. 35 (1941); Report of the ABA Commission to Study the Federal Trade Commission (1969).

8 W. Gellhorn & C. Byse, Administrative Law, Cases and Comments 878–79 (5th ed. 1970).

9 Austern, Sanctions in Silhouette, Lecture at the Harvard Law School, March 22, 1960,

quoted in W. Gellhorn & C. Byse, Administrative Law, Cases and Comments 672 (4th ed. 1960).

10 Freeman, Administrative Procedures, 22 Bus. Law. 891, 897 (1967).

11 437 F.2d 397 (2d Cir. 1971).

12 397 U.S. 254, 264 (1970).

13 R. Caves, Air Transport and Its Regulators 362 (1962); see Moss v. CAB, 430 F.2d 891 (D.C. Cir. 1970).

14 In addition, an individual who is subject to an agency's continuing supervision may sometimes accede to an agency demand in the belief that too-frequent resistance may, in the long run, jeopardize his relationship with the agency.

15 1967 HEW Ann. Rep. 198.

16 K. Davis, Administrative Law, Cases – Text – Problems 73–74 (1965).

17 21 C.F.R. § 3.85 (1972).

18 1967 HEW Ann. Rep. 197.

19 430 F.2d 891 (D.C. Cir. 1970).

Chapter 19: Structuring the use of summary action

1 § 4(c), 7 U.S.C. § 135b(c) (1970).

2 108 Cong. Reg. 17,366 (1962) (remarks of Senator Eastland).

3 Universal Camera Corp. v. NLRB, 340 U.S. 474, 487 (1951).

4 See, e.g., K. Davis, Discretionary Justice: A Preliminary Inquiry (1969); H. Friendly, The Federal Administrative Agencies (1962); Wright, Beyond Discretionary Justice, 81 Yale L.J. 575 (1972); Kennecott Copper Corp. v. EPA, 462 F.2d 846 (D. C. Cir. 1972); United States v. Bryant, 439 F.2d 642, 652 & n.22 (D.C. Cir. 1971); Holmes v. New York City Housing Authority, 398 F.2d 262 (2d Cir. 1968).

5 5 U.S.C. § 552(a) (1970).

6 See Reiss, Research on Administrative Discretion and Justice, 23 J. Legal Ed. 69, 73 (1970) (footnote omitted): "The literature on decision-making strongly suggests that an increase in alternatives reduces the capacity to discriminate among them. This seems to be true for all forms of cognitive discrimination. . . . Injustice may arise as much from many rules as it does from a relative lack of them."

7 12 C.F.R. § 547.1 (1972).

8 401 U.S. 402 (1971). See Camp v. Pitts, 411 U.S. 138 (1973). The Administrative Procedure Act's requirement that "[a]ll decisions, including initial, recommended, and tentative decisions . . . include a statement of – (A) findings and conclusions, and the reasons or basis therefor," does not apply to summary action; it is limited to instances in which there has been a hearing required by statute. 5 U.S.C. § 557(a), (c)(3) (1970).

9 Interstate Commerce Act §§ 15(7), 216(g), 218(c), 406(e), 907(g), 49 U.S.C. §§ 15(7), 216(g), 218(c), 406(e), 907(g) (1970). Statutes modeled after the Interstate Commerce Act appear at Chapter 16, note 13.

10 See, e.g., Burlington Truck Lines, Inc. v. United States, 371 U.S. 156 (1962); SEC v. Chenery Corp., 318 U.S. 80 (1943).

11 In addition to the two decisions discussed in the text, see Dunlop v. Bachowski, 421 U.S. 560 (1975); Brooks v. AEC, 476 F.2d 924 (D.C. Cir. 1973); Medical Comm. for Human Rights v. SEC, 432 F.2d 659 (D.C. Cir. 1970), *vacated as moot*, 404 U.S. 403 (1972); Environmental Defense Fund, Inc. v. Hardin, 428 F.2d 1093 (D.C. Cir. 1970); United States v. Broyles, 423 F.2d 1299 (4th Cir. 1970).

12 439 F.2d 584 (D.C. Cir. 1971).

13 465 F.2d 528 (D.C. Cir. 1972).

14 In both *Environmental Defense Fund* cases the court required a statement of reasons for administrative decisions *not* to take summary action – decisions "not ordinarily . . . made in a matter of moments, or even hours or days." 465 F.2d at 539.

15 Statements of reasons should not be required, of course, when the volume of the agency's business would prevent it from preparing meaningful statements. The Interstate Commerce Commission, for example, would have great practical difficulty preparing a statement of reasons each time it permitted one of the hundreds of thousands of proposed tariffs filed with it annually to take effect without suspension. Situations of this kind would be appropriate exceptions from a blanket requirement that reasons be given for each decision to take, or not to take, summary action.

16 Spritzer, Uses of the Summary Power to Suspend Rates: An Examination of Federal Regulatory Agency Practices, 120 U. Pa. L. Rev. 39, 61–62 (1971).

17 Gardner, The Procedures by Which Informal Action Is Taken, 24 Ad. L. Rev. 155, 163–64 (1972). The only similar provision of present law, Section 558(c) of the Administrative Procedure Act, 5 U.S.C. § 558(c) (1970), is limited: It prohibits an agency from suspending a license unless the licensee has been given written notice before institution of proceedings and an "opportunity to demonstrate or achieve compliance," except when the "public health, interest, or safety requires otherwise," the classic circumstances in which summary action is justified.

18 Compare Moss v. CAB, 430 F.2d 891 (D.C. Cir. 1970) , with Public Util. Comm'n v. United States, 356 F.2d 236 (9th Cir.), *cert. denied,* 385 U.S. 816 (1966).

19 334 F.2d 570 (D.C. Cir. 1964).

20 437 F.2d 397 (2d Cir. 1971).

21 162 F. Supp. 350 (E.D. Wis. 1958), *appeal dismissed,* 266 F.2d 246 (7th Cir.), *cert. denied,* 361 U.S. 823 (1959).

22 See, e.g., Federal Insecticide, Fungicide, and Rodenticide Act § 4(c), 7 U.S.C. § 135b(c) (1970); Food, Drug, and Cosmetic Act § 404, 21 U.S.C. § 344 (1970).

23 § 19(a)(4), 15 U.S.C. § 78s(a)(4) (1970); § 15(c)(5), 15 U.S.C. § 78o(c)(5) (1970). But the commission often "tacks" one ten-day suspension period onto another if it determines that circumstances require continuation of the suspension period.

24 Interstate Commerce Act § 15(7), 49 U.S.C. § 15(7) (1970); see Arrow Transp. Co. v. Southern Ry., 372 U.S. 658 (1963).

25 Congress could mitigate the impact that limiting the effective period of summary orders might have on enforcement policy and practice by providing that an agency need only commence an adjudicatory hearing to toll the limitation. Assuming that the agency did not prolong the hearing unnecessarily, the summary order would then remain in effect until the hearing was completed. Such a provision would create an incentive for the agency to move expeditiously to a hearing (although inadequacies of staff and resources could still prevent it from acting) and yet permit a more deliberative hearing than could be conducted within the limitation period.

26 See, e.g., Federal Meat Inspection Act §§ 402–03, 21 U.S.C. §§ 672–73 (1970); National Housing Act § 407(k)(2), 12 U.S.C. § 1730(k)(2) (1970).

27 See, e.g., Arrow Transp. Co. v. Southern Ry., 372 U.S. 658 (1963); Abbott Laboratories v. Gardner, 387 U.S. 136 (1967); Hahn v. Gottlieb, 430 F.2d 1243 (1st Cir. 1970); Nor-Am Agricultural Prods., Inc. v. Hardin, 435 F.2d 1151, *rev'g on rehearing en banc* 435 F.2d 1133 (7th Cir. 1970), *petition for cert. dismissed,* 402 U.S. 935 (1971); Greater Del. Valley Fed. Sav. & Loan Ass'n v. FHLBB, 262 F.2d 371 (3d Cir. 1958).

28 See, e.g., Goldberg v. Kelly, 397 U.S. 254 (1970); Abbott Laboratories v. Gardner, 387 U.S. 136 (1967).
29 1 E. Burke, Works 379 (rev. ed. 1865) (orig. ed. 1770).

Chapter 20: The challenge of administrative legitimacy

1 Dicey, The Development of Administrative Law in England, 31 L.Q. Rev. 148 (1915); A. Dicey, An Introduction to the Study of the Law of the Constitution (1885); F. Maitland, Constitutional History 505–06 (1908).
2 F. Frankfurter & J. Davison, Cases and Other Materials on Administrative Law vii (1932).
3 F. Frankfurter & J. Davison, Cases and Other Materials on Administrative Law viii (1932).

Bibliography

A comprehensive bibliography of books on administrative·law and the administrative process would comprise a book-length volume in itself. The books included on the following selected list are those that I found particularly useful in the course of thinking about the questions discussed in this book.

Abrahamson, Mark, *The Professional in the Organization* (Chicago: Rand McNally and Co., 1967).

Allen, Carleton K., *Bureaucracy Triumphant* (London: Oxford Univ. Press, 1931).

Appleby, Paul H., *Policy and Administration* (University, Ala.: Univ. of Alabama Press, 1949).

Attorney General's Committee on Administrative Procedure, *Final Report* (Washington, D.C.: U.S. Government Printing Office, S. Doc. No. 8, 77th Cong., 1st Sess., 1941).

Auerbach, Jerold S., *Unequal Justice: Lawyers and Social Change in Modern America* (New York: Oxford Univ. Press, 1975).

Barber, James D., *The Presidential Character: Predicting Performance in the White House* (Englewood Cliffs, N.J.: Prentice-Hall, 1972).

Barber, Sotirios A., *The Constitution and the Delegation of Congressional Power* (Chicago: Univ. of Chicago Press, 1975).

Beck, James M., *Our Wonderland of Bureaucracy: A Study of the Growth of Bureaucracy in the Federal Government and Its Destructive Effect Upon the Constitution* (New York: Macmillan Co., 1932).

Bendix, Reinhard, *Max Weber: An Intellectual Portrait* (Garden City, N.Y.: Doubleday and Company, 1960).

Bentley, Arthur F., *The Process of Government: A Study of Social Pressures* (Chicago: Univ. of Chicago Press, 1908).

Berger, Raoul, *Impeachment: The Constitutional Problems* (Cambridge, Mass.: Harvard Univ. Press, 1973).

Berman, Harold J., ed., *Talks on American Law* (New York: Vintage Books, 1961).

Bernstein, Marver H., *The Job of the Federal Executive* (Washington, D.C.: Brookings Institution, 1958).

   Regulating Business by Independent Commission (Princeton, N.J.: Princeton Univ. Press, 1955).

Bickel, Alexander M., *The Least Dangerous Branch: The Supreme Court at the Bar of Politics* (Indianapolis, Ind.: Bobbs-Merrill Co., 1962).

   The Morality of Consent (New Haven, Conn.: Yale Univ. Press, 1975).

   The New Age of Political Reform (New York: Harper & Row, 1968).

304

Politics and the Warren Court (New York: Harper & Row, 1965).

The Supreme Court and the Idea of Progress (New York: Harper & Row, 1970).

Black, Charles L., Jr., *The People and the Court: Judicial Review in a Democracy* (New York: Macmillan Co., 1960).

Blau, Peter M., *The Dynamics of Bureaucracy: A Study of Interpersonal Relationships in Two Government Agencies* (Chicago: Univ. of Chicago Press, rev. 2d ed. 1963).

Blau, Peter M., and Marshall W. Meyer, *Bureaucracy in Modern Society* (New York: Random House, 2d ed. 1971).

Blumrosen, Alfred W., *Black Employment and the Law* (New Brunswick, N.J.: Rutgers Univ. Press, 1971).

Brandeis, Louis D., *Other People's Money and How the Bankers Use It* (New York: Frederick A. Stokes Co., 1914).

Carr, Cecil T., *Concerning English Administrative Law* (New York: Columbia Univ. Press, 1941).

Cary, William L., *Politics and the Regulatory Agencies* (New York: McGraw-Hill Book Co., 1967).

Clark, John M., *Social Control of Business* (Chicago: Univ. of Chicago Press, 1926).

Commission on Organization of the Executive Branch of the Government, *Reports* (Washington, D.C.: U.S. Government Printing Office, 1949; 1955).

Cooper, Frank E., *State Administrative Law* (Indianapolis, Ind.: Bobbs-Merrill Co., 2 vols. 1965).

Corwin, Edward S., *The President, Office and Powers* (New York: New York Univ. Press, rev. 4th ed. 1957).

Cushman, Robert E., *The Independent Regulatory Commissions* (New York: Oxford Univ. Press, 1941).

Dahl, Robert A., *After the Revolution? Authority in a Good Society* (New Haven, Conn.: Yale Univ. Press, 1970).

Polyarchy: Participation and Opposition (New Haven, Conn.: Yale Univ. Press, 1971).

A Preface to Democratic Theory (Chicago: Univ. of Chicago Press, 1956).

Davis, Kenneth C., *Administrative Law Treatise* (St. Paul, Minn.: West Publishing Co., 4 vols. 1958, Supplement 1970).

Administrative Law of the Seventies (Rochester, N.Y.: Lawyers Co-Operative Publishing Co., 1976).

Discretionary Justice: A Preliminary Inquiry (Baton Rouge, La.: Louisiana State Univ. Press, 1969).

Discretionary Justice in Europe and America (Urbana, Ill.: Univ. of Illinois Press, 1976).

Dawson, Robert M., *The Principle of Official Independence* (London: P.S. King and Son, 1922).

de Bedts, Ralph F., *The New Deal's SEC: The Formative Years* (New York: Columbia Univ. Press, 1964).

Dickinson, John, *Administrative Justice and the Supremacy of Law in the United States* (Cambridge, Mass.: Harvard Univ. Press, 1927).

Dole, Charles F., *The American Citizen* (Indianapolis, Ind.: D.C. Heath and Co., 1891).

Douglas, Paul H., *Ethics in Government* (Cambridge, Mass.: Harvard Univ. Press, 1952).

Douglas, William O., *Democracy and Finance* (New Haven, Conn.: Yale Univ. Press, 1940).

Points of Rebellion (New York: Random House, 1970).

We the Judges: Studies in American and Indian Constitutional Law from Marshall to Mukherjea (Garden City, N.Y.: Doubleday and Company, 1956).

Downs, Anthony, *Inside Bureaucracy* (Boston, Mass.: Little, Brown and Co., 1967).

Edelman, Murray, *The Symbolic Uses of Politics* (Urbana, Ill.: Univ. of Illinois Press, 1964).

Bibliography

Evan, William M., ed., *Law and Sociology* (Glencoe, Ill.: The Free Press, 1962).

Fenno, Richard F., Jr., *Congressmen in Committees* (Boston, Mass.: Little, Brown and Co., 1973).

The Power of the Purse: Appropriations Politics in Congress (Boston, Mass.: Little, Brown and Co., 1966).

Finer, Herman, *The Presidency: Crisis and Regeneration* (Chicago: Univ. of Chicago Press, 1960).

Forcey, Charles, *The Crossroads of Liberalism: Croly, Weyl, Lippmann and the Progressive Era, 1900–1925* (New York: Oxford Univ. Press, 1961).

Frank, Jerome, *Courts on Trial: Myth and Reality in American Justice* (Princeton, N.J.: Princeton Univ. Press, 1949).

If Men Were Angels: Some Aspects of Government in a Democracy (New York: Harper and Brothers, 1942).

Frankel, Charles, *High on Foggy Bottom: An Outsider's Inside View of the Government* (New York: Harper & Row, 1969).

Frankfurter, Felix, *The Public and Its Government* (New Haven, Conn.: Yale Univ. Press, 1930).

and J. Forrester Davison, eds., *Cases and Other Materials on Administrative Law* (New York: Commerce Clearing House, 1932).

Freund, Ernst, *Administrative Powers over Persons and Property: A Comparative Survey* (Chicago: Univ. of Chicago Press, 1928).

Cases on Administrative Law Selected from Decisions of English and American Courts (St. Paul, Minn.: West Publishing Co., 1911).

Freund, Ernst, et al., *The Growth of American Administrative Law* (St. Louis, Mo.: Thomas Law Book Co., 1923).

Freund, Ernst, *Standards of American Legislation* (Chicago: Univ. of Chicago Press, 2d ed. 1965).

Friedman, Lawrence M., *A History of American Law* (New York: Simon and Schuster, 1973).

Friedman, Milton, *Capitalism and Freedom* (Chicago: Univ. of Chicago Press, 1962).

Friendly, Henry J., *Benchmarks* (Chicago: Univ. of Chicago Press, 1967).

The Federal Administrative Agencies: The Need for Better Definition of Standards (Cambridge, Mass.: Harvard Univ. Press, 1962).

Federal Jurisdiction: A General View (New York: Columbia Univ. Press, 1973).

Fuess, Claude M., *Joseph B. Eastman, Servant of the People* (New York: Columbia Univ. Press, 1952).

Galbraith, John K., *The Affluent Society* (Boston, Mass.: Houghton Mifflin Co., rev. ed. 1971).

Economics and the Public Purpose (Boston, Mass.: Houghton Mifflin Co., 1973).

Gellhorn, Ernest, *Administrative Law and Process in a Nutshell* (St. Paul, Minn.: West Publishing Co., 1972).

Gellhorn, Walter, *Individual Freedom and Governmental Restraints* (Baton Rouge, La.: Louisiana State Univ. Press, 1956).

Ombudsmen and Others: Citizens' Protectors in Nine Countries (Cambridge, Mass.: Harvard Univ. Press, 1966).

When Americans Complain: Governmental Grievance Procedures (Cambridge, Mass.: Harvard Univ. Press, 1966).

Gellhorn, Walter, and Clark Byse, *Administrative Law, Cases and Comments* (Mineola, N.Y.: Foundation Press, 4th ed. 1960; 5th ed. 1970; 6th ed. 1974).

Gerth, Hans, and C. Wright Mills, *From Max Weber: Essays in Sociology* (New York: Oxford Univ. Press, 1946).

Giddens, Anthony, *Politics and Sociology in the Thought of Max Weber* (London: Macmillan Press, 1972).

Goldman, Eric F., *Rendezvous with Destiny* (New York: Alfred A. Knopf, 1952).

Goodnow, Frank J., *Politics and Administration: A Study in Government* (New York: Russell and Russell, 1900).

    The Principles of the Administrative Law of the United States (New York: G. P. Putnam's Sons, 1905).

Goodwin, Richard N., *The American Condition* (Garden City, N.Y.: Doubleday and Company, 1974).

Gwyn, William B., *The Meaning of the Separation of Powers* (New Orleans, La.: Vol. 9, Tulane Studies in Political Science, 1965).

Hamilton, Walton, *The Politics of Industry* (New York: Alfred A. Knopf, 1957).

Hamson, Charles J., *Executive Discretion and Judicial Control: An Aspect of the French Conseil d'Etat* (London: Stevens and Sons, 1954).

Hand, Learned, *The Bill of Rights* (Cambridge, Mass.: Harvard Univ. Press, 1958).

Handler, Joel F., and Ellen J. Hollingsworth, *The Deserving Poor: A Study of Welfare Administration* (Chicago: Markham Publishing Co.. 1971).

Handlin, Oscar, and Mary Handlin, *The Wealth of the American People: A History of American Affluence* (New York: McGraw-Hill Book Co., 1975).

Harris, Josepn P., *Congressional Control of Administration* (Washington, D.C.: Brookings Institution, 1964).

Hawley, Ellis W., *The New Deal and the Problem of Monopoly: A Study in Economic Ambivalence* (Princeton, N.J.: Princeton Univ. Press, 1966).

Henderson, Gerard C., *The Federal Trade Commission* (New Haven, Conn.: Yale Univ. Press, 1924).

Herring, Edward P., *Public Administration and the Public Interest* (New York: McGraw-Hill Book Co., 1936).

Hewart, Gordon, *The New Despotism* (London: Ernest Benn, 1929).

Hofstadter, Richard, *The Age of Reform: From Bryan to F.D.R.* (New York: Alfred A. Knopf, 1955).

    The American Political Tradition (New York: Alfred A. Knopf, 1948).

    Anti-intellectualism in American Life (New York: Alfred A. Knopf, 1963).

Holmes, Oliver W., Jr., *Collected Legal Papers* (New York: Harcourt, Brace and Co., 1920).

Humbert, Willard H., *The Pardoning Power of the President* (Washington, D.C.: American Council on Public Affairs, 1941).

Hurst, James W. *The Growth of American Law: The Law Makers* (Boston, Mass.: Little, Brown and Co., 1950).

Hyneman, Charles S., *Bureaucracy in a Democracy* (New York: Harper and Brothers, 1950).

Jackson, Robert H., *The Struggle for Judicial Supremacy: A Study of a Crisis in American Power Politics* (New York: Alfred A. Knopf, 1941).

Jacoby, Henry, *The Bureaucratization of the World* (Berkeley, Calif.: Univ. of California Press, 1974).

Jaffe, Louis L., *Judicial Control of Administrative Action* (Boston, Mass.: Little, Brown and Co., 1965).

Jaffe, Louis L., and Nathaniel L. Nathanson, *Administrative Law: Cases and Materials* (Boston, Mass.: Little, Brown and Co., 3d ed. 1968; 4th ed. 1976).

Jowell, Jeffrey L., *Law and Bureaucracy* (Port Washington, N.Y.: Dunellen Pub. Co., 1975).

Kaufman, Herbert, *Administrative Feedback: Monitoring Subordinates' Behavior* (Washington, D.C.: Brookings Institution, 1973).

Bibliography

Kirst, Michael W., *Government Without Passing Laws: Congress' Non-statutory Techniques for Appropriations Control* (Chapel Hill, N.C.: Univ. of North Carolina Press, 1969).

Kissinger, Henry A., *The Necessity for Choice* (New York: Harper & Row, 1961).

Koch, Adrienne, *Madison's "Advice to My Country"* (Princeton, N.J.: Princeton Univ. Press, 1966).

Kohlmeier, Louis M., Jr., *The Regulators: Watchdog Agencies and the Public Interest* (New York: Harper & Row, 1969).

Kolko, Gabriel, *Railroads and Regulation, 1877–1916* (Princeton, N.J.: Princeton Univ. Press, 1965).

Krislov, Samuel, and Lloyd D. Muslof, eds., *The Politics of Regulation: A Reader* (Boston, Mass.: Houghton Mifflin Co., 1964).

Landis, James M., *The Administrative Process* (New Haven, Conn.: Yale Univ. Press, 1938).
  Report on Regulatory Agencies to the President-Elect, Submitted by the Chairman of the Subcomm. on Administrative Practice and Procedure of the Senate Comm. on the Judiciary (Washington, D.C.: U.S. Government Printing Office, Comm. Print, 86th Cong., 2d Sess., 1960).

Lazarus, Simon, *The Genteel Populists* (New York: McGraw-Hill Book Co., 1974).

Leuchtenburg, William E., *Franklin D. Roosevelt and the New Deal, 1932–1940* (New York: Harper & Row, 1963).

Linde, Hans A., and George Bunn, *Legislative and Administrative Processes* (Mineola, N.Y.: Foundation Press, 1976).

Link, Arthur S., *Woodrow Wilson and the Progressive Era: 1910–1917* (New York: Harper & Row, 1954).

Lippmann, Walter, *Drift and Mastery: An Attempt to Diagnose the Current Unrest* (New York: Mitchell Kennerley Co., 1914).
  Public Opinion (New York: Harcourt, Brace and Co., 1922).

Lipset, Seymour M., *Political Man: Essays on the Sociology of Democracy* (Garden City, N.Y.: Doubleday and Company, 1963).

Llewellyn, Karl N., *The Common Law Tradition: Deciding Appeals* (Boston, Mass.: Little, Brown and Co., 1960).
  Jurisprudence: Realism in Theory and Practice (Chicago: Univ. of Chicago Press, 1962).

Lowell, Abbott L., *Public Opinion and Popular Government* (New York: Longmans, Green and Co., 1913).

Lowi, Theodore J., *The End of Liberalism* (New York: W. W. Norton and Co., 1969).
  The Politics of Disorder (New York: Basic Books, 1971).

MacAvoy, Paul W., ed., *The Crisis of the Regulatory Commissions* (New York: W. W. Norton and Co., 1970).

McCloskey, Robert G., ed., *The Works of James Wilson* (Cambridge, Mass.: Harvard Univ. Press, 1967).

McConnell, Grant, *Private Power and American Democracy* (New York: Random House, 1966).

McIlwain, Charles H., *Constitutionalism: Ancient and Modern* (Ithaca, N.Y.: Cornell Univ. Press, rev. ed. 1958).

MacRae, Donald G., *Max Weber* (New York: Viking Press, 1974).

Maine, Sir Henry J., *Ancient Law* (New York: Henry Holt and Son, 1874).

Manley, John F., *The Politics of Finance: The House Committee on Ways and Means* (Boston, Mass.: Little, Brown and Co., 1970).

Mann, Dean E., and Jameson W. Doig, *The Assistant Secretaries: Problems and Processes of Appointment* (Washington, D.C.: Brookings Institution, 1965).

Mannheim, Karl, *Ideology and Utopia: An Introduction to the Sociology of Knowledge* (New York: Harcourt, Brace and Co., 1954).

Marx, Fritz M., *The Administrative State: An Introduction to Bureaucracy* (Chicago: Univ. of Chicago Press, 1957).

Mayhew, Leon, *Law and Equal Opportunity: A Study of the Massachusetts Commission Against Discrimination* (Cambridge, Mass.: Harvard Univ. Press, 1968).

Mendelson, Wallace, ed., *Felix Frankfurter: A Tribute* (New York: Reynal and Co., 1964).

Felix Frankfurter: The Judge (New York: Reynal and Co., 1964).

Merton, Robert K., *Social Theory and Social Structure* (New York: The Free Press, rev. ed. 1968).

Milgram, Stanley, *Obedience to Authority* (New York: Harper & Row, 1974).

Mommsen, Wolfgang J., *The Age of Bureaucracy: Perspectives on the Political Sociology of Max Weber* (New York: Harper & Row, 1974).

Nisbet, Robert, *Twilight of Authority* (New York: Oxford Univ. Press, 1975).

Niskanen, William A., Jr., *Bureaucracy and Representative Government* (Chicago: Aldine Publishing Co., 1971).

Noll, Roger G., *Reforming Regulation: An Evaluation of the Ash Council Proposals* (Washington, D.C.: Brookings Institution, 1971).

Nonet, Philippe, *Administrative Justice: Advocacy and Change in a Government Agency* (New York: Russell Sage Foundation, 1969).

Okun, Arthur M., *Equality and Efficiency: The Big Tradeoff* (Washington, D.C.: Brookings Institution, 1975).

Olson, Mancur, Jr., *The Logic of Collective Action* (Cambridge, Mass.: Harvard Univ. Press, 1965).

Packer, Herbert L., *The Limits of the Criminal Sanction* (Stanford, Calif.: Stanford Univ. Press, 1968).

Parrish, Michael E., *Securities Regulation and the New Deal* (New Haven, Conn.: Yale Univ. Press, 1970).

Piven, Frances F., and Richard A. Cloward, *Regulating the Poor: The Functions of Public Welfare* (New York: Pantheon Books, 1971).

President's Advisory Council on Executive Organization, *A New Regulatory Framework* (Washington, D.C.: U.S. Government Printing Office, 1971).

President's Committee on Administrative Management, *Report of the Committee with Studies of Administration in Federal Government* (Washington, D.C.: U.S. Government Printing Office, 1937).

Redford, Emmette S., *Democracy in the Administrative State* (New York: Oxford Univ. Press, 1969).

The Regulatory Process (Austin, Tex.: Univ. of Texas Press, 1969).

Reedy, George, *The Twilight of the Presidency* (New York: World Publishing Co., 1970).

Rehfuss, John, *Public Administration as Political Process* (New York: Charles Scribner's Sons, 1973).

Robinson, Glen O., *The Forest Service: A Study in Public Land Management* (Baltimore, Md.: Johns Hopkins Univ. Press, 1975).

Robinson, Glen O., and Ernest Gellhorn, *The Administrative Process* (St. Paul, Minn.: West Publishing Co., 1974).

Robson, William A., *The Governors and the Governed* (Baton Rouge, La.: Louisiana State Univ. Press, 1964).

Roueche, Berton, *The Orange Man* (Boston, Mass.: Little, Brown and Co., 1971).

Rourke, Francis E., *Bureaucracy, Politics, and Public Policy* (Boston, Mass.: Little, Brown and Co., 1969).

Bibliography

Sax, Joseph L., *Defending the Environment* (New York: Alfred A. Knopf, 1971).
Schlesinger, Arthur M., Jr., *The Coming of the New Deal* (Boston, Mass.: Houghton Mifflin Co., 1959).
 The Crisis of the Old Order: 1919–33 (Boston, Mass.: Houghton Mifflin Co., 1957).
 The Imperial Presidency (Boston, Mass.: Houghton Mifflin Co., 1973).
 The Politics of Upheaval (Boston, Mass.: Houghton Mifflin Co., 1960).
Schwartz, Bernard, *Administrative Law* (Boston, Mass.: Little, Brown and Co., 1976).
Schwartz, Bernard, and H. W. R. Wade, *Legal Control of Government: Administrative Law in Britain and the United States* (Oxford: Oxford Univ. Press, 1972).
Seidman, Harold, *Politics, Position, and Power: The Dynamics of Federal Organization* (New York: Oxford Univ. Press, 1970).
Selznik, Philip, *TVA and the Grass Roots: A Study in the Sociology of Formal Education* (Berkeley, Calif.: Univ. of California Press, 1949).
Shapiro, Martin M., *Freedom of Speech: The Supreme Court and Judicial Review* (Englewood Cliffs, N.J.: Prentice-Hall, 1966).
 The Supreme Court and Administrative Agencies (New York: The Free Press, 1968).
Simon, Herbert A., *Administrative Behavior* (New York: Macmillan Co., 2d ed. 1957).
Sovern, Michael I., *Legal Restraints on Racial Discrimination in Employment* (New York: Twentieth Century Fund, 1966).
Stanley, David T., Dean E. Mann, and Jameson W. Doig, *Men Who Govern: A Biographical Profile of Federal Political Executives* (Washington, D.C.: Brookings Institution, 1967).
Stigler, George J., and Manuel F. Cohen, *Can Regulatory Agencies Protect the Consumer?* (Washington, D.C.: American Enterprise Institute for Public Policy Research, 1971).
Thompson, Victor A., *Without Sympathy or Enthusiasm: The Problem of Administrative Compassion* (University, Ala.: Univ. of Alabama Press, 1975).
Trilling, Lionel, *The Liberal Imagination: Essays on Literature and Society* (New York: Charles Scribner's Sons, 1950).
Truman, David B., *The Governmental Process: Political Interests and Public Opinion* (New York: Alfred A. Knopf, 1950).
Tugwell, Rexford, *The Emerging Constitution* (New York: Harper's Magazine Press, 1974).
Vanderbilt, Arthur T., *The Doctrine of the Separation of Powers and Its Present-Day Significance* (Lincoln, Neb.: Univ. of Nebraska Press, 1953).
Vile, Maurice J., *Constitutionalism and the Separation of Powers* (Oxford: Oxford Univ. Press, 1967).
Vreeland, Hamilton, Jr., *Twilight of Individual Liberty* (New York: Charles Scribner's Sons, 1944).
Wade, H. W. R., *Administrative Law* (Oxford, Oxford Univ. Press, 3d ed. 1971).
 Towards Administrative Justice (Ann Arbor, Mich.: Univ. of Michigan Press, 1963).
Wallace, Robert A., *Congressional Control of Federal Spending* (Detroit, Mich.: Wayne State Univ. Press, 1960).
Weber, Max, *The Theory of Social and Economic Organization* (Parsons, Talcott, ed.) (New York: The Free Press, 1947).
Wechsler, Herbert, *Principles, Politics, and Fundamental Law* (Cambridge, Mass.: Harvard Univ. Press, 1961).
Weisband, Edward, and Thomas M. Franck, *Resignation in Protest: Political and Ethical Choices Between Loyalty to Team and Loyalty to Conscience in American Public Life* (New York: Viking Press, 1975).
Wheare, K. C., *Maladministration and Its Remedies* (London: Stevens and Sons, 1973).
Whyte, William H., Jr., *The Organization Man* (New York: Simon and Schuster, 1956).

Wildavsky, Aaron, *The Politics of the Budgetary Process* (Boston, Mass.: Little, Brown and Co., 2d ed. 1974).

Wilson, Woodrow, *A Crossroads of Freedom: The Campaign Speeches of Woodrow Wilson* (Davidson, John W., ed.) (New Haven, Conn.: Yale Univ. Press, 1956).

Constitutional Government in the United States (New York: Columbia Univ. Press, 1908).

The New Freedom (Leuchtenburg, William E., ed.) (Englewood Cliffs, N.J.: Prentice-Hall, 1961).

Wolfman, Bernard, Jonathan Silver, and Marjorie Silver, *Dissent Without Opinion: The Behavior of Justice William O. Douglas in Federal Tax Cases* (Philadelphia, Pa.: Univ. of Pennsylvania Press, 1975).

Woll, Peter, *Administrative Law, The Informal Process* (Berkeley, Calif.: Univ. of California Press, 1963).

Wright, Benjamin F., ed., *The Federalist* (Cambridge, Mass.: Harvard Univ. Press, 1961).

Index

Index

Civil Rights Act of 1964: (cont.)
enforcement of by individuals, 107–12;
importance of, 106–7; Title VII, 105–12,
114; voluntary compliance with, 108–12
Civil Service Commission, 4, 222–3; role of in
selecting hearing examiners, 162–3, 165,
170, 181
Clark, John Maurice: on keeping government
"out of politics," 58
Cohen, Manuel F., 196–7, 198; on "bureaucratic ossification," 37, 122
Columbia Research Corp. v. Schaffer, 185–9,
200
combination of functions: and administrative
organization, 17, 24, 26, 142–3, 146–9,
172–91; Administrative Procedure Act's
provisions on, 173–91, 270; and bias,
178, 181, 237–8; and delegation, 172–3;
discontent with, 172–3; investigative and
judicial functions, 194–203; necessity of,
in administration, 61, 172–3, 174, 190–1,
197; and Office of Foreign Direct Investments, 146–9, 165, 173–90, 199–202;
and separation of inconsistent functions,
26, 146–9, 190, 199; and succession, in
violation of Constitution, 198, 202–3;
threat to impartiality in, 182, 185–90; see
also *Wong Yang Sung v. McGrath*
Commerce, Department of, 141, 142, 145,
165: and Appeals Board, 145–9, 173
commerce, secretary of, 137, 138, 139,
143–7, 153, 157, 168
Commission on Organization of the Executive
Branch of Government, 8, 49, 63, 236
common law: contrasted with administrative
law, 23–4
Common Law, The, 31
community antenna television systems
(CATV), 81
conciliation: as method of administrative
enforcement, 107–12; and powers of
Equal Employment Opportunity Commission, 107–8
Congress, 9; administration and, 10; and
administrative procedure, creation of,
265–6; as an adversary, 35; and agency
independence, effort to insure, 60–1, 64;
and appointments to administrative
agencies, 102: appropriations by, 67,
102–3, 113–14; and banking, 218–19;
and combination of functions, 142–3,
172–91, 192–8, 203: and confirmation of
agency appointees, 19, 63, 68; and
control of administrative agencies, 62,
66–9, 70, 76; cooperation between
bureaucracy and, 35; delegation of

legislative power by, 66–7, 78–94, 212,
263; delegation to agencies by, 5, 21, 32,
50, 54, 79–90, 128, 141, 212; delegation
to President by, 92; direction of administration given by, 191; and economic
regulation, 34, 263; and elderly, policy
regarding the, 117; and employment discrimination laws, 105–15; encouragement
of agencies' policymaking by, 70, 193;
and enforcement procedures of agencies,
107–12, 151–3; failure by to evolve more
definite standards, 34–5, 50, 56–7;
failure by to furnish Federal Communications Commission with intelligible
standard, 34; hearing examiners' role
legislated by, 161–71; hearing requirements in agencies legislated by, 158–60;
and influence of agency decisions, 62;
and intrusiveness into administrative
matters, 67, 103: lawmaking power of,
78–89; legislative veto of, 73; limiting of
agency powers by, 107–12, 114–15,
116–17; nullification of agency rulings
by, 34–5; political support for legislation
in, 109, 112, 114; President and, 61;
President sometimes authorized by to
participate in agency decision making,
65; pressures by members of on agencies,
68; pressures by private interests on, 102;
procedures imposed on agency by, 243;
and proposal that it place time limit on
summary orders, 252–3; and proposal
that it require prompt hearings after
summary action, 252–5; proposals for
stimulating revision of standards by,
244–5, 251; and regulatory agencies, 107;
and responsibility for insuring that agency
does not appear biased, 238; review
function of, 99; rules for decision making
infrequently required of agency by,
247–9; and Securities and Exchange Commission, empowering of, 99; and
summary authority, 210, 211–32, 233,
235, 242; and silence as to extent of
judicial review allowable, 253–5;
vagueness of standards initially prescribed
by, 34, 50, 56–7, 79, 126
congressional committees, 75, 128; and
appropriations committee, 81: appropriations process, 67; and duty of oversight,
67; investigations by, 67–8; pressure on
agencies by, 70
congressmen: interest by in particular administrative proceedings, 68
Constitution: adjudicatory hearing, and
specifications for, 209, 214, 227; and

319

Index

Hutcheson, Joseph C., Jr., 192
Huxley, Aldous: on legitimacy of governments, 127

idealized conception of administrative process, 44, 46, 76
Immigration and Nationality Act, 153
Immigration and Naturalization Service, 175
impeachment of the President, 86–8
informal administrative process: and banking supervision, 218–19; and bulk of agency work, 207–10; implications of reliance on, 242; increased use of, 242; and negotiation and settlement, 242; and publicity, 238; and SEC "stop orders," 239; and seizure of property, 214; and summary action pending adjudicatory hearing, 207–10; uses and limits of, 208–9; and war as justification for summary process, 214–15
Informal Procedure Act of 1980, proposal for, 249
inquisitorial procedure: in Social Security hearings, 23
Interior, Department of, 4
internal revenue, commissioner of, 118, 209, 234, 238
Internal Revenue Code of 1954, 118, 239
Internal Revenue Service: system of internal review, 237
Interstate Commerce Act, 106, 247
Interstate Commerce Commission (ICC), 4, 59, 161, 169, 235, 248, 252; complacency of, 36: creation of, 36; and hearing examiners, 166–7; and Suspension Board, 250

Jackson, Andrew, 45
Jackson, Robert H., 3; on "malaise" in administrative process, 8; on value to government of due process, 150
Jaffe, Louis L.: on Ernst Freund's theory of nondelegation, 80; on diminution in agency creativity, 283 n17
James, William, 31
Johnson, Lyndon B., 137, 138, 152–3
Joint Anti-Fascist Refugee Committee v. McGrath, 211
judicial process: American admiration of, 7, 21, 24, 27, 29, 261; contrasted with administrative process, 21–30; limitations of, 21–2, 24, 26–7, 28–30, 111–12, 125, 261; limited powers of investigation by, 22–4, 27, 38
judicial review: administrative discretion and, 26, 68, 72–3, 128, 130: and alien exclusion proceedings, 26; and bias, effect on, 62, 192: and certiorari, 64;

common law of, 254: considerations governing extent of, 7, 45–6, 254–5; disqualification for bias in, 62; and expertise of agency, 45–6; and foreign affairs, 158–60; and Presidential decisions, 158; presumption of, 254; scope of, 45; and standing, 47; substantial evidence in, 163; trial de novo, 26; volume of cases, 5–6
jurisdictional fact, doctrine of, 26
Justice Department: Antitrust Division, 102; role of attorney general, 64, 221, 222, 245

Kafka, Franz, 41
Kennedy, John F., 8, 10, 27, 64–5, 106, 121, 137
Kent, James: on doctrine of necessity, 200
Kent v. Dulles, 83–5, 88
Kesey, Ken, 41
Kilbourn v. Thompson, 16
King, Martin Luther, Jr., 27
Kirkpatrick, Miles W.: as chairman of Federal Trade Commission, 121
Korematsu v. United States, 157–8

Labor, Department of, 118
LaFollette, Robert M., 45
laissez-faire, nineteenth-century doctrine of, 31
Landis, James M., 8, 44–5, 46, 51, 60, 101, 121, 172
Landis Report, 8, 49, 63
Laski, Harold J.: on bureaucracy, 37; on limitations of expertise, 52–3, 55
Law and Sociology, 105
legal realists, 28
legislative facts: distinguished from adjudicative facts, 154–5
legislative power: contrasted with judicial power, 29; ratemaking as exercise of, 29; *see also* delegation of legislative power
Legislative Reorganization Act of 1946, 67
legislative veto, 73
licensing: as alternative to competition in entry, 100
Lippmann, Walter, 45, 59
Llewellyn, Karl N.: on importance of generalists, 54
Lloyd-LaFollette Act, 222, 224, 225
Local Government Board v. Arlidge, 21
Locke, John, 15, 78
Long, Huey P., 73
Love v. Pullman Company, 110

McCulloch v. Maryland, 85–6
MacKay v. McAlexander, 195

320

Index